A MULTITUDE OF COUNSELLORS

BEING A COLLECTION OF CODES, PRECEPTS AND RULES OF LIFE FROM THE WISE OF ALL AGES

EDITED, WITH AN INTRODUCTORY ESSAY ON THE ANCIENT AND MODERN KNOWLEDGE OF GOOD AND EVIL, BY
J. N. LARNED

LONDON
GAY AND BIRD
22 BEDFORD STREET, STRAND
1901

ACKNOWLEDGMENTS

THANKS are due to the following-named gentlemen for permission kindly given to use selections from certain translations and texts, each of which is specified in its place as it appears : —

Rev. Drummond P. Chase, M. A., D. D., London; Prof. Robert K. Douglas, London ; Dr. F. J. Furnivall, London, for the Early English Text Society; Thomas Bailey Saunders, M. A., British Museum; Messrs. Swan Sonnenschein & Co., London ; and James Thornton, Esq., Oxford.

CONTENTS

PAGE

INTRODUCTORY ESSAY "ON THE ANCIENT AND MODERN KNOWLEDGE OF GOOD AND EVIL," BY THE EDITOR . . . 1

PRECEPTS OF PTAH-HOTEP, THE EGYPTIAN; FROM "THE OLDEST BOOK IN THE WORLD" 32

THE DECALOGUE, OR TEN COMMANDMENTS 41

FURTHER MOSAIC COMMANDMENTS, FROM THE BOOK OF LEVIT-ICUS 44

THE FIFTEENTH PSALM 46

PRECEPTS SELECTED FROM THE BOOK OF PROVERBS. . . . 47

PRECEPTS SELECTED FROM ECCLESIASTES. 58

PRECEPTS SELECTED FROM THE HINDU CODE OF MANU . . 64

HESIOD'S ADVICE TO PERSES; FROM "WORKS AND DAYS" . 71

"THE SEVEN WISE MEN OF GREECE;" GREEK EPIGRAM, TRANSLATED BY LORD NEAVES 76

THE EIGHT PRECEPTS AND TEN COMMANDMENTS OF BUDDHISM 77

THE BUDDHIST BEATITUDES 79

PRECEPTS SELECTED FROM THE DHAMMAPADA (ONE OF THE SACRED BOOKS OF THE BUDDHIST CANON) 82

THE GOLDEN VERSES OF PYTHAGORAS 85

THE PYTHAGORIC SENTENCES OF DEMOPHILUS 90

PRECEPTS SELECTED FROM THE MAHA-BHARATA (THE GREAT HINDU EPIC) 95

PRECEPTS SELECTED FROM CONFUCIUS 99

PRECEPTS SELECTED FROM "THE STORY OF AHIKAR" . . . 103

PRECEPTS SELECTED FROM THE "NICHOMACHEAN ETHICS" OF ARISTOTLE 106

PRECEPTS SELECTED FROM ECCLESIASTICUS (THE WISDOM OF JESUS THE SON OF SIRACH) 113

CICERO ON THE GOOD THAT MAKES LIFE HAPPY 126

CHRIST'S SERMON ON THE MOUNT 130

SENECA'S RULES FOR A HAPPY LIFE 137

MARTIAL'S IDEAL OF A HAPPY LIFE, WITH FIVE TRANSLA-TIONS 143

PRECEPTS SELECTED FROM THE "ENCHIRIDION" OF EPICTETUS 148

PRECEPTS SELECTED FROM THE MEDITATIONS OF MARCUS AURELIUS 155

OPINIONS OF THE SPIRIT OF WISDOM (ZOROASTRIAN) . . . 163

COUNSEL OF MAIMONIDES TO HIS SON, IN HIS LAST WILL . 165

WELSH MORAL TRIADS 171

DYING WORDS OF SAINT LOUIS TO HIS SON 173

MEDIÆVAL PRECEPTS ; FROM THE ROMANCES, AND FROM "STANS PUER AD MENSAM" 178

INSTRUCTIONS OF THE KNIGHT OF LA TOUR-LANDRY TO HIS DAUGHTERS 185

WYCLIF'S "SHORT RULE OF LIFE" 192

LETTER OF WILLIAM DE LA POLE, DUKE OF SUFFOLK, TO HIS SON 199

PRECEPTS SELECTED FROM THOMAS À KEMPIS'S "LITTLE GARDEN OF ROSES" 202

"THE RULE OF HONEST LIVING," FROM HUGH RHODES'S "BOKE OF NURTURE" 205

THE "OLD MEN'S DIALOGUE" AND "THE SCHOOLMASTER'S ADMONITIONS ;" FROM THE "COLLOQUIES" OF ERASMUS . 210

ROGER ASCHAM'S ADVICE TO HIS BROTHER-IN-LAW, LORD WARWICK'S SERVANT 219

ANCIENT MEXICAN CODE OF MORAL PRECEPTS 221

LETTERS OF SIR THOMAS WYATT TO HIS SON 230

TEN PRECEPTS OF LORD BURLEIGH, ADDRESSED TO HIS SON . 238

LETTER OF SIR HENRY SIDNEY TO HIS SON, SIR PHILIP SIDNEY 245

MONTAIGNE ON THE CULTIVATION OF LIFE 248

SIR WALTER RALEIGH'S "INSTRUCTIONS TO HIS SON AND TO POSTERITY" 253

LYLY'S EUPHUES ON THE EDUCATION OF YOUTH 259

LORD BACON'S "PRECEPTS OF THE DOCTRINE OF ADVANCEMENT IN LIFE" 264

THE EARL OF ESSEX'S LETTER OF ADVICE TO THE YOUNG EARL OF RUTLAND, ATTRIBUTED TO BACON 269

THE ADVICE OF POLONIUS TO LAERTES ; FROM SHAKESPEARE'S "HAMLET" 280

SIR HENRY WOTTON'S "THE HAPPY LIFE" 282

PRECEPTS SELECTED FROM BALTHASAR GRACIAN 284

PRECEPTS SELECTED FROM THE "ENCHIRIDION" OF FRANCIS QUARLES 288

SELECTIONS FROM FRANCIS OSBORNE'S "ADVICE TO A SON" 293

PROVISIONAL RULES OF CONDUCT FRAMED BY DESCARTES FOR HIMSELF 296

PRECEPTS SELECTED FROM SIR THOMAS BROWNE'S "LETTER
TO A FRIEND" AND FROM HIS "CHRISTIAN MORALS" . . 299
MORAL TEACHINGS FROM THOMAS FULLER'S "HOLY STATE" 305
SELECTIONS FROM AN ENGLISH TRANSLATION OF MAXIMS AND
MORAL SENTENCES OF THE DUKE DE LA ROCHEFOUCAULD 309
PASSAGES FROM LORD HALIFAX'S "MORAL THOUGHTS AND
REFLECTIONS" 313
SELECTIONS FROM LORD HALIFAX'S "ADVICE TO A DAUGH-
TER" 316
THE "THUS I THINK" OF JOHN LOCKE 321
SELECTED "REFLECTIONS AND MAXIMS RELATING TO THE
CONDUCT OF LIFE," FROM WILLIAM PENN'S "FRUITS OF
SOLITUDE" 324
WILLIAM PENN'S ADVICE TO HIS CHILDREN 330
FÉNELON'S RULES FOR A CHRISTIAN LIFE 342
MASSILLON ON THE USE OF TIME 345
DEAN SWIFT ON GOOD MANNERS 348
ADDISON'S METHODS FOR FILLING UP EMPTY SPACES OF LIFE 351
TRAITS OF MORAL COURAGE IN EVERY-DAY LIFE, BY STANIS-
LAUS, KING OF POLAND 356
PRECEPTS SELECTED FROM CHESTERFIELD'S LETTERS TO HIS
SON 360
PRECEPTS SELECTED FROM "THE ECONOMY OF HUMAN LIFE,"
ATTRIBUTED TO CHESTERFIELD 362
RESOLUTIONS OF JONATHAN EDWARDS 365
FRANKLIN'S CATALOGUE OF VIRTUES AND PLAN FOR ACQUIR-
ING THEM 375
LORD CHATHAM'S LETTER TO HIS NEPHEW 385
COWPER'S DELINEATION OF THE HAPPY MAN, FROM "THE
TASK" 393
WASHINGTON'S LETTERS TO HIS NEPHEWS, AND A SELECTION
FROM HIS "RULES OF CIVILITY" 397
JEFFERSON'S LETTERS OF ADVICE TO YOUNG FRIENDS . . . 405
PRECEPTS SELECTED FROM GOETHE'S "MAXIMS AND REFLEC-
TIONS" 412
SELECTIONS FROM THE "PENSÉES" OF JOUBERT 418
ROBERT BURNS'S POETICAL "EPISTLE TO A YOUNG FRIEND". 420
JEAN PAUL FRIEDRICH RICHTER'S RULES OF LIFE, FROM
"QUINTUS FIXLEIN" 424
WORDSWORTH'S "CHARACTER OF THE HAPPY WARRIOR" . . 428
PRECEPTS FROM ZSCHOKKE'S "MEDITATIONS ON LIFE, DEATH,
AND ETERNITY" 432

SELECTIONS FROM THE "AIRELLES" AND "THOUGHTS" OF MADAME SWETCHINE 436

SELECTED PASSAGES FROM SCHOPENHAUER'S "APHORISMS ON THE WISDOM OF LIFE" 439

CARLYLE'S "THE EVERLASTING YEA;" FROM "SARTOR RESARTUS" 446

PRECEPTS SELECTED FROM LACORDAIRE'S "THE MORAL LIFE" AND "LETTERS TO YOUNG MEN" 451

RULES FROM EMERSON'S "CONDUCT OF LIFE" 455

THOREAU ON THE MAKING OF LIFE DELIBERATE AND SIMPLE; FROM "WALDEN" 461

A MULTITUDE OF COUNSELLORS

INTRODUCTORY ESSAY

ON THE ANCIENT AND MODERN KNOWLEDGE OF GOOD AND EVIL

THE book that is believed to be the oldest in the world — the earliest piece of literature known to have escaped destruction and forgetfulness and to have survived to our day — is a collection of precepts of morals and manners, compiled in Egypt well-nigh fifty centuries ago. It is a manuscript known as "The Papyrus Prisse," taking the name from a gentleman, M. Prisse d'Avennes, who acquired it at Thebes, in 1847, and presented it to the National Library in Paris. This most interesting message from the remotest antiquity out of which any voice has reached us is in two parts. The first part, which is brief and probably fragmentary, contains a few rules of behavior ascribed to one Kaqimna, of the time of Snefrou, who reigned among the Pharaohs of the third dynasty. The second part is a more extended and important treatise of the same character. Its author introduces himself as "The prefect, the feudal lord, Ptah-hotep, under the majesty of the king of the South and the North, Assa." Assa was a monarch of the Fifth Dynasty, and the latest reckonings of Egyptian chronology, by Professor Petrie, place his reign somewhere between 3700 and 3500 years before Christ, or considerably more than two thousand years before the time of Moses and the exodus of Israel.

Hence the precepts of Ptah-hotep are probably older than the oldest books of the Jewish Sacred Scriptures by more than twenty centuries, even if the latter came from Moses.

Aside from their extraordinary antiquity, the precepts of Ptah-hotep have a remarkable interest of their own. They are the first of a long series of writings in which thoughtful and wise men of every age have deliberately undertaken to prescribe, for themselves or for others, the rules of right, prudent, and seemly conduct that have appeared most important in their several views of life. Each one of such monitory writings may be looked upon as reflecting, incompletely, of course, but with more or less fidelity, the ideas of a good life, or a successful life, that colored the conduct of the better men and women of the age and the region from which it comes. I can think of no study more likely to be profitable and pleasant than a comparative review of the admonitions in such a series.

When I read the " good sayings," as he has rightly called them, of Ptah-hotep, in translations that have been made by the patient and long study of many scholars, I have the feeling that I am being introduced to the primitive archetype of all gentlemen. He may worship, as the venerable Ptah-hotep would enjoin him to do, " the god with the two crocodiles ; " he may abase himself to the earth before a man greater than himself ; but he has the thinking and the feeling that have made gentlemen from his day to ours. In conversation with one who displays ignorance, he will not answer the unfortunate in a crushing way, to bring him to shame, but will treat him with courtesy and allow the subject to be dropped. He will always " speak without heat," and yet know how to make his answers " penetrate." He will ever " respect knowledge and calmness of language." He will answer the evil words of a hot-headed disputant with silence. He will not despise one whose opinion differs from his own, nor be angry with one who is wrong. If he has " become great after having been little," or " rich after having been poor," he will not harden his heart, but will remember that he has " become only the steward of the good things of God." He will remember those who were faithful to him in his low estate. He will despise flattery. He will listen with patience and kindness to petitioners, and not be abrupt with them. He will be neither haughty nor mean. He will keep himself from the " fatal malady " of bad humor, — from grumbling, — from little irritations, — from rudeness. He will keep his countenance cheerful. If he hears extravagances of hasty language he will not repeat them. He will let his thoughts be abundant, but keep his mouth under restraint. His lips will be just when he speaks, his eyes when he gazes, his ears when he hears. If he is powerful he will not seize the goods of others. He will not inspire men with fear. He will love his wife and cherish her. He will make no improper advances to a woman. He will treat his dependents well. He will " train his son to be a teachable man." He will understand that " love for the work they accomplish transports men to God." Is not that to be a gentleman, in almost the highest sense in which we use the word to-day ?

Remember that this outlines a standard of right conduct which was set before men some centuries before Abraham, — thousands of years before Homer — before Athens had risen — before the foundations of a city were laid on the seven hills of Rome. And the standard set is very high. It makes lofty demands on one who would live up to it. It will fit no life that is not lifted to an elevation above petty things, where the mind becomes tolerant, the spirit magnanimous, the temper serene. Its limitations, indeed, are in the lower, not the upper range of ethical obligations, as though its author scorned to assume that the people for whom he wrote could need to be admonished against low inclinations or gross crimes. The whole tone of his teaching forbids us, for example, to believe that Ptah-hotep would have overlooked drunkenness, if drunkenness had been a vice of his time, or failed to enjoin helpfulness to the needy, if suffering poverty had been common in the land. Thus even the omissions of the treatise cannot lessen the astonishment with which we find such conceptions of conduct and character matured at so early a day.

From Ptah-hotep we pass a long interval of time before we find another code of conduct given to mankind, and that one, the second in our series, is the code delivered to Moses on Mount Sinai, with the awful sanctions of a divine command. As an ethical standard, it offers a strange contrast to the standard marked by the old Egyptian. Of its mandates, four are religious, forbidding polytheism, idolatry, and profanity in speech, and enjoining the observance of the Sabbath day; six only are purely moral laws. These touch the right and the wrong of human conduct in six very important particulars, but touch them only on their grosser side. It is not violence that the Decalogue condemns, but murder; not unchastity, but adultery; not dishonesty, but stealing; not untruthfulness, but false-witnessing; not grasping and malign dispositions generally, but covetousness; and it enjoins, not respect for age and wisdom, but filial reverence, only. If we construe this strangely limited code in the largest possible way, there are heights and depths and reaches of temper, passion, thought, conduct, on which it leaves us with no light!

The Decalogue is supplemented, however, by another

Mosaic code, in the nineteenth chapter of Leviticus, which covers a larger ground of morals. This requires the owners of fields and vineyards to leave gleanings for the poor; forbids fraudulent dealing as well as theft, and lying as well as the bearing of false witness. It condemns oppression and injustice, hatred, vengeance, and ill-will, and it gives that great, comprehensive commandment, which received emphasis from Christ, — " Thou shalt love thy neighbor as thyself." In that commandment we have really the whole principle of social morality — the essence of everything ethical in the relations between man and man. Rightly interpreted, it sums up the obligations of each to each more completely than the Golden Rule, to which it is collateral. The difference between the two is the difference between a principle and a rule. One generalizes the feeling that ought to govern all our conduct toward our fellows; the other lays down a clear, simple, straight line of reciprocity, to which the conduct itself must be squared, in every particular, and which tests it with no possibility of mistake.

The Mosaic codes are far cruder and more primitive, generally, in their ethical tone and spirit, than the teaching of the Egyptian; but the later Jewish canon of morals, which we find in the Book of Proverbs, rises to a higher level. It is a collection of precepts and sayings ascribed mostly to Solomon, but probably gathered from many sources. They denounce envy, jealousy, pride, haughtiness, knavery, treachery, lying, slander, mischief-making, cruelty, harlotry, contention, drunkenness, slothfulness; and they extol thrift, industry, liberality, benevolence, mercifulness, cheerfulness, reticence; while Wisdom, Understanding, and Righteousness are generalized in praises that run through the book like the refrain of a song. Though some of these proverbial admonitions seem almost empty of significance, there is great beauty and a finely spiritual insight in many among them. For example : " He that is of a cheerful heart hath a continual feast ; " — what philosophy and what poetry are in that ! And again : " There is that maketh himself rich, yet hath nothing ; there is that maketh himself poor, yet hath great wealth." That has been said in other words many times, but never with more simple impressiveness. And two, at least, of the thoughts that underlie and are inspiration for the very highest of all states of moral feeling are expressed here in a striking way. " If thine enemy be hungry, give him bread to eat ; and if he be thirsty, give him water to drink : for thou shalt heap coals of fire upon his head, and the Lord shall reward thee." There we have the proposal of an attitude of spirit that is almost the noblest and nearly the most difficult that man can assume, and which nothing but high culture or native greatness of character makes possible. It is not a disposition, let us admit, that is consistently or repeatedly inculcated in the Old Testament; but something is added to one's estimate of human nature when we find even a single preacher of magnanimity at so early a stage of human history. Much the same may be said of the other sentiment to which I have referred : " He that is slow to anger is better than the mighty ; and he that ruleth his spirit is better than he that taketh a city." Possibly this is the earliest formulation we can find of the grand doctrine of self-mastery, which holds the golden secret of moral greatness in character and life. The discipline of it is practically implied in the older teaching of Ptah-hotep, the Egyptian ; but he did not lead his disciples back from the practice to the principle behind it. Nor does the doctrine seem ever to have become as fundamental in the moral philosophy of the Jews at it did elsewhere in the ancient world, even though we find it thus early in their proverbs.

In the later Hebrew "wisdom-book," called Ecclesiastes, or Koheleth, The Preacher, there is a loftier eloquence, a deeper thoughtfulness, a profounder sense of the mysteries of the divine government of the world, than in the Book of Proverbs; but the view of life is gloomy almost to despair, and the counsels are stern and limited in range. The still later Apocryphal book of Jewish moral teaching, called "The Wisdom of Jesus the Son of Sirach," is quite different. It contains, in a scattered way, intermingled with noble prayers and fragments of religious discourse, a large collection of the most practical precepts, extending to common details in all departments of human affairs. The character of these is exceedingly mixed. In some the moral tone is quite elevated, in others decidedly low, indicating no advance in moral sentiment from the time of the earlier wisdom-literature.

In the very old Hindu collection of laws and precepts known as the Code of Manu, the fundamental importance of the doctrine of self-mastery receives far more emphasis than in the Jewish Scriptures; and quite possibly its recognition there antedates its appearance in the Book of Proverbs; for, in the opinion of Sir William Jones, the Code of Manu was compiled as early as the thirteenth century before Christ, or three centuries before Solomon. Other scholars assign it to an age nearly contemporary with Solomon; while some make it several centuries later. Among the "Ācāra" or rules of conduct in that ancient Hindu code is the following, as translated by Sir Monier Monier-Williams, in his interesting work entitled "Indian Wisdom:" —

> "E'en as a driver checks his restive steeds,
> Do thou, if thou art wise, restrain thy passions,
> Which, running wild, will hurry thee away."

The same idea is repeated with an enlargement in these words : —

> " The man who keeps his senses in control,
> His speech, heart, actions pure and ever guarded,
> Gains all the fruit of holy study; he
> Needs neither penance nor austerity."

And a third time it appears, in the following " decalogue," as it may be called, of Hindu morals, which offers an interesting comparison with the Decalogue of Moses : —

> " Contentment, patience under injury,
> Self-subjugation, honesty, restraint
> Of all the sensual organs, purity,
> Devotion, Knowledge of the Deity,
> Veracity, and Abstinence from Anger,
> These form the tenfold summary of duty."

There is a more limited but splendid expression given to the same thought of self-control in the " Dhammapada," or Buddhist precepts of the law, as translated by Professor Max Müller : " He who holds back rising anger like a rolling chariot, him I call a real driver ; other people are but holding the reins." And again : " Self is the lord of self; who else could be the lord ? With self well subdued, a man finds a lord such as few can find."

Whatever may have been the prevalent, practical morality of the ancient Hindus, their sense of rightness in feeling and conduct, and their perception of the reason in morals, were singularly advanced, as is shown in their sacred literature, both Brahmanical and Buddhistic. From their great epic poem, " The Maha-bharata," Sir Monier Monier-Williams has translated a selection of precepts that are most remarkable in their ethical significance. The poem is some centuries older than Christianity ; but it contains the Golden Rule twice formulated in different words. First this : —

> " Do naught to others which if done to thee
> Would cause thee pain; this is the sum of duty."

Then this : —

> " This is the sum of all true righteousness: —
> Treat others as thou wouldst thyself be treated.
> Do nothing to thy neighbor which hereafter
> Thou wouldst not have thy neighbor do to thee.
> In causing pleasure, or in giving pain,
> In doing good or injury to others,
> In granting or refusing a request,
> A man obtains a proper rule of action
> By looking on his neighbor as himself."

This golden rule of reciprocity represents what may be called relative altruism, or the determination of duty to others by one's own claims. But a more absolute altruism of feeling is inculcated in the same poem : —

> " Enjoy thou the prosperity of others,
> Although thyself unprosperous; noble men
> Take pleasure in their neighbor's happiness."

Again : —

> " To injure none by thought or word or deed,
> To give to others, and be kind to all —
> This is the constant duty of the good.
> High-minded men delight in doing good,
> Without a thought of their own interest."

The Code of Manu teaches the same absolute considerateness for the feelings as well as for the rights of others : —

> " Wound not another, though by him provoked,
> Do no one injury by thought or deed,
> Utter no word to pain thy fellow-creatures."

And where in all ethical literature is there a more sublime injunction than this, in the same Code, which throws the final and true motive of right conduct back to the soul's own consciousness of right ?

> " The soul is its own witness, yea the soul
> Itself is its own refuge; grieve thou not,
> O man, thy soul, the great internal witness."

Among the Chinese, who, since the sixth century before Christ, have taken their teaching in morals from Confucius, there seems never to have been recognized so absolute a principle of right in spirit and conduct; but Confucius set forth the Golden Rule most distinctly. In the "Confucian Analects," as translated by Professor Legge, Tsze-kung asked : " Is there one word which may serve as a rule of practice for all one's life ? " to which the Master replied : " Is not *Reciprocity* such a word? What you do not want done to yourself, do not do to others." Apparently Confucius regarded this as a simple rule of expediency — the suggestion to a practical mind of the plan of dealings between men most likely to make their intercourse satisfactory to each and all. Indeed, it is wholly a practical, expedient wisdom that we find in the teachings of Confucius. There is rarely, in his injunctions, the glimpse of a principle out of which other rules might be drawn ; but almost always the Confucian precept is an indisputable decision of common sense, applied concretely to some of the circumstances of life. In one respect, however, Confucius was far advanced beyond all other ancient teachers of the East. That was in his urgency of teaching. " Instruct sons and younger brothers; " "make much of the colleges and seminaries ; " " describe and explain the laws ; " instruct others ; learn from others ; question others ; — this is largely the burden of the admonitions of the Master and his disciples. And the appeal was effective. If their apprehension of what is valuable in knowledge had equalled the zeal for education with which Confucius inspired them, the Chinese would probably be the best educated among the peoples of the world to-day.

If we now turn westward again, in the world of antiquity, and come back to the Mediterranean, this time arriving on its northern shore, among the Greeks, we shall meet first a counsellor of morals whose views are as worldly-wise and plainly practical as those of Confucius, and whose teachings hardly rise to the height of the doctrine of Reciprocity. It is Hesiod, the ancient bard, who, in one part of his "Works and Days," addresses moral advice to a certain Perses, apparently his brother. The advice all tends correctly enough to good conduct, — to respect for virtue, to desire for wisdom, to piety, to hospitality, to neighborly good-will, to general prudence and decency of life. But the motives appealed to are not high, as may be seen in a few passages taken out of the translation made by Mr. C. A. Elton: —

> "Bid to thy feast a friend; thy foe forbear."

And: —

> "Love him who loves thee ; to the kind draw nigh ;
> Give to the giver, but the churl pass by.
> Men fill the giving, not the ungiving hand."

Another sentiment of the poem is significant of the prevalence of bad faith among the Greeks : —

> "Not e'en thy brother on his word believe,
> But, as in laughter, set a witness by."

If Hesiod, who is supposed to have lived in the eighth century before Christ, represented the moral ideas of the better-cultured Greeks of his time, and if the "Golden Verses" ascribed to Pythagoras were composed in the sixth or fifth century before Christ, the moral advance made in the intervening two or three hundred years was very great. In the "Golden Verses" there is no trace of utilitarianism, either practical or philosophical. The appeal is always to the soul itself, as its own monitor: —

> "Let rev'rence of thyself thy thoughts control,
> And guard the sacred temple of thy soul."
> "Let no example, let no soothing tongue,

> Prevail upon thee with a syren's song,
> To do thy soul's immortal essence wrong."
> " Let not the stealing god of sleep surprise,
> Nor creep in slumbers on thy weary eyes,
> E'er ev'ry action of the former day
> Strictly thou dost and righteously survey.
> With rev'rence at thy own tribunal stand,
> And answer justly to thy own demand :
> Where have I been ?   In what have I transgress'd ?
> What good or ill has this day's life express'd ?
> Where have I failed in what I ought to do ?
> In what to God, to man, or to myself I owe ? . . .
> If evil were thy deeds, repenting mourn,
> And let thy soul with strong remorse be torn.
> If good, the good with peace of mind repay,
> And to thy secret self with pleasure say,
> Rejoice, my heart, for all went well to-day."

I quote from a translation made by the old English dramatist, Nicholas Rowe. This undoubtedly takes some modernness of tone from the translator, as the poetry of the ancients is almost sure to do ; but the fine spirit of it is readily seen.

Thus far all the ethical teachings we have reviewed have come from what Principal Sir Alexander Grant, of the University of Edinburgh, has called " the era of popular or unconscious morals." We are now, in Greece, approaching the beginnings of such inquisitive thinking upon the nature and sources of moral obligation as produce, first, a " skeptic or sophistic era," in Principal Grant's division, and then a " conscious or philosophic era." From the Greek sophists, little or nothing seems to have embodied itself in lasting precepts. Nor is anything of that description to be got from the teachings of Socrates and Plato, who made the passage for Greek thought from sophistic to philosophic morals. Of all the teachers ever given to mankind, Socrates was the least dogmatic, — the least likely to frame a positive precept or rule of conduct.

His mission was to cure men's minds of half-thinking, — to drive them to the end of a thought, — force them to rummage the contents of an idea, and find all that belongs to it. As Plato's dialogues represent him, he pulled to pieces the Greek notions of virtue and the virtues, one after another : temperance, or moderation, for example, in the dialogue called "Charmides," and courage in the "Laches" and the "Protagoras," with the result that no positive definitions are found, and none seem discoverable. The constant inference to be drawn from the destructive dialectic of Socrates is, that all virtue is substantially one and indivisible, and that a man may possess its complete guidance in his own consciousness, if he will improve himself in wisdom, with which it is really identified.

With Aristotle, who succeeded Plato in the founding of great schools of Greek thought, moral philosophy, strictly speaking, had its birth. He was the first of all men to attempt the construction of a logical science of the principles of human conduct, and to explain its rightness and wrongness on rational grounds. Since his day, no subject of speculative philosophy has received more thought, and system after system of the theory of ethics has been worked out and discussed. Of the intellectual value of such theories and the discussion of them, as part of the process of the enlightenment of the human mind, contributing essentially to its comprehension of itself and of the Cosmos, there can be no doubt. But that the practical morality of mankind has been much influenced by systems of moral philosophy seems doubtful in the extreme.

From the beginning, these systems have been divided by a single main contention, and have followed one or the other of two lines of theory, namely : the stoical and the epicurean, or the intuitive and the inductive, or the absolute and the utilitarian. In one view, Right and Wrong are absolute facts, belonging to the nature of things ; the human mind is endowed with the power to recognize them, and the recognition carries with it an inherent feeling of obligation on the side of Right, which is the " ought to " of our sense of duty. In the other view, Right and Wrong in human conduct are mere backward reflections from its consequences, and our recognition of them is derived from our observation of what is and what is not conducive to happiness. To the stoic, virtue is the end, happiness a result from it — an incident. To the epi- curean, on the contrary, happiness (which the utilitarian of modern times explains to be " the greatest happiness of the greatest number ") is the end, and virtue the ne- cessary means to the attainment of it. The stoic doctrine lifts morality to the nobler level, and gives a dignity to right conduct that is wholly denied by the epicurean or utilitarian philosophy. It has a powerful attraction, therefore, for noble minds ; it is congenial to noble spirits; they incline naturally to the acceptance of it, as a true representation of what they find in themselves. But how far different would they have found the springs of conduct in themselves if they had never known the philosophic doctrine ? It has satisfied them intellectually, but how far has it influenced them morally ? I suspect that the influence has really been small, and that the practical im- portance, as affecting motives and conduct, of all that has been written in systematic moral philosophy, by philoso- phers of either school, from Aristotle to Mill, is estimated commonly with much exaggeration.

Plutarch, who wrote moral essays on the cure of anger, on envy and hatred, on tranquillity of mind, and like topics, was neither a moral philosopher nor a maker of precepts; and neither a stoic nor an epicurean. He wrote against epicureanism, but rather in protest against sensual notions of happiness than in support of any philosophical theory of ethics; and he moralizes in his essays by the pleasant method of anecdote and example, more than by pointed admonition.

The two great representatives of stoic morality among the ancients were Epictetus, the slave, and Marcus Aurelius, the Roman emperor. In no proper sense of the term were they moral philosophers, as they are frequently called. They were greater than philosophers, — they were practical moralists, of the sublimest order. They did not support the stoic philosophy by any systematic writing, but they illustrated the ethical ideas of stoicism by their lives and by the precepts they formulated; and the stoic creed has influenced morals a thousand times more through the pregnant injunctions and examples of these two men, the slave and the emperor, than through the logic of all its philosophers. Stoicism as a philosophy founds itself, as I have said, on the belief in an intuitive cognition of right and wrong, — an innate moral sense. Stoicism as a doctrine of life is the acted consciousness of an eternal superiority in the soul of man to all the conditions of its existence in a body of clay. It was an inspiring faith in the world before Zeno composed a philosophy to support it. It was voiced, as we have seen, in the most ancient moral poetry of the Hindus. Socrates illuminated it in his life and in everything that he taught. It was set forth broadly and strongly by Aristotle. But the great stoic moralists made it conspicuous, as never before, — supreme above other considerations that bear on conduct and life. Sovereignty of spirit over flesh, of reason over passion, is the surpassing attainment through moral discipline, in the stoic view. Thence come temperance, or moderation in all things; fortitude, or courage to deal with vicissitudes, both good and ill; faithfulness to duty; submissiveness to the divine ordering of the world; contentment. "Require not things to happen," said Epictetus, "as you wish; but wish them to happen as they do happen; and all will go on well." Another of his sayings is this: "Remember that you are an actor in a drama, of such a kind as the author pleases to make it. If short, of a short one; if long, of a long one. If it be his pleasure that you should act a poor man, a cripple, a governor, or a private person, see that you act it naturally. For this is your business, to act well the character assigned you: to choose it is another's." To the same purpose said Marcus Aurelius: "Live with the gods. And he does live with the gods who constantly shows them that his own soul is satisfied with that which is assigned to him." Again: "Think not so much of what thou hast not as of what thou hast; but of the things which thou hast, select the best, and then reflect how eagerly they would have been sought if thou hadst them not." Among the many fine injunctions of the great emperor there is none finer than this: "Men exist for one another. Teach them then, or bear with them." And this: "Let it make no difference to thee whether thou art cold or warm, if thou art doing thy duty; and whether thou art drowsy or satisfied with sleep; and whether ill-spoken of or praised; and whether dying or doing something else. For it is one of the acts of life, this act by which we die; it is sufficient, then, in this act also, to do well what we have in hand."

These are pagan morals. Has Christianity improved on them? The question is now timely, for we have arrived, in our hasty survey, within the Christian era. The life of Epictetus was in its first century; that of Marcus Aurelius in the second. It is improbable that either of them knew aught of the teachings of Christ.

In the Sermon on the Mount we have the greater part of the moral prescriptions of Jesus gathered up. With some additions to be made to it from the parables and other portions of the gospels, it may be called the Moral Code of Christianity. In most of its precepts, the Sermon on the Mount differs little from older codes. It repeats the Golden Rule, already formulated in the East. It urges righteousness and purity of heart in general terms. It enjoins humility, meekness, mercifulness, forgiveness, kindly feeling towards one's enemies, sincerity in speech, self-examination, good example. It condemns anger, contention, retaliation, hypocrisy, ostentation in almsgiving and prayer, mammon-worship, anxiety for the future, censoriousness, the taking of oaths. Thus far it contains nothing that is not common to the moralists of earlier times and other regions. In a single point, only, I should say, it reveals a depth of moral perception not discovered before. That is where lustfulness is tracked from the lustful deed to the lustful thought, and the breaking of marriage except for one cause is forbidden. But that alone cannot lift it to any great supremacy above other moral codes.

Nevertheless, there is a difference, very great, between the higher moral notions of antiquity and the higher moral notions of the modern Christian world. What is it? From what does it arise? I think the answer is this: The difference is one, not of quality, but of breadth — of amplitude — of practical range; and Jesus gave the key to a moral dispensation as distinctly new as the religious dispensation that he introduced was new, when he answered the lawyer's question, " Who is my neighbor? " by the parable of the Good Samaritan ; and when, to the amazement of his disciples, he talked with the woman of Samaria, and abode two days in that alien city, teaching its people. This would seem to have been the starting-point of an effective wakening of mankind to the larger sense of human fellowship, — of fellowship between men as men, extending beyond tribal lines and race lines, embracing all. The higher civilizations of antiquity had developed a full understanding, as it seems to me, of all the essential principles of moral law, but shrunk them to a narrow application. All that makes Right in the conduct of one man towards another was perfectly recognized, as between two who stood related in some familiar way, as members of the same family group, the same tribe, the same city, the same state. Dimly the recognition might stretch sometimes, and in some particulars, over the large kinship of race; but it has rarely gone to that limit in any primitive society of either ancient or modern times. Within such bounds of obligation, Ptah-hotep, the Egyptian of five thousand years ago, the composers of the Hebrew proverbs, the authors of the Hindu epics and of the Laws of Manu, had little to learn of moral duty or restraint from our Christian twentieth century. The laws of rectitude between their "neighbors" and themselves they knew well; but their "neighbors" dwelt closely around them, worshipped the same gods, obeyed the same king, spoke the same language, followed the same habits of life. For the "stranger," outside the gates of their community, they held a very different moral code.

From the time of Christ to our day, two influences have been steadily, slowly working together, to expand that narrowness and littleness of moral view which seems so inveterate in the human mind. One of those influences — and I dare not say that it is the more potent one — has been the teaching that compelled the disciples of Christ, first to see a "neighbor" in even the detested Samaritan, and finally to become "brethren" to the whole Gentile world. The other influence has been the widening and quickening of intercourse, in modern times, between men of different countries, races, classes, and creeds. Increasing acquaintance has been erasing, one by one, the artificial bounds that cribbed their sympathies and their discernment of right. Thus justice, benevolence, charity, tolerance, honesty, magnanimity, have come to mean vastly more than they did in former times, not by anything newly found in the essence of them, but simply by the expanding of their application. It is that which has uprooted slavery,— even, at last, the enslavement of black-skinned by white-skinned races. It is that which slowly makes the instructed feel responsible for the ignorant, the fortunate for the unfortunate, the strong for the weak. It is that which is taking vindictiveness out of law, and ferocity out of war, and which will, in time, — not soon, but after some centuries, perhaps,— put tribunals in place of armies and substitute arbitration for war.

Neither of those influences, neither Christian teaching of human fellowship nor widened intercourse in the world, came speedily into effective operation. The voice of Christ was almost silenced for centuries by the din of theological disputes. His precepts were forgotten in the angry war of dogmas. Then, with the fall of the Roman Empire, there came a cloud of darkness over the world, in which men groped apart, and became strangers, and neighborhood and fellowship were lost, as much as they had been in the ancient days. Out of that long period of the Middle Ages there has come to us little that I discover of practical moralizing from the purest and most meditative minds; and the little that we do find is singularly limited in scope. Moral sentiment was absorbed in religious sentiment, and lost its distinctiveness. The Church had become keeper of consciences; the standards of right were hidden in its confessionals; there was little thought of examining them. Even when the mediæval darkness begins to break, and there are monitory voices heard once more, from lips as pure and as noble as have ever spoken for righteousness, the monition is almost strictly a religious one; the appeal for right-doing is made to motives of piety, rather than to the obligation of Right, considered absolutely, in itself. We find it so in the deathbed admonitions that good St. Louis of France addressed to his son, as reported by the Sire de Joinville. We find it in the precepts ascribed to Thomas à Kempis, and in Wyclif's "Short Rule of Life." An exception to it is furnished by the great Jewish Rabbi of the Middle Ages, Moses Maimonides, whose injunctions to his son Abraham, contained in his last will, form a noble moral code. They make plain the needful showing, that rightness does not lie on the surface of conduct, but has a root that runs deep down into the heart of man and into the everlasting verity of things. They are full, too, of a profound practical wisdom. "Accustom yourself," he says, "to good morals; for the nature of man dependeth upon habit, and habit taketh root in nature." "There is no nobility like that of morality, and there is no inheritance like faithfulness." "Let not bill, witnesses, or possession, be stronger in your sight than a promise made by word of mouth, whether in public or in private. Refrain from and disdain all deep reserves, cunning subterfuges, tricky pretexts, sharp practices, and flaws and evasions."

After the Renaissance and the Reformation there came a great revival of attentiveness to the counselling of the young, in definite particulars of conduct and behavior, for their practical guidance through life. The literature of the sixteenth and seventeenth centuries is suddenly rich in letters, and other forms of discourse, addressed to sons, or to youthful friends, or to the world at large, by thoughtful and notable men of the day, giving advice, point by point, on the courses to take in life, the aims to pursue, the principles to be governed by. The composition of sententious precepts and rules was also much in vogue, and much interest was evidently taken in them. To a great extent, the moralizing of that period was of the prudential kind, looking to success and smoothness in life, rather than to high spiritual motives and a fine self-culture. Even Shakespeare, when he framed the advice of Polonius to Laertes, exemplified the fashionable worldly-wisdom of his age, in prudential maxims. It is only at the end that he puts a higher meaning into the old man's words, and makes him say: —

> " This above all, — To thine own self be true;
> And it must follow, as the night the day,
> Thou canst not then be false to any man."

Of the moralists of that extraordinary age there are none who show a shrewder worldly-wisdom than Montaigne ; but his was the wisdom of a profounder consideration of life, from the egoistic standpoint, than most of those who wrote of it had given. In that essay of Book III., in which he tells of his love of life, and how thoughtfully he cultivates it and makes the most of it, he says : " Others are sensible of the sweetness of contentment and of prosperity ; I feel it, too, as well as they, but not as it slides and passes by ; a man ought to study, taste, and ruminate upon it, to render worthy thanks to Him that grants it to us. . . . I *consult* myself about a contentment ; I do not skim, but sound it ; and bend my reason, now grown perverse and ill-humored, to entertain it." In that we have contentment sublimated, and the enjoyment of life erected into both a science and an art. Elsewhere in the same essay he says : " The great and glorious masterpiece of man is to know how to live to purpose ; all other things, to reign, to lay up treasure, to build, are at the most but mere appendixes and little props." Further : " Grandeur of soul consists, not so much in mounting and in proceeding forward, as in knowing how to govern and circumscribe itself. It takes everything for great that is enough ; and shows its height better in loving moderate than eminent things. There is nothing so handsome and lawful as well and duly to play the man ; nor science so hard as well to know how to live in this life." And again : "Of the experience I have of myself, I find enough to make me wise, if I were but a good scholar. . . . The life of Cæsar himself has no greater examples for us than our own."

Lord Bacon is believed to have written, for the Earl of Essex, a letter of rare wisdom which was addressed, in the name of the latter, to the young Earl of Rutland. " Behavior," his lordship is told, " is but a garment, and it is easy to make a comely garment for a body that is itself well proportioned." Hence, the essential matter is the shaping and cultivation of one's mind. The excellences of the mind are the same as those found in the physical body, namely, — health, strength, and beauty. By health of mind we are kept from things evil and base. " Strength of mind is that active power which maketh us to perform good things and great things." Beauty of mind is shown in sweetness and gracefulness of behavior. As for the attaining of such an admirable condition of mind, the young man is pithily told that one " may mend his faults with as little labor as cover them." It would not be easy to put more food for moral thinking into a dozen words.

Among the moralists of the next generation after Bacon, the favorite, apparently, was Francis Quarles, whose " Enchiridion," or manual of precepts, enjoyed an extraordinary popularity in its day. Many of its maxims are trite, and they carry a little too plainly the marks of an artful and conscious workmanship ; but in some of them, on the other hand, so fine an expression is given to an old idea that it carries a new effect. I quote a few examples : —

" Hath any wronged thee ? be bravely revenged : slight it, and the work 's begun ; forgive it, and 't is finished. He is below himself that is not above an injury."

" In the commission of evil, fear no man so much as thy own self. Another is but one witness against thee ; thou art a thousand : another thou mayest avoid ; thyself thou canst not."

" Demean thyself more warily in thy study, than in the street. . . . The multitude looks but *upon* thy actions ; thy conscience looks *into* them."

" If thou seest anything in thyself which may make thee proud, look a little further, and thou shalt find enough to humble thee."

" If thou wouldst have a good servant, let thy servant find a wise master."

One of the contemporaries of Quarles was Sir Thomas Browne, who wrote a " Letter to a Friend " on subjects of conduct, and afterwards expanded it into a treatise on " Christian Morals." Like everything that came from that most delightful old physician, it is full of meat for meditation. " Be substantially great in thyself," he writes, " and more than thou appearest unto others, and let the world be deceived in thee as they are in the lights of heaven."

" When thou lookest upon the imperfections of others, allow one eye for what is laudable in them, and the balance they have from some excellency, which may render them considerable."

"Owe not thy humility unto humiliation by adversity, but look humbly down in that state when others look upward upon thee."

"Be charitable before wealth makes thee covetous, and lose not the glory of the mite. If riches increase, let thy mind hold pace with them."

When we find a crafty statesman, like Lord Robert Burleigh, addressing to his son Robert "Ten Precepts" which prove to be counsels of worldly prudence, just tinctured with a formal piety, we are not surprised. But one expects something more from Sir Walter Raleigh, and it is disappointing to discover scarcely more than a thrifty view of life in the "Instructions" which he left "To his Son and to Posterity." A somewhat higher tone appears in two letters of formal advice that were written from Spain by Sir Thomas Wyatt, the poet and diplomatist, to his only son, Thomas, and in a similar epistle by Sir Henry Sidney, to his famous son, the knightly Sir Philip; but neither is at all remarkable.

In Spain, a little later, there was a maker of maxims, Balthasar Gracian, whose sayings have been greatly admired. Discreetness and taste, rather than loftiness of sentiment, are the qualities that permeate them; but they are wise in their kind and most cleverly framed. "Look into the inside of things," says Gracian; "they are usually very different from what they seem." "Have something left to wish for, so as not to be unhappy from very happiness. If there is nothing to desire, there is everything to fear." "Know how to do good to people a little at a time and often." "Have no days of carelessness. Destiny loves to play tricks, and will pile chance on chance to take us unawares."

The eloquent admonitions of old Thomas Fuller, in his classic discourses on " The Holy State and the Profane State," are almost purely religious; but there are fine gleanings of strictly moral precept in them. For example : he does not condemn anger, in itself, as the moralists commonly do, but commends it, if rightly controlled and directed. " Anger," he says, " is one of the sinews of the soul. He that wants it hath a maimed mind." But " to be angry for every toy, debases the worth of thy anger ; " and " he will make a strange combustion in the state of his soul, who at the landing of every cockboat sets the beacons on fire." There is a deeper wisdom in this than in the customary deprecation of all anger. So, too, in his counsels concerning recreation. He extols it, as " the breathing of the soul ; " but, he pleads, " Spill not the morning (the quintessence of the day) in recreations. For sleep itself is a recreation ; add not therefore sauce to sauce." And, in conclusion : " Choke not thy soul with immoderate pouring in of the cordial of pleasures."

From the Puritan writers of that strange time we get little of the kind of ethic teaching that is the object of my present search. It is not in Puritanism, but in Quakerism, that we find the sense of righteousness uplifted again, and purged of worldly prudence, and made a very living force. Religion, as the followers of George Fox conceived it, included moral rightness in a way and a degree which the professors of religion have not always understood. It made them scrupulous of many things, such as war, and slavery, and the vanities of pomp and title, which mere fervors of emotional piety have often failed to waken the consciences of men against. It made the plain yea and nay of daily human intercourse as sacred to them as the worship of God. And that, I think, is why William Penn became a disciple of George Fox. He was the truest and purest moralist of his generation.   His meditative mind concerned itself as much with the life that is as with the life to come, and he was spiritually drawn to a conception of religion which resolutely broke down the distinctions between righteousness and piety that men are forever trying to build up.

Penn was one of the most admirable writers of his generation, and when he put his thoughts on conduct into precepts, as in a little collection which he entitled " Fruits of Solitude," he gave many of them an almost perfect form.

" If thou thinkest twice," he wrote, " before thou speakest once, thou wilt speak twice the better for it."

" Knowledge is the treasure, but judgment is the treasurer of a wise man."

" Let nothing be lost, said our Saviour ; but that is lost which is misused."

" Hospitality is good if the poorer sort are the subjects of our bounty."

" Never marry but for love ; but see that thou lovest what is lovely."

" Seek not to be rich, but to be happy.   The one lies in bags ; the other in content."

" Nothing needs a trick but a trick.   Sincerity loathes one."

Penn's little book of the " Fruits of Solitude " fell into the hands of Robert Louis Stevenson one day, at San Francisco, and delighted him so that he made it for a time his constant companion.   At last he sent it to a London friend, with this note written in it : " If ever in all my ' human conduct ' I have done a better thing to any fellow creature than handing on to you this sweet, dignified, and wholesome book, I know I shall hear of it on the last day.   To write a book like this were impossible ; at least one can hand it on — with a wrench — one to another. My wife cries out and my own heart misgives me, but still here it is. . . . Even the copy was dear to me, printed in the colony that Penn established, and carried in my pocket all about the San Francisco streets, read in street cars and ferry boats, when I was sick unto death, and found in all times and places a peaceful and sweet companion."

But the principles of right conduct were discussed in a broader and more influential way by Penn in the "Advice to his Children" which he published in 1699. As a treatise of practical ethics, spiritualized, or interfused with religious motive, I doubt if anything better can be found in literature.

When we arrive at the eighteenth century, we are at the opening of the new age of industry and politics through which the civilized world has been passing ever since : the age, that is, of great progress in science, mechanism and democracy. At the beginning, at least, it was a most prosaic time, and the ideals in it were not high, — which fact shows in nothing more plainly than in the moralizing of the age. Whoever it may be that undertakes to frame rules for himself, or to give advice to young or old, on conduct, or on the use of time, or on the management of life, the advice has seldom any thought but the wary thought of prudence behind it. Even Addison, when he attempts, in one of the essays of "The Spectator," to propose to people who are wasting the greater part of their existence, "certain methods for filling up the empty spaces of their lives," drops into the veriest commonplaces, and makes it plain that either he cannot or dare not hold up to his readers the high conceptions of life, and duty, and good, and happiness, and self-cultivation, that would have suggested themselves to such a man, on such an occasion, in many earlier times. Our own Franklin, thrifty, shrewdly forethoughtful, kindly, public-spirited, ever busy in doing good to all around him, but politic and practical in everything, and having no glimmer of idealism or spirituality in his mind, was the typical moralist, I should say, of his age. It would be unfair to the age to make Chesterfield its representative in this matter, though his letters to his son, in their frank world-liness, and in the earnestness of their plea for the surface polish to be put on behavior by polite manners, are very much in the spirit of their time. Lord Chatham wrote letters to his nephew that are on about the same level of suggestion, though inspired by far more of moral earnest-ness. Nearly the same is to be said of the excellent let-ters of advice which Washington and Jefferson addressed to young friends; and, indeed, it would be hardly reason-able to expect more from men — even the greatest — whose lives have been given, not to meditation, but to heroic and laborious deeds.

Even the supreme genius of Goethe was affected, in no slight degree, by the hardness and coldness in the temper of the eighteenth century. He was not a moralist; he had the larger wisdom of the great poet, realizing Mat-thew Arnold's definition of poetry, that it is a "criticism of life." He was, *par excellence*, the critic of life, from all view-points, including the moral. The abundant "Maxims and Reflections" that he left are rich in ethi-cal suggestion; but they are not of the quality most in-spired or inspiring. They never flash such a light on man and on the life of man as we get sometimes from the sayings of Marcus Aurelius, and from others whom I have quoted in this slight review. Yet there is great and valu-able wisdom in them.

"Ingratitude," says Goethe, " is always a kind of weakness. I have never known men of ability to be ungrateful."

"It is not enough to know, we must apply; it is not enough to will, we must also do."

"Perfection is the measure of heaven, and the wish to be perfect the measure of man."

"Use well the moment ; what the hour
  Brings for thy use is in thy power ;
  And what thou best canst understand,
  Is just the thing lies nearest to thy hand."

"Art thou little, do that little well, and for thy comfort know,
  The biggest man can do his biggest work no better than just so."

There is nothing more fundamental in the ethics of Goethe than the doctrine embodied in these last two injunctions. They convey one of the teachings with which Goethe most inspired Carlyle — "Do the duty that lies nearest thee." In his cynical and vehement way, the latter took it up and made it ring into the ears of his own generation with a passion of eloquence that reverberates yet. "Produce! produce!" he cries, in "Sartor Resartus," "were it but the pitifulest infinitessimal fraction of a product, produce it in God's name! 'T is the utmost thou hast in thee : out with it, then. Up, up! Whatsoever thy hand findeth to do, do it with thy whole might. Work while it is called To-day; for the Night cometh, wherein no man can work." It is an old gospel ; but it came with wholesome force to the modern world from Goethe and Carlyle. So, too, did that other bitter-tonic doctrine, which both preached, that no man need think he has any right to happiness. It was an old annunciation even when the stoics found it ; yet Carlyle startled our fathers, sixty years ago, and put no little new thinking into their minds, when he cried to them : "What act of Legislature was there that *thou* shouldst be Happy? A little while ago thou hadst no right to *be* at all. What if thou wert born and predestined not to be Happy, but to be Unhappy! Art thou nothing other than a Vulture, then, that fliest through the Universe seeking after somewhat to *eat*, and shrieking dolefully because carrion enough is not given thee? Close thy Byron; open thy Goethe."

As Carlyle cried "Produce, produce!" so Thoreau cried "Simplify, simplify life!" and he was scornful of the much-bragged-of *work* of the world. "As for work," he said, "we have n't any of any consequence. We have the St. Vitus's dance, and cannot possibly keep our heads still." Now, put the two doctrines of practical living together, — simplify life as Thoreau would have it, then do the duty that lies nearest, as Carlyle enjoins, and we have the groundwork, it seems to me, of the life best worth living.

No two men of our day have won more attention to their views of life than Carlyle and Thoreau on these two points of duty-work and of simplicity which they singled out for emphasis. Therefore I have quoted them in this connection, though they do not belong among the systematic preceptors whose maxims I have been discussing. Indeed, the counsellors and maxim-makers of that world-old school which dates from Ptah-hotep seem now to be disappearing. Men who meditate on Life and Conduct and Duty and Happiness seem no longer willing to attempt to pack their thoughts into a little bead-string of precepts and apothegms, or into the brevity of a letter of fatherly advice. It may be that life has widened so, and the considerations which bear on it have so multiplied, that they demand ampler and fuller treatment. At all events, whatever the cause, it is in rounded essays and many-chaptered books that the counsels for right and happy living have mostly been given of late years.

These books I will not open, but end my hasty survey here. I end it with a deepened conviction that the knowledge of Good and Evil has been complete in the world from the beginning of history, and that mankind has had nothing to learn since but the application of it.

THE OLDEST BOOK IN THE WORLD

SOME account of the discovery of the papyrus containing the precepts of Ptah-hotep, and of the conclusions reached by Egyptologists with regard to the period of antiquity from which it has come down, are given in the introductory essay. Among the eminent scholars who have devoted time and labor to the decipherment and study of the papyrus, M. Philippe Virey appears to have been the most patient. The results of his "Études sur le Papyrus Prisse," begun in 1881, were published at Paris in 1887. Three years later he contributed an English translation of the "Precepts of Ptah-hotep" to the third volume of Professor Sayce's "Records of the Past," from which translation the following selection of a few among the precepts is taken.

A SELECTION FROM THE PRECEPTS OF PTAH-HOTEP.

(From "Records of the Past," edited by A. H. Sayce, N. S., v. 3.)

Precepts of the prefect the feudal lord Ptah-hotep, under the majesty of the king of the South and North, Assa, living eternally forever.

The prefect, the feudal lord Ptah-hotep says : O God with the two crocodiles, my lord, the progress of age changes into senility. Decay falls [upon man] and decline takes the place of youth. A vexation weighs upon him every day; sight fails; the ear becomes deaf; his strength dissolves without ceasing. The mouth is silent, speech fails him; the mind decays, remembering not the day before. The whole body suffers. That which is good becomes evil; taste completely disappears. Old age makes a man altogether miserable; the nose is stopped up, breathing no more from exhaustion. Standing or sitting there is here a condition (?) of . . . Who will cause me to have authority to speak? that I may declare to him the words of those who have heard the counsels of former days? And the counsels heard of the gods, who (will give me authority to declare them?) Cause that it be so and that evil be removed from those that are enlightened; send the double . . .

The majesty of this god says: Instruct him in the sayings of former days.* It is this which constitutes the merit of the children of the great. All that which makes the soul equal penetrates him who hears it, and that which it says produces no satiety.

Beginning of the arrangement of the good saying(s), spoken by the noble lord, the divine father, beloved of God, the son of the king, the first-born of his race, the prefect (and) feudal lord Ptah-hotep, so as to instruct the ignorant in the knowledge of the arguments of the good saying(s). It is profitable for him who hears them, it is a loss to him who shall transgress them.

He says to his son: Be not arrogant because of that which thou knowest; deal with the ignorant as with the learned; for the barriers of art are not closed, no artist being in possession of the perfection to which he should aspire. [But] good (words) are more difficult to find than the emerald, for it is by slaves that that is discovered among the rocks of pegmatite.

If thou findest a disputant while he is hot, and if he is superior to thee in ability, lower the hands, bend the back, do not get into a passion with him. As he will not let thee destroy his words, it is utterly wrong to interrupt him; that proclaims that thou art incapable of keeping thyself calm when thou art contradicted.

If, then, thou hast to do with a disputant while he is

hot, imitate one who does not stir. Thou hast the advantage over him if thou keepest silence when he is uttering evil words. "The better (of the two) is he who is impassive," say the bystanders, and thou art right in the opinion of the great.

If thou findest a disputant while he is hot, do not despise him, because thou art not of the same opinion. Be not angry against him when he is wrong; away with such a thing. He fights against himself; require him not [further] to flatter thy feelings.* Do not amuse thyself with the spectacle which thou hast before thee; it is odious, [it is] mean, [it is the part] of a despicable soul [so to do]. As soon as thou lettest thyself be moved by thy feelings, combat this [desire] as a thing that is reproved by the great.

. . . .

Inspire not men with fear, [else] God will fight against [thee] in the same manner.

. . . .

If thou art an agriculturist, gather the crops (?) in the field which the great God has given thee, fill not thy mouth in the house of thy neighbors; it is better to make one's self dreaded by the possessor. As for him who, master of his own way of acting, being all-powerful, seizes [the goods of others] like a crocodile in the midst [even] of watchmen, his children are an object of malediction, of scorn and of hatred on account of it, while [his] father is grievously distressed, and [as for] the mother who has borne [him], happy is another rather than herself. [But] a man becomes a god when he is chief of a tribe which has confidence in following him.

If thou abasest thyself in obeying a superior, thy conduct is entirely good before God. Knowing who ought to obey and who ought to command, do not lift up thy heart against him. As thou knowest that in him is authority, be respectful towards him as belonging to him. Fortune comes only at her own good-will, and her caprice only is her law; as for him who . . . God, who has created his superiority, turns himself from him and he is overthrown.

Be active during the time of thy existence, doing more than is commanded. Do not spoil the time of thy activity; he is a blameworthy person who makes a bad use of his moments. Do not lose the daily opportunity of increasing that which thy house possesses. Activity produces riches, and riches do not endure when it slackens.

If thou art a wise man, bring up a son who shall be pleasing to God. If he conforms his conduct to thy way and occupies himself with thy affairs as is right, do to him all the good thou canst; he is thy son, a [person] attached [to thee] whom thine own self hath begotten. Separate not thy heart from him. . . . [But] if he conducts himself ill and trangresses thy wish, if he rejects all counsel, if his mouth goes according to the evil word, strike him on the mouth in return. Give orders without hesitation to those who do wrong, to him whose temper is turbulent; and he will not deviate from the straight path, and there will be no obstacle to interrupt the way.

.   .   .   .

If thou art a leader, setting forward thy plans according to that which thou decidest, perform perfect actions which posterity may remember, without letting the words prevail [with thee] which multiply flattery, [which] excite pride and produce vanity.

If thou art a leader of peace, listen to the discourse of the petitioner. Be not abrupt with him; that would trouble him. Say not to him: " Thou hast [already] recounted this." Indulgence will encourage him to accomplish the object of his coming. As for being abrupt with the complainant because he described what passed when the injury was done, instead of complaining of the injury itself, let it not be! The way to obtain a clear explanation is to listen with kindness.

If thou desirest to excite respect within [the house] thou enterest, for example [the house] of a superior, a friend or any person of consideration, [in short] every-where where thou enterest, keep thyself from making advances to a woman, for there is nothing good in so doing. There is no prudence in taking part in it, and thousands of men destroy themselves in order to enjoy a moment, brief as a dream, while they gain death, so as to know it. It is a villainous *intention* (?), that of a man who [thus] excites himself (?) ; if he goes on to carry it out, his mind abandons him. For as for him who is without repugnance for such an [act] there is no good sense at all in him.

If thou desirest that thy conduct should be good and preserved from all evil, keep thyself from [every] attack of bad humor. It is a fatal malady which leads to discord, and there is no longer any existence for him who gives way to it. For it [introduces] *discord* (?) between fathers and mothers, as well as between brothers and sisters; it causes the wife [and] the husband to hate each other; it contains all kinds of wickedness, it embodies all kinds of wrong. When a man has established his just equilibrium and walks in this path, there where he makes his dwelling, there is no room for bad humor.

Be not of an irritable temper as regards that which happens beside thee; grumble (?) not over thy [own] affairs. Be not of an irritable temper in regard to thy neighbors; better is a compliment to that which displeases than rudeness. It is wrong to get into a passion with one's neighbors, to be no longer master of one's words. When there is only a little irritation, one creates for oneself an affliction for the [time when one will again be] cool.

If thou art wise, look after thy house; love thy wife without alloy. Fill her stomach, clothe her back, these are the cares [to be bestowed] on her person. Caress her, fulfil her desires during the time of her existence; it is a kindness which does honor to its possessor. Be not *brutal* (?); *tact* (?) will influence her better than violence; her . . . behold to what she aspires, at what she aims, what she regards. It is that which fixes her in thy house; if thou repellest her, it is an *abyss* (?). Open thy *arms* (?) for her, [respondent] to her arms; call her, display to her [thy] love.

Treat thy dependents well, in so far as it belongs to thee [to do so]; [and] it belongs to those whom God has favored.

. . . .

Do not repeat any extravagance of language; do not listen to it; it is a thing which has escaped from a hasty mouth. If it is repeated, look, without hearing it, towards the earth; say nothing in regard to it. Cause him who speaks to thee to know what is just, even him who provokes to injustice; cause that [which is just] to be done, cause it to triumph. As for that which is hateful according to the law, condemn it by unveiling it.

If thou art a wise man, sitting in the council of thy lord, direct thy thought towards that which is wise. Be silent rather than scatter thy words. When thou speakest, know that which can be brought against thee. To speak in the council is an art, and speech is criticised more than any [other] labor; it is contradiction which puts it to the proof.

If thou art powerful, respect knowledge and calmness of language. Command only to direct; to be absolute is to run into evil. Let not thy heart be haughty, neither let it be mean. Do not let thy orders remain unsaid, and cause thy answers to penetrate; but speak without heat, assume a serious countenance. As for the vivacity of an ardent heart, temper it; the gentle man penetrates [all] obstacles. He who agitates himself all the day long has not a good moment; and he who amuses himself all the day long keeps not his fortune. Aim at fulness like pilots; once one is seated another works, and seeks to obey [one's] orders.

Disturb not a great man; weaken not the attention of him who is occupied. His care is to embrace [his task], and he strips his person through the love which he puts into it. That transports men to God, [even] the love for the work which they accomplish. Compose [then thy] face (?) [even] in trouble, that peace may be with thee, when agitation is with . . . These are the people who succeed in what they desire.

. . . .

If thou art annoyed at a thing, if thou art tormented by some one who is acting within his right, get out of his sight, and remember him no more when he has ceased to address thee.

If thou hast become great after having been little, [if] thou hast become rich after having been poor, [when thou art at the] head of the city, know how not to take advantage of the fact that thou hast reached the first rank; *harden* (?) not thy heart because of thy elevation; thou art become [only] the steward of the good things of God. Put not behind thee the neighbor who is like unto thee; be unto him as a companion.

. . . .

If thou aimest at polished manners, call not him whom thou accostest. Converse with him especially in such a way as not to annoy him. Enter on a discussion with him only after having left him time to saturate his mind with the subject of the conversation. If he lets his ignorance display itself, and if he gives thee an opportunity to disgrace him, treat him with courtesy rather; proceed not to drive him [into a corner]; do not . . . the word to him; answer not in a crushing manner; crush him not; worry him not; in order that in his turn he may not return [to the subject], but depart to the profit of thy conversation.

Let thy countenance be cheerful during the time of thy existence. . . .

Distinguish the superintendent who directs from the workman, for manual labor is little elevated; the inaction [of the hands] is honorable. If a man is not in the evil way, that which places him [there] is the want of subordination to authority.

.   .   .   .

The wise man is satiated by knowledge; he is a great man through his own merits. His tongue is in accord with his mind; just are his lips when he speaks, his eyes when he gazes, his ears when he hears. The advantage of his son is to do that which is just without deceiving himself.

.   .   .   .

When a son receives the instruction of his father, there is no error in all his plans. Train thy son to be a teachable man whose wisdom is agreeable to the great. Let him direct his mouth according to that which has been said to him; in the docility of a son is discovered his wisdom. His conduct is perfect, while error carries away the unteachable. To-morrow knowledge will support him, while the ignorant will be destroyed.

As for the man without experience who listens not, he effects nothing whatsoever. He sees knowledge in ignorance, profit in loss ; he commits all kinds of error, always accordingly choosing the contrary of what is praiseworthy. He lives on that which is mortal, in this fashion. His food are evil words whereat he is filled with astonishment. That which the great know to be mortal he lives upon every day, flying from that which would be profitable to him, because of the multitude of errors which present themselves before him every day.

.   .   .   .

Let thy thoughts be abundant [but] let thy mouth be under restraint, and thou shalt argue with the great. Put thyself in unison with the ways of thy master ; cause him to say : " He is my son," so that those who shall hear it shall say : " Praise be to [her who] has borne him to him ! " Apply thyself while thou speakest ; speak [only] of perfect things ; and let the great who shall hear thee say : " Twice good [is] that which issues from his mouth ! "

Do that which thy master bids thee. Twice good is the precept of our father, from whom we have issued, from his flesh. What he tells us, let it be [fixed in our] heart ; to satisfy him greatly let us do for him more than he has prescribed. Verily a good son is one of the gifts of God, [a son] who does [even] better than he has been told [to do]. For his master he does what is satisfactory, putting himself with all his heart on the part [of right].

So I shall bring it about that thy body shall be healthful, that the king shall be satisfied [with thee] in all circumstances, and that thou shalt obtain years of life without default.

It has caused me on earth to obtain 110 years of life, along with the gift of the favor of the king among the first of those whom their works (?) have ennobled, satisfying the king in a place of dignity.

THE DECALOGUE, OR TEN COMMANDMENTS

(Exodus xix.–xx., Revised Version.)

AND it came to pass on the third day, when it was morning, that there were thunders and lightnings, and a thick cloud upon the mount, and the voice of a trumpet exceeding loud ; and all the people that were in the camp trembled. And Moses brought forth the people out of the camp to meet God ; and they stood at the nether part of the mount. And mount Sinai was altogether on smoke, because the LORD descended upon it in fire : and the smoke thereof ascended as the smoke of a furnace, and the whole mount quaked greatly. And when the voice of the trumpet waxed louder and louder, Moses spake, and God answered him by a voice. And the LORD came down upon mount Sinai, to the top of the mount : and the LORD called Moses to the top of the mount ; and Moses went up. And the LORD said unto Moses, Go down, charge the people, lest they break through unto the LORD to gaze, and many of them perish. And let the priests also, which come near to the LORD, sanctify themselves, lest the LORD break forth upon them. And Moses said unto the LORD, The people cannot come up to mount Sinai : for thou didst charge us, saying, Set bounds about the mount, and sanctify it. And the LORD said unto him, Go, get thee down ; and thou shalt come up, thou, and Aaron with thee : but let not the priests and the people break through to come up unto the LORD, lest he break forth upon them. So Moses went down unto the people, and told them.

And God spake all these words, saying,

I am the LORD thy God, which brought thee out of the land of Egypt, out of the house of bondage.

1. Thou shalt have none other gods before me.

2. Thou shalt not make unto thee a graven image, nor the likeness of any form that is in heaven above, or that is in the earth beneath, or that is in the water under the earth: thou shalt not bow down thyself unto them, nor serve them: for I the LORD thy God am a jealous God, visiting the iniquity of the fathers upon the children, upon the third and upon the fourth generation of them that hate me ; and shewing mercy unto thousands, of them that love me and keep my commandments.

3. Thou shalt not take the name of the LORD thy God in vain; for the LORD will not hold him guiltless that taketh his name in vain.

4. Remember the sabbath day, to keep it holy. Six days shalt thou labour, and do all thy work : but the seventh day is a sabbath unto the LORD thy God: *in it* thou shalt not do any work, thou, nor thy son, nor thy daughter, thy manservant, nor thy maidservant, nor thy cattle, nor thy stranger that is within thy gates : for in six days the LORD made heaven and earth, the sea, and all that in them is, and rested the seventh day ; wherefore the LORD blessed the sabbath day, and hallowed it.

5. Honour thy father and thy mother : that thy days may be long upon the land which the LORD thy God giveth thee.

6. Thou shalt do no murder.

7. Thou shalt not commit adultery.

8. Thou shalt not steal.

9. Thou shalt not bear false witness against thy neighbour.

10. Thou shalt not covet thy neighbour's house, thou shalt not covet thy neighbour's wife, nor his manservant, nor his maidservant, nor his ox, nor his ass, nor anything that is thy neighbour's.

FURTHER MOSAIC COMMANDMENTS

(Leviticus xix. 1–19, Revised Version.)

AND the LORD spake unto Moses, saying, Speak unto all the congregation of the children of Israel, and say unto them, Ye shall be holy: for I the LORD your God am holy. Ye shall fear every man his mother, and his father, and ye shall keep my sabbaths: I am the LORD your God. Turn ye not unto idols, nor make to yourselves molten gods: I am the LORD your God. And when ye offer a sacrifice of peace offerings unto the LORD, ye shall offer it that ye may be accepted. It shall be eaten the same day ye offer it, and on the morrow: and if aught remain until the third day, it shall be burnt with fire. And if it be eaten at all on the third day, it is an abomination; it shall not be accepted: but every one that eateth it shall bear his iniquity, because he hath profaned the holy thing of the LORD: and that soul shall be cut off from his people. And when ye reap the harvest of your land, thou shalt not wholly reap the corners of thy field, neither shalt thou gather the gleaning of thy harvest. And thou shalt not glean thy vineyard, neither shalt thou gather the fallen fruit of thy vineyard; thou shalt leave them for the poor and for the stranger: I am the LORD your God. Ye shall not steal; neither shall ye deal falsely, nor lie one to another. And ye shall not swear by my name falsely, so that thou profane the name of thy God: I am the LORD. Thou shalt not oppress thy neighbour, nor rob him: the wages of a hired servant shall not abide with thee all night until the morning. Thou shalt not curse the deaf, nor put a stumbling block before the blind, but thou shalt fear thy God: I am the LORD. Ye shall do no unrighteousness in judgement: thou shalt not respect the person of the poor, nor honour the person of the mighty: but in righteousness shalt thou judge thy neighbour. Thou shalt not go up and down as a talebearer among thy people: neither shalt thou stand against the blood of thy neighbour: I am the LORD. Thou shalt not hate thy brother in thine heart: thou shalt surely rebuke thy neighbour, and not bear sin because of him. Thou shalt not take vengeance, nor bear any grudge against the children of thy people, but thou shalt love thy neighbour as thyself: I am the LORD.

THE FIFTEENTH PSALM

THE fifteenth Psalm is one of the Psalms ascribed to David, and with considerable probability in favor of David's authorship, according to the opinion of many modern critics. Ewald includes it in the list of Psalms which he selected, on internal grounds, as most likely to have been composed by the royal lyrist; and Canon Driver concludes that "if Davidic Psalms are to be preserved in the Psalter, we may say safely that they are to be found among those which Ewald has selected."

Lord, who shall sojourn in thy tabernacle?
Who shall dwell in thy holy hill?
He that walketh uprightly, and worketh righteousness,
And speaketh truth in his heart.
He that slandereth not with his tongue,
Nor doeth evil to his friend,

Nor taketh up a reproach against his neighbour.
In whose eyes a reprobate is despised;
But he honoureth them that fear the LORD.
He that sweareth to his own hurt, and changeth not.
He that putteth not out his money to usury,
Nor taketh reward against the innocent.
He that doeth these things shall never be moved.

THE BOOK OF PROVERBS

THE Book of Proverbs is plainly made up, as critics have pointed out, of eight distinct parts: The first part, extending from the beginning of chapter i. to the end of ch. ix., is (notwithstanding the introductory words, "The Proverbs of Solomon, the son of David, king of Israel") a poetical discourse in praise of wisdom. The second part, extending from the beginning of ch. x. to verse 16 of ch. xxii., bears likewise the title, "The Proverbs of Solomon," and this time the title is accurate. The contents *are* proverbs in the strict sense of the term. The third part, beginning with verse 17 of ch. xxii. and ending with verse 22 of ch. xxiv., is made up of admonitions, described as "words of the wise," which, as remarked by Professor Driver, are "less a collection of individual proverbs than a body of maxims, in which proverbs are interwoven." The fourth part embraces only the remainder of ch. xxiv. from verse 23 to the end, under the title, "These also are sayings of the wise." Part the fifth introduces a new collection, with the title, "These also are Proverbs of Solomon, which the men of Hezekiah, king of Judah, copied out," and these fill chapters xxv. to xxix., both inclusive. The sixth part covers ch. xxx., under the title, "The words of Agur, the son of Jakeh, the oracle." In part seven there are only the first nine verses of ch. xxxi., given as "The words of Lemuel, a king; the oracle which his mother taught him." The eighth and last part, covering the remainder of ch. xxxi., has no title, but is a poem descriptive of a virtuous woman.

Says Professor Driver: "From the very different character of the various collections of which the Book is composed, it is apparent that the Book must have been formed gradually. According to the common opinion, the oldest collection is 10, 1–22, 16," — that is, the second part described above. He adds: "At what date this collection was formed cannot be determined with precision; but from the general picture of society which the proverbs seem to reflect, and especially from the manner in which the king is uniformly alluded to, it is generally referred to the golden days of the monarchy: Delitzsch thinks of the reign of Jehoshaphat; Ewald assigns it to the beginning of the eighth century." As to the authorship of the proverbs ascribed to Solomon, the professor holds the most probable view to be that those in part two are "a collection of proverbs by different ' wise men ' living under the monarchy, including a nucleus, though we cannot determine its limits or ascribe particular proverbs to it, actually the work of the Wise King (in accordance with the tradition, 1 Kings, 4, 32)." The same remarks, he thinks, will apply to the proverbs in part five of the division described above.

SELECTIONS FROM THE BOOK OF PROVERBS.

I.

The fear of the LORD is the beginning of knowledge:
But the foolish despise wisdom and instruction.
My son, hear the instruction of thy father,
And forsake not the law of thy mother:
For they shall be a chaplet of grace unto thy head,
And chains about thy neck.
My son, if sinners entice thee,
Consent thou not.
If they say, Come with us,
Let us lay wait for blood,
Let us lurk privily for the innocent without cause;
Let us swallow them up alive as Sheol,
And whole, as those that go down into the pit;
We shall find all precious substance,
We shall fill our houses with spoil;
Thou shalt cast thy lot among us;
We will all have one purse:
My son, walk thou not in the way with them;

Refrain thy foot from their path:
For their feet run to evil,
And they make haste to shed blood.
For in vain is the net spread,
In the eyes of any bird :
And these lay wait for their own blood,
They lurk privily for their own lives.
So are the ways of every one that is greedy of gain ;
It taketh away the life of the owners thereof.

III.

Happy is the man that findeth wisdom,
And the man that getteth understanding.
For the merchandise of it is better than the merchandise
     of silver,
And the gain thereof than fine gold.
She is more precious than rubies :
And none of the things thou canst desire are to be com-
     pared unto her.
Length of days is in her right hand ;
In her left hand are riches and honour.
Her ways are ways of pleasantness,
And all her paths are peace.
She is a tree of life to them that lay hold upon her:
And happy is every one that retaineth her.
Withhold not good from them to whom it is due,
When it is in the power of thine hand to do it.
Say not unto thy neighbour, Go, and come again,
And to-morrow I will give ;
When thou hast it by thee.
Devise not evil against thy neighbour,
Seeing he dwelleth securely by thee.
Strive not with a man without cause,
If he have done thee no harm.

Envy thou not the man of violence,
And choose none of his ways.
For the perverse is an abomination to the LORD;
But his secret is with the upright.
The curse of the LORD is in the house of the wicked;
But he blesseth the habitation of the righteous.
Surely he scorneth the scorners,
But he giveth grace unto the lowly.
The wise shall inherit glory;
But shame shall be the promotion of fools.

v.

My son, attend unto my wisdom;
Incline thine ear to my understanding:
That thou mayest preserve discretion,
And that thy lips may keep knowledge.
For the lips of a strange woman drop honey,
And her mouth is smoother than oil:
But her latter end is bitter as wormwood,
Sharp as a two-edged sword.
Her feet go down to death;
Her steps take hold on Sheol;
So that she findeth not the level path of life:
Her ways are unstable *and* she knoweth *it* not.
Now therefore, *my* sons, hearken unto me,
And depart not from the words of my mouth.
Remove thy way far from her,
And come not nigh the door of her house.

VI.

My son, if thou art become surety for thy neighbour,
If thou hast stricken thy hands for a stranger,
Thou art snared with the words of thy mouth,
Thou art taken with the words of thy mouth.

Do this now, my son, and deliver thyself,
Seeing thou art come into the hand of thy neighbour;
Go, humble thyself, and importune thy neighbour.
Give not sleep to thine eyes,
Nor slumber to thine eyelids.
Deliver thyself as a roe from the hand *of the hunter*,
And as a bird from the hand of the fowler.
Go to the ant, thou sluggard;
Consider her ways, and be wise:
Which having no chief,
Overseer, or ruler,
Provideth her meat in the summer,
And gathereth her food in the harvest.
How long wilt thou sleep, O sluggard?
When wilt thou arise out of thy sleep?
Yet a little sleep, a little slumber,
A little folding of the hands to sleep:
So shall thy poverty come as a robber,
And thy want as an armed man.
There be six things which the LORD hateth;
Yea, seven which are an abomination unto him:
Haughty eyes, a lying tongue,
And hands that shed innocent blood;
An heart that deviseth wicked imaginations,
Feet that be swift in running to mischief;
A false witness that uttereth lies,
And he that soweth discord among brethren.

x.

He becometh poor that dealeth with a slack hand:
But the hand of the diligent maketh rich.
He that gathereth in summer is a wise son:
But he that sleepeth in harvest is a son that causeth
    shame.

He is in the way of life that heedeth correction:
But he that forsaketh reproof erreth.
He that hideth hatred is of lying lips;
And he that uttereth a slander is a fool.
In the multitude of words there wanteth not transgression.
But he that refraineth his lips doeth wisely.
The tongue of the righteous is as choice silver:
The heart of the wicked is little worth.
The lips of the righteous feed many:
But the foolish die for lack of understanding.

XI.

A false balance is an abomination to the LORD;
But a just weight is his delight.
When pride cometh, then cometh shame:
But with the lowly is wisdom.
The integrity of the upright shall guide them:
But the perverseness of the treacherous shall destroy them.
Riches profit not in the day of wrath:
But righteousness delivereth from death.
He that despiseth his neighbour is void of wisdom:
But a man of understanding holdeth his peace.
He that goeth about as a talebearer revealeth secrets:
But he that is of a faithful spirit concealeth the matter.
Where no wise guidance is, the people falleth:
But in the multitude of counsellors there is safety.
He that is surety for a stranger shall smart for it:
But he that hateth suretiship is sure.
A gracious woman retaineth honour:
And violent men retain riches.
The merciful man doeth good to his own soul:
But he that is cruel troubleth his own flesh.
The liberal soul shall be made fat:
And he that watereth shall be watered also himself.

He that withholdeth corn, the people shall curse him:
But blessing shall be upon the head of him that selleth it.
He that diligently seeketh good seeketh favour:
But he that searcheth after mischief, it shall come unto
him.
He that trusteth in his riches shall fall:
But the righteous shall flourish as the green leaf.

XII.

A righteous man regardeth the life of his beast:
But the tender mercies of the wicked are cruel.

XIII.

The soul of the sluggard desireth, and hath nothing:
But the soul of the diligent shall be made fat.
A righteous man hateth lying:
But a wicked man is loathsome, and cometh to shame.
Righteousness guardeth him that is upright in the way:
But wickedness overthroweth the sinner.
There is that maketh himself rich, yet hath nothing:
There is that maketh himself poor, yet hath great wealth.
The ransom of a man's life is his riches:
But the poor heareth no threatening.
The light of the righteous rejoiceth:
But the lamp of the wicked shall be put out.
By pride cometh only contention:
But with the well-advised is wisdom.
Wealth gotten by vanity shall be diminished:
But he that gathereth by labour shall have increase.
Hope deferred maketh the heart sick:
But when the desire cometh, it is a tree of life.
Walk with wise men, and thou shalt be wise:
But the companion of fools shall smart for it.

XIV.

He that is slow to anger is of great understanding:
But he that is hasty of spirit exalteth folly.
A sound heart is the life of the flesh:
But envy is the rottenness of the bones.
He that oppresseth the poor reproacheth his Maker:
But he that hath mercy on the needy honoureth him.

XV.

A soft answer turneth away wrath:
But a grievous word stirreth up anger.
The tongue of the wise uttereth knowledge aright:
But the mouth of fools poureth out folly.
He that is of a cheerful heart *hath* a continual feast.
Better is little with the fear of the LORD,
Than great treasure and trouble therewith.
Better is a dinner of herbs where love is,
Than a stalled ox and hatred therewith.

XVI.

Pleasant words are *as* an honeycomb,
Sweet to the soul, and health to the bones.

XVII.

He that spareth his words hath knowledge:
And he that is of a cool spirit is a man of understanding.
Even a fool, when he holdeth his peace, is counted wise:
When he shutteth his lips he is *esteemed* as prudent.

XVIII.

He also that is slack in his work
Is brother to him that is a destroyer.

XIX.

He that hath pity upon the poor lendeth unto the LORD,
And his good deed will he pay him again.

XX.

Wine is a mocker, strong drink a brawler ;
And whosoever erreth thereby is not wise.
Divers weights and divers measures,
Both of them alike are an abomination to the LORD.
Even a child maketh himself known by his doings,
Whether his work be pure, and whether it be right.
The hearing ear, and the seeing eye,
The LORD hath made even both of them.
Love not sleep, lest thou come to poverty ;
Open thine eyes, *and* thou shalt be satisfied with bread.
It is naught, it is naught, saith the buyer :
But when he is gone his way, then he boasteth.

XXI.

He that loveth pleasure shall be a poor man :
He that loveth wine and oil shall not be rich.

XXII.

Make no friendship with a man that is given to anger ;
And with a wrathful man thou shalt not go :
Lest thou learn his ways,
And get a snare to thy soul.
Be thou not one of them that strike hands,
Or of them that are sureties for debts :
If thou hast not wherewith to pay,
Why should he take away thy bed from under thee ?
Remove not the ancient landmark,
Which thy fathers have set.

Seest thou a man diligent in his business? he shall stand
    before kings.

XXIII.

Be not among winebibbers;
Among gluttonous eaters of flesh:
For the drunkard and the glutton shall come to poverty.
Who hath woe? who hath sorrow? who hath contentions?
Who hath complaining? who hath wounds without cause?
Who hath redness of eyes?
They that tarry long at the wine;
They that go to seek out mixed wine.
Look not thou upon the wine when it is red,
When it giveth its colour in the cup,
When it goeth down smoothly:
At the last it biteth like a serpent,
And stingeth like an adder.

XXV.

Go not forth hastily to strive,
Lest *thou know not* what to do in the end thereof,
When thy neighbour hath put thee to shame.
Debate thy cause with thy neighbour *himself*,
And disclose not the secret of another:
Lest he that heareth it revile thee,
And thine infamy turn not away.
A word fitly spoken
Is *like* apples of gold in baskets of silver.
Let thy feet be seldom in thy neighbour's house;
Lest he be weary of thee, and hate thee.
If thine enemy be hungry, give him bread to eat;
And if he be thirsty, give him water to drink:
For thou shalt heap coals of fire upon his head,
And the LORD shall reward thee.

XXVI.

For lack of wood the fire goeth out:
And where there is no whisperer, contention ceaseth,
As coals are to hot embers, and wood to fire,
So is a contentious man to inflame strife.

XXVII.

Boast not thyself of to-morrow;
For thou knowest not what a day may bring forth.
Let another man praise thee, and not thine own mouth;
A stranger, and not thine own lips.
Wrath is cruel, and anger is outrageous;
But who is able to stand before jealousy?
Better is open rebuke
Than love that is hidden.

ECCLESIASTES, OR THE PREACHER

SAYS Professor Cheyne: "Jewish tradition, while admitting a Hezekian or post-Hezekian redaction to the book, assigns the original authorship of Ecclesiastes to Solomon." But he adds: "Whichever way we look, whether to the social picture, or to the language, or to the ideas of the book, its recent origin forces itself upon us. . . . The judgment of Ewald, as already expressed in 1837, appears to me on the whole satisfactory: ' One might easily imagine Koheleth [by which Hebrew name, signifying The Preacher, the book Ecclesiastes is commonly known among the critics] to be the very latest book in the Old Testament. . . . But though not the latest, it cannot have been written till long after Aramaic had begun powerfully to influence Hebrew, and therefore not before the last century of the Persian rule ' " — in other words, not before the fourth century B. C.

SELECTIONS FROM ECCLESIASTES.

CHAPTER V.

Be not rash with thy mouth, and let not thine heart be hasty to utter any thing before God ; for God is in heaven, and thou upon earth: therefore let thy words be few. For a dream cometh with a multitude of business ; and a fool's voice with a multitude of words. When thou vowest a vow unto God, defer not to pay it ; for he hath no pleasure in fools : pay that which thou vowest. Better is it that thou shouldest not vow, than that thou shouldest vow and not pay. Suffer not thy mouth to cause thy flesh to sin ; neither say thou before the angel, that it was an error: wherefore should God be angry at thy voice, and destroy the work of thine hands? For *thus it cometh to pass* through the multitude of dreams and vanities and many words: but fear thou God.

If thou seest the oppression of the poor, and the violent taking away of judgement and justice in a province, marvel not at the matter: for one higher than the high regardeth; and there be higher than they. Moreover, the profit of the earth is for all: the King *himself* is served by the field.

He that loveth silver shall not be satisfied with silver, nor he that loveth abundance with increase: this also is vanity. When goods increase, they are increased that eat them: and what advantage is there to the owner thereof, saving the beholding of them with his eyes? The sleep of a labouring man is sweet, whether he eat little or much: but the fulness of the rich will not suffer him to sleep.

There is a grievous evil which I have seen under the sun, *namely*, riches kept by the owner thereof to his hurt: and those riches perish by evil adventure; and if he hath begotten a son, there is nothing in his hand. As he came forth of his mother's womb, naked shall he go again as he came, and shall take nothing for his labour, which he may carry away in his hand. And this also is a grievous evil, that in all points as he came, so shall he go: and what profit hath he that he laboureth for the wind?

VII.

A *good* name is better than precious ointment; and the day of death than the day of one's birth. It is better to go to the house of mourning, than to go to the house of feasting: for that is the end of all men; and the living will lay it to his heart. Sorrow is better than laughter:

for by the sadness of the countenance the heart is made glad. The heart of the wise is in the house of mourning; but the heart of fools is in the house of mirth. It is better to hear the rebuke of the wise, than for a man to hear the song of fools. For as the crackling of thorns under a pot, so is the laughter of the fool: this also is vanity. Surely extortion maketh a wise man foolish; and a gift destroyeth the understanding. Better is the end of a thing than the beginning thereof: *and* the patient in spirit is better than the proud in spirit. Be not hasty in thy spirit to be angry: for anger resteth in the bosom of fools. Say not thou, What is the cause that the former days were better than these? for thou dost not inquire wisely concerning this. Wisdom is as good as an inheritance: yea, more excellent is it for them that see the sun. For wisdom is a defence, even as money is a defence: but the excellency of knowledge is, that wisdom preserveth the life of him that hath it. Consider the work of God: for who can make that straight, which he hath made crooked? In the day of prosperity be joyful, and in the day of adversity consider: God hath even made the one side by side with the other, to the end that man should not find out any thing *that shall be* after him.

VIII.

Because sentence against an evil work is not executed speedily, therefore the heart of the sons of men is fully set in them to do evil. Though a sinner do evil an hundred times, and prolong his *days*, yet surely I know that it shall be well with them that fear God, which fear before him: but it shall not be well with the wicked, neither shall he prolong *his* days, *which are* as a shadow; because he feareth not before God. There is a vanity which is done upon the earth; that there be righteous men, unto whom it happeneth according to the work of the wicked; again, there be wicked men, to whom it happeneth according to the work of the righteous : I said that this also is vanity. Then I commended mirth, because a man hath no better thing under the sun, than to eat, and to drink, and to be merry : for that shall abide with him in his labour *all* the days of his life which God hath given him under the sun.

IX.

Go thy way, eat thy bread with joy, and drink thy wine with a merry heart; for God hath already accepted thy works. Let thy garments be always white; and let not thy head lack ointment. Live joyfully with the wife whom thou lovest all the days of the life of thy vanity, which he hath given thee under the sun, all the days of thy vanity : for that is thy portion in life, and in thy labour wherein thou labourest under the sun. Whatsoever thy hand findeth to do, do *it* with thy might; for there is no work, nor device, nor knowledge, nor wisdom, in the grave, whither thou goest.

I returned, and saw under the sun, that the race is not to the swift, nor the battle to the strong, neither yet bread to the wise, nor yet riches to men of understanding, nor yet favour to men of skill; but time and chance happeneth to them all. For man also knoweth not his time : as the fishes that are taken in an evil net, and as the birds that are caught in the snare, even so are the sons of men snared in an evil time, when it falleth suddenly upon them.

XI.

Cast thy bread upon the waters : for thou shalt find it after many days. Give a portion to seven, yea, even unto eight; for thou knowest not what evil shall be upon the earth. If the clouds be full of rain, they empty themselves upon the earth: and if a tree fall toward the south, or toward the north, in the place where the tree falleth, there shall it be. He that observeth the wind shall not sow; and he that regardeth the clouds shall not reap. As thou knowest not what is the way of the wind, *nor* how the bones *do grow* in the womb of her that is with child; even so thou knowest not the work of God who doeth all. In the morning sow thy seed, and in the evening withhold not thine hand: for thou knowest not which shall prosper, whether this or that, or whether they both shall be alike good. Truly the light is sweet, and a pleasant thing it is for the eyes to behold the sun. Yea, if a man live many years, let him rejoice in them all; but let him remember the days of darkness, for they shall be many. All that cometh is vanity.

Rejoice, O young man, in thy youth; and let thy heart cheer thee in the days of thy youth, and walk in the ways of thine heart, and in the sight of thine eyes: but know thou, that for all these things God will bring thee into judgement. Therefore remove sorrow from thy heart, and put away evil from thy flesh: for youth and the prime of life are vanity.

XII.

Remember also thy Creator in the days of thy youth, or ever the evil days come, and the years draw nigh, when thou shalt say, I have no pleasure in them; or ever the sun, and the light, and the moon, and the stars, be darkened, and the clouds return after the rain: in the day when the keepers of the house shall tremble, and the strong men shall bow themselves, and the grinders cease because they are few, and those that look out of the windows be darkened, and the doors shall be shut in the street; when the sound of the grinding is low, and one shall rise up at the voice of a bird, and all the daughters of music shall be brought low ; yea, they shall be afraid of *that which is* high, and terrors *shall be* in the way ; and the almond tree shall blossom, and the grasshopper shall be a burden, and the caper-berry shall fail: because man goeth to his long home, and the mourners go about the streets : or ever the silver cord be loosed, or the golden bowl be broken, or the pitcher be broken at the fountain, or the wheel broken at the cistern ; and the dust return to the earth as it was, and the spirit return unto God who gave it. Vanity of vanities, saith the Preacher; all is vanity.

And furthermore, my son, be admonished: of making many books there is no end ; and much study is a weariness of the flesh.

This is the end of the matter; all hath been heard: fear God, and keep his commandments; for this is the whole duty of man. For God shall bring every work into judgement, with every hidden thing, whether it be good or whether it be evil.

THE CODE OF MANU

(Of unknown antiquity.)

THE collection of laws and precepts commonly called "The Code of Manu" is the oldest and most celebrated of many books of the law that were compiled among the ancient Hindus for the purpose of giving more definiteness to the vague injunctions of the Vedic hymns. Sir William Jones assigned the work to as early a date as 1280 B. C. Mr. Elphinstone placed it 900 years B. C. In the opinion of Sir Monier Monier-Williams, it can scarcely, in its present form, be placed earlier or later than the fifth century B. C. Says the latter: "We must beware of imagining that Manu's Law-book is a record of national ordinances and institutions prevalent over the whole" of India. "No doubt ultimately it worked its way to acceptance with the entire Hindu community; and certainly in the end it not only secured for itself a high place in popular estimation and a degree of reverence only second to that accorded to the Veda, but it became, moreover, the chief authority as a basis of Hindu jurisprudence." "Some of its moral precepts are worthy of Christianity itself."

In Sir Monier's interesting work entitled "Indian Wisdom," he gives, "as literally as possible," a metrical version of some of Manu's most noteworthy precepts, selected from different parts of the Code, under the four heads of $\bar{A}$ćāra, rules of conduct; Vyavahāra, rules of government and judicature; Prāyaś-ćitta, penance; Karma-phala, rewards and punishments of acts. The following is his version of the "Āćāra, or Rules of Conduct."

ĀĆĀRA, OR RULES OF CONDUCT.

(From the Code of Manu.)

Think constantly, O son, how thou mayest please
Thy father, mother, teacher — these obey.
By deep devotion seek thy debt to pay.
This is thy highest duty and religion.

(ii. 228.)

Who finds around him only wicked sons,
When called by fate to pass the gloom of death,
Is like a man who seeks to cross a flood
Borne on a raft composed of rotten wood.

(ix. 161.)

Even though wronged, treat not with disrespect
Thy father, mother, teacher, elder brother.

(ii. 226.)

From poison thou mayest take the food of life,
The purest gold from lumps of impure earth,
Examples of good conduct from a foe,
Sweet speech and gentleness from e'en a child,
Something from all; from men of low degree
Lessons of wisdom, if thou humble be.

(ii. 238, 239.)

Wound not another, though by him provoked,
Do no one injury by thought or deed,
Utter no word to pain thy fellow-creatures.

(ii. 161.)

Say what is true, speak not agreeable falsehood.

(iv. 138.)

Treat no one with disdain, with patience bear
Reviling language; with an angry man
Be never angry; blessings give for curses.

(vi. 47, 48.)

E'en as a driver checks his restive steeds,
Do thou, if thou art wise, restrain thy passions,
Which, running wild, will hurry thee away.

(ii. 88.)

When asked, give something, though a very trifle,
Ungrudgingly and with a cheerful heart,
According to thy substance ; only see
That he to whom thou givest worthy be.

(iv. 227, 228.)

Pride not thyself on thy religious works,
Give to the poor, but talk not of thy gifts.
By pride religious merit melts away,
The merit of thy alms by ostentation.

(iv. 236, 237.)

None sees us, say the sinful in their hearts ;
Yes, the gods see them, and the omniscient Spirit
Within their breasts.   Thou thinkest, O good friend,
' I am alone,' but there resides within thee
A Being who inspects thy every act,
Knows all thy goodness and thy wickedness.

(viii. 85, 91.)

The soul is its own witness, yea, the soul
Itself is its own refuge ; grieve thou not,
O man, thy soul, the great internal Witness.

(viii. 84.)

The Firmament, the Earth, the Sea, the Moon,
The Sun, the Fire, the Wind, the Night, and both
The sacred Twilights, and the Judge of souls,
The god of Justice, and the Heart itself —
All constantly survey the acts of men.

(viii. 86.)

When thou hast sinned, think not to hide thy guilt
Under a cloak of penance and austerity.

(iv. 198.)

No study of the Veda, nor oblation,
No gift of alms, nor round of strict observance
Can lead the inwardly depraved to heaven.

(ii. 97.)

If with the great Divinity who dwells
Within thy breast thou hast no controversy,
Go not to Ganges' water to be cleansed,
Nor make a pilgrimage to Kuru's fields.

(viii. 92.)

Iniquity once practised, like a seed,
Fails not to yield its fruit to him who wrought it,
If not to him, yet to his sons and grandsons.

(iv. 173.)

Contentment is the root of happiness,
And discontent the root of misery.
Wouldst thou be happy, be thou moderate.

(iv. 12.)

Honour thy food, receive it thankfully,
Eat it contentedly and joyfully,
Ne'er hold it in contempt; avoid excess,
For gluttony is hateful, injures health,
May lead to death, and surely bars the road
To holy merit and celestial bliss.

(ii. 54, 57.)

Desire is not extinguished by enjoyment,
Fire is not quenched by offerings of oil,
But blazes with increased intensity.

(ii. 94.)

Shrink thou from worldly honour as from poison,
Seek rather scorn; the scorn'd may sleep in peace,
In peace awake; the scorner perishes.

Daily perform thy own appointed work
Unweariedly; and to obtain a friend —

A sure companion to the future world —
Collect a store of virtue like the ants
Who garner up their treasures into heaps;
For neither father, mother, wife, nor son,
Nor kinsman, will remain beside thee then,
When thou art passing to that other home —
Thy virtue will thy only comrade be.

(iv. 238, 239.)

Single is every living creature born,
Single he passes to another world,
Single he eats the fruit of evil deeds,
Single, the fruit of good; and when he leaves
His body like a log or heap of clay
Upon the ground, his kinsmen walk away;
Virtue alone stays by him at the tomb
And bears him through the dreary trackless gloom.

(iv. 240, 242.)

Thou canst not gather what thou dost not sow;
As thou dost plant the tree so will it grow.

(ix. 40.)

Depend not on another, rather lean
Upon thyself; trust to thine own exertions.
Subjection to another's will gives pain;
True happiness consists in self-reliance.

(iv. 160.)

Strive to complete the task thou hast commenced;
Wearied, renew thy efforts once again;
Again fatigued, once more the work begin,
So shalt thou earn success and fortune win.

(ix. 300.)

Never despise thyself, nor yet contemn
Thy own first efforts, though they end in failure;
Seek Fortune with persistency till death,
Nor ever deem her hard to be obtained.

(iv. 137.)

Success in every enterprise depends
On Destiny and man combined, the acts
Of Destiny are out of man's control ;
Think not on Destiny, but act thyself.

(vii. 205.)

Be courteous to thy guest who visits thee ;
Offer a seat, bed, water, food enough,
According to thy substance, hospitably ;
Naught taking for thyself till he be served ;
Homage to guests brings wealth, fame, life, and heaven.

(iii. 106, iv. 29.)

He who possessed of ample means bestows
His gifts on strangers while his kindred starve,
Thinks to enjoy the honey of applause,
But only eating poison dies despised —
Such charity is cruelty disguised.

(xi. 9.)

He who pretends to be what he is not,
Acting a part, commits the worst of crimes,
For, thief-like, he abstracts a good man's heart.

(iv. 255.)

Though thou mayst suffer for thy righteous acts,
Ne'er give thy mind to aught but honest gain.

(iv. 171.)

So act in thy brief passage through this world
That thy apparel, speech, and inner store
Of knowledge be adapted to thy age,
Thy occupation, means, and parentage.

(iv. 18.)

The man who keeps his senses in control,
His speech, heart, actions, pure and ever guarded,
Gains all the fruit of holy study ; he
Needs neither penance nor austerity.

(ii. 160.)

But if a single organ fail, by that defect
His knowledge of the truth flows all away
Like water leaking from a leathern vessel.

(ii. 99.)

Contentment, patience under injury,
Self-subjugation, honesty, restraint
Of all the sensual organs, purity,
Devotion, knowledge of the Deity,
Veracity, and abstinence from anger,
These form the tenfold summary of duty.

(vi. 92.)

Long not for death, nor hanker after life;
Calmly expect thine own appointed time,
E'en as a servant reckons on his hire.

(iv. 45.)

This mansion of the soul, composed of earth,
Subject to sorrow and decrepitude,
Inhabited by sicknesses and pains,
Bound by the bonds of ignorance and darkness,
Let a wise man with cheerfulness abandon.

(vi. 77.)

Quitting this body, he resembles merely
A bird that leaves a tree.　Thus is he freed
From the fell monster of an evil world.

(vi. 78.)

HESIOD

(Eighth century, B. C.)

"IT is from the ' Works and Days ' and the introduction to the ' Theogony ' that we learn all we know about Hesiod's life. His father came from Cyme in Æolia and settled in Ascra, at the foot of Mount Helicon, in Bœotia. There, as far as we know, Hesiod spent his life. After his father's death he lost his share of his father's property in a lawsuit brought against him by his brother, Persês, who obtained a verdict by bribing the judges. This, however, seems not to have prevented Hesiod from obtaining, by careful farming, a livelihood sufficient to enable him to give assistance to his brother subsequently, when Persês was in need of aid. Nor did the work which he had to do prevent him from composing didactic poetry. . . .

"The lawsuit with his brother was the occasion of Hesiod's composing the poem which now forms the first part of the ' Works and Days '; the appeals of Persês for assistance afforded him the opportunity for giving the advice contained. . . . Under the title ' Works and Days ' there are comprised in all probability two works. There is the ' Works and Days ' proper, consisting of advice about farming and husbandry generally, and constituting the second half of the poem as it now stands. There is also another poem addressed to Hesiod's brother and containing moral advice, which makes the first half of the poem in its present form. . . .

"Hesiod's verses are not in themselves beautiful, nor does his subject, even when it of itself suggests poetical treatment, exalt his style above his ordinary prosaic level. He lacks imagination. But it is unfair to convert this into a reproach. His object was to give sound practical advice, and this he does in a practical if prosaic manner. . . . Verse was the proper vehicle for his ideas, not because they required poetical rendering, but because it was an aid to the memory." — F. B. JEVONS, " History of Greek Literature," pt. i. bk. i. ch. 6.

"The Hesiodic poems contain certain pretended reminiscences, and one of them, the 'Erga,' is largely made up of addresses to Persês, assumed to be the poet's erring friend — in one part, his brother. We have seen that the reminiscences are fictions, and presumably Persês is a fiction too. If a real man had treacherously robbed Hesiod of his patrimony by means of bribes to 'man-devouring princes,' Hesiod would scarcely have remained on intimate terms with him. Persês is a lay figure for the didactic epos to preach at, and as such he does his duty. . . . We have, then, no information of what Hesiod was — only a tradition of what Hesiod was supposed to be." — GILBERT MURRAY, "History of Ancient Greek Literature," ch. 2.

ADVICE TO PERSÊS.

(From Hesiod's "Works and Days," translated by C. A. Elton.)

Most simple Persês! I the good perceive,
And willing tell thee, wouldst thou but believe:
Choose Sin, by troops she shall beside thee stand:
Smooth is the track, her mansion is at hand:
Where Virtue dwells the gods have placed before
The dropping sweat that springs from every pore;
And ere the foot can reach her high abode,
Long, rugged, steep th' ascent, and rough the road:
The ridge once gain'd, the path so hard of late
Runs easy on, and level to the gate.
Far best is he whom conscious wisdom guides,
Who, first and last, the right and fit decides;
He too is good that to the wiser friend
His docile reason can submissive bend;
But worthless he that Wisdom's voice defies,
Nor wise himself, nor duteous to the wise.

But thou, O Persês! what my words impart
Let memory bind forever on thy heart.
O son of Dios! labour evermore,
That hunger turn abhorrent from thy door;
That Ceres bless'd with spiky garland crown'd,
Greet thee with love, and bid thy barns abound.

Still on the sluggard hungry want attends;
The scorn of man, the hate of Heaven impends;
While he, averse from labour, drags his days,
Yet greedy on the gains of others preys;
E'en as the stingless drones devouring seize
With glutted sloth the harvest of the bees.

Love every seemly toil, that so the store
Of foodful seasons heap thy garner's floor.

.   .   .   .

Shame of ill sort shall still the needy bind;
Shame, which or greatly helps or hurts mankind:
Shame leads to want; to courage wealth is given;
No ravish'd riches; best the boon of Heaven.
He that shall heaps of hoarded gold command,
By fraudful tongue, or by rapacious hand;
As oft betides, when lucre lights the flame,
And shamelessness expels the better shame;
Him shall the god cast down, in darkness hurl'd,
And that man's house be wasted from the world;
The wealth, for which he pawn'd his soul, decay,
The breath and shining bubble of a day.

Alike the man of sin is he confess'd,
Who spurns the suppliant, and who wrongs the guest;
Who climbs, by lure of stol'n embraces led,
With ill-timed act, a brother's marriage bed;
Who dares by crafty wickedness abuse
His trust, and robs the orphans of their dues;
Who, on the threshold of afflictive age

His hoary parent stings with taunting rage;
On him shall Jove in anger look from high,
And deep requite the dark iniquity:
But wholly thou from these refrain thy mind,
Weak as it is, and wavering as the wind.

With thy best means perform the ritual part,
Outwardly pure, and spotless at the heart;
Now burn choice portions to the gods; dispense
Wine-offerings now, and smoke of frankincense;
When on the nightly couch thy limbs repose,
Or sacred light from far its coming shows:
So shall they yearn to thee with soul benign,
And thou buy others' land, not others thine.

Bid to thy feast a friend; thy foe forbear;
Let a next neighbour chief thy welcome share;
In household calls th' ungirded neighbours run,
But kinsmen gird them when thy work is done.
As the good neighbour is our prop and stay,
So is the bad a pitfall in our way:
Thus bless'd or curs'd, we this or that obtain,
The first a blessing, and the last a bane.
How should thine ox by chance untimely die?
The evil neighbour looks and passes by.

Measure thy neighbour's loan, and strict repay;
Give more, if more thou canst; some future day
His ready hand thy needy call supplies;
But shun bad gains, those losses in disguise.
Love him who loves thee; to the kind draw nigh;
Give to the giver, but the churl pass by.
Men fill the giving, not th' ungiving hand;
The gift is good, but Rapine walks the land,
Squand'ring the seeds of death; though much he give,
The willing donor shall rejoice and live:
Th' extortioner of bold unblushing sin,
Though small the plunder, feels a thorn within.

If with a little thou a little blend
Continual, mighty shall the heap ascend.
Who bids his gather'd substance gradual grow
Shall see not livid hunger's face of woe.
No bosom pang attends the home-laid store,
But fraught with loss the food without thy door.
'T is good to take from hoards, and pain to need
What is far from thee : — give the precept heed.
Spare the mid-cask ; when broach'd or low, drink free ;
Bad is the thrift that spares it on the lee.
Let thy friend's service guerdon fit receive ;
Not e'en thy brother on his word believe,
But, as in laughter, set a witness by ;
Mistrust destroys us, and credulity.

THE SEVEN WISE MEN OF GREECE

(Seventh and sixth centuries before Christ.)

THEIR NAMES AND PRINCIPAL SAYINGS.

(From a Greek epigram, translated by Lord Neaves, in "The Greek Anthology" ["Ancient Classics for English Readers"].)

I 'LL tell the names and sayings and the places of their
    birth,
Of the Seven great ancient Sages, so renowned on Gre-
    cian earth:
The Lindian Cleobulus said — "The mean was still the
    best:"
The Spartan Chilo, "know thyself," a heav'n-born phrase
    confessed:
Corinthian Periander taught, "Our anger to command:"
"Too much of nothing," Pittacus, from Mitylene's strand:
Athenian Solon this advised, "Look to the end of life:"
And Bias from Prienè showed, "Bad men are the most
    rife:"
Milesian Thales urged that "None should e'er a surety
    be:"
Few were their words, but, if you look, you 'll much in
    little see.

BUDDHISM

(Sixth century before Christ.)

THE founder of the religion known as Buddhism was Gautama, son of the Rajah of the Sakyas, an Aryan tribe, whose capital town was called Kapilavastu (identified with the modern village of Nagara), about one hundred miles northeast of Benares, in India. The date of his birth has not been determined with certainty, but it was probably not far from the middle of the sixth century before Christ. Early in life Gautama became profoundly impressed with the misery and suffering in the world, and in his twenty-ninth year he suddenly abandoned his home, his princely station, his wife and child, and devoted himself, in a life of mendicancy, to the search for knowledge that might cure the sorrows of mankind. One teacher after another disappointed his hopes, but light reached him at last, and he became Buddha — that is, the Enlightened. The secret of human misery that he believed to have been revealed to him is substantially this : that suffering and sorrow are inseparable from the consciousness of individuality ; that the world, acting on that consciousness, through the senses, produces in men cravings and affections which torment them, and a lust of life that life cannot satisfy. To overcome this lust of life is to win emancipation from individual consciousness, and so escape from sorrow. The means by which such a conquest is attained are right views, right feelings, right words, right behavior, right mode of livelihood, right exertion, right memory, right meditation and tranquillity ; and the ten evil states of mind to be conquered are delusion of self, doubt, dependence on rites, sensuality, hatred, love of life on earth, desire for life in heaven, pride, self - righteousness, ignorance. Buddhism, therefore, is not so much a religion as an ethical system, or system of moral culture.

THE EIGHT PRECEPTS AND TEN COMMANDMENTS OF BUDDHISM.

(From " Buddhism," by T. W. Rhys Davids.)

1. One should not destroy life.

2. One should not take that which is not given.

3. One should not tell lies.

4. One should not become a drinker of intoxicating liquors.

5. One should refrain from unlawful sexual intercourse — an ignoble thing.

6. One should not eat unseasonable food at night.

7. One should not wear garlands or use perfumes.

8. One should sleep on a mat spread on the ground.

Such, they say, is the eight-fold sacred formula declared by Buddha, who came amongst us to put an end to sorrows. . . . With regard to these commandments, the first five, placed above in the mouth of Gautama himself, . . . are called the five commandments, *par excellence*, . . . and are binding on every Buddhist. . . . These eight precepts, together with two others — viz. 9, to abstain from dancing, music, singing and stage plays; and, 10, to abstain from the use of gold and silver — are the Ten Commandments binding on the mendicants. . . .

Besides the above division of moral duties into the five obligatory and three permissive precepts, there is another division into ten sins, which are :

Three of the body :

Taking life.

Theft (taking what has not been given).

Unlawful sexual intercourse.

Four of speech :

Lying.

Slander ("saying here what one hears there").
Abuse (swearing).
Vain conversation.
Three of the mind:
Covetousness.
Malice.
Skepticism.

BUDDHIST BEATITUDES.

(From a translation quoted by T. W. Rhys Davids in "Buddhism.")

A deva speaks —

1. Many angels and men
   Have held various things blessings,
   When they were yearning for happiness.
   Do thou declare to us the chief good.

Gautama answers —

2. Not to serve the foolish,
   But to serve the wise;
   To honour those worthy of honour:
       This is the greatest blessing.

3. To dwell in a pleasant land,
   Good works done in a former birth,
   Right desires in the heart:
       This is the greatest blessing.

4. Much insight and education,
   Self-control and pleasant speech,
   And whatever word be well-spoken:
       This is the greatest blessing.

5. To support father and mother,
   To cherish wife and child,
   To follow a peaceful calling:
      This is the greatest blessing.

6. To bestow alms and live righteously,
   To give help to kindred,
   Deeds which cannot be blamed:
      These are the greatest blessing.

7. To abhor, and cease from sin,
   Abstinence from strong drink,
   Not to be weary in well-doing,
      These are the greatest blessing.

8. Reverence and lowliness,
   Contentment and gratitude,
   The hearing of the Law at due seasons,
      This is the greatest blessing.

9. To be long-suffering and meek,
   To associate with the tranquil (*i. e.* Buddhist
      monks),
   Religious talk at due seasons,
      This is the greatest blessing.

10. Self-restraint and purity,
    The knowledge of the Noble Truths,
    The realization of Nirvāna,
       This is the greatest blessing.

11. Beneath the stroke of life's changes,
    The mind that shaketh not,
    Without grief or passion, and secure,
       This is the greatest blessing.

12. On every side are invincible
    They who do acts like these,
    On every side they walk in safety,
        And theirs is the greatest blessing.

SELECTIONS FROM THE DHAMMAPADA

(Translated by F. Max Müller, "Sacred Books of the East," v. 10.)

"THE DHAMMAPADA" is one of the canonical sacred books of the Buddhists. Its title has been interpreted in various ways, as meaning "Footsteps of Religion," "Paths of Religion," "Path of Virtue," "Sentences of Religion."

In his introduction to the translation from which the subjoined precepts are quoted, Professor F. Max Müller says: "I cannot see any reason why we should not treat the verses of the Dhammapada, if not as the utterances of Buddha, at least as what were believed by the members of the Council under Asoka, in 242 B. C., to have been the utterances of the founder of their religion."

He who lives without looking for pleasures, his senses well controlled, moderate in his food, faithful and strong, him Mâra will certainly not overthrow, any more than the wind throws down a rocky mountain.

Earnestness is the path of immortality (Nirvâna), thoughtlessness the path of death. Those who are in earnest do not die; those who are thoughtless are as if dead already.

If a traveller does not meet with one who is his better, or his equal, let him firmly keep to his solitary journey; there is no companionship with a fool.

Do not have evil-doers for friends, do not have low people for friends; have virtuous people for friends, have for friends the best of men.

If a man would hasten towards the good, he should

keep his thought away from evil; if a man does what is good slothfully, his mind delights in evil.

If a man does what is good, let him do it again; let him delight in it: happiness is the outcome of good.

Let no man think lightly of evil, saying in his heart, It will not come nigh unto me. Even by the falling of water-drops a water-pot is filled; the fool becomes full of evil, even if he gather it little by little.

Do not speak harshly to anybody; those who are spoken to will answer thee in the same way. . . .

If a man hold himself dear, let him watch himself carefully; during one at least out of the three watches a wise man should be watchful.

Self is the lord of self, who else could be the lord? With self well subdued, a man finds a lord such as few can find.

Let no one forget his own duty for the sake of another's, however great. . . .

Rouse thyself! do not be idle! Follow the law of virtue! The virtuous rests in bliss in this world and in the next.

Look upon the world as a bubble, look upon it as a mirage: the king of death does not see him who thus looks down upon the world.

Let us live happily then, not hating those who hate us! Among men who hate us, let us dwell free from hatred.

Let us live happily then, free from greed among the greedy! Among men who are greedy let us dwell free from greed.

Let us live happily then, though we call nothing our own! We shall be like the bright gods, feeding on happiness!

Victory breeds hatred, for the conquered is unhappy. He who has given up both victory and defeat, he, the contented, is happy.

He who holds back rising anger like a rolling chariot, him I call a real driver; other people are but holding the reins.

Let a man overcome anger by love, let him overcome evil by good, let him overcome the greedy by liberality, the liar by truth.

Speak the truth, do not yield to anger; give, if thou art asked for little; by these three steps thou wilt go near the gods.

Let a wise man blow off the impurities of his self, as a smith blows off the impurities of silver, one by one, little by little, and from time to time.

Life is easy to live for a man who is without shame, a crow hero, a mischief-maker, an insulting, bold, and wretched fellow.

But life is hard to live for a modest man, who always looks for what is pure, who is disinterested, quiet, spotless, and intelligent.

If by leaving a small pleasure one sees a great pleasure, let a wise man leave the small pleasure and look to the great.

Rouse thyself by thyself, examine thyself by thyself, thus self-protected and attentive wilt thou live happily. . . .

What is the use of platted hair, O fool! what of the raiment of goat-skins? Within thee there is ravening, but the outside thou makest clean.

PYTHAGORAS

(Probably of the sixth century before Christ.)

OF Pythagoras, the Greek philosopher, many legends were current in later times among the Greeks, but almost no information that is trustworthy has been found. Some have suspected that a myth is concealed under his name; but it is probable that a real Pythagoras — a primitive man of science and a born teacher and leader of men — did exist at some time in the sixth century before Christ; that he was a native of Samos, but established himself as a teacher at Crotona, in Italy; that he founded there and elsewhere in Magna Græcia a brotherhood of disciples, who made a secret, to some extent, of their knowledge and their beliefs, and who became, for some reason, obnoxious to the people, and were mercilessly attacked. The Pythagorean brotherhood survived persecution, and continued for some time, in various cities of Magna Græcia, to be known as a philosophical or religious sect. Its members believed in the transmigration of souls, and there seems to be little doubt that this was fundamental in the teaching of Pythagoras. Their doctrines in morals were of a high order, and they probably derived them, in the main, from their greatly venerated master. There seems to be, moreover, no reason to doubt that he made important discoveries in mathematics, in astronomy, and in the principles of musical harmony, which the Pythagoreans attributed to him. But various writings ascribed to him are fully believed to be the work of disciples, at a later time. Among them are the so-called "Golden Verses of Pythagoras," of which a translation is given below. We are only permitted to believe that these verses may represent somewhat nearly the morals that Pythagoras taught. The same is possible in the case of the appended "Pythagoric Sentences of Demophilus," the nominal author of which is entirely unknown.

THE GOLDEN VERSES OF PYTHAGORAS.

(Translated from the Greek by Nicholas Rowe.)

First to the Gods thy humble Homage pay ;
The greatest this, and first of Laws obey :
Perform thy Vows, observe thy plighted Troth,
And let Religion bind thee to thy Oath.
The Heroes next demand thy just regard,
Renown'd on Earth, and to the Stars preferr'd,
To Light and endless Life their Virtues sure Reward.
Due Rites perform and Honours to the Dead,
To ev'ry Wise, to ev'ry pious Shade.
With lowly Duty to thy Parents bow,
And Grace and Favour to thy Kindred show :
For what concerns the rest of Human-kind,
Chuse out the Man to Virtue best inclin'd ;
Him to thy Arms receive, him to thy Bosom bind.
Possest of such a Friend, preserve him still ;
Nor thwart his Counsels with thy stubborn Will ;
Pliant to all his Admonitions prove,
And yield to all his Offices of Love :
Him, from thy Heart, so true, so justly dear,
Let no rash Word nor light Offences tear.
Bear all thou canst, still with his Failings strive,
And to the utmost still, and still forgive ;
For strong Necessity alone explores,
The secret Vigour of our latent Pow'rs,
Rouses and urges on the lazy Heart,
Force, to its self unknown before, t' exert.
By use thy stronger Appetites asswage,
Thy Gluttony, thy Sloath, thy Lust, thy Rage :
From each dishonest Act of Shame forbear ;
Of others, and thy self, alike beware.

Let Rev'rence of thy self thy Thoughts controul,
And guard the sacred Temple of thy Soul.
Let Justice o'er thy Word and Deed preside,
And Reason ev'n thy meanest Actions guide :
For know that Death is Man's appointed Doom.
Know that the Day of great Account will come,
When thy past Life shall strictly be survey'd,
Each Word, each Deed be in the Ballance laid,
And all the Good and all the Ill most justly be repaid.
For Wealth the perishing, uncertain Good,
Ebbing and flowing like the fickle Flood,
That knows no sure, no fix'd abiding Place,
But wandering Loves from Hand to Hand to pass,
Revolve the Getter's Joy and Looser's Pain,
And think if it be worth thy while to gain.
Of all those Sorrows that attend Mankind,
With Patience bear the Lot to thee assign'd ;
Nor think it Chance, nor murmur at the Load ;
For know what Man calls Fortune is from God.
In what thou mayst from Wisdom seek Relief,
And let her healing Hand asswage the Grief ;
Yet still whate'er the Righteous Doom ordains,
What Cause soever multiplies thy Pains,
Let not those Pains as Ills be understood,
For God delights not to afflict the Good.

The Reas'ning Art to various Ends apply'd,
Is oft a sure, but oft an erring Guide.
Thy Judgment, therefore, sound and cool preserve,
Nor lightly from thy Resolution swerve ;
The dazzling Pomp of Words does oft deceive,
And sweet Persuasion wins the easie to believe.

When Fools and Liars labour to persuade,
Be dumb, and let the Bablers vainly plead.

This above all, this Precept chiefly learn,
This nearly does, and first, thy self concern;
Let no Example, let no soothing Tongue,
Prevail upon thee with a Syren's Song,
To do thy Soul's Immortal Essence wrong.
Of Good and Ill by Words or Deeds exprest,
Chuse for thy self, and always chuse the best.

Let wary thought each Enterprize forerun,
And ponder on thy Task before begun,
Lest Folly should the wretched Work deface,
And mock thy fruitless Labours with Disgrace.
Fools huddle on and always are in haste,
Act without Thought, and thoughtless Words they waste,
But thou in all thou dost, with early Cares
Strive to prevent at first a Fate like theirs;
That Sorrow on the End may never wait,
Nor sharp Repentance make thee Wise too late.
Beware thy medling Hand in ought to try,
That does beyond thy reach of Knowledge lye;
But seek to know, and bend thy serious Thought
To search the profitable Knowledge out.
So Joys on Joys for ever shall encrease,
Wisdom shall crown thy Labours, and shall bless
Thy Life with Pleasure, and thy End with Peace.
Nor let the Body want its Part, but share
A just Proportion of thy tender Care:
For Health and Welfare prudently provide,
And let its lawful Wants be all supply'd.
Let sober Draughts refresh, and wholsome Fare
Decaying Nature's wasted Force repair;
And sprightly Exercise the duller Spirits chear.
In all Things still which to this Care belong,
Observe this Rule, to guard thy Soul from Wrong.

By virtuous Use thy Life and Manners frame,
Manly and simply pure, and free from Blame.
Provoke not Envy's deadly Rage, but fly
The glancing Curse of her malicious Eye.
Seek not in needless Luxury to waste
Thy Wealth and Substance, with a Spendthrift's Haste;
Yet flying these, be watchful, lest thy Mind,
Prone to Extreams, an equal Danger find,
And be to sordid Avarice inclin'd.
Distant alike from each, to neither lean,
But ever keep the happy Golden Mean.
Be careful still to guard thy Soul from Wrong,
And let thy Thought prevent thy Hand and Tongue.
Let not the stealing God of Sleep surprize
Nor creep in Slumbers on thy weary Eyes,
E'er ev'ry Action of the former Day
Strictly thou dost and righteously survey.
With Rev'rence at thy own Tribunal stand,
And answer justly to thy own Demand:
Where have I been? In what have I transgress'd?
What Good or Ill has this Day's Life express'd?
Where have I fail'd in what I ought to do?
In what to God, to Man, or to my self I owe?
Inquire severe whate'er from first to last,
From Morning's Dawn 'till Ev'ning's Gloom has past.
If Evil were thy Deeds, repenting mourn,
And let thy Soul with strong Remorse be torn.
If Good, the Good with Peace of Mind repay,
And to thy secret Self with Pleasure say,
Rejoice, my Heart, for all went well to Day.
These Thoughts and chiefly these thy Mind should move,
Employ thy Study, and engage thy Love.
These are the Rules which will to Virtue lead,
And teach thy Feet her Heav'nly Paths to tread.

THE PYTHAGORIC SENTENCES OF DEMOPHILUS.

(Translated from the Greek by Thomas Taylor.)

1. Request not of Divinity such things as, when obtained, you cannot preserve; for no gift of Divinity can ever be taken away; and on this account he does not confer that which you are unable to retain.

2. Be vigilant in your intellectual part; for sleep about this has an affinity with real death.

3. Divinity sends evil to men, not as being influenced by anger, but for the sake of purification; for anger is foreign from Divinity, since it arises from circumstances taking place contrary to the will; but nothing contrary to the will can happen to a god.

4. When you deliberate whether or not you shall injure another, you will previously suffer the evil yourself which you intended to commit. But neither must you expect any good from the evil; for the manners of every one are correspondent to his life and actions. Every soul, too, is a repository, that which is good, of things good, and that which is evil, of things depraved.

5. After long consultation, engage either in speaking or acting; for you have not the ability to recall either your words or deeds.

6. Divinity does not principally esteem the tongue, but the deeds of the wise; for a wise man, even when he is silent, honours Divinity.

7. A loquacious and ignorant man both in prayer and sacrifice contaminates a divine nature. The wise man, therefore, is alone a priest, is alone the friend of Divinity, and only knows how to pray.

8. The wise man being sent hither naked, should naked invoke him by whom he was sent; for he alone is heard by Divinity, who is not burdened with foreign concerns.

9. It is impossible to receive from Divinity any gift greater than virtue.

10. Gifts and victims confer no honour on Divinity, nor is he adorned with offerings suspended in temples ; but a soul divinely inspired solidly conjoins us with Divinity ; for it is necessary that like should approach to like.

11. It is more painful to be subservient to passions than to tyrants themselves.

12. It is better to converse more with yourself than with others.

13. If you are always careful to remember, that in whatever place either your soul or body accomplishes any deed, Divinity is present as an inspector of your conduct; in all your words and actions you will venerate the presence of an inspector from whom nothing can be concealed, and will, at the same time, possess Divinity as an intimate associate.

14. Believe that you are furious and insane in proportion as you are ignorant of yourself.

15. It is necessary to search for those wives and children which will remain after a liberation from the present life.

16. The self-sufficient and needy philosopher lives a life truly similar to Divinity, and considers the non-possession of external and unnecessary goods as the greatest wealth. For the acquisition of riches sometimes inflames desire ; but not to act in any respect unjustly is sufficient to the enjoyment of a blessed life.

17. True goods are never produced by indolent habits.

18. Esteem that to be eminently good, which, when communicated to another, will be increased to yourself.

19. Esteem those to be eminently your friends, who assist your soul rather than your body.

20. Consider both the praise and reproach of every

foolish person as ridiculous, and the whole life of an ignorant man as a disgrace.

21. Endeavour that your familiars may reverence
rather than fear you; for love attends upon reverence,
but hatred upon fear.

22. The sacrifices of fools are the aliment of the fire;
but the offerings which they suspend in temples are the
supplies of the sacrilegious.

23. Understand that no dissimulation can be long concealed.

24. The unjust man suffers greater evil while his soul
is tormented with a consciousness of guilt, than when his
body is scourged with whips.

25. It is by no means safe to discourse concerning
Divinity with men of false opinions; for the danger is
equally great in speaking to such as these, things either
fallacious or true.

26. By every where using reason as your guide, you
will avoid the commission of crimes.

27. By being troublesome to others, you will not easily
escape molestation yourself.

28. Consider that as great erudition, through which
you are able to bear the want of erudition in the ignorant.

29. He who is depraved does not listen to the divine
law, and on this account lives without law.

30. A just man who is a stranger, is not only superior
to a citizen, but is even more excellent than a relation.

31. As many passions of the soul, so many fierce and
savage despots.

32. No one is free who has not obtained the empire of
himself.

33. Labour together with continence precedes the acquisition of every good.

34. Be persuaded that those things are not your riches

which you do not possess in the penetralia of the reasoning power.

35. Do that which you judge to be beautiful and honest, though you should acquire no glory from the performance ; for the vulgar is a depraved judge of beautiful deeds.

36. Make trial of a man rather from his deeds than his discourses ; for many live badly and speak well.

37. Perform great things, at the same time promising nothing great.

38. Since the roots of our natures are established in Divinity, from which also we are produced, we should tenaciously adhere to our root; for streams also of water, and other offspring of the earth, when their roots are cut off become rotten and dry.

39. The strength of the soul is temperance ; for this is the light of a soul destitute of passions ; but it is much better to die than to darken the soul through the intemperance of the body.

40. You cannot easily denominate that man happy who depends either on his friends or children, or on any fleeting and fallen nature ; for all these are unstable and uncertain ; but to depend on oneself and on Divinity is alone stable and firm.

41. He is a wise man, and beloved by Divinity, who studies how to labour for the good of his soul, as much as others labour for the sake of the body.

42. Yield all things to their kindred and ruling nature except liberty.

43. Learn how to produce eternal children, not such as may supply the wants of the body in old age, but such as may nourish the soul with perpetual food.

44. It is impossible that the same person can be a lover of pleasure, a lover of body, a lover of riches, and a lover

of Divinity. For a lover of pleasure is also a lover of body; but a lover of body is entirely a lover of riches; a lover of riches is necessarily unjust; and the unjust is necessarily profane towards Divinity, and lawless with respect to men. Hence, though he should sacrifice hecatombs, he is only by this mean the more impious, unholy, atheistical, and sacrilegious, with respect to his intention: and on this account it is necessary to avoid every lover of pleasure as an atheist and polluted person.

45. The Divinity has not a place in the earth more allied to his nature than a pure and holy soul.

THE MAHA-BHARATA

(Probably from the fifth century before Christ.)

THE MAHA-BHARATA, one of the two great epic poems of the Hindus, is, says Sir Monier Monier-Williams, "probably by far the longest epic poem that the world has ever produced. Its main design is to describe the great contest between the descendants of King Bharata. He was the most renowned monarch of the Lunar dynasty, and is alleged to have reigned in the neighborhood of Hastinapur or ancient Delhi, and to have extended his authority over a great part of India, so that India to this day is called by the natives Bharata-varsha. The great epic, however, is not so much a poem with a single subject as a cyclopedia or thesaurus of Hindu mythology, legendary history, ethics, and philosophy. The work, as we now possess it, cannot possibly be regarded as representing the original form of the poem. Its compilation appears to have proceeded gradually for centuries." In the opinion of Sir Monier, the first version of the poem should be dated early in the fifth century before Christ.

In his excellent work on the sacred and philosophical literature of India, entitled "Indian Wisdom," Sir Monier gives some translations from the moral precepts of the Maha-bharata, and the following selections are borrowed from them: —

SELECTIONS FROM THE MORAL PRECEPTS OF THE MAHA-BHARATA.

(From "Indian Wisdom," by Sir Monier Monier-Williams.)

> Conquer a man who never gives by gifts;
> Subdue untruthful men by truthfulness;
> Vanquish an angry man by gentleness;
> And overcome the evil man by goodness.
>
> (iii. 13253.)

To injure none by thought or word or deed,
To give to others, and be kind to all —
This is the constant duty of the good.
High-minded men delight in doing good,
Without a thought of their own interest ;
When they confer a benefit on others,
They reckon not on favours in return.

(iii. 16782, 16796.)

Two persons will hereafter be exalted
Above the heavens — the man with boundless power
Who yet forbears to use it indiscreetly,
And he who is not rich and yet can give.

(v. 1028.)

Bear railing words with patience, never meet
An angry man with anger, nor return
Reviling for reviling, smite not him
Who smites thee ; let thy speech and acts be gentle.

(v. 1270, 9972.)

If thou art wise, seek ease and happiness
In deeds of virtue and of usefulness ;
And ever act in such a way by day
That in the night thy sleep may tranquil be ;
And so comport thyself when thou art young,
That when thou art grown old, thine age may pass
In calm serenity.   So ply thy task
Throughout thy life, that when thy days are ended,
Thou may'st enjoy eternal bliss hereafter.

(v. 1248.)

Esteem that gain a loss which ends in harm ;
Account that loss a gain which brings advantage.

(v. 1451.)

Do naught to others which if done to thee
Would cause thee pain ; this is the sum of duty.

(v. 1517.)

He who lets slip his opportunity,
And turns not the occasion to account,
Though he may strive to execute his work,
Finds not again the fitting time for action.

(xii. 3814.)

Enjoy thou the prosperity of others,
Although thyself unprosperous ; noble men
Take pleasure in their neighbour's happiness.

(xii. 3880.)

Be active now,
While thou art young, and time is still thine own.
This very day perform to-morrow's work,
This very morning do thy evening's task.
When duty is discharged, then if thou live,
Honour and happiness will be thy lot,
And if thou die, supreme beatitude.

(xii. 6534.)

This is the sum of all true righteousness —
Treat others, as thou would'st thyself be treated.
Do nothing to thy neighbour, which hereafter
Thou would'st not have thy neighbour do to thee.
In causing pleasure, or in giving pain,
In doing good, or injury to others,
In granting, or refusing a request,
A man obtains a proper rule of action
By looking on his neighbour as himself.

(xiii. 5571.)

Before infirmities creep o'er thy flesh ;
Before decay impairs thy strength and mars
The beauty of thy limbs ; before the Ender,
Whose charioteer is sickness, hastes towards thee,
Breaks up thy fragile frame and ends thy life,
Lay up the only treasure : do good deeds ;

Practice sobriety and self-control ;
Amass that wealth which thieves cannot abstract,
Nor tyrants seize, which follows thee at death,
Which never wastes away, nor is corrupted.

(xiii. 12084.)

CONFUCIUS

(B. C. 551–478.)

THE birth of Confucius is believed to have occurred in the year 551 B. C. "Of the parents of the Sage we know but little, except that his father, Shuh-leang Heîh, was a military officer, eminent for his commanding stature, his great bravery, and immense strength, and that his mother's name was Yen Ching-tsai. The marriage of this couple took place when Heîh was seventy years old, and the prospects, therefore, of his having an heir having been but slight, unusual rejoicings commemorated the birth of the son, who was destined to achieve such everlasting fame. . . . Of the early years of Confucius we have but scanty record. It would seem that from his childhood he showed ritualistic tendencies, and we are told that as a boy he delighted to play at the arrangement of vessels and at postures of ceremony. As he advanced in years he became an earnest student of history, and looked back with love and reverence to the time when the great and good Yaou and Shun [sovereigns of the legendary dawn of Chinese history] reigned in —

'A golden age, fruitful of golden deeds.'

"At the age of fifteen 'he bent his mind to learning,' and when he was nineteen years old he married a lady from the state of Sung. As has befallen many other great men, Confucius's married life was not a happy one, and he finally divorced his wife, not, however, before she had borne him a son.

"Soon after his marriage, at the instigation of poverty, Confucius accepted the office of keeper of the stores of grain, and in the following year he was promoted to be guardian of the public fields and lands. . . . At the age of twenty-two we find Confucius released from the toils of office and devoting his time to the more congenial task of imparting instruction to a band of admiring and earnest students." From about the age of thirty until his death the career of Confucius may be described as that of an itinerant teacher and reformer. He journeyed from court to court of the struggling, ephemeral states which composed the troubled empire, offering counsel to the rulers in turn and sometimes holding important offices for a season, but having little success on the whole. He had faithful disciples who adhered to him throughout, and his fame as a sage grew great even in his lifetime. He died in 478 B. C. at the age of seventy-three.

"There is nothing spiritual in the teachings of Confucius. He rather avoided all references to the supernatural. In answer to a question about death, he answered, 'While you do not know life, how do you know about death.' Life, then, was his study, and life as represented by man as he exists." — ROBERT K. DOUGLAS, "Confucianism and Taouism."

SIXTEEN CONFUCIAN MAXIMS.

(From " Confucianism and Taouism," by Robert K. Douglas.)

Towards the close of the seventeenth century the Emperor K'ang-he . . . issued sixteen maxims, founded on the teachings of the Sage [Confucius], for the guidance of the people, whose morality "had for some time been daily declining, and whose hearts were not as of old." He thus summed up, as it were, all the essential points in the Confucian doctrine, and thus he wrote : —

1. Esteem most highly filial piety and brotherly submission, in order to give due prominence to the social relations.

2. Behave with generosity to the branches of your kindred, in order to illustrate harmony and benignity.

3. Cultivate peace and concord in your neighbourhoods, in order to prevent quarrels and litigations.

4. Recognise the importance of husbandry and the culture of the mulberry-tree, in order to ensure a sufficiency of clothing and food.

5. Show that you prize moderation and economy, in order to prevent the lavish waste of your means.

6. Make much of the colleges and seminaries, in order to make correct the practice of the scholars.

7. Discountenance and banish strange doctrines, in order to exalt the correct doctrine.

8. Describe and explain the laws, in order to warn the ignorant and obstinate.

9. Exhibit clearly propriety and yielding courtesy, in order to make manners and customs good.

10. Labour diligently at your proper callings, in order to give settlement to the aims of the people.

11. Instruct sons and younger brothers, in order to prevent them from doing what is wrong.

12. Put a stop to false accusations, in order to protect the honest and the good.

13. Warn against sheltering deserters, in order to avoid being involved in their punishments.

14. Promptly and fully pay your taxes, in order to avoid the urgent requisition of your quota.

15. Combine in hundreds and tithings, in order to put an end to thefts and robbery.

16. Study to remove resentments and angry feelings, in order to show the importance due to the person and life.

CONFUCIAN ANALECTS.

(From " The Life and Teachings of Confucius," by James Legge.)

Tsze-kung asked, saying, " Is there one word which may serve as a rule of practice for all one's life ? " The Master said, " Is not RECIPROCITY such a word ? What you do not want done to yourself, do not do to others."

Confucius said, " There are three things which the superior man guards against. In youth, when the physical powers are not yet settled, he guards against lust. When he is strong, and the physical powers are full of vigour, he guards against quarrelsomeness. When he is old, and the animal powers are decayed, he guards against covetousness."

Confucius said, "The superior man has nine things which are subjects with him of thoughtful consideration. In regard to the use of his eyes, he is anxious to see clearly. In regard to the use of his ears, he is anxious to hear distinctly. In regard to his countenance, he is anxious that it should be benign. In regard to his demeanour, he is anxious that it should be respectful. In regard to his speech, he is anxious that it should be sincere. In regard to his doing of business, he is anxious that it should be reverently careful. In regard to what he doubts about, he is anxious to question others. When he is angry, he thinks of the difficulties his anger may involve him in. When he sees gain to be got, he thinks of righteousness."

THE STORY OF AHIKAR

MR. F. C. CONYBEARE, Dr. J. Rendel Harris, and Mrs. Agnes Smith Lewis, published, in 1898, six versions, from the Syriac, the Arabic, the Armenian, the Ethiopic, the Greek, and the Slavonic languages, of a story of great antiquity, which has been found in many forms, among many peoples, and the nucleus of which they believe to have been Biblical or semi-Biblical in origin. It seems to have come to modern notice first in connection with the tales of the Arabian Nights. "Whether," says Dr. Harris in his introduction, "it be actually a part of the recitations by which for 1001 nights the faithful and ingenious Scheherezade whiled away the impatience and wore out the mistrust and wrath of the Sultan, or whether it is only a supplement to that collection, is not of immediate importance." That it comes from a very early time and was told far and wide in the ancient Eastern world is clearly shown.

Ahikar, or Haykar, of whom the story is told, and whose maxims and wise sayings may be called the very marrow of it, is represented to have been the vizier of Sennacherib, king of Assyria, and "famous amongst men for his wisdom in all that concerned morality and politics." He had no son, but adopted a nephew, Nadan, or Nathan, to whom his precepts are addressed. Nadan, handsome in person, crafty in mind, specious in manner, proved to be "a goodly apple rotten at the core," and his heartless ingratitude to the generous Ahikar is the theme of the tale.

The precepts which follow are chosen from the Armenian version of the story, as translated in the work mentioned above.

SELECTIONS FROM THE STORY OF AHIKAR.

Son, be not like the olive tree, which is first to bloom and last to ripen its fruit. But be like the mulberry, which is last to bloom and first to ripen its fruit.

Son, be thou not over-sweet, so that they swallow thee down, nor over-bitter, so that they spit thee out. But do thou be gentle, tranquil in the works of thy paths and in all thy words.

Son, while the boot is on thy foot, tread down the thorns and make a path for thy sons.

Son, eat not bread that is not thine own, even though thou be very hungry.

Son, if thy doorposts be loftily built to heaven as it were seven ells, whenever thou enterest, bow thy head.

Son, take not from others with a big weight and give back to them with a little weight, and say: I have made a profit. For God gives it not, but will be wroth; and thou wilt die of starvation.

Son, swear not false, that of thy days there be no fail.

Son, if lofty be the lintels of thy house, and thy friend be sick, say not: What shall I send him? but go on foot and see him with thy eyes; for that is better for him than a thousand talents of gold and silver.

Son, keep thy tongue from evil speaking and thine eye from immodest glances, and thy right hand from stealing; and it will be well for thee with God and man. For whether it be gold or little things that one steals, the punishment and the slaying is one and the same.

Son, it is better to be blind of eye than blind of mind; for he that is blind of eye is quick to learn the coming and going of the road. But the blind in mind forsakes the straight road, and walks according to his will.

Son, it is better to garner with poverty than to squander with riches.

Son, examine the word in thy heart and then utter it. For if thou alter the word, thou art a fawner.

Son, if thou hearest an evil word about any one, hide it in thy heart seven fathoms deep; so that the evil die and the good be fulfilled.

Son, I have eaten endive and I have drunk gall, and it was not more bitter than poverty. I have lifted salt and I have lifted lead, and it was not heavier than is debt.

Son, it is better if they steal thy goods than that they detect theft in thee.

Son, that which seems evil unto thee, do not to thy companion; and what is not thine own, give not unto others.

Son, love the truth and hate lawlessness and falsehood. Give ear unto the commandments of God, and fear not the evil one. For the commandment of God is the rampart of man.

They asked the sage and said: What is the most pleasing thing on earth? He replied: Modesty. He that hath a modest face is pleasing. For all evils are born of impudence and folly.

ARISTOTLE

(B. C. 384-322.)

"ARISTOTLE was born in the year 384 B. C., at Stageira, a Grecian colony and seaport town on the Strymonic Gulf in Thrace, not far from Mount Athos — and, what is more important, not far from the frontier of Macedonia, and from Pella, the residence of the Macedonian king Amyntas. To Stageira, his birthplace, he owed the world-famous appellation of ' the Stagirite,' given to him by scholiasts and schoolmen in later days. . . . Aristotle's family were purely Hellenic, and probably the colonists of Stageira lived in strict conformity with Greek ideas, and not without contempt for the surrounding ' barbarians.' . . . Probably the mere locality of his birth produced but little influence upon him, except so far as it led to his subsequent connection with the court of Macedon. His father, Nicomachus, was physician to King Amyntas, and it is possible that the youthful Aristotle was taken at times to the court, and thus made the acquaintance of his future patron, Philip of Macedon, who was about his own age. But all through the time of Aristotle's boyhood, affairs in Macedonia were troubled and unprosperous. . . . Up to the time when he left his native city there had appeared no indication of that which afterwards occurred, — that Macedonia would conquer the East, and become mistress of the entire liberties of Greece. . . . About the year 367 B. C., when he was seventeen years old, his father having recently died, he was sent by his guardian, Proxenus of Atarneus, to complete his studies at Athens, the ' metropolis of wisdom.' There he continued to reside for twenty years, during the greater part of which time he attended the school of philosophy which Plato had founded in the olive-groves of Academus, on the banks of the Cephisus. . . . Among his fellow-pupils in the Academe he is said to have got the sobriquet of ' the Reader '; while Plato himself called him ' the Mind of the

School,' in recognition of his quick and powerful intelligence. . . .

"The writings of Aristotle are quite consistent with the tradition that he was for twenty years a pupil of the Academic School. They show a long list of thoughts and expressions borrowed from the works of Plato, and also not unfrequently refer to the oral teaching of Plato. They contain a logical, ethical, political, and metaphysical philosophy which is evidently, with some modifications, the organization and development of rich materials often rather suggested than worked out in the Platonic dialogues. Aristotle thus, in constructing a system of knowledge which was destined immensely to influence the thoughts of mankind, became, in the first place, the disciple of Plato and the intellectual heir of Socrates; and summed up all the best that had been arrived at by the previous philosophers of Greece."

In the year that Plato died, 347 B. C., Aristotle left Athens and resided for a few years, first at Atarneus, in Asia Minor, where he married, and then at Mitylene, in the island of Lesbos. He was then invited by Philip of Macedon to become the tutor of Alexander, and resided at the Macedonian court until after the assassination of Philip (336 B. C.), when he returned to Athens. On the death of Alexander, 323 B. C., Aristotle was driven from Athens by the anti-Macedonian party, and retired to Chalcis in Eubœa, where he died the following year.

"Perhaps it may be said, in a word, that Aristotle has contributed more than any one man to the scientific education of the world. The amount of the influence which he has exercised may be inferred from the traces which his system has left in all the languages of modern Europe. Our everyday conversation is full of Aristotelian ' fossils,' that is, remnants of his peculiar phraseology." — SIR ALEXANDER GRANT, "Aristotle" ("Ancient Classics for English Readers").

INJUNCTIONS FOR THE KEEPING OF "THE MEAN" BETWEEN EXCESS AND DEFECT.

(From "The Nichomachean Ethics of Aristotle," book 2, chap. ii. and ix. ; translated by D. P. Chase.)

That we are to act in accordance with Right Reason is a general maxim, and may for the present be taken for granted. . . . But let this point be first thoroughly understood between us, that all which can be said on moral action must be said in outline, as it were, and not exactly : for . . . such reasoning only must be required as the nature of the subject-matter admits of, and matters of moral action and expediency have no fixedness any more than matters of health. And if the subject in its general maxims is such, still less in its application to particular cases is exactness attainable : because these fall not under any art or system of rules, but it must be left in each instance to the individual agents to look to the exigencies of the particular case, as it is in the art of healing, or that of navigating a ship. Still, though the present subject is confessedly such, we must try and do what we can for it.

First, then, this must be noted, that it is the nature of such things to be spoiled by defect and excess ; as we see in the case of health and strength (since for the illustration of things which cannot be seen we must use those that can), for excessive training impairs the strength as well as deficient : meat and drink, in like manner, in too great or too small quantities, impair the health : while in due proportion they cause, increase, and preserve it.

Thus it is, therefore, with the habits of perfected Self-Mastery and Courage and the rest of the Virtues : for the man who flies from and fears all things, and never stands up against any thing, comes to be a coward ; and he who fears nothing, but goes at every thing, comes to be rash. In like manner, too, he that tastes of every pleasure and abstains from none, comes to lose all self-control ; while he who avoids all, as do the dull and clownish, comes as it were to lose his faculties of perception : that is to say, the habits of perfected Self-Mastery and Courage are spoiled by the excess and defect, but by the mean state are preserved.

Furthermore, not only do the origination, growth, and marring of the habits come from and by the same circumstances, but also the acts of working after the habits are formed will be exercised on the same : for so it is also with those other things which are more directly matters of sight, strength for instance : for this comes by taking plenty of food and doing plenty of work, and the man who has attained strength is best able to do these : and so it is with the Virtues, for not only do we by abstaining from pleasures come to be perfected in Self-Mastery, but when we have come to be so we can best abstain from them : similarly too with courage : for it is by accustoming ourselves to despise objects of fear and stand up against them that we come to be brave ; and after we have come to be so we shall be best able to stand up against such objects.

And for a test of the formation of the habits we must take the pleasure or pain which succeeds the acts ; for he is perfected in Self-Mastery who not only abstains from the bodily pleasures but is glad to do so ; whereas he who abstains but is sorry to do it has not Self-Mastery : he again is brave who stands up against danger either with positive pleasure or at least without any pain ; whereas he who does it with pain is not brave. . . .

There are principally three things moving us to choice, and three to avoidance, the honourable, the expedient, the pleasant; and their three contraries, the dishonourable, the hurtful, and the painful ; now the good man is apt to go right, and the bad man wrong, with respect to all these of course, but most specially with respect to pleasure : because not only is this common to him with all animals, but also it is a concomitant of all those things which move to choice, since both the honourable and the expedient give an impression of pleasure. . . .

That Moral Virtue is a mean state, and how it is so, and that it lies between two faulty states, one in the way of excess and another in the way of defect, and that it is so because it has an aptitude to aim at the mean both in feelings and actions, all this has been set forth fully and sufficiently.

And so it is hard to be good : for surely hard it is in each instance to find the mean, just as to find the mean point or centre of a circle is not what any man can do, but only he who knows how: just so to be angry, to give money, and be expensive, is what any man can do and easy : but to do these to the right person, in due propor- tion, at the right time, with a right object, and in the right manner, this is not as before what any man can do nor is it easy : and for this cause goodness is rare and praiseworthy and noble.

Therefore he who aims at the mean should make it his first care to keep away from that extreme which is more contrary than the other to the mean ; just as Calypso in Homer advises Ulysses —

"Clear of this smoke and surge thy barque direct ; "
because of the two extremes the one is always more, and the other less erroneous : and, therefore, since to hit exactly on the mean is difficult, one must take the least of the evils as the safest plan ; and this a man will be doing if he follows this method.

We ought also to take into consideration our own natural bias; which varies in each man's case and will be ascertained from the pleasure and pain arising in us. Furthermore, we should force ourselves off in the contrary direction, because we shall find ourselves in the mean after we have removed ourselves far from the wrong side, exactly as men do in straightening bent timber.

But in all cases we must guard most carefully against what is pleasant, and pleasure itself because we are not impartial judges of it.

We ought to feel in fact towards pleasure as did the old counsellors toward Helen, and in all cases pronounce a similar sentence: for so by sending it away from us we shall err the less.

Well, to speak very briefly, these are the precautions by adopting which we shall be best able to attain the mean.

Still, perhaps, after all, it is a matter of difficulty, and especially in the particular instances: it is not easy, for instance, to determine exactly in what manner, with what persons, for what causes, and for what length of time, one ought to feel anger: for we ourselves sometimes praise those who are defective in this feeling, and we call them meek; at another we term the hot-tempered manly and spirited.

Then again, he who makes a small deflection from what is right, be it on the side of too much or too little, is not blamed, only he who makes a considerable one, for he cannot escape observation. But to what point or degree a man must err in order to incur blame it is not easy to determine exactly in words: nor in fact any of those points which are matter of perception by the Moral Sense: such questions are matters of detail and the decision of them rests with the Moral Sense.

At all events thus much is plain, that the mean state is in all things praiseworthy, and that practically we must deflect sometimes towards excess, sometimes towards defect, because this will be the easiest method of hitting on the mean, that is, on what is right.

ECCLESIASTICUS

(Second century before Christ.)

IN his work on "Job and Solomon, or the Wisdom of the Old Testament," Professor Cheyne gives the following account of the Apocryphal book entitled "The Wisdom of Jesus the Son of Sirach, or Ecclesiasticus:" "The author was, beyond reasonable doubt, a contemporary of 'Simon the high priest, the son of Onias.' Now there were five high priests who bore the name of Simon or Simeon, two of whom, Simon I. (B. C. 310–290) and Simon II. (B. C. 219–199), have by different critics been thought of. The weight of argument is in favor of the second of the name, who was certainly the more important of the two, and who is referred to in the Talmud under the name of Simeon the Righteous. This is in accordance with the Greek translator's statement in his preface, that he was the grandson of the author, and we may conjecturally fix the composition of the book at about 180 B. C. The translator himself came into Egypt, as he tells us, in the 38th year of King Euergetes (comp. Luke xxii. 25). Now Euergetes II., Physkon, who must be here intended, began to reign jointly with his brother Philometer B. C. 170; his brother died B. C. 145, and he reigned alone for twenty-five years longer (till B. C. 116). Hence the translator's arrival in Egypt and possibly the translation itself fall within the year 132. The object of his work, we gather from the preface, was to correct the inequalities of moral and religious culture among the Jews of Egypt by setting before them a standard and a lesson book of true religious wisdom."

SELECTIONS FROM "THE WISDOM OF JESUS THE SON OF SIRACH, OR ECCLESIASTICUS."

(From the Apocrypha.)

CHAPTER III.

Honour thy father and mother both in word and deed, that a blessing may come upon thee from them.

My son, help thy father in his age, and grieve him not as long as he liveth.

And if his understanding fail, have patience with him; and despise him not when thou art in thy full strength.

He that forsaketh his father is as a blasphemer; and he that angereth his mother is cursed of God.

My son, go on with thy business in meekness; so shalt thou be beloved of him that is approved.

The greater thou art, the more humble thyself, and thou shalt find favour before the Lord.

Seek not out the things that are too hard for thee, neither search the things that are above thy strength.

But what is commanded thee, think thereupon with reverence; for it is not needful for thee to see with thine eyes the things that are in secret.

Be not curious in unnecessary matters: for more things are shewed unto thee than men understand.

For many are deceived by their own vain opinion; and an evil suspicion hath overthrown their judgment.

A stubborn heart shall fare evil at the last; and he that loveth danger shall perish therein.

IV.

My son, defraud not the poor of his living, and make not the needy eyes to wait long.

Make not a hungry soul sorrowful; neither provoke a man in his distress.

Add not more trouble to a heart that is vexed; and defer not to give to him that is in need.

Reject not the supplication of the afflicted; neither turn away thy face from a poor man.

Turn not away thine eye from the needy, and give him none occasion to curse thee:

For if he curse thee in the bitterness of his soul, his prayer shall be heard of him that made him.

Get thyself the love of the congregation, and bow thy head to a great man.

Let it not grieve thee to bow down thine ear to the poor, and give him a friendly answer with meekness.

Deliver him that suffereth wrong from the hand of the oppressor; and be not faint-hearted when thou sittest in judgment.

Be as a father unto the fatherless, and instead of a husband unto their mother: so shalt thou be as a son of the Most High, and he shall love thee more than thy mother doth.

Observe the opportunity, and beware of evil; and be not ashamed when it concerneth thy soul.

For there is a shame that bringeth sin; and there is a shame which is glory and grace.

In no wise speak against the truth; but be abashed of the error of thine ignorance.

Be not ashamed to confess thy sins; and force not the course of the river.

Make not thyself an underling to a foolish man; neither accept the person of the mighty.

Strive for the truth unto death, and the Lord shall fight for thee.

Be not hasty in thy tongue, and in thy deeds slack and remiss.

Be not as a lion in thy house, nor frantic among thy servants.

Let not thy hand be stretched out to receive, and shut when thou shouldst repay.

v.

Set not thy heart upon thy goods; and say not, I have enough for my life.

Follow not thine own mind and thy strength, to walk in the ways of thy heart.

And say not, Who shall control me for my works? for the Lord will surely revenge thy pride.

Say not, I have sinned, and what harm hath happened unto me? for the Lord is long-suffering, he will in no wise let thee go.

Set not thy heart upon goods unjustly gotten: for they shall not profit thee in the day of calamity.

Winnow not with every wind, and go not into every way: for so doth the sinner that hath a double tongue.

Be steadfast in thine understanding; and let thy word be the same.

Be swift to hear; and let thy life be sincere; and with patience give answer.

If thou hast understanding, answer thy neighbour; if not, lay thy hand upon thy mouth.

Honour and shame is in talk: and the tongue of man is his fall.

Be not called a whisperer, and lie not in wait with thy tongue; for a foul shame is upon the thief, and an evil condemnation upon the double tongue.

Be not ignorant of any thing in a great matter or a small.

vi.

Instead of a friend become not an enemy; [for thereby] thou shalt inherit an ill name, shame, and reproach: even so shall a sinner that hath a double tongue.

Sweet language will multiply friends: and a fair-speaking tongue will increase kind greetings.

Be in peace with many: nevertheless have but one counsellor of a thousand.

If thou wouldst get a friend, prove him first, and be not hasty to credit him.

For some man is a friend for his own occasion, and will not abide in the day of thy trouble.

And there is a friend, who, being turned to enmity and strife, will discover thy reproach.

Again, some friend is a companion at the table, and will not continue in the day of thine affliction.

But in thy prosperity he will be as thyself, and will be bold over thy servants.

If thou be brought low, he will be against thee, and will hide himself from thy face.

Separate thyself from thine enemies, and take heed of thy friends.

A faithful friend is a strong defence: and he that hath found such a one hath found a treasure.

Nothing doth countervail a faithful friend, and his excellency is invaluable.

A faithful friend is the medicine of life; and they that fear the Lord shall find him.

VII.

Laugh no man to scorn in the bitterness of his soul: for there is one which humbleth and exalteth.

Devise not a lie against thy brother: neither do the like to thy friend.

Use not to make any manner of lie: for the custom thereof is not good.

Use not many words in a multitude of elders, and make not much babbling when thou prayest.

Hate not laborious work, neither husbandry, which the Most High hath ordained.

Change not a friend for any good, by no means; neither a faithful brother for the gold of Ophir.

Forego not a wise and good woman: for her grace is above gold.

Whereas thy servant worketh truly, entreat him not evil, nor the hireling that bestoweth himself wholly for thee.

Let thy soul love a good servant, and defraud him not of liberty.

Hast thou cattle? have an eye to them: and if they be for thy profit, keep them with thee.

Hast thou children? instruct them, and bow down their neck from their youth.

Hast thou a wife after thy mind? forsake her not: but give not thyself over to a light woman.

Honour thy father with thy whole heart, and forget not the sorrows of thy mother.

And stretch thy hand unto the poor, that thy blessing may be perfected.

Fail not to be with them that weep, and mourn with them that mourn.

Be not slow to visit the sick: for that shall make thee to be beloved.

Whatsoever thou takest in hand, remember the end, and thou shalt never do amiss.

VIII.

Strive not with a mighty man, lest thou fall into his hands.

Be not at variance with a rich man, lest he overweigh thee: for gold hath destroyed many, and perverted the hearts of kings.

Strive not with a man that is full of tongue, and heap not wood upon his fire.

Jest not with a rude man, lest thine ancestors be disgraced.

Reproach not a man that turneth from sin, but remember that we are all worthy of punishment.

Dishonour not a man in his old age : for even some of us wax old.

Rejoice not over thy greatest enemy being dead, but remember that we die all.

Despise not the discourse of the wise, but acquaint thyself with their proverbs.

Be not surety above thy power : for if thou be surety, take care to pay it.

Consult not with a fool, for he cannot keep counsel.

Do no secret thing before a stranger ; for thou knowest not what he will bring forth.

Open not thy heart to every man, lest he requite thee with a shrewd turn.

IX.

Be not jealous over the wife of thy bosom, and teach her not an evil lesson against thyself.

Give not thy soul unto a woman to set her foot upon thy substance.

Meet not with a harlot, lest thou fall into her snares.

Forsake not an old friend ; for the new is not comparable to him : a new friend is as new wine ; when it is old, thou shalt drink it with pleasure.

Envy not the glory of a sinner : for thou knowest not what shall be his end.

Delight not in the thing that the ungodly have pleasure in : but remember they shall not go unpunished unto their grave.

XI.

Blame not before thou hast examined the truth: understand first, and then rebuke.

Answer not before thou hast heard the cause: neither interrupt men in the midst of their talk.

Strive not in a matter that concerneth thee not; and sit not in judgment with sinners.

XII.

When thou wilt do good, know to whom thou doest it; so shalt thou be thanked for thy benefits.

Do good to the godly man, and thou shalt find a recompense; and if not from him, yet from the Most High.

Give unto the good, and help not the sinner.

A friend cannot be known in prosperity: and an enemy cannot be hid in adversity.

In the prosperity of a man, enemies will be grieved; but in his adversity, even a friend will depart.

XIII.

He that toucheth pitch shall be defiled therewith; and he that hath fellowship with a proud man shall be like unto him.

The heart of a man changeth his countenance, whether it be for good or evil: and a merry heart maketh a cheerful countenance.

XVIII.

My son, blemish not thy good deeds, neither use uncomfortable words when thou givest any thing.

Shall not the dew assuage the heat? so is a word better than a gift.

Lo, is not a word better than a gift? but both are with a gracious man.

A fool will upbraid churlishly, and a gift of the envious consumeth the eyes.

Learn before thou speak, and use physic or ever thou be sick.

When thou hast enough, remember the time of hunger: and when thou art rich, think upon poverty and need.

Go not after thy lusts, but refrain thyself from thine appetites.

If thou givest thy soul the desires that please her, she will make thee a laughing-stock to thine enemies that malign thee.

Take not pleasure in much good cheer, neither be tied to the expense thereof.

Be not made a beggar by banqueting upon borrowing, when thou hast nothing in thy purse: for thou shalt lie in wait for thine own life, and be talked on.

XIX.

A labouring man that is given to drunkenness shall not be rich: and he that contemneth small things shall fall by little and little.

Wine and women will make men of understanding to fall away: and he that cleaveth to harlots will become impudent.

He that can rule his tongue shall live without strife; and he that hateth babbling shall have less evil.

Rehearse not unto another that which is told unto thee, and thou shalt fare never the worse.

Whether it be to a friend or foe, talk not of other men's lives; and if thou canst without offence, reveal them not.

If thou hast heard a word, let it die with thee; and be bold, it will not burst thee.

A fool travaileth with a word, as a woman in labour of a child.

As an arrow that sticketh in a man's thigh, so is a word within a fool's belly.

Admonish a friend, it may be he hath not done it: and if he have done it, that he do it no more.

Admonish thy friend, it may be he hath not said it: and if he have, that he speak it not again.

Admonish a friend: for many times it is a slander, and believe not every tale.

XX.

A wise man will hold his tongue, till he see opportunity: but a babbler and a fool will regard no time.

To slip upon a pavement is better than to slip with the tongue: so the fall of the wicked shall come speedily.

A wise sentence shall be rejected when it cometh out of a fool's mouth; for he will not speak it in due season.

A thief is better than a man that is accustomed to lie: but they both shall have destruction to heritage.

XXVIII.

Forgive thy neighbour the hurt that he hath done unto thee, so shall thy sins also be forgiven when thou prayest.

One man beareth hatred against another, and doth he seek pardon from the Lord?

He sheweth no mercy to a man, which is like himself: and doth he ask forgiveness of his own sins?

Abstain from strife, and thou shalt diminish thy sins: for a furious man will kindle strife.

Many have fallen by the edge of the sword: but not so many as have fallen by the tongue.

Look that thou hedge thy possession about with thorns, and bind up thy silver and gold.

And weigh thy words in a balance, and make a door and bar for thy mouth.

Help the poor for the commandment's sake, and turn him not away because of his poverty.

Lose thy money for thy brother and thy friend, and let it not rust under a stone to be lost.

Lay up thy treasure according to the commandments of the Most High, and it shall bring thee more profit than gold.

Shut up alms in thy storehouses; and it shall deliver thee from all affliction.

It shall fight for thee against thine enemies better than a mighty shield and strong spear.

An honest man is surety for his neighbour: but he that is impudent will forsake him.

Forget not the friendship of thy surety, for he hath given his life for thee.

XXX.

He that loveth his son causeth him oft to feel the rod, that he may have joy of him in the end.

He that chastiseth his son shall have joy of him, and shall rejoice in him among his acquaintance.

Cocker thy child, and he shall make thee afraid: play with him, and he will bring thee to heaviness.

Laugh not with him, lest thou have sorrow with him, and lest thou gnash thy teeth in the end.

Give him no liberty in his youth, and wink not at his follies.

Bow down his neck while he is young, and beat him on the sides while he is a child, lest he wax stubborn, and be disobedient unto thee, and so bring sorrow to thy heart.

Health and good estate of body are above all gold, and a strong body above infinite wealth.

Give not over thy mind to heaviness, and afflict not thyself in thine own counsel.

The gladness of the heart is the life of man, and the joyfulness of a man prolongeth his days.

Envy and wrath shorten the life, and carefulness bringeth age before the time.

XXXII.

Do nothing without advice; and when thou hast once done, repent not.

Go not in a way wherein thou mayest fall, and stumble not among the stones.

Be not confident in a plain way.

And beware of thy own children.

In every good work trust thy own soul; for this is the keeping of the commandment.

XXXIII.

Give not thy son and wife, thy brother and friend, power over thee while thou livest, and give not thy goods to another: lest it repent thee, and thou entreat for the same again.

As long as thou livest and hast breath in thee, give not thyself over to any.

For better it is that thy children should seek to thee, than that thou shouldest stand to their courtesy.

XXXVII.

My son, prove thy soul in thy life, and see what is evil for it, and give not that unto it.

For all things are not profitable for all men, neither hath every soul pleasure in every thing.

Be not unsatiable in any dainty thing, nor too greedy upon meats.

XLII.

Of these things be not thou ashamed, and accept no person to sin thereby:

Of the law of the Most High, and his covenant; and of judgment to justify the ungodly;

Of reckoning with thy partners and travellers; or of the gift of the heritage of friends;

Of exactness of balance and weights; or of getting much or little;

And of merchants' indifferent selling; of much correction of children; and to make the side of an evil servant to bleed.

Sure keeping is good, where an evil wife is; and shut up, where many hands are.

Deliver all things in number and weight; and put all in writing that thou givest out, or receivest in.

CICERO

(B. C. 106–43.)

MARCUS TULLIUS CICERO, the great Roman orator, statesman, and philosopher, was born at Arpinum, a town of Latium, about seventy miles from Rome, on the 3d of January, B. C. 106. His father, of the same name, was a man of wealth, and Cicero received the best education that could be given him, applying special study to law. He acquired early distinction as an orator, and was little past thirty years of age when he began to be called to high offices in the state. In the year 63 B. C. he became consul, and performed his greatest service to the Roman Republic in defeating the conspiracy of Catiline. To accomplish this he was obliged to overstep the bounds of law, which gave his enemies an opportunity to assail him with prosecutions when his term of office had expired. He withdrew from Rome in consequence, and resided for a time in Greece, but was triumphantly recalled in September, 57 B. C. On the outbreak of the civil war between Cæsar and Pompey, Cicero, after long hesitation, took sides with the Pompeians. The victorious Cæsar treated him with magnanimity, and he lived in undisturbed privacy until Cæsar's death, devoting himself to the composition of philosophical and rhetorical works, many of which have survived to claim the undying admiration of the world. After Cæsar's assassination, Cicero made common cause with the assassins, and ruined himself by vehement orations against Marc Antony. He was doomed by the defeat of the republicans. His name was put into the list of the proscribed, when Antony, Octavian, and Lepidus agreed on the destruction of their enemies, and he was slain by a party of their soldiers on the 7th of December, B. C. 43.

Among the more philosophical works of Cicero "The Tusculan Disputations" hold a high place. They are discussions supposed to have taken place in Cicero's villa at Tusculum, in the mountains near Rome.

THE GOOD THAT MAKES LIFE HAPPY.

(From "The Tusculan Disputations" of Cicero ; literally translated by C. D. Yonge.)

As the perturbations of the mind make life miserable, and tranquillity renders it happy ; and as these perturbations are of two sorts, grief and fear, proceeding from imagined evils, and as immoderate joy and lust arise from a mistake about what is good, and as all these feelings are in opposition to reason and counsel ; when you see a man at ease, quite free and disengaged from such troublesome commotions, which are so much at variance with one another, can you hesitate to pronounce such an one a happy man ? Now the wise man is always in such a disposition, therefore the wise man is always happy. Besides, every good is pleasant ; whatever is pleasant may be boasted and talked of ; whatever may be boasted of is glorious, but whatever is glorious is certainly laudable, and whatever is laudable doubtless, also, honourable ; whatever, then, is good is honourable ; (but the things which they reckon as goods, they themselves do not call honourable ;) therefore what is honourable alone is good. Hence it follows that a happy life is comprised in honesty alone. Such things, then, are not to be called or considered goods, when a man may enjoy an abundance of them, and yet be most miserable. Is there any doubt but that a man who enjoys the best health, and who has strength and beauty, and his senses flourishing in their utmost quickness and perfection ; suppose him likewise, if you please, nimble and active, nay, give him riches, honours, authority, power, glory ; now, I say, should this person, who is in possession of all these, be unjust, intemperate, timid, stupid, or an idiot, could you hesitate to call such an one miserable? What, then, are those goods in the possession of which you may be very miserable? Let us see if a happy life is not made up of parts of the same nature, as a heap implies a quantity of grain of the same kind. And if this be once admitted, happiness must be compounded of different good things which alone are honourable; if there is any mixture of things of another sort with these, nothing honourable can proceed from such a composition; now, take away honesty, and how can you imagine anything happy? For whatever is good is desirable on that account; whatever is desirable must certainly be approved of; whatever you approve of must be looked on as acceptable and welcome. You must consequently impute dignity to this; and if so, it must necessarily be laudable; therefore, everything that is laudable is good. Hence it follows that what is honourable is the only good. And should we not look upon it in this light, there will be a great many things which we must call good.

I forbear to mention riches, which, as any one, let him be ever so unworthy, may have them, I do not reckon amongst goods; for what is good is not attainable by all. I pass over notoriety and popular fame, raised by the united voice of knaves and fools. Even things which are absolute nothings may be called goods; such as white teeth, handsome eyes, a good complexion, and what was commended by Euryclea, when she was washing Ulysses's feet, the softness of his skin and the mildness of his discourse. If you look on these as goods, what greater encomiums can the gravity of a philosopher be entitled to than the wild opinion of the vulgar and the thoughtless crowd? The Stoics give the name of excellent and choice to what the others call good: they call them so indeed, but they do not allow them to complete a happy life. But these others think that there is no life happy without them; or, admitting it to be happy, they deny it to be the most happy. But our opinion is that it is the most happy, and we prove it from that conclusion of Socrates. For thus that author of philosophy argued: that as the disposition of a man's mind is, so is the man: such as the man is, such will be his discourse: his actions will correspond with his discourse, and his life with his actions. But the disposition of a good man's mind is laudable: the life, therefore, of a good man is laudable: it is honourable, therefore, because laudable: the unavoidable conclusion from which is that the life of good men is happy.

THE SERMON ON THE MOUNT

"WHAT is the Sermon on the Mount? It is the moral law of the kingdom of Christ, or in other words it occupies in the New Testament the place which in the Old Testament is occupied by the Ten Commandments. It is thus an excellent example of the relation of the two divine ' testaments,' or rather covenants, to one another. . . . We may say with truth that the Sermon on the Mount supersedes the Ten Commandments; but it supersedes them by including them in a greater, deeper, and more positive whole." — CHARLES GORE, "The Sermon on the Mount," ch. i.

(Matthew v., Revised Version.)

And seeing the multitudes, he went up into the mountain: and when he had sat down, his disciples came unto him : and he opened his mouth and taught them, saying,

Blessed are the poor in spirit: for theirs is the kingdom of heaven.

Blessed are they that mourn: for they shall be comforted.

Blessed are the meek: for they shall inherit the earth.

Blessed are they that hunger and thirst after righteousness: for they shall be filled.

Blessed are the merciful: for they shall obtain mercy.

Blessed are the pure in heart: for they shall see God.

Blessed are the peacemakers: for they shall be called sons of God.

Blessed are they that have been persecuted for righteousness' sake: for theirs is the kingdom of heaven.

.   .   .   .

Ye have heard that it was said to them of old time, Thou shalt not kill; and whosoever shall kill shall be in danger of the judgement: but I say unto you, that every one who is angry with his brother shall be in danger of the judgement; and whosoever shall say to his brother, Raca, shall be in danger of the council; and whosoever shall say, Thou fool, shall be in danger of the hell of fire. If therefore thou art offering thy gift at the altar, and there rememberest that thy brother hath aught against thee, leave there thy gift before the altar, and go thy way, first be reconciled to thy brother, and then come and offer thy gift. Agree with thine adversary quickly, whiles thou art with him in the way; lest haply the adversary deliver thee to the judge, and the judge deliver thee to the officer, and thou be cast into prison. Verily I say unto thee, Thou shalt by no means come out thence, till thou have paid the last farthing.

Ye have heard that it was said, Thou shalt not commit adultery; but I say unto you, that every one that looketh on a woman to lust after her hath committed adultery with her already in his heart. And if thy right eye causeth thee to stumble, pluck it out, and cast it from thee; for it is profitable for thee that one of thy members should perish, and not thy whole body be cast into hell. And if thy right hand causeth thee to stumble, cut it off, and cast it from thee: for it is profitable for thee that one of thy members should perish, and not thy whole body go into hell. It was said also, Whosoever shall put away his wife, let him give her a writing of divorcement: but I say unto you, that every one that putteth away his wife, saving for the cause of fornication, maketh her an adulteress: and whosoever shall marry her when she is put away committeth adultery.

Again, ye have heard that it was said to them of old

time, Thou shalt not forswear thyself, but shalt perform unto the Lord thine oaths: but I say unto you, Swear not at all; neither by the heaven, for it is the throne of God; nor by the earth, for it is the footstool of his feet; nor by Jerusalem, for it is the city of the great King. Neither shalt thou swear by thy head, for thou canst not make one hair white or black. But let your speech be, Yea, yea; Nay, nay; and whatsoever is more than these is of the evil *one*.

Ye have heard that it was said, An eye for an eye, and a tooth for a tooth: but I say unto you, Resist not him that is evil: but whosoever smiteth thee on thy right cheek, turn to him the other also. And if any man would go to law with thee, and take away thy coat, let him have thy cloke also. And whosoever shall compel thee to go one mile, go with him twain. Give to him that asketh thee, and from him that would borrow of thee turn not thou away.

Ye have heard that it was said, Thou shalt love thy neighbour, and hate thine enemy: but I say unto you, Love your enemies, and pray for them that persecute you; that ye may be sons of your Father which is in heaven: for he maketh his sun to rise on the evil and the good, and sendeth rain on the just and the unjust. For if ye love them that love you, what reward have ye? do not even the publicans the same? And if ye salute your brethren only, what do ye more than others? do not even the Gentiles the same? Ye therefore shall be perfect, as your heavenly Father is perfect.

VI.

Take heed that ye do not your righteousness before men, to be seen of them: else ye have no reward with your Father which is in heaven.

When therefore thou doest alms, sound not a trumpet before thee, as the hypocrites do in the synagogues and in the streets, that they may have glory of men. Verily I say unto you, They have received their reward. But when thou doest alms, let not thy left hand know what thy right hand doeth : that thine alms may be in secret : and thy Father which seeth in secret shall recompense thee.

And when ye pray, ye shall not be as the hypocrites : for they love to stand and pray in the synagogues and in the corners of the streets, that they may be seen of men. Verily, I say unto you, They have received their reward. But thou, when thou prayest, enter into thine inner chamber, and having shut thy door, pray to thy Father which is in secret, and thy Father which seeth in secret shall recompense thee. And in praying use not vain repetitions, as the Gentiles do : for they think that they shall be heard for their much speaking. Be not therefore like unto them : for your Father knoweth what things ye have need of, before ye ask him. After this manner therefore pray ye : Our Father which art in heaven, Hallowed be thy name. Thy kingdom come. Thy will be done, as in heaven, so on earth. Give us this day our daily bread. And forgive us our debts, as we also have forgiven our debtors. And bring us not into temptation, but deliver us from the evil *one*. For if ye forgive men their trespasses, your heavenly Father will also forgive you. But if ye forgive not men their trespasses, neither will your Father forgive your trespasses.

Moreover, when ye fast, be not, as the hypocrites, of a sad countenance : for they disfigure their faces, that they may be seen of men to fast. Verily I say unto you, They have received their reward. But thou, when thou fastest, anoint thy head, and wash thy face ; that thou be not seen of men to fast, but of thy Father which is in secret :

and thy Father, which seeth in secret, shall recompense thee.

Lay not up for yourselves treasures upon the earth, where moth and rust doth consume, and where thieves break through and steal: but lay up for yourselves treasures in heaven, where neither moth nor rust doth consume, and where thieves do not break through nor steal: for where thy treasure is, there will thy heart be also. The lamp of the body is the eye: if therefore thine eye be single, thy whole body shall be full of light. But if thine eye be evil, thy whole body shall be full of darkness. If therefore the light that is in thee be darkness, how great is the darkness! No man can serve two masters: for either he will hate the one, and love the other; or else he will hold to one, and despise the other. Ye cannot serve God and mammon. Therefore I say unto you, Be not anxious for your life, what ye shall eat, or what ye shall drink; nor yet for your body, what ye shall put on. Is not the life more than the food, and the body than the raiment? Behold the birds of the heaven, that they sow not, neither do they reap, nor gather into barns; and your heavenly Father feedeth them. Are not ye of much more value than they? And which of you by being anxious can add one cubit unto his stature? And why are ye anxious concerning raiment? Consider the lilies of the field, how they grow; they toil not, neither do they spin; yet I say unto you, that even Solomon in all his glory was not arrayed like one of these. But if God doth so clothe the grass of the field, which to-day is, and to-morrow is cast into the oven, shall he not much more clothe you, O ye of little faith? Be not therefore anxious, saying, What shall we eat? or, What shall we drink? or, Wherewithal shall we be clothed? For after all these things do the Gentiles seek; for your heavenly

Father knoweth that ye have need of all these things. But seek ye first his kingdom, and his righteousness; and all these things shall be added unto you. Be not therefore anxious for the morrow: for the morrow will be anxious for itself. Sufficient unto the day is the evil thereof.

VII.

Judge not, that ye be not judged. For with what judgement ye judge, ye shall be judged: and with what measure ye mete, it shall be measured unto you. And why beholdest thou the mote that is in thy brother's eye, but considerest not the beam that is in thine own eye? Or how wilt thou say to thy brother, Let me cast out the mote out of thine eye; and lo, the beam is in thine own eye? Thou hypocrite, cast out first the beam out of thine own eye; and then shalt thou see clearly to cast out the mote out of thy brother's eye.

Give not that which is holy unto the dogs, neither cast your pearls before the swine, lest haply they trample them under their feet, and turn and rend you.

Ask, and it shall be given you; seek, and ye shall find; knock, and it shall be opened unto you: for every one that asketh receiveth; and he that seeketh findeth; and to him that knocketh it shall be opened. Or what man is there of you, who, if his son shall ask him for a loaf, will give him a stone; or if he shall ask for a fish, will give him a serpent? If ye then, being evil, know how to give good gifts unto your children, how much more shall your Father which is in heaven give good things to them that ask him? All things therefore whatsoever ye would that men should do unto you, even so do ye also unto them, for this is the law and the prophets.

Enter ye in by the narrow gate: for wide is the gate, and broad is the way, that leadeth to destruction, and many be they that enter in thereby. For narrow is the gate, and straitened the way, that leadeth unto life, and few be they that find it.

Beware of false prophets, which come to you in sheep's clothing, but inwardly are ravening wolves. By their fruits ye shall know them. Do *men* gather grapes of thorns, or figs of thistles? Even so every good tree bringeth forth good fruit; but the corrupt tree bringeth forth evil fruit. A good tree cannot bring forth evil fruit, neither can a corrupt tree bring forth good fruit. Every tree that bringeth not forth good fruit is hewn down, and cast into the fire. Therefore by their fruits ye shall know them.

SENECA

(First century of the Christian era.)

LUCIUS ANNÆUS SENECA was a moralist, or a moralizing philosopher, whose precepts were not happily illustrated in his life, and in whose character there is not much to admire. He was born in Spain, about 4 B. C., but brought to Rome in childhood by his father, a man of wealth, belonging to the equestrian class. Rising to eminence as a pleader he incurred, after some years, the hostility of Messalina, the wife of the emperor Claudius, and was banished to Corsica for eight years. The second wife of Claudius, Agrippina, procured his recall, and made him the teacher of Domitius, her son by a former husband, who subsequently received the name of Nero and became the worst of emperors. For some time after Nero's accession to the throne, Seneca's influence over the young emperor was great, and was used generally for good, though not unselfishly; for the teacher and adviser improved his opportunities to acquire vast wealth. As the foul and fiendish propensities of Nero came more and more to light, Seneca yielded to them, and became, in a measure, accessory to some of the worst of his early crimes, especially the murder of his mother, Agrippina. But wickeder men than Seneca could possibly be were needed soon to satisfy Nero's demands for counsel and aid, and the philosopher was easily supplanted in imperial favor. The wealth he had accumulated then excited the greed of the vile harpies of the court, and his destruction was decreed. A conspiracy against the emperor was opportunely discovered; Seneca was accused of participation in it; he was ordered to die, and obeyed the order by opening his veins and bleeding to death — A. D. 65.

Theoretically, Seneca was a Stoic; practically he may be said to have exemplified Stoicism in nothing but the calmness and dignity of his death. But his moral writings are eloquent, forcible, and true, and they have conveyed profitable teaching to all the generations since his time.

SENECA'S RULES FOR A HAPPY LIFE.

'(From " Minor Dialogues; " translated by Aubrey Stewart.)

It will come to the same thing, if I say, " The highest good is a mind which despises the accidents of fortune, and takes pleasure in virtue ; " or, " It is an unconquerable strength of mind, knowing the world well, gentle in its dealings, showing great courtesy and consideration for those with whom it is brought into contact." Or we may choose to define it by calling that man happy who knows good and bad only in the form of good or bad minds : who worships honour and is satisfied with his own virtue, who is neither puffed up by good fortune nor cast down by evil fortune, who knows no other good than that which he is able to bestow upon himself, whose real pleasure lies in despising pleasures. If you choose to pursue this digression further, you can put this same idea into many other forms, without impairing or weakening its meaning : for what prevents our saying that a happy life consists in a mind which is free, upright, undaunted, and steadfast, beyond the influence of fear or desire, which thinks nothing good except honour, and nothing bad except shame, and regards everything else as a mass of mean details which can neither add anything to nor take anything away from the happiness of life, but which come and go without either increasing or diminishing the highest good ? A man of these principles, whether he will or no, must be accompanied by continual cheerfulness, a high happiness, which come, indeed, from on high, because he delights in what he has, and desires no greater pleasures than those which his home affords. Is he not right in allowing these to turn the scale against petty, ridiculous, and shortlived movements of his wretched body ? On the day on which he becomes proof against pleasure he also becomes proof against pain. See, on the other hand, how evil and guilty a slavery the man is forced to serve who is dominated in turn by pleasures and pains, those most untrustworthy and passionate of masters. We must, therefore, escape from them into freedom. This nothing will bestow upon us save contempt of Fortune: but if we attain to this, then there will dawn upon us those invaluable blessings, the repose of a mind that is at rest in a safe haven, its lofty imaginings, its great and steady delight at casting out errors and learning to know the truth, its courtesy, and its cheerfulness, in all of which we shall take delight, not regarding them as good things, but as proceeding from the proper good of man. . . . What answer are we to make to the reflection that pleasure belongs to good and bad men alike, and that bad men take as much delight in their shame as good men in noble things? This was why the ancients bade us lead the highest, not the most pleasant life, in order that pleasure might not be the guide but the companion of a right-thinking and honourable mind; for it is Nature whom we ought to make our guide: let our reason watch her, and be advised by her. To live happily, then, is the same thing as to live according to Nature: what this may be, I will explain. If we guard the endowments of the body and the advantages of nature with care and fearlessness, as things soon to depart and given to us only for a day; if we do not fall under their dominion, nor allow ourselves to become the slaves of what is no part of our own being; if we assign to all bodily pleasures and external delights the same position which is held by auxiliaries and light-armed troops in a camp; if we make them our servants, not our masters, then and then only are they of value to our minds. A man should be unbiassed and not to be conquered by external things : he ought to admire himself alone, to feel confidence in his own spirit, and so to order his life as to be ready alike for good or for bad fortune. Let not his confidence be without knowledge, nor his knowledge without steadfastness : let him always abide by what he has once determined, and let there be no erasure in his doctrines. It will be understood, even though I append it not, that such a man will be tranquil and composed in his demeanour, high-minded and cour- teous in his actions. Let reason be encouraged by the senses to seek for the truth, and draw its first principles from thence : indeed it has no other base of operations or place from which to start in pursuit of truth : it must fall back upon itself. Even the all-embracing universe and God who is its guide extends himself forth into outward things, and yet altogether returns from all sides back to himself. Let our mind do the same thing : when, fol- lowing its bodily senses, it has by means of them sent itself forth into the things of the outward world, let it remain still their master and its own. By this means we shall obtain a strength and an ability which are united and allied together, and shall derive from it that reason which never halts between two opinions, nor is dull in forming its perceptions, beliefs, or convictions. Such a mind, when it has ranged itself in order, made its various parts agree together, and, if I may so express myself, har- monized them, has attained to the highest good : for it has nothing evil or hazardous remaining, nothing to shake it or make it stumble : it will do everything under the guidance of its own will, and nothing unexpected will be- fall it, but whatever may be done by it will turn out well, and that, too, readily and easily, without the doer having recourse to any underhand devices : for slow and hesitat- ing actions are the signs of discord and want of settled purpose. You may, then, boldly declare that the highest good is singleness of mind: for where agreement and unity are, there must the virtues be: it is the vices that are at war one with another. . . . It is the act of a generous spirit to proportion its efforts not to its own strength but to that of human nature, to entertain lofty aims, and to conceive plans which are too vast to be carried into execution even by those who are endowed with gigantic intellects, who appoint for themselves the following rules: " I will look upon death or upon a comedy with the same expression of countenance: I will submit to labours, however great they may be, supporting the strength of my body by that of my mind: I will despise riches when I have them as much as when I have them not; if they be elsewhere I will not be more gloomy, if they sparkle around me I will not be more lively than I should otherwise be: whether Fortune comes or goes I will take no notice of her; I will view all lands as though they belong to me, and my own as though they belonged to all mankind: I will so live as to remember that I was born for others, and will thank Nature on this account: for in what fashion could she have done better for me? she has given me alone to all, and all to me alone. Whatever I may possess, I will neither hoard it greedily nor squander it recklessly. I will think that I have no possessions so real as those which I have given away to deserving people: I will not reckon benefits by their magnitude or number, or by anything except the value set upon them by the receiver: I never will consider a gift to be a large one if it be bestowed upon a worthy object. I will do nothing because of public opinion, but everything because of conscience: whenever I do anything alone by myself I will believe that the eyes of the Roman people are upon me while I do it. In eating and drinking my object shall be to quench the desires of Nature, not to fill and empty my belly. I will be agreeable with my friends, gentle and mild to my foes: I will grant pardon before I am asked for it, and will meet the wishes of honourable men half way: I will bear in mind that the world is my native city, that its governors are the gods, and that they stand above and around me, criticising whatever I do or say. Whenever either Nature demands my breath again, or reason bids me dismiss it, I will quit this life, calling all to witness that I have loved a good conscience, and good pursuits: that no one's freedom, my own least of all, has been impaired through me." He who sets up these as the rules of his life will soar aloft and strive to make his way to the gods.

MARTIAL

(First century.)

LITTLE is known concerning Martial, the Latin poet, whose epigrammatic summary of the essentials of happiness in life has been translated and imitated by many modern poets. He was born in Spain, in the year 43 A. D., and he died in 104.

THE HAPPY LIFE.

(From Martial's "Epigrams," lib. x., ep. xlv.)

Vitam quæ faciunt beatiorem,
Jucundissime Martialis, hæc sunt:
Res non parta, labore, sed relicta;
Non ingratus ager, focus perennis,
Lis nunquam; toga rara; mens quieta;
Vires ingenuæ; salubre corpus;
Prudens simplicitas; pares amici;
Convictis facilis; sine arte mensa;
Nox non ebria, sed soluta curis;
Non tristis torus, et tamen pudicus;
Somnus, qui faciat breves tenebras;
Quod sis, esse velis, nihilque malis:
Summum nec metuas diem, nec optes.

(Translation by Henry Howard, Earl of Surrey.)

Martial, the things that do attain
  The happy life be these, I find —
The riches left, not got with pain;
  The fruitful ground, the quiet mind,

The equal friend; no grudge, no strife;
  No charge of rule, nor governance;
Without disease, the healthful life;
  The household of continuance;

The mean diet, no delicate fare;
  True wisdom joined with simpleness;
The night discharged of all care,
  Where wine the wit may not oppress;

The faithful wife, without debate;
  Such sleeps as may beguile the night;
Contented with thine own estate,
  Ne wish for Death, ne fear his might.

(Translation by Sir Richard Fanshawe.)

The things that make a life to please
(Sweetest Martial), they are these:
Estate inherited, not got:
A thankful field, hearth always hot:
City seldom, law-suits never:
Equal friends agreeing ever:
Health of body, peace of mind:
Sleeps that till the morning bind:
Wise simplicity, plain fare:
Not drunken nights, yet loos'd from care:
A sober, not a sullen spouse:
Clean strength, not such as his that plows;
Wish only what thou art, to be;
Death neither wish, nor fear to see.

(Translation by Abraham Cowley.)

Since, dearest friend, 't is your desire to see
A true receipt of happiness from me;

These are the chief ingredients, if not all:
Take an estate neither too great nor small,
Which *quantum sufficit* the doctors call.
Let this estate from parents' care descend;
The getting it too much of life does spend.
Take such a ground, whose gratitude may be
A fair encouragement for industry.
Let constant fires the winter's fury tame;
And let thy kitchen's be a vestal flame.
Thee to the town let never suit at law,
And rarely, very rarely, business draw.
Thy active mind in equal temper keep,
In undisturbed peace, yet not in sleep.
Let exercise a vigorous health maintain,
Without which all the composition's vain.
In the same weight prudence and innocence take,
And of each does the just mixture make.
But a few friendships wear, and let them be
By nature and by fortune fit for thee.
Instead of art and luxury in food,
Let mirth and freedom make thy table good.
If any cares into thy day-time creep,
At night, without wine's opium, let them sleep.
Let rest, which nature does to darkness wed,
And not lust, recommend to thee thy bed.
Be satisfied, and pleas'd with what thou art,
Act cheerfully and well th' allotted part;
Enjoy the present hour, be thankful for the past,
And neither fear, nor wish, th' approaches of the last.

(Free translation or imitation by Alexander Pope.)

Happy the man whose wish and care
   A few paternal acres bound,
Content to breath his native air,
       In his own ground.

Whose herds with milk, whose fields with bread,
  Whose flocks supply him with attire,
Whose trees in summer yield him shade,
      In winter fire.

Blest, who can unconcern'dly find
  Hours, days, and years slide soft away,
In health of body, peace of mind,
      Quiet by day.

Sound sleep by night; study and ease,
  Together mixt; sweet recreation;
And Innocence, which most does please
      With meditation.

Thus let me live, unseen, unknown,
  Thus unlamented let me die,
Steal from the world, and not a stone
      Tell where I lie.

(Translation by C. Merivale.)

What makes the happiest life below,
A few plain rules, my friend, will show.
A good estate, not earn'd with toil,
  But left by will, or giv'n by fate;
A land of no ungrateful soil,
  A constant fire within your grate:

No laws; few cares; a quiet mind;
  Strength unimpair'd, a healthful frame;
Wisdom with innocence combin'd;
  Friends equal both in years and fame;

Your living easy, and your board
With food, but not with luxury stored;

A bed, though chaste, not solitary ;
　　Sound sleep, to shorten night's dull reign ;
Wish nothing that is yours to vary ;
　　Think all enjoyments that remain ;
And for the inevitable hour,
Nor hope it nigh, nor dread its power.

EPICTETUS

(First century of the Christian era.)

DURING some considerable part of his life, Epictetus, the Stoic philosopher, was a slave. His master, Epaphroditus, had been himself a slave, had become a freedman, had risen to favor in the court of the emperor Nero, whom he served as librarian or secretary. "Epictetus was probably born in about the fiftieth year of the Christian era; but we do not know the exact date of his birth, nor do we even know his real name. 'Epictetus' means 'bought' or 'acquired,' and is simply a servile designation. He was born at Hierapolis, in Phrygia. . . . What were the accidents — or rather, what was 'the unseen Providence, by man nicknamed chance' — which assigned Epictetus to the house of Epaphroditus, we do not know. To a heart refined and noble there could hardly have been a more trying position. . . . The slaves of a Roman *familia* were crowded together in immense gangs; they were liable to the most violent and capricious punishments; they might be subjected to the most degraded and brutalizing influences. . . . An anecdote has been handed down to us by several writers which would show that Epictetus was treated with atrocious cruelty. Epaphroditus, it is said, once gratified his cruelty by twisting his slave's leg in some instrument of torture. 'If you go on you will break it,' said Epictetus. The wretch did go on, and did break it. 'I told you that you would break it,' said Epictetus quietly, not giving vent to his anguish by a single word or a single groan. . . . Another authority tells us that Epictetus became lame in consequence of a natural disease. . . . At some period of his life, but how or when we do not know, Epictetus was manumitted by his master, and was henceforward regarded by the world as free. . . . We are told that he lived in a cottage of the simplest and even meanest description: it neither needed nor possessed a fastening of any kind, for within it there was no furniture except a lamp and the poor straw pallet on which he slept. . . . But, in spite of his deep poverty, it must not be supposed that there was anything eccentric or ostentatious in the life of Epictetus." Banished, with other philosophers, from Rome, by the emperor Domitian, he went to Nicopolis, in Epirus. "Whether he ever revisited Rome is uncertain, but it is probable that he did so, for we know that he enjoyed the friendship of several eminent philosophers and statesmen, and was esteemed and honored by the emperor Hadrian himself. He is said to have lived to a good old age, surrounded by affectionate and eager disciples, and to have died with the same noble simplicity which had marked his life. The date of his death is as little known as that of his birth. . . . It is nearly certain that Epictetus never committed any of his doctrines to writing. Like his great exemplar, Socrates, he contented himself with oral instruction, and the bulk of what has come down to us in his name consists in the ' Discourses ' reproduced for us by his pupil Arrian. It was the ambition of Arrian ' to be to Epictetus what Xenophon had been to Socrates.' . . . With this view he wrote four books on Epictetus: a life, which is now unhappily lost; a book of conversations or ' table talk,' which is also lost; and two books which have come down to us, viz., the ' Discourses ' and the ' Manual.' . . . The ' Manual ' is a kind of abstract of Epictetus's ethical principles." — F. W. FARRAR, "Seekers after God."

It is from the "Manual" or "Enchiridion" of Epictetus that the subjoined precepts are selected.

SELECTIONS FROM THE PRECEPTS OF EPICTETUS.

(From the " Works of Epictetus," translated by Elizabeth Carter.)

Of Things, some are in our Power, and others not. In our Power are Opinion, Pursuit, Desire, Aversion, and, in one Word, whatever are our own Actions. Not in our Power, are Body, Property, Reputation, Command, and, in one Word, whatever are not our own Actions.

Now, the Things in our Power are, by Nature, free, un-restrained, unhindered ; but those not in our Power, weak, slavish, restrained, belonging to others. Remember, then, that, if you suppose Things by Nature slavish, to be free ; and what belongs to others, your own ; you will be hin-dered ; you will lament ; you will be disturbed ; you will find fault both with Gods and Men. But if you sup-pose that only to be your own which is your own ; and what belongs to others, such as it really is ; no one will ever compel you ; no one will restrain you : you will find fault with no one ; you will accuse no one ; you will do no one Thing against your Will : no one will hurt you : you will not have an Enemy : for you will suffer no Harm. . . .

Remember that *Desire* promises the Attainment of that of which you are desirous ; and *Aversion* promises the Avoiding of that to which you are averse : that he who fails of the Object of his Desire, is disappointed : and he who incurs the Object of his Aversion, wretched. If then, you confine your Aversion to those Objects only which are contrary to that natural Use of your Faculties which you have in your own Power, you will never incur any thing to which you are averse. But if you are averse to Sick-ness, or Death, or Poverty, you will be wretched. Re-move Aversion, then, from all Things that are not in our Power, and transfer it to Things contrary to the Nature of what is in our Power. But, for the present, totally suppress Desire ; for if you desire any of the Things not in our own Power, you must necessarily be disappointed ; and of those which are, and which it would be laudable to desire, nothing is yet in your Possession. . . .

Men are disturbed, not by Things, but by the Princi-ples and Notions which they form concerning Things. Death, for Instance, is not terrible, else it would have appeared so to *Socrates*. But the Terror consists in our Notion of Death, that it is terrible. When therefore we are hindered, or disturbed, or grieved, let us never impute it to others, but to ourselves; that is, to our own Principles.

Require not Things to happen as you wish; but wish them to happen as they do happen; and you will go on well. . . .

Never say of any thing, "I have lost it," but, "I have restored it." Is your child dead? It is restored. Is your wife dead? She is restored. Is your Estate taken away? Well: and is not that likewise restored? "But he who took it away is a bad Man." What is that to you, by whose Hands He, who gave it, hath demanded it back again? While He gives you to possess it, take care of it; but as of something not your own, as Passengers do of an Inn. . . .

Remember that you must behave [in Life] as at an Entertainment. Is any thing brought round to you? Put out your Hand, and take your Share, with Moderation. Doth it pass by you? Do not stop it. Is it not yet come? Do not stretch forth your Desire towards it, but wait till it reaches you. Thus [do] with regard to Children, to a Wife, to public Posts, to Riches: and you will be some time or other a worthy Partner of the Feasts of the Gods. And if you do not so much as take the Things which are set before you, but are able even to despise them, then you will not only be a Partner of the Feasts of the Gods, but of their Empire also. . . .

Remember that you are an Actor in a Drama, of such a Kind as the Author pleases to make it. If short, of a short one; if long, of a long one. If it be his Pleasure you should act a poor man, a Cripple, a Governor, or a private Person, see that you act it naturally. For this is your Business, to act well the Character assigned you : to chuse it, is another's. . . .

Remember, that not he who gives Ill-Language, or a Blow, affronts ; but the Principle, which represents these Things as affronting. When, therefore, any one provokes you, be assured, that it is your own Opinion which provokes you. . . .

If you ever happen to turn your Attention to Externals, so as to wish to please any one, be assured, that you have ruined your Scheme of Life. . . .

Be for the most part silent : or speak merely what is necessary, and in few Words. We may however enter, though sparingly, into Discourse sometimes, when Occasion calls for it ; but not on any of the common Subjects, of Gladiators, or Horse Races, or athletic Champions, or Feasts ; the vulgar Topics of Conversation : but principally not of Men, so as either to blame, or praise, or make Comparisons. . . .

Let not your Laughter be much, nor on many Occasions, nor profuse.

Avoid Swearing, if possible, altogether ; if not, as far as you are able.

Avoid public and vulgar Entertainments : but, if ever an Occasion calls you to them, keep your Attention upon the Stretch, that you may not imperceptibly slide into vulgar Manners. . . .

Provide Things relating to the Body no farther than mere Use ; as Meat, Drink, Clothing, House, Family. But strike off, and reject, everything relating to Show and Delicacy. . . .

If any one tells you, that such a Person speaks ill of you, do not make Excuses about what is said of you, but answer : " He doth not know my other Faults, else he would not have mentioned only these." . . .

In Parties of Conversation, avoid a frequent and excessive mention of your own Actions, and Dangers. For, however agreeable it may be to yourself to mention the Risques you have run, it is not equally agreeable to others to hear your Adventures. Avoid, likewise, an Endeavour to excite Laughter. For this is a slippery Point, which may throw you into vulgar Manners; and, besides, may be apt to lessen you in the esteem of your Acquaintance. Approaches to indecent Discourse are likewise dangerous. . . .

When you do any thing, from a clear Judgment that it ought to be done, never shun the being seen to do it, even though the World should make a wrong Supposition about it: for, if you do not act right, shun the Action itself; but, if you do, why are you afraid of those who censure you wrongly? . . .

It is a Mark of Want of Genius, to spend much Time in Things relating to the Body. . . .

Every Thing hath two Handles; the one, by which it may be borne; the other, by which it cannot. If your Brother acts unjustly, do not lay hold on the Action by the Handle of his Injustice; for by that it cannot be borne: but by the Opposite, that he is your Brother, that he was brought up with you: and thus you will lay hold on it, as it is to be borne. . . .

Whatever Rules you have deliberately proposed to yourself [for the Conduct of Life] abide by them, as so many Laws, and as if you would be guilty of Impiety in transgressing any of them. . . . Let whatever appears to be the best, be to you an inviolable Law. And if any instance of Pain, or Pleasure, or Glory, or Disgrace be set before you, remember, that now is the Combat, now the *Olympiad* comes on, nor can it be put off; and that, by once being worsted, and giving way, Proficiency is lost, or [by the contrary] preserved.   Thus *Socrates* became perfect, improving himself by every thing ; attending to nothing but Reason.   And though you are not yet a *Socrates*, you ought however to live as one desirous of becoming a *Socrates*.

MARCUS AURELIUS

(A. D. 121–180.)

"' It is more delightful,' says the great historian Niebuhr, 'to speak of Marcus Aurelius than of any man in history; for if there is any sublime human virtue it is his. He was certainly the noblest character of his time, and I know no other man who combined such unaffected kindness, mildness, and humility, with such conscientiousness and severity towards himself. We possess innumerable busts of him, for every Roman of his time was anxious to possess his portrait, and if there is anywhere an expression of virtue it is in the heavenly features of Marcus Aurelius.'

"Marcus Aurelius was born on April 26, A. D. 121. His more correct designation would be Marcus Antoninus, but since he bore several different names at different periods of his life, and since at that age nothing was more common than a change of designation, it is hardly worth while to alter the name by which he is most popularly recognized. His father, Annius Verus, who died in his Prætorship, drew his blood from a line of illustrious men who claimed descent from Numa, the second King of Rome. His mother, Domitia Calvilla, was also a lady of consular and kingly race. The character of both seems to have been worthy of their high dignity. Of his father he can have known little, since Annius died when Aurelius was a mere infant. . . . The childhood and boyhood of Aurelius fell during the reign of Hadrian. . . . Hadrian, though an able, indefatigable, and, on the whole, beneficial emperor, was a man whose character was stained with serious faults. It is, however, greatly to his honour that he recognized in Aurelius, at the early age of six years, the germs of those extraordinary virtues which afterwards blessed the empire and elevated the sentiments of mankind. . . . Towards the end of his long reign, worn out with disease and weariness, Hadrian, being childless, had adopted as his son L. Ceionius Commodus, a man who had few recommendations but his personal beauty. Upon his [Ceionius's] death, which took place a year afterwards, Hadrian, assembling the senators round his sick bed, adopted and presented to them as their future emperor Arrius Antoninus, better known by the surname of Pius, which he won by his gratitude to the memory of his predecessor. Had Aurelius been older — he was then but seventeen — it is known that Hadrian would have chosen *him*, and not Antoninus, for his heir. The latter, indeed, who was then fifty-two years old, was only selected on the express condition that he should in turn adopt both Marcus Aurelius and the son of the deceased Ceionius. Thus, at the age of seventeen, Aurelius, who, even from his infancy, had been loaded with conspicuous distinctions, saw himself the acknowledged heir to the Empire of the world. . . . On the death of Hadrian in A. D. 138, Antoninus Pius succeeded to the throne, and, in accordance with the late emperor's conditions, adopted Marcus Aurelius and Lucius Commodus. . . . The long reign of Antoninus Pius is one of those happy periods that have no history." It was ended in A. D. 161 by his death.

Marcus Aurelius then came to the throne, in association with his adoptive brother. The latter died in 169. "Marcus was now the undisputed lord of the Roman world. He was seated on the dizziest and most splendid eminence which it was possible for human grandeur to obtain. But this imperial elevation kindled no glow of pride or self-satisfaction in his meek and chastened nature. He regarded himself as being in fact the servant of all. It was his duty, like that of the bull in the herd, or the ram among the flocks, to confront every peril in his own person, to be foremost in all the hardships of war and most deeply immersed in all the toils of peace. . . . His ' Meditations ' were written amid the painful self-denial and distracting anxieties of his wars with the Quadi and the Marcomanni, and he was the author of other works, which unhappily have perished." He died in Pannonia on the 17th of March, A. D. 180. — F. W. FARRAR, "Seekers after God."

"The reading of Marcus Aurelius strengthens, but it does not console: it leaves a void in the soul which is at once cruel and delightful, which one would not exchange for full satisfaction. Humility, renunciation, severity towards self, were never carried further. Glory — that last illusion of great souls — is reduced to nothingness. It is needful to do right without disturbing one's self as to whether any one knows that we do it. . . . The consequences of this austere philosophy might have been hardness and obstinacy. It is here that the rare goodness of Marcus Aurelius shines out in its full brilliancy. His severity is only for himself. The fruit of his great tension of soul is an infinite benevolence. All his life was a study of how to return good for evil. . . . One moment, thanks to him, the world was governed by the best and greatest man of his age. Frightful decadences followed; but the little casket which contained the ' Thoughts ' on the banks of the Granicus was saved. From it came forth that incomparable book in which Epictetus was surpassed. . . . Veritable, eternal Evangel, the book of ' Thoughts ' which will never grow old, because it asserts no dogma." — ERNEST RENAN, "Marcus Aurelius " ("English Conferences," trans. by Clara Erskine Clement).

SELECTIONS FROM THE THOUGHTS OF MARCUS AURELIUS.

(Translated by George Long.)

Begin the morning by saying to thyself, I shall meet with the busybody, the ungrateful, arrogant, deceitful, envious, unsocial. All these things happen to them by reason of their ignorance of what is good and evil. But I who have seen the nature of the good, that it is beautiful, and of the bad, that it is ugly, and the nature of him who does wrong, that it is akin to me, not [only] of the same blood or seed, but that it participates in [the same] intelligence and [the same] portion of the divinity, I can neither be injured by any of them, for no one can fix on me what is ugly, nor can I be angry with my kinsman, nor hate him. For we are made for co-operation, like feet, like hands, like eyelids, like the rows of the

upper and lower teeth.   To act against one another then
is contrary to nature; and it is acting against one another
to be vexed and to turn away.

Every moment think steadily as a Roman and a man,
to do what thou hast in hand with perfect and simple
dignity, and feeling of affection, and freedom, and justice;
and to give thyself relief from all other thoughts.   And
thou wilt give thyself relief, if thou doest every act of thy
life as if it were the last, laying aside all carelessness and
passionate aversion from the commands of reason, and all
hypocrisy, and self-love, and discontent with the portion
which has been given to thee.   Thou seest how few the
things are, the which if a man lays hold of, he is able to
live a life which flows in quiet, and is like the existence of
the gods ; for the gods on their part will require nothing
more from him who observes these things.

This thou must always bear in mind, what is the nature
of the whole, and what is my nature, and how this is related to that, and what kind of a part it is of what kind
of a whole ; and that there is no one who hinders thee
from always doing and saying the things which are according to the nature of which thou art a part.

Though thou shouldst be going to live three thousand
years, and as many times ten thousand years, still remember that no man loses any other life than this which he
now lives, nor lives any other than this which he now
loses.   The longest and shortest are thus brought to the
same.   For the present is the same to all. . . .

Labor not unwillingly, nor without regard to the common interest, nor without due consideration, nor with dis-
traction ; nor let studied ornament set off thy thoughts,
and be not either a man of many words, or busy about too
many things. . . .

If thou findest in human life anything better than

justice, truth, temperance, fortitude, and, in a word, anything better than thy own mind's self-satisfaction in the things which it enables thee to do according to right reason, and in the condition that is assigned to thee without thy own choice ; if, I say, thou seest anything better than this, turn to it with all thy soul, and enjoy that which thou hast found to be the best. . . .

If thou workest at that which is before thee, following right reason seriously, vigorously, calmly, without allowing anything else to distract thee, but keeping thy divine part pure, as if thou shouldest be bound to give it back immediately ; if thou holdest to this, expecting nothing, fearing nothing, but satisfied with thy present activity according to nature, and with heroic truth in every word and sound which thou utterest, thou wilt live happy. And there is no man who is able to prevent this.

Do not act as if thou wert going to live ten thousand years. Death hangs over thee. While thou livest, while it is in thy power, be good.

Occupy thyself with few things, says the philosopher, if thou wouldst be tranquil. — But consider if it would not be better to say, Do what is necessary, and whatever the reason of the animal which is naturally social requires, and as it requires. For this brings not only the tranquillity which comes from doing well, but also that which comes from doing few things. For the greatest part of what we say and do being unnecessary, if a man takes this away, he will have more leisure and less uneasiness. . . .

Love the art, poor as it may be, which thou hast learned, and be content with it; and pass through the rest of life like one who has intrusted to the gods with his whole soul all that he has, making thyself neither the tyrant nor the slave of any man.

In the morning when thou risest unwillingly, let this thought be present — I am rising to the work of a human being. Why then am I dissatisfied if I am going to do the things for which I exist and for which I was brought into the world? . . .

Such as are thy habitual thoughts, such also will be the character of thy mind; for the soul is dyed by the thoughts. Dye it then with a continuous series of such thoughts as these: for instance, that where a man can live, there he can also live well. . . .

Live with the gods. And he does live with the gods who constantly shows to them that his own soul is satisfied with that which is assigned to him. . . .

Let it make no difference to thee whether thou art cold or warm, if thou art doing thy duty; and whether thou art drowsy or satisfied with sleep; and whether ill-spoken of or praised; and whether dying or doing something else. For it is one of the acts of life, this act by which we die: it is sufficient then in this act also to do well what we have in hand.

The best way of avenging thyself is not to become like the wrong doer.

It is a shame for the soul to be first to give way in this life, when thy body does not give way.

Adapt thyself to the things with which thy lot has been cast: and the men among whom thou hast received thy portion, love them, but do it truly [sincerely].

Be not ashamed to be helped; for it is thy business to do thy duty like a soldier in the assault on a town. How then, if being lame thou canst not mount up on the battlements alone, but with the help of another it is possible?

Let not future things disturb thee, for thou wilt come to them, if it shall be necessary, having with thee the same reason which now thou usest for present things.

When a man has done thee any wrong, immediately consider with what opinion about good or evil he has done wrong. For when thou hast seen this, thou wilt pity him, and wilt neither wonder nor be angry. . . .

Think not so much of what thou hast not as of what thou hast: but of the things which thou hast select the best, and then reflect how eagerly they would have been sought, if thou hadst them not. . . .

In everything which happens keep before thy eyes those to whom the same things happened, and how they were vexed, and treated them as strange things, and found fault with them: and now where are they? Nowhere. . . .

It is a ridiculous thing for a man not to fly from his own badness, which is indeed possible, but to fly from other men's badness, which is impossible.

Remember that to change thy opinion and to follow him who corrects thy error is as consistent with freedom as it is to persist in thy error. . . .

Men exist for the sake of one another. Teach them then or bear with them.

When thou art offended with any man's shameless conduct, immediately ask thyself, Is it possible then that shameless men should not be in the world? It is not possible. Do not then require what is impossible. . . .

When thou hast assumed these names, good, modest, true, rational, a man of equanimity, and magnanimous, take care that thou dost not change these names; and if thou shouldst lose them, quickly return to them. . . .

No longer talk about the kind of man that a good man ought to be, but be such.

The safety of life is this, to examine everything all through, what it is itself, what is its material, what its formal part; with all thy soul to do justice and to say the truth. What remains except to enjoy life by joining one good thing to another so as not to leave even the smallest intervals between?

How small a part of the boundless and unfathomable time is assigned to every man? for it is very soon swallowed up in the eternal. And how small a part of the whole substance? and how small a part of the universal soul? and on what a small clod of the whole earth thou creepest? Reflecting on all this, consider nothing to be great, except to act as thy nature leads thee, and to endure that which the common nature brings.

OPINIONS OF THE SPIRIT OF WISDOM

(About the seventh century.)

"THE Pahlavi phrase, Dînâ-î Maînôg-î Khirad, ' Opinions
of the Spirit of Wisdom,' " says E. W. West, from whose
translation the following selections are taken, "is a name
applied to sixty-two enquiries, or series of enquiries, on subjects connected with the religion of the Mazda-worshippers,
made by an anonymous wise man and answered by the Spirit
of Wisdom. . . . By the Spirit of Wisdom the author
means the innate wisdom of Aûharmazd. . . . It was originally created by Aûharmazd, and is superior to the archan-
gels. . . . The author was evidently a devoted Mazda-
worshipper, and probably a layman. . . . Whether he wrote
before or after the Arab conquest of Persia (A. D. 632–651)
is doubtful." Two translations of this work have been made
by Mr. West. The later one, from the original Pahlavi
text, appeared in 1885, in the great collection of "The
Sacred Books of the East," edited by Professor Max Müller.
It is from the introduction to this that the quotations above
are taken. The earlier translation, published in 1871, was
from an Indian (Pâzand-Sanskrit) version, in which the work
bears the name Mainyô-î Khard. The following Rules of
Life were selected from the last-mentioned translation by
Mr. Moncure D. Conway for his "Sacred Anthology," and
are here borrowed from that compilation.

RULES OF LIFE.

The sage asked the Spirit of Wisdom, How is it possible to seek the preservation and prosperity of the body,
without injury to the soul, and the deliverance of the soul
without injury of the body?

The Spirit of Wisdom replied : —

Slander not, lest ill-fame and wickedness come to thee

therefrom; for it is said every other demon attacks in the front, but Slander, which assaults from behind.

Form no covetous desire, that avarice may not deceive thee, and that the benefit of the world may not be tasteless to thee, and that of the spirit unheeded.

Practice not wrathfulness, since a man, when he practises wrath, becomes then forgetful of his duties and good works.

Suffer not anxiety, since he that is anxious is heedless of the enjoyment of the world and of the spirit, and decay results to his body and soul.

Commit no lustfulness, lest, from thine own actions, injury and regret come to thee.

Bear no envy, that life may not be tasteless for thee.

Commit no sin through shame.

Practice not slothful sleep, lest the duties and good works which it is necessary for thee to do remain undone.

Utter no ill-timed gossip.

Be diligent and discreet, and eat of thine own regular industry; and form a portion for God and the good. This practice, in thy occupation, is the greatest good work.

Plunder not from the wealth of others, lest thy own industry become unheeded; since it is said that whoever eats anything not from his own regular industry, but from another, is as one who devours men's heads.

With enemies, struggle with equity.

With friends, proceed with their approbation.

With a malicious man, carry on no conflict, and nowise molest him.

With the covetous man, be not a partner, and trust him not with the leadership.

With an ignorant man, be not a confederate; with a foolish man, make no dispute; from an ill-natured man, take no loan.

With a slanderer, go not to the door of kings.

MAIMONIDES

(A. D. 1135–1204.)

MOSES BEN MAIMON, or MAIMONIDES, the greatest of mediæval Jews, was born in Cordova, Spain, A. D. 1135, while that city remained in possession of the Moors, and during the reign of the Almoravides. On the fall of the Almoravid dynasty, which occurred in 1147, the more fanatical Almohades, then in power, began religious persecutions which drove the family of Maimonides, with other Jews, from the country. Moses settled finally at Fostat (Cairo), where the remainder of his life (which ended A. D. 1204) was spent. He became famous as a physician and as a scholar, and was the recognized spiritual head of the Jews of Cairo. He was a writer of extraordinary diligence, and his works, religious, philosophical, and medical, are numerous and extensive. His lasting fame rests mainly on the great philosophical treatise entitled "Mōrēh Nebūhchīm," or "Guide of the Perplexed," the importance of which in the history of philosophical thought has been increasingly recognized within recent times. An English translation of the work, by M. Friedländer, was published in 1885.

MAIMONIDES, TO HIS SON IN HIS LAST WILL.

Let me implore you to discern the excellency of light over darkness, to reject death and evil, and to choose life and good; for the option is given to you! Accustom yourself to good morals, for the nature of man dependeth upon habit, and habit taketh root in nature. Know ye that the perfection of the body precedes the perfection of the soul, and is like the key which openeth the inner saloon. Let, therefore, the chief purpose of perfecting your body be to perfect your soul, improve your morals, and open before you the gates of heaven. Conduct yourselves with care and with honour ; beware of associating with the wanton, of sitting in the streets, and of sporting with the young men, for thence proceedeth bad fruit. Always be found among respectable and learned men, only with humility and meekness and deference. Incline your head, and open the ears of your heart, to hearken and to listen to their words, what they praise and what they blame ; weigh their ideas and compare them, and then ye shall be wise and prosper. Keep your mouth and your tongue from wearying them with redundancy of speech. Measure your words with judgment, for by multiplying your words you will increase your errors. Be not proud or haughty in their presence, and be not ashamed to inquire about anything which is obscure to you, but let it be done in proper time and in proper language. Consider and weigh the word well, ere you let it go forth from your mouth, for you cannot bring it back afterward.

Love wisdom, seek her, and search for her as for silver and hid treasures. Attend on the threshold of the houses of the wise men, them that learn and teach : there shall be your recreation, there you will be delighted in hearing lectures on the sciences and on morals, new things, and the argument of the students. Be jealous of the men of knowledge, and despise the ignorant in your heart. When you ask a question or reply to one, be not rash, speak not precipitately, cry not aloud, nor speak with stammering lips. Speak in choice language, and in a pure tongue, in a moderate voice, and with points of the subject; as one who seeketh to learn, and who searcheth for truth, and not as one who quarreleth and is eager for victory. . . .

Love truth and righteousness, and cleave unto them ; for by them you will be sure to prosper, like unto one who buildeth upon a flinty rock. Hate falsehood and injustice, and " be not desirous of their dainties ; " for it is as one who buildeth upon sand, and to him apply the scriptural passage, " Say unto them who daub it with untempered mortar, that it shall fall." (Ezekiel xi. 13.)

Let therefore truth, by which you may apparently lose, be more acceptable unto you than falsehood and injustice, by which you may apparently profit. Thus says the wise man in his Proverbs, " buy the truth and sell it not." (Prov. xxiii. 23.) Know ye that truth and justice are the ornaments of the soul, and give strength, security, and stability to the body. Indeed, I have found no remedy for weakness of heart like the pursuit of truth and justice. . . .

Keep firm to your word, let not bill, witnesses, or possession, be stronger in your sight than a promise made by word of mouth, whether in public or in private. Refrain from and disdain all deep reserves, cunning subterfuges, tricky pretexts, sharp practice, and flaws and evasions. Woe to him who buildeth his house upon them, for "it shall leave him in the midst of his days, and in his end he shall be a fool." Live by innocence, uprightness, and by purity ; and touch not that which is not yours, be it great or small. Taste not the least of anything which is not clearly and decidedly yours, flee far from doubtful possessions, but, on the contrary, establish them firmly in the possession of those they belong to. Know that the tasting of doubtful goods causeth to be weary of sure goods, the tasting of little to be weary of much, and the tasting of the secret to be weary of the revealed, so that one becometh a confirmed and hardened thief and robber. Flee from such a man's face ; whosoever buys of him will not rejoice, and whoever selleth to him will have to regret it, he will be ashamed in his life and be confounded in his death. All this I have seen and put it to my heart. Whoever conceiveth chaff bringeth forth stubble, but he 'who to himself sows righteousness shall reap in mercy.' Ennoble yourself by moral strictness and be satisfied of your faithfulness, for there is no nobility like that of morality, and there is no inheritance like faithfulness. Bring near to you those that are far, bow to the little ones, cause your face to shine upon the humble, have compassion upon the needy, and those that are ashamed of their poverty rejoice in your joy, and visit them in your festivals and appointed days " according to the good hand of God upon you." Take care that their faces be not put to the blush and shame on account of your gifts. Cease not doing good to whomever you can do good, and befriend the deserving whoever he may be. Despise inactivity and abhor indolence, for they are the causes of the destruction of the body, of want, of penury, of self-contempt, of frowardness of mouth, and of perverseness of lips ; they constitute the ladder to Satan and his satellites. All these evils are the pernicious fruits of sluggishness, whilst " in all labour there is profit." Do not make yourselves abominable by quarrelsomeness and petulance, which waste the body, the soul, and the property, and what else remains ? I have seen the white ones become black, the low brought still lower, families expatriated, princes deposed from their greatness, great cities laid in ruins, assemblies dispersed, pious men destroyed, and men of faith lost, honourable men rejected and despised, — all on account of quarrelsomeness. . . . Glory in forbearance, because that is the true strength and real victory ; for in your taking revenge there is a doubt ; perhaps ye may not attain it, and your heart will grow sick by hope deferred, and ye may perhaps increase your shame in case of failure, like unto one who flings a stone which redounds back upon his head. . . .

Conduct yourselves with meekness and humility, for they are the steps of the ladder by which ye may climb the highest hill of virtue and excellency, and then ye hardly need forbearance. Know that there is no ornament so beautiful as that of humility. Behold the master of all prophets (Moses) was not so distinguished in Scripture for any of his high attributes as for that of humility. Keep a bridle upon your tongue and a muzzle upon your mouth. . . .

If the spiritual part, the understanding, rules and subdues the physical desires, the latter will succumb and seek but that which is necessary, will be satisfied with the little, and disdain superfluities; he will be contented in life and comforted in death. Eat that ye may live, and condemn all that is superfluous. Believe not that the multitude of eating and drinking enlarges the body and increases the understanding, as a sack which is filled by that which is put therein: for it is just the contrary. . . . Be careful in taking wine, for it destroys the mighty and disgraces the honourable. . . .

Know, that Expenditure is divided into four classes: Profit, Loss, Disgrace, and Honour. Profit is the expenditure of charity and benevolence, the interest of which ye enjoy in this world, whilst the capital is laid up as an endowment for the future. Loss is gambling, by which man loseth his money, his respect, and his time; for if he gaineth, he weaveth spiders' webs, and " it is a trespass he hath certainly trespassed." Disgrace is that which is extravagantly spent in eating and drinking. Honour is the expenditure for garments for his skin. Dress, therefore, as well as your means will possibly allow; but eat less than your means, only sufficient to preserve your lives. Despise gambling, and keep aloof from gamblers. " Sow in righteousness," that is, spend in alms even somewhat more than your means will permit, and " ye will reap in mercy." Live happily in the society of your friends, and with the wife of your youthful years; but touch not the one which is not yours, for " she hath cast down many wounded: yea, many strong men have been slain by her." . . . Serve your friends and your friendless with all your physical power and might, " according to the good hand of the Lord upon you "; but take heed lest ye serve them with your souls, for they are a godly portion. Remember this, my son Abraham; and the Lord, blessed be he, shall have mercy upon thee!

WELSH TRIADS

(12th–14th centuries.)

A FAVORITE form of mediæval Welsh literature was that of the sententious compositions known as "triads," in which thoughts or subjects were grouped by threes. Considerable collections of these have survived, and some writers have endeavored to trace their origin to Druidical times; but recent Celtic scholars seem to be generally persuaded that the triads have no earlier source than among the Welsh bards of the twelfth century and afterwards. The following is a collection grouped as "Moral Triads:"

MORAL TRIADS

(From "Ecclesiastical Antiquities of the Cymry," by Rev. John Williams, p. 28.)

1. The three primary principles of wisdom: obedience to the laws of God, concern for the welfare of mankind, and suffering with fortitude all the accidents of life.

2. The three great laws of man's actions: what he forbids in another, what he requires from another, and what he cares not how it is done by another.

3. Three things well understood will give peace: the tendencies of nature, the claims of justice, and the voice of truth.

4. There are three ways of searching the heart of man: in the thing he is not aware of, in the manner he is not aware of, and at the time he is not aware of.

5. There are three things, and God will not love him

that loves to look at them: fighting, a monster, and the pomposity of pride.

6. Three things produce wisdom: truth, consideration, and suffering.

7. The three great ends of knowledge: duty, utility, and decorum.

8. There are three men that all ought to look upon with affection: he that with affection looks at the face of the earth, that is delighted with rational works of art, and that looks lovingly on little infants.

9. Three men will not love their country: he that loves luxurious food, he that loves riches, and he that loves ease.

10. The three laughs of a fool: at the good, at the bad, and at he knows not what.

11. Three things corrupt the world: pride, superfluity, and indolence.

SAINT LOUIS

(A. D. 1215–1270.)

OF Louis IX., king of France, who reigned from A. D. 1226 to 1270, and who became "Saint Louis" in the calendar of the Roman Church by the canonizing decree of Pope Boniface VIII. in 1297, M. Guizot says: "The world has seen more profound politicians on the throne, greater generals, men of more mighty and brilliant intellect, princes who have exercised a more powerful influence over later generations and events subsequent to their own time; but it has never seen such a king as this St. Louis; never seen a man possessing sovereign power and yet not contracting the vices and passions which attend it; displaying upon the throne in such a high degree every human virtue purified and ennobled by Christian faith. St. Louis did not give any new or permanent impulse to his age; he did not strongly influence the nature or the development of civilization in France; whilst he endeavored to reform the gravest abuses of the feudal system by the introduction of justice and public order, he did not endeavor to abolish it, either by the substitution of a pure monarchy, or by setting class against class in order to raise the royal authority high above all. He was neither an egotist nor a scheming diplomatist; he was in all sincerity in harmony with his age, and sympathetic alike with the faith, the institutions, the customs, and the tastes of France in the thirteenth century. And yet, both in the thirteenth century and in later times, St. Louis stands apart as a man of profoundly original character; an isolated figure, without any peer among his contemporaries or his successors; so far as it was possible in the Middle Ages, he was an ideal man, king, and Christian."

ST. LOUIS'S INSTRUCTIONS TO HIS SON.

(From " St. Louis, King of France," by the Sire de Joinville; translated by James Hutton.)

" After he had landed at Tunis, before the Castle of Carthage, he was seized with dysentery, for which he took to bed, and was sensible that he must soon pass from this world to the next. Thereupon he called Monseigneur Philip, his son, and commanded him to observe, as if it were a will, all the instructions he left him, which instructions the king, it is said, wrote out with his own sainted hand.

" 'Fair son, the first thing I teach thee is to mould thy heart to love God ; for without that no one can be saved. Take care not to do anything which may displease God, to wit, a deadly sin ; on the contrary, thou shouldst endure all sorts of outrage and torture rather than commit a deadly sin. If God send thee adversity, accept it patiently, and render thanks to our Lord, and think that thou hast deserved it, and that it will turn wholly to thy advantage. If He bestows upon thee prosperity, thank Him humbly, so that thou art not worse through pride or other cause when thou oughtest to be better, for no one ought to war against God with gifts. Confess thyself frequently, and choose as confessor a man of discretion, who shall teach thee what thou oughtest to do and what thou oughtest to avoid. And thou shouldst bear and comport thyself in such manner that thy confessor and friends may venture to reprove thee for thy misdeeds. Attend devoutly to the service of the Holy Church, both with heart and mouth, especially at mass during the consecration. Let thy heart be gentle and compassionate towards the poor, the unfortunate, and the afflicted, and comfort and help them so far as in thee lies. Maintain the good customs of thy kingdom, and put down the bad. Be not covetous against thy people, and do not load thy conscience with imposts and taxes. If thou hast any sorrow at heart, tell it straightway to thy confessor, or to some discreet man who is not full of idle words; then thou wilt bear it more easily. Take care to have in thy company discreet and loyal persons, whether religious or secular, who are not full of covetousness, and converse frequently with them; but flee and avoid the society of the wicked. Listen gladly to the word of God, and keep it in thy heart; and seek earnestly for prayers and indulgences. Love what is good and profitable; hate whatever is evil, wherever it be. Let no one be so bold as to utter before thee any word that may lead to or excite a sin, or to speak evil of others behind their backs; neither suffer any profane thing to be said of God in thy presence. Render thanks frequently to God for all the good things He has bestowed upon thee, so that thou be worthy of still greater blessings. In administering justice and doing right to thy subjects be loyal and firm, without turning to the right hand or to the left; but help the right, and uphold the complaint of the poor man until the truth be made manifest. And if any one has an action against thee, do not believe anything until thou knowest the whole truth; for then thy counsellors will judge more boldly according to truth, either for or against thee. If thou hast anything that belongeth to another, either through thee or thy predecessors, and the thing be certain, make restitution without delay; but if the thing be doubtful, institute an inquiry into it by means of wise men, promptly and diligently. It is thy duty to take care that thy people and subjects live under thee in peace and uprightness. Above all, keep the good towns and customs of thy kingdom in the condition and liberties in which thy predecessors preserved them; and if there be anything to amend, amend and redress it, and keep them in favour and affection; for because of the power and riches of the great cities thy subjects and foreigners will fear to do anything against thee, especially thy peers and thy barons. Honour and love all persons belonging to the Holy Church, and take heed that no one wrests from them, or diminishes the gifts and alms which thy predecessors have bestowed. It is related of King Philip, my grand-father, that on one occasion one of his counsellors told him that the people of the Holy Church did him much wrong in that they infringed his rights and encroached upon his jurisdiction, and that it was great marvel he suffered it; and the good king answered, that he was well aware of it; but when he reflected upon the goodness and favour God had shown to himself, he preferred to lose something of his rights than to have any dispute with the people of the Holy Church. To thy father and thy mother show honour and respect, and keep their commandments. Bestow the benefices of the Holy Church upon persons of worth and of unspotted lives; and act by the advice of wise and honourable men. Take care not to undertake a war against a Christian prince without grave deliberation; and if it be necessary for thee to do so, watch over the Holy Church and those who have done thee no wrong. If wars and disputes arise between thy subjects, appease them as speedily as thou canst. Be careful to have good provosts and bailiffs, and make frequent inquiries about them and the people of thy household, as to how they conduct themselves, and if they are guilty of overmuch greed, or of treachery or deceit. Labour to root out of thy kingdom all vile sinfulness; especially put down with all thy might profane oaths and heresy. Take heed that the charges of thy household be reasonable. Lastly, sweet son, cause masses to be chanted and prayers offered up for my soul throughout thy kingdom; and grant me a special and positive part in all the good that thou shalt do. Fair, dear son, I bestow upon thee all the benedictions that a good father can give unto a son. And may the blessed Trinity preserve and defend thee from all evil; and may God give thee grace, to do always His will, so that He may be honoured by thee, and that thou and I, after this mortal life, may be together with Him, and praise Him without end. Amen.' "

MEDIÆVAL PRECEPTS

(From Thomas Wright's "History of Domestic Manners and Sentiments in England," chapter viii.)

"THE early metrical romances of the Carlovingian cycle give us an insight into what were considered as the praiseworthy features in the character of the feudal knight. In 'Doon of Mayence,' for example, when the aged count Guy sends his young son Doon into the world, he counsels him thus: 'You shall always ask questions of good men, and you shall never put your trust in a stranger. Every day, fair son, you shall hear the holy mass, and give to the poor whenever you have money, for God will repay you double. Be liberal in gifts to all; for the more you give, the more honour you will acquire, and the richer you will be; for a gentleman who is too sparing will lose all in the end, and die in wretchedness and disgrace; but give without promising whenever you can. Salute all people when you meet them, and, if you owe anything, pay it willingly; but if you cannot pay, ask for a respite. When you come to the hostelry, don't stand squabbling, but enter glad and joyously. When you enter the house, cough very loud, for there may be something doing which you ought not to see, and it will cost you nothing to give this notice of your approach, while those who happen to be there will love you the better for it. Do not quarrel with your neighbour, and avoid disputing with him before other people; for if he know anything against you, he will let it out, and you will have the shame of it. When you are at court, play at tables, and if you have any good points of behaviour (depors), show them; you will be the more prized, and gain the more advantage. Never make a noise or joke in church; this is only done by unbelievers, whom God loves not. Honour all the clergy, and speak fairly to them, but leave them as little of your goods as you can; the more they get from you, the more you will be laughed at; you will never profit by enriching them. And if you wish to save your honour undiminished, meddle with nothing you do not understand, and don't pretend to be a proficient in what you have never learnt. And if you have a valet, take care not to seat him at the table by you, or take him to bed with you; for the more honour you do to a low fellow, the more will he despise you. If you should know anything that you would wish to conceal, tell it by no means to your wife, if you have one; for if you let her know it, you will repent of it the first time you displease her.'

"With these counsels of a father, we may compare those of a mother to her son. In the romance of 'Huon de Bordeaux,' when the youthful hero leaves his home to repair to the court of Charlemagne, the duchess addresses her son as follows: 'My child,' she said, 'you are going to be a courtier; I require you, for God's love, have nothing to do with a treacherous flatterer; make the acquaintance of wise men. Attend regularly at the service of holy church, and show honour and love to the clergy. Give your goods willingly to the poor; be courteous, and spend freely, and you will be the more loved and cherished.' On the whole, higher sentiments are placed in the mouth of the lady than in that of the baron."

SELECTED RULES OF GOOD BEHAVIOR FROM A BOOK ENTITLED "STANS PUER AD MENSAM."

(From Thomas Wright's "History of Domestic Manners," ch. ix.)

EVERY one was considered to show his good manners best, or at least to be expected to do so, in the hall at table, and manners at table were among those in which the scholar was first instructed. Among the most common of the pieces in Latin verse, composed for the purpose of which I am here speaking, is one bearing, under rather different forms, the title of 'Stans Puer ad Mensam' — (the boy standing at table), as it gives directions for his conduct under those circumstances. Several copies of this piece, which is written in Latin hexameters, are found among the mediæval manuscripts of the British Museum of different dates. One of these occurs in the Harl. MS., No. 1002, in a handwriting of the fifteenth century, the age in which the outward forms of mediæval manners were perhaps most insisted upon, and from this copy I will give a review of its teaching and doctrines. " While you are standing at your lord's table," the scholar is told, " learn the good maxims " —

Stans puer ad mensam domini, bona dogmata discas.

Attention is first called to the personal bearing of the boy. He is while talking to "keep at perfect ease, and his fingers, hands, and feet quiet, to hold his countenance undisturbed, and not to roll his eyes about in every direction ; nor is he to fix his eyes upon the wall as if it were a looking-glass, or lean upon the post as if it were a walking-staff " —

Dum loqueris digitique manus in pace pedes sint.
Sis simplex vultu, visum nec ubique revolvas,
Nec paries speculum, baculus nec sit tibi postis.

Still less ought he in such company to pick his nose or to scratch himself, or to lean his head, but to look in the face of the one speaking —

Non nares fodeas, carnem propriam neque scalpus,
Nec caput inclines, facies sit in ore loquentis.

He is to go demurely in walking in the streets and ways —

Pergas in pace per vicos atque plateas.

He was not to let the colour in his face change suddenly through levity; nor to burst into horse-laughs in the presence of his lord — " despise laughing, by which you may be brought into contempt " —

Nec coram domino debes monastrare cachinnos ;
Sperne cachinnare, poteris quo vilificari.

" Hold to these maxims, if thou wilt be considered polite " —

Hæc documenta tene, si vis urbanus haberi.

Next come the directions for behaviour at eating in the feudal meal. The first is, " Never take your food with unwashed hands " —

Illotis manibus escam ne sumpseris unquam ;

and " take the seat which the host has pointed out to you; never presuming on a high place, unless you have been ordered to take it " —

Atque loco sedeas tibi quem signaverit hospes ;
Altum sperne locum tibi sumere sis nisi jussus.

" Touch not the bread and wine till the dishes are placed, or you will be said to be starved or gluttonous " —

Fercula donec sint sita, pani parce meroque,
Ne fame captus dicaris, sive gulosus ;

" Nor eat anything until grace has been said " —

Nec escas capias donec benedictio fiat.

"Let thy nails be clean, lest perchance they offend thy neighbour " —

Mundi sint ungues, noceant ne forte sodali.

" Eat all that has been served to you, or let it be given to the poor " —

Morsellum totum comedas, vel detur egenis.

It was customary at the mediæval table, in the course of carving, to lay aside a portion of the provisions for the poor, for whom there was a basket, or some large vessel, in the hall, in which all the offal was placed, and it was sent out in charity to the beggars, who assembled at the hall-door in the court. Hence it was considered a part of genteel behaviour in hall to put aside the part of your own share of provisions which you were unable to eat yourself, and add it to that which was sent to the poor.

You are taught to be quiet at table, and not to indulge in much chattering.

Pace fruens multis caveas garrire loquelis.

" Avoid swelling out your cheeks by taking a great lump into your mouth at once " —

Maxillamque bolo caveas expandere magno.

"Nor eat your food on both sides of your mouth at once " —

Nec gemina parte vescaris cibis simul oris.

" Never laugh or talk with your mouth full " —

Nunquam ridebis nec faberis ore repleto.

Directions are then given with regard to your plate. You are not to make a noise in it by overeating; the spoon is not to be left standing in it, nor lying on its edge, for fear of fouling the table-cloth ; nor must you return to the dish a morsel once taken up ; and call not back to the table a dish which has been taken away —

In disco nunquam cochlear stet, nec super oram
Ipsius jaceat, ne mappam polluat udo.
In discum tacta buccella retrograda non sit;
Discum de mensa sublatum nec revocabis.

" Never spit over the table or upon it " —

Non ultra mensam spueris nec desuper unquam.

" Scrape not nor scratch your own skin with your fingers; always avoid wiping your nose with a clean hand," — handkerchiefs were not in use at the time, — " and at table avoid picking your teeth with your knife " —

Non carnem propriam digitis verres neque scalpas;
Semper munda manus devitet tergere nasum;
Mensa cultello dentes mundare caveto.

" Drink not at table while you have food in your mouth " —

Ore tenens escas potum superaddere noli.

" Never bring to table what may offend your companions " —

Quod noceat sociis in mensa ne refer unquam.

This refers to familiarity with animals — " Be careful at table not to handle the cat or the dog " —

Mensa murilegum caveas palpare canemque.

The young guest was admonished to beware of staining the table-cloth with his knife —

Mensa cultello mappam maculare caveto.

And he has to wipe his mouth before drinking —

Oreque polluto non potabis nisi terso.

. . . This Latin metrical code of good manners concludes with the wish that all who refuse to conform to these teachings should be banished from every polite table —

Privetur mensa qui spernit hæc documenta.

In the Harleian MS., this poem ends with the statement that the author of this code was the celebrated Robert Grosseteste, Bishop of Lincoln, one of the bright stars of English literature and learning in the thirteenth century—

Hæc qui me docuit, Grossum-caput est sibi nomen.
Præsul et ille fuit, cui det felix Deus omen.

THE KNIGHT OF LA TOUR-LANDRY

(A. D. 1381.)

THE late Mr. Thomas Wright, in introducing a translation of "The Book of the Knight of La Tour-Landry, compiled for the instruction of his Daughters," says that the book was first translated from the original French into English in the reign of Henry VI. The author of it was Geoffroy de la Tour, lord of the feudal castle of La Tour-Landry, in the province of Anjou. The ruins of the old castle are still to be seen. The book was begun in 1381, for the instruction and guidance of his three motherless daughters. Mention is made in the text of a previous book, which he had compiled for the use of his sons, but no MS. of it is known to exist. In compiling this work for his daughters the knight followed the practice of mediæval times, of teaching morals and religion by means of popular stories and historical narratives. In collecting these anecdotes he employed two priests and two clerks.

"A very large proportion of the stories given by Geoffroy de la Tour-Landry are taken from the Scriptures and from the lives of saints and other similar productions; but, like other moralists of his age, he adopted the stories of the fabliaux, and the tales of the popular conteur, whenever they seemed to suit his purpose, and in his choice he has not rejected some which were better fitted by their want of delicacy to the ears of his contemporaries than to those of modern times. There then existed very little of refinement in word or thought, and, in the best society, both sexes often conversed in terms and on subjects which are in strange discordance with our modern sentiments.

"No doubt under the pretext of instructing his own daughters, Geoffroy's design was to write a treatise on the domestic education of women, and his plan appears to have extended still further, and to have been intended to embrace the other sex also. We learn positively from several passages in the present book, that he had already compiled a similar book for the use of his sons, and, from the way in which he speaks of it, the compilation of this other work must have preceded the book for the instruction of his daughters by some years. ' And, therefore,' he says at the end of his prologue, ' y have made .ij. bokes, one for my sones, another for my doughtres.' In another place, in warning his daughters against drunkenness, he says, ' as ye shal finde it more pleinly in the boke of youre brethren;' and again, at the close of the book, in Caxton's translation, the knight is made to say, ' as hit is reherced in the booke of my two sonnes.' At least one other allusion to this book is found in the French text; yet, strange to say, nobody has ever heard of the existence of a copy of this treatise for the instruction of the Knight's sons, nor has any trace of it ever been discovered except in the mention of it in the book of which the translation is now published.

"The book which Geoffroy de la Tour-Landry compiled for the instruction of his daughters, on the contrary, appears to have become extremely popular. Nearly a dozen copies of the original text are known to exist in manuscript, of which seven are in the Bibliothèque Imperial in Paris, and one in the Library of the British Museum. . . .

"The popularity of this book soon extended to foreign lands, and it was translated into several languages. The two earliest printed translations appeared in Germany and England very nearly at the same date. . . .

"The first edition in English, as we are informed in the colophon at the end, was translated by our first printer, William Caxton, and printed by him. . . .

"There existed, however, an English translation of the Book of Geoffroy de la Tour-Landry long anterior to that of Caxton, though it was never printed. It is anonymous, and we have no means whatever of ascertaining the name of the author, or in fact, anything whatever of its history. It is contained in a manuscript in the Harleian collection in the British Museum. . . . This translation is in many respects superior to that of Caxton. . . . This earlier translation, moreover, furnishes a far more elegant and interesting monument of the English language in the fifteenth century. It is for these reasons that I have chosen it for the text of the

present volume.   Unfortunately, it is an imperfect manuscript, for there are one or two lacunæ in the body of the
work, and it is truncated at the end by nearly one-fifth of
the whole.   Under these circumstances, the only resource
was to supply from Caxton's text the parts which are wanting
in the inedited manuscript."

PASSAGES FROM "THE BOOK OF THE KNIGHT OF LA
TOUR–LANDRY."

(Early English Text Society, Publication 33.)

HOW AND WHY THE BOOK WAS MADE.

In the yere of the incarnacion of oure Lord M^{le} iijc
lxxj, as y was in a gardin, al heui and fulle of thought, in
the shadow, about the ende of the monthe of Aprille, but
a litelle y reioysed me of the melodie and song of the
wilde briddes ; thei sang there in her langages, as the thrus-
tille, the thrusshe, the nytinggale, and other briddes, the
which were fulle of mirthe and ioye ; and thaire suete
songe made my herte to lighten, and made me to think of
the tyme that is passed of my youthe, how loue in gret
distresse had holde me, and how y was in her seruice mani
tymez fulle of sorugh and gladnesse, as mani lovers ben.
But my sorw was heled, and my seruice wel ysette and
quitte, for he gaue [me a] fayr wyff, and that was bothe
faire and good, [who had knowleche of alle honoure, alle
good, and of fayre mayntenynge,] and of alle good she
was bell and the floure ; and y delited me so moche in her
that y made for her loue songges, balades, rondelles, viro-
layes, and diuerse [other] thinges in the best wise that y
couthe.   But dethe, that on alle makithe werre, toke her
from me, the whiche hathe made me haue mani a sorufulle
thought and gret heuinesse.   And so it is more than .xx.
yeere that I haue ben for her ful of gret sorugh.   For a

true loveris hert forgetith neuer the woman that enis he
hathe truli loued.   And as y was in the saide gardein,
thinkynge of these thought[s], y sawe come towardes me
my .iij. doughters, of the whiche I was ioyful, and had grete
desire that thei shuld turne to good and worship aboue
alle ertheli thinges, for thei were yonge and had but tendir
witte ; and so atte the begynnyng a man aught to lerne
his doughters with good ensaumples, ye vinge as dede the
quene Proues of Hongrie, that faire and goodly chastised
and taught her doughters, as it [is] contened in her boke.
. . . Therefor y purposed to make a litelle boke in the
whiche y wolde write the good condiciones and dedes of
ladies and gentille women, that for her goodnesse were
worshipped, honoured, praised, and renomed the tyme
passed, and euer shalle be, for her weldoinge and goodnes,
to that entent that my doughtres shulde take ensaumple
of faire continuaunce and good manere.   And also y wol
make write the manere contrarie of goodnesse, the whiche
is called the boke of hurting of euelle women, that hath
vsed to do euelle and had blames, to that entent that who
so luste may kepe hem from harme ther thei might erre,
as thei that yet be blamed, dishonoured, and shamed. &
for these causes aforesaid, y thought to make this litelle
boke to my yong doughtres, wherupon thei might rede and
studie, to that entent that thei might lerne and see both
good and euelle of the tyme passed, and for to kepe hem in
good clennesse, and from alle euelle in tyme comyng. . . .
Ther for the resones that y haue saide you, y parted and
yede out of the gardein, and fonde in my way .ij. prestes
and .ij. clerkes that y had.   And y said to hem that y
wolde make a boke of ensaumples, for to teche my doughtres, that thei might vnderstond how thei shulde gouerne
hem, and knowe good from euell.   And so y made hem
extraie me ensaumples of the Bible and other bokes that

y had, as the gestis of kinges, the croniclez of Fraunce, Grece, of Inglond, and of mani other straunge londes. And y made hem rede me eueri boke; and ther that y fonde a good ensaumple, y made extraie it oute. And thanne y made this boke. But y wolde not sette it in ryme, but in prose, forto abregge it, and that it might be beter and more pleinly to be understond. And y made this boke for the gret loue that y had to my said doughtres. . . .

CHAPTER X.

HOW WOMEN SHULDE BEHAUE HEM CURTESLY AND MEKELY.

Affter, doughtres, ye must be meke and curteys, for there nis none so grete a vertu to gete the grace of God and the loue of alle peple; for humilite and curtesie ouercomithe alle proude hertys that be felle, as a sparhauke, be he neuer so ramageus, ye may ouercome hym with goodly and curteys demening, ye may make hym come from the tre to youre honde. And yef ye fare rudely and be cruelle with hym, he will fle his way and neuer come atte you. And sethe that curtesye and softenesse may ouercome a wilde bridde, that hathe no reson, nedes it aught to refraine felons proude herte of man and woman. And humilite is the furst entre and wey of frenship and wordely loue, and that ouercomithe gret hertis, and suagithe ire and wrathe of alle persones. Ther was a lorde that y knew, that conquered the knightes and squiers by his curtesie and humilite to do hem [more] plesaunce in the tyme of his werre, than other lordes couthe gete with her gold and siluer or ani other yeftes. And also y haue know mani ladies and gentille women that haue gote hem moche loue of gret and smale for her curtesie and humilite. And therfor y rede you be curteys and humble to gret and smale, and to do curtesie and reuerence, and speke to hem faire, and to be meke in ansuere to the pore, and thei wol praise you, and bere forthe of you good worde and good fame more than wolle the grete that ye make curtesie to; for to grete ye make curtesie of right, the whiche is dew to hem, but the curtesie that is made to poure gentilmen, or to other of lasse degre, it comithe of fre and gentille curteys and humble hert. And the smalle peple that the curtesye and humblesse is done to, holdithe hem worshipped therby, and thanne, ouer alle there thei comithe, thei praisithe and spekithe good of hym that dothe hem reuerence and curtesie. And of the pore that curtesie is done to, comithe gret loos and good name fro tyme to tyme, and gettithe loue of the peple; as it happed as y was not longe sethe with a companie of knyhtes and ladies, a gret ladi dede of her hode and bowed her ayenst a taillour. And one of the knyghtes saide, "Madame, ye haue done of youre hode to a taillour." And she said that she was gladder that she had do it of to hym thanne to a lorde. And thei alle sawe her mekenesse and wisdom, and helde her wyse, and the knight leuid that tolde her of the tailour. . . .

CHAPTER XXXVIII.

OF GOOD EXAMPLES.

And there be other be wyse, that haue her herte and hope of God. And for the loue and fere that thei haue in hym, thei kepe hem clene and fytithe ayenst temptaciones, and the braydes of the fyre of lecherye, and kepithe hem suerly withoute delycious metes, for the flesshe is tempted by delycious metes and drinkes, the which bene leteres and kindelers of the brondes of lecherye; and other that haue grace to thenke that they haue suffisaunce, and that is ayenst couetise. And there be other that haue free hert, true and iuste, and be not riotous; for who that sekithe ryot gladly, he metithe therewith, for many men for anger betithe hym selff with his owne staffe, and sekithe hym sorw from day to day. And God blessithe in the gospelle the meke and the humble hert. And all these men that kepithe hem selff clene, and in the loue and drede of God, and of his neighboures, shewithe welle who is her fader, and that is God the fader, of the which they kepe his comaundementis as holy chirche techithe hem. And they haue free hert to witholde good ensaumples of lyff, and ioye perdurable, and of saluation. And therfor, faire doughters, haue night and day youre hertes to hym and loue hym, and drede hym, and he wille kepe you and saue you from perille and temptaciones. And therfor, my faire doughters, y wille shewe you and declare you by this boke the good ladyes that God preisithe in the Bybille, and for thaire holy lyff shal euer be praised, and therfor takithe ensaumple to lyue clenly and honestly as thei dede. And also y wille declare you sum euelle women that were diuerse and cruelle, the whiche made and hadde euelle ende, to that entent that ye may take hede by hem to kepe you from the euelle, that ye falle not inne.

WYCLIF

(A. D. 1320–1384.)

"WYCLIF, Langland, and Chaucer are the three great figures of English literature in the Middle Ages.

"Wyclif belonged to the rich and respected family of the Wyclifs, lords of the manor of Wyclif, in Yorkshire. He was born about 1320, and devoted himself early to a scientific and religious calling. He studied at Oxford, where he soon attracted notice, being one of those men of character who occupy from the beginning of their lives, without seeking for it, but being, as it seems, born to it, a place apart amid the limp multitude of men. The turn of his mind, the originality of his views, the firmness of his will, his learning, raised him above others; he was one of those concerning whom it is at once said they are ' some one; ' and several times in the course of his existence he saw the University, the King, the country even, turn to him when ' some one ' was needed.

"He was hardly thirty-five when, the college of Balliol at Oxford having lost its master, he was elected to the post. In 1366 Parliament ruled that the Pope's claim to the tribute promised by King John should no longer be recognized, and Wyclif was asked to draw up a pamphlet justifying the decision. In 1374 a diplomatic mission was entrusted to him, and he went to Bruges, with several other ' ambassatores,' to negotiate with the Pope's representatives. He then had the title of doctor of divinity.

"Various provincial livings were successively bestowed upon him: that of Fillingham in 1361; that of Ludgarshall in 1368; that of Lutterworth, in Leicestershire, in 1374, which he kept till his death. He divided his time between his duties as rector, his studies, his lectures at Oxford, and his life in London, where he made several different stays, and preached some of his sermons.

"These quiet occupations were interrupted from time to time owing to the storms raised by his writings. But so great was his fame, and so eminent his personality, that he escaped the terrible consequences that heresy then involved. He had at first alarmed religious authority by his political theories on the relations of Church and State, next on the reformation of the Church itself; finally he created excessive scandal by attacking dogmas and by discussing the sacraments. . . .

"Besides his writings and his speeches, he used, in order to popularize his doctrines, his ' simple priests,' or ' poor priests,' who, without being formed into a religious order, imitated the wandering life of the friars, but not their mendicity, and strove to attain the ideal which the friars had fallen short of. They went about preaching from village to village, and the civil authority was alarmed by the political and religious theories expounded to the people by these wanderers, who journeyed ' from county to county, and from town to town, in certain habits under dissimulation of great holiness, without license of our Holy Father the Pope, or of the ordinary of the diocese.' Wyclif justified these unlicensed preachings by the example of St. Paul, who, after his conversion, ' preechide fast, and axide noo leve of Petir herto, for he hadde leve of Jesus Crist.'

"From this time forth Wyclif began to circulate on the sacraments, and especially on the Eucharist, opinions that Oxford even was unable to tolerate; the University condemned them. Conformably to his own theory, which tended, as did that of the Commons, towards a royal supremacy, Wyclif appealed not to the Pope but to the king, and in the meantime refused to submit. This was carrying boldness very far. John of Gaunt separates from his *protégé;* Courtenay, bishop of London, calls together a Council, which condemns Wyclif and his adherents (1382); the followers are pursued, and retract or exile themselves; but Wyclif continues to live in perfect quiet. Settled at Lutterworth, from whence he now rarely stirred, he wrote more than, ever, with a more and more caustic and daring pen. The papal schism, which had begun in 1378, had cast discredit on the Holy See; Wyclif's work was made the easier by it. At last Urban VI., the Pope whom England recognized, summoned him to appear in his presence, but an attack of paralysis came on, and Wyclif died in his parish on the last day of the year 1384. . . . By order of the Council of Constance, his ashes were afterwards thrown to the winds, and the family of the Wyclifs of Wyclif, firmly attached to the old faith, erased him from their genealogical tree." — T. J. JUSSERAND, "A Literary History of the English People."

WYCLIF'S SHORT RULE OF LIFE.

FOR EACH MAN IN GENERAL, AND FOR PRIESTS, AND LORDS, AND LABOURERS, IN PARTICULAR, HOW EACH SHALL BE SAVED IN HIS DEGREE.

First, When thou risest, or fully wakest, think upon the goodness of thy God; how for his own goodness, and not for any need, he made all things out of nothing, both angels and men, and all other creatures, good in their kind.

The second time, think on the great sufferings, and willing death that Christ suffered for mankind. When no man might make satisfaction for the guilt of Adam and Eve, and others more, neither any angel might make satisfaction therefore, then Christ, of his endless charity, suffered such great passion and painful death that no creature could suffer so much.

Think the third time, how God hath saved thee from death and other mischief, and suffered many thousands to be lost that night, some in water, some in fire, and some by sudden death; and some to be damned without end. And for this goodness and mercy thank thy God with all thine heart. And pray him to give thee grace to spend in that day, and evermore, all the powers of thy soul, as mind, understanding, reason, and will; and all the powers of thy body, as strength, beauty, and thy five senses, in his service and worship, and in nothing against his commandments; but in ready performance of his works of mercy, and to give good example of holy life, both in word and deed, to all men about thee.

Look afterward that thou be well occupied, and no time idle, for the danger of temptation. Take meat and drink in measure, not too costly nor too lickerous, and be not too curious thereabout. But such as God sendeth thee with health, take it in such measure that thou be fresher in mind and understanding to serve God. And always thank him for such gifts. Besides this, look thou do right and equity to all men, thy superiors, equals, and subjects or servants; and stir all to love truth, and mercy, and true peace, and charity; and suffer no men to be at dissension, but accord them if thou canst in any good manner.

Also, most of all fear God and his wrath; and most of all love God and his law, and his worship; and ask not principally for worldly reward, but in all thine heart desire the bliss of heaven in mercy of God, and thine own good life; and think much of the dreadful doom of pains of hell, to keep thee out of sin; and on the endless great joys of heaven, to keep thee in virtuous life; and according to thy skill teach others the same doing.

In the end of the day think wherein thou hast offended God, and how much and how oft, and therefore have entire sorrow, and amend it while thou mayest. And think how many God hath suffered to perish that day, many ways, and to be damned everlastingly, and how graciously he hath saved thee; not for thy desert, but for his own mercy and goodness, and therefore thank him with all thine heart. And pray him for grace that thou mayest dwell and end in his true and holy service and real love, and to teach other men the same doing.

If thou art a PRIEST, and especially a curate, live thou holily, surpassing other men in holy prayer, desire, and thinking, in holy speaking, counselling, and true teaching. And that God's commands, his gospel, and virtues, be ever in thy mouth; and ever despise sin to draw men therefrom; and that thy deeds be so rightful that no man shall blame them with reason, but that thy open deeds be a true book to all subjects and unlearned men, to serve God and do his commands thereby. For example of good life, open and lasting, more stirreth rude men than true preaching by word only. And waste not thy goods in great feasts of rich men, but live a humble life, of poor men's alms and goods, both in meat, and drink, and clothes, and the remainder give truly to poor men that have not of their own, and may not labour for feebleness or sickness, and thus thou shalt be a true priest both to God and man.

If thou art a LORD, look that thou live a rightful life in thine own person, both in respect to God and man, keeping the commands of God, doing the works of mercy, ruling well thy five senses, and doing reason and equity, and good conscience to all men. In the second place, govern well thy wife, thy children, and thy household attendants in God's law, and suffer no sin among them, neither in word nor in deed, that they may be examples of holiness and righteousness to all others; for thou shalt be condemned for their evil life and their evil example, unless thou amend it according to thy might. In the third place, govern well thy tenants, and maintain them in right and reason, and be merciful to them in their rents and worldly mercements, and suffer not thine officers to do them wrong nor be extortionate to them. And chastise in good manner them that are rebels against God's commands and virtuous life, more than for rebellion against thine own cause; or else for that thou lovest more thine own cause than God's, and thyself more than God Almighty, thou wert then a false traitor to God. And love, reward, praise, and cherish the true and virtuous of life more than if thou sought only thine own profit. And reverence and maintain truly, according to thy skill and might, God's law and true preachers thereof, and God's servants, in rest and peace. For thereby thou holdest the lordship of God, and if thou failest of this thou misdoest against God, and all thy lordship, in body and in soul. And principally if thou maintainest antichrist's disciples in their errors against Christ's life and his teaching, for blindness, covetousness, and worldly friendship; and helpest to slander and pursue true men that teach Christ's gospel and his life, and warn the people of their great sins, and of false prophets and hypocrites that deceive Christian men in faith, virtuous life, and worldly goods.

If thou art a LABOURER, live in meekness, and truly and willingly do thy labour, that thy lord or thy master if he be a heathen man, by thy meekness, willing and true service, may not have to grudge against thee, nor slander thy God, nor thy Christian profession; but rather be stirred to come to Christianity. And serve not Christian lords with grudgings; not only in their presence, but truly and willingly, and in absence. Not only for worldly dread, or worldly reward, but for dread of God and conscience, and for reward in heaven. For God that putteth thee in such service knoweth what state is best for thee, and will reward thee more than all earthly lords may, if thou dost it truly and willingly for his ordinance. And in all things beware of grudging against God and his visitation, in great labour, and long or great sickness, and other adversities. And beware of wrath, of cursing, of speaking evil, of banning man or beast; and ever keep patience, meekness, and charity, both to God and man. And thus each man in the three states ought to live, to save himself, and to help others; and thus should good life, rest, peace, and love, be among Christian men, and they be saved, and heathen men soon converted, and God magnified greatly in all nations and sects that now despise him and his law, for the false living of wicked Christian men.

WILLIAM DE LA POLE

(A. D. ——–1450.)

WILLIAM DE LA POLE, Earl and afterwards Duke of Suffolk, was the chief counsellor and minister, for a time, of the unfortunate King Henry VI., of England. He negotiated the marriage of the young king to Margaret of Anjou, with the hope that it might be influential in bringing about peace with France. The marriage was hateful to English feeling, and seems to have started against Suffolk the host of enemies by whom he was soon pursued. But the time was one of fierce and selfish factions, when no special provocation was needed for savage hostility to an influential public man. How far, if at all, Suffolk deserved the hatred with which he was hunted to death is not likely to be ever made clear. After five or six years of supremacy in the king's councils, he was impeached in Parliament and ordered into banishment by Henry (1450). Escaping with difficulty from a furious London mob, he got on board a ship sailing to Flanders; but was pursued by assassins, overtaken and murdered at sea.

This bare story of his career does not greatly recommend William de la Pole to our confidence; but one can hardly read the subjoined letter of admonition, which he wrote to his son a short time before he came to his tragical end, without wishing that his memory might be cleared of all the doubts that rest upon it. The epistle appears (No. 26) in Fenn's edition of the Paston Letters. His wife, of whom he speaks so lovingly to their son, was a grand-daughter of Chaucer, the poet.

LETTER OF THE DUKE OF SUFFOLK TO HIS SON.

(From the Paston Letters.)

My dear and only well-beloved son, I beseech our Lord in Heaven, the Maker of all the World, to bless you, and to send you ever grace to love him, and to dread him, to the which, as far as a father may charge his child, I both charge you, and pray you to set all your spirits and wits to do, and to know his holy laws and commandments, by the which ye shall, with his great mercy, pass all the great tempests and troubles of this wretched world.

And that also, weetingly, ye do nothing for love nor dread of any earthly creature that should displease him. And there as (*whenever*) any frailty maketh you to fall, beseech his mercy soon to call you to him again with repentance, satisfaction, and contrition of your heart, never more in will to offend him.

Secondly, next him above all earthly things, to be true liegeman in heart, in will, in thought, in deed, unto the king our aldermost (*greatest*) high and dread sovereign lord, to whom both ye and I be so much bound to; charging you as father can and may, rather to die than to be the contrary, or to know anything that were against the welfare or prosperity of his most royal person, but that as far as your body and life may stretch ye live and die to defend it, and to let his highness have knowledge thereof in all the haste ye can.

Thirdly, in the same wise, I charge you, my dear son, alway as ye be bounden by the commandment of God to do, to love, to worship, your lady and mother; and also that ye obey alway her commandments, and to believe her counsels and advices in all your works, the which dread not but shall be best and truest to you. And if any other body would steer you to the contrary, to flee the counsel in any wise, for ye shall find it naught and evil.

Furthermore, as far as father may and can, I charge you in any wise to flee the company and counsel of proud men, of covetous men, and of flattering men, the more especially and mightily to withstand them, and not to draw nor to meddle with them, with all your might and power; and to draw to you and to your company good and virtuous men, and such as be of good conversation, and of truth, and by them shall ye never be deceived nor repent you of.

Moreover, never follow your own wit in nowise, but in all your works, of such folks as I write of above, ask your advice and counsel, and doing thus, with the mercy of God, ye shall do right well, and live in right much worship, and great heart's rest and ease.

And I will be to you as good lord and father as my heart can think.

And last of all, as heartily and as lovingly as ever father blessed his child in earth, I give you the blessing of Our Lord and of me, which of his infinite mercy increase you in all virtue and good living; and that your blood may by his grace from kindred to kindred multiply in this earth to his service, in such wise as after the departing from this wretched world here, ye and they may glorify him eternally amongst his angels in heaven.

Written of mine hand,

The day of my departing fro this land.

Your true and loving father,

SUFFOLK.

APRIL, 1450, 28 H. VI.

THOMAS À KEMPIS

(A. D. 1380–1471.)

THOMAS HAMERKEN, known to fame as Thomas à Kempis, the reputed author of the "Imitation of Christ," was born at Kempen near Cologne, in 1380, entered the Augustinian monastery of Mt. St. Agnes, near Zwolle, in 1400, was ordained a priest in 1413, and was elected sub-prior in 1425. He died in 1471. He wrote a number of books; but his name is immortally associated with the "Imitation of Christ," which is believed to have had more readers than any other book in Christian literature except the Bible. That Thomas à Kempis was the author is not certain; but opinion among those who have investigated the question inclines in his favor.

The "Imitation of Christ" is so purely religious that its teachings do not come within the scope of this collection. The subjoined precepts are selected from an English translation of other writings, published a few years ago under the title of "The Little Garden of Roses."

SELECTIONS FROM "THE LITTLE GARDEN OF ROSES."

Every virtue has its particular sweetness to refresh him that worketh well; but he that clings to vice begets an evil end, makes shipwreck of his honour, destroys repose, lays up for himself a store of infirmities, increases sorrow, and deprives himself of the relish of what is good and virtuous; but he that denies himself lawful pleasures, increases the surety of resisting such as are unlawful.

He that muzzles the mouth of the hound need not fear his bark; so he that keeps strict silence shall not offend with his lips.

He that lives retired and in silence is far removed from

falsehood and bickering; from cursing and detraction; from anger and murmuring.

He that hearkens not to evil discourse, and shuts his eyes on the vanities of this world, more easily avoids its snares, and turns away his thoughts from its vain imaginations; for a watch over the senses is the foundation of purity, the discipline of peace, the mirror of devotion.

When wrath takes possession of the breast wisdom takes to flight even from the wise. He that speaks hastily is like a snarling hound; but a meek answer breaks the violence of wrath, and gives to the afflicted roses in the stead of thorns.

Blessed is the prudent tongue, for it heals the wounds of the hasty.

He that resisteth his evil inclinations in their birth, when they show themselves but young and limber, shall more easily destroy them than when their roots are deep.

He that preserves purity in soul and body is like God's angels; but he that yields to his evil inclinations, and takes pleasure in the depravity of his thoughts, is the bond-slave of Satan.

Publish not scandal, for it is well to be silent; proclaim the truth, for it is salutary; be modest, for it is reasonable; hurt no one, for it is just; be useful to all, for such is piety; and edify thy neighbour by word and deed, for such is religion.

The prudent man thinks before he acts; changes not unreasonably; speaks with reserve of what he is ignorant of; and affirms not lightly what is doubtful.

Look carefully into your own faults, and you will find little leisure or inclination to weigh in the balance the actions of others.

Be faithful in little things, and your talent shall be vastly increased in the kingdom of heaven.

Be neither idle in solitude, nor a babbler in public, and the evil one, overcome by your diligence and silence, shall depart from you.

Trample pride under foot, and you shall find much.

HUGH RHODES'S "BOKE OF NURTURE"

(A. D. 1577.)

A CURIOUS collection of mediæval writings, which illustrate the ideas of nurture and training for children that prevailed in England during the latter part of the Middle Ages, was made for the Early English Text Society by Mr. Frederick J. Furnivall, the eminent student of early English literature, and published in 1868. The injunctions, rules and precepts of the collection relate mainly to manners, and more to table-manners than to behavior in other circumstances and places, — so much so that "Manners and Meals in Olden Time" is a general title given to the volume by Mr. Furnivall. Its principal contents are "The Babees Book, or How young people should behave," from a MS. of about 1475; "Stans Puer ad Mensam" (already referred to); Hugh Rhodes's "Boke of Nurture;" John Russell's "Boke of Nurture;" Wynkyn de Worde's "Boke of Seruyce and Keruynge [Carving] and Sewynge," and several other "bokes of curtasye" and "bokes of demeanor." The injunctions most distinctly moral are in the following series, entitled "The Rule of Honest Living," found in the fifth edition of Rhodes's "Boke of Nurture," published in 1577, — the first edition having been printed in 1554. Of the first edition of this "boke" Mr. Furnivall knew of but one copy existing when he wrote of it; of the fifth edition he mentions two, in the British Museum and the Bodleian Library. Of Hugh Rhodes it is known, only, that he was "of the king's chapel" and that he was born and bred in Devonshire.

THE RULE OF HONEST LIVING.

(From Publications of the Early English Text Society, No. 32, p. 105.)

If thou desyre temperance, cut away all superfluitye, and brydle in thy desyres within thy mynde; consyder to thy selfe what nature req[u]yreth, and not what sensuall concupiscence appeteth.

Put a brydle & a measure to thy concupiscence, & cast away the things that draw thy mynde with secrete pleasure.

Eate without surfet.

Drinke without dronkennesse.

Let thy lyuing be of light repaste; come not for wanton pleasure, but for desyre of meate; let hunger moue thy appetyte and not sauery sauces.

Think that all thing may be suffred but villany and dishonesty; abstayn euer from wordes of rybaudry, for a tongue euer lyberall nourisheth folly.

Loue rather wordes profytable than eloquent and plesaunte, right wordes then flattering.

Thou shalt sometyme mixe with sadnesse thy merry iestes, but temperately, and without hurt of thy dignitye and honesty; for laughing is reproueable if it be out of measure; if lyke a chylde, it is effuse and wanton; if lyke a woman, foolish.

If thou be a continent man, auoyde flattery, & let it be as paynefull to thee to be praysed of lewd and inhonest persons, as if thou be praysed for lewd and inhonest deedes.

Be more ioyous and glad when thou displeasest euill persons; and take the euill iudgements of them touching thee, as a true prayse of thee.

It is a very hard work of continence to repell the paynting glose of flatterings whose words resolue the hart with plesure.

Alure not the loue of any man by flattery, nor set not open the waye by that meane to get thee loue and friendshyp; thou shalte not be mad hardye, nor presumptyous; submit thy selfe and stoope not to low, but keepe a meane grauity.

Be aduertised with good wil, and take rebuke paciently.

If any man chyde thee with cause, be thou assured that he doeth profyte thee. If so be without thanke, that hee wylleth thy profyte.

Thou shalte not feare sharp words, but dread fayre wordes.

If thou be a continent man, regard the moouinges and afflictions of thy soule and body, that they be not out of order; nor therfore doe not set lighte by them, because they be vnknown, for it forceth not if no man see them, whan thou thy selfe seest them.

Be actiue and styrring, but not of light fashyon, constant, but not obstynate: let it not be vnknown nor greuous to thee thou hast not knowledge of any thing.

Cherish al that be thy Peeres; disdayne not thy inferyours by pryde; cast not away thy superiours that liues vpright.

In requyting a good tourne, shew not thy selfe negligent, nor contrarye: bee not an exactour of another man.

Be lyberall to euery man.

To no man flattering.

Familier but to few.

Equall to all men.

Be not light of credens to new raysed tales, nor crymes, nor suspicious to maligne no man.

Slack and slow to yre.

Prone, inclyned to mercy.

Stable in aduersytye.

And hider of vertue, as other be of vice.

Be a dyspyser of vayne glorye, and no busy bragger of the vertues with the which thou art indued.

Despyse no man's follye and ignoraunce: be thou of fewe wordes, but suffer other to speake.

Be sharpe, but not cruell, nor despyse him that is merry.

Be desyrous of wysedome, and apte to learne it.

Men learne when they teache.

Be content to departe to a man wylling to learne suche thinges as thou knowest, without arrogance and pride.

Desyre to haue knowledge of suche thinges which thou knowest not, wythout concealement of thy ignoraunce.

> He that spendeth much
> 　and getteth nought,
> He that oweth much
> 　and hath nought,
> He that looketh in his purse
> 　and fyndeth nought,
> He may be sorry
> 　and say nought.

> He that may and will not,
> He then that would shall not,
> He that would and cannot,
> May repent and sighe not.

> He that sweareth
> 　tyll no man trust him,
> He that lyeth
> 　tyll no man beleue him,

He that boroweth
   tyll no man will lende him,
Let him go where no
   man knoweth him.

He that hath a good Mayster
   and cannot keepe him,
He that hath a good seruaunt
   and not content with hym,
He that hath such condicions
   that no man loueth hym,
May well know other,
   but few men wyll knowe hym.

Thus endeth the Booke of Nurture or gouer-
naunce of Youth, with Stans Puer
ad mensam. Compyled by
Hugh Rhodes of the
Kinges Chap-
pell.

ERASMUS

(A. D. 1465 (?) –1536.)

ERASMUS, the most accomplished scholar and admired writer of the Reformation, was the son of parents whose sad story has been charmingly told, with close fidelity to fact, by Charles Reade, in his romance entitled "The Cloister and the Hearth." His father, Gerard, and his mother, Margaret, were betrothed by a solemn ceremony which they looked upon as marriage. The malice of some evil-disposed persons drove Gerard, soon afterwards, from his home (near Rotterdam, in Holland), to seek fortune, as an artist, elsewhere. He made his way to Rome, and prospered so well that he expected to return soon to his betrothed — to his wife, as she was in his thoughts. Then a letter came to him, forged by the same malice that had driven him abroad — announcing her death. In his grief he entered a monastery and took the irrevocable vows which made marriage forever impossible to him. Years afterwards, he returned to Holland and found Margaret living, faithful to his memory, and faithfully rearing a son who had been born to them. That son, thus born out of wedlock, was known in youth as Geert Geerts, or Gerhard Gerhards, — that is, Geert's or Gerhard's son; but he afterwards assumed a name composed of the Latin and Greek equivalents of Gerhard, or Gerard — Desiderius Erasmus.

The birth of Erasmus occurred between 1465 and 1467 — the year is uncertain. He became an orphan in 1478, with some property, of which his guardians sought to defraud him. Their efforts were successful in forcing him to enter a monastery, though he shrank from the monastic life. Study was his delight, but the Church did not attract him. Though he became a priest in 1492, he does not seem to have ever performed priestly duties. He succeeded in living mostly the life of a scholar and teacher. In 1506 he obtained from the pope a dispensation from his monastic dress, and ten years later he was absolved from his vows. He travelled much, and resided in several countries, staying two years in England, where he acquired the friendship of Sir Thomas More and others, among the choicer spirits of the time. His death occurred in Switzerland, in 1536.

Erasmus was one of the most effective assailants of the corruption in the Roman Church, and his writings did much to promote the movement of the Reformation; but he had little interest in doctrinal disputes, and was never heartily enlisted under the Lutheran banners.

The most celebrated of the writings of Erasmus were his "Colloquies," from an English translation of which the subjoined passages are taken, and his "Praise of Folly." From his published "Letters," Mr. Froude, the historian, has gleaned a most interesting book.

THE OLD MEN'S DIALOGUE.

(From "The Colloquies of Erasmus," translated by N. Bailey.)

[One of the colloquies of Erasmus is between five old men, who had been students together at Paris in their youth, and who meet in a coach after forty-two years of separation. One of the number, Glycion, is observed to show much less appearance of age than his companions, and they beg him to tell them how he has been able to preserve himself so much from the common marks of time. The account he then gives of the manner in which his life has been ruled may be supposed to embody the counsels that Erasmus wished to give.

After telling of his marriage, in which he made his choice "with judgment first, and then loved afterwards," and of his employment, which he carefully selected, Glycion proceeds as follows: —]

Gl. Envy always is a Concomitant of a pompous Felicity, but a Mediocrity is safe; this was always my Study, not to make any Advantage to myself from the

Disadvantages of other People. I embraced as much as I could, that which the *Greeks* call Freedom from the Encumbrance of Business. I intermeddled with no one's affairs; but especially I kept myself clear from those that could not be meddled with without gaining the ill Will of a great many. If a Friend wants my Assistance, I so serve him, as thereby not to procure any Enemies to myself. In Case of any Misunderstanding between me and any Persons, I endeavour to soften it by clearing myself of Suspicion, or to set all right again by good Offices, or to let it die without taking Notice of it: I always avoid Contention, but if it shall happen, I had rather lose my Money than my Friend. Upon the Whole, I act the part of *Mitio* in the Comedy, I affront no Man, I carry a chearful Countenance to all, I salute and re-salute affably, I find no Fault with what any Man pur-poses to do or does, I don't prefer myself before other People; I let every one enjoy his Opinion; what I would have kept as a Secret, I tell to no Body: I never am curious to pry in the Privacies of other Men. If I happen to come to the Knowledge of any thing, I never blab it. As for absent Persons, I either say nothing at all of them, or speak of them with Kindness and Civility. Great Part of the Quarrels that arise between Men, come from the Intemperance of the Tongue. I never breed Quarrels or heighten them; but where-ever Opportunity happens, I either moderate them, or put an End to them. By these Methods I have hitherto kept clear of Envy, and have maintained the Affections of my fellow Citizens.

Pa. Did you not find a single Life irksome to you?

Gl. Nothing happened to me in the whole Course of my Life, more afflicting than the Death of my Wife, and I could have passionately wish'd that we might have grown old together, and might have enjoy'd the Comfort of the common Blessing, our Children: But since Providence saw it meet it should be otherwise, I judged that it was best for us both, and therefore did not think there was Cause for me to afflict myself with Grief, that would do no good, neither to me nor the Deceased.

Pol. What, had you never an Inclination to marry again, especially the first having been so happy a match to you?

Gl. I had an Inclination so to do, but as I married for the Sake of Children, so for the Sake of my Children I did not marry again.

Pol. But 't is a miserable Case to lie alone whole Nights without a Bedfellow.

Gl. Nothing is hard to a willing Mind. And then do but consider the Benefits of a single Life: There are some People in the World, who will be for making the worst of every Thing; such a one *Crates* seemed to be, or an Epigram under his Name, summing up the Evils of human Life. And the Resolution is this, that it is best not to be born at all. Now *Metrodorus* pleases me a great Deal better, who picks out what is good in it; this makes Life the pleasanter. And I brought my Mind to that Temper of Indifference never to have a violent Aversion or Fondness for any thing. And by this it comes to pass, that if any good Fortune happens to me, I am not vainly transported, or grow insolent; or if any thing falls out cross, I am not much perplex'd.

Pa. Truly if you can do this, you are a greater Philosopher than *Thales* himself.

Gl. If any uneasiness in my Mind rises (as mortal Life produces many of them) I cast it immediately out of my Thoughts, whether it be from the Sense of an Affront offered, or any Thing done unhandsomely.

Pol. Well, but there are some Provocations that would

raise the Anger of the most patient Man alive: As the Sauciness of Servants frequently are.

Gl. I suffer nothing to stay long enough in my Mind to make an Impression. If I can cure them I do it, if not, I reason thus with myself, What good will it do me to torment myself about that which will be never the better for it? In short, I let Reason do that for me at first, which after a little While Time itself would do. And this I be sure take Care of, not to suffer any Vexation, be it never so great, to go to Bed with me.

Eu. No wonder that you don't grow old, who are of that Temper.

Gl. Well, and that I may n't conceal any thing from Friends, in an especial Manner I have kept this Guard upon myself, never to commit any Thing that might be a Reflection either on my own Honour or that of my Children. For there is nothing more troublesome than a guilty Conscience. And if I have committed a Fault I don't go to Bed before I have reconcil'd myself to God. To be at Peace with God is the Fountain of true Tranquillity of Mind, or, as the *Greeks* call it, εὐθυμία. For they who live thus, Men can do them no great Injury.

Eu. Have you never any anxious Thoughts upon the Apprehension of Death?

Gl. No more than I have for the Day of my Birth. I know I must die, and to live in the Fear of it may possibly shorten my Life, but to be sure it would never make it longer. So that I care for nothing else but to live piously and comfortably, and leave the rest to Providence; and a Man can't live happily that does not live piously.

Pa. But I should grow old with the Tiresomeness of living so long in the same Place, tho' it were *Rome* itself.

Gl. The changing of Place has indeed something of Pleasure in it; but then, as for long Travels, tho' perhaps they may add to a Man's Experience, yet they are liable to a great many Dangers. I seem to myself to travel over the whole World in a Map, and can see more in Histories than if I had rambled through Sea and Land for Twenty Years together, as *Ulysses* did. I have a little Country-House about two Miles out of Town, and there sometimes, of a Citizen I become a Country-Man, and having recreated myself there, I return again to the City a new Comer, and salute and am welcom'd as if I had return'd from the new-found Islands.

Eu. Don't you assist Nature with a little Physick?

Gl. I never was let Blood, or took Pills nor Potions in my Life yet. If I feel any Disorder coming upon me, I drive it away with spare Diet or the Country Air.

Eu. Don't you study sometimes?

Gl. I do. In that is the greatest Pleasure of my Life: But I make a Diversion of it, but not a Toil. I study either for Pleasure or Profit of my Life, but not for Ostentation. After Meat I have a Collation of learned Stories, or else somebody to read to me, and I never sit to my Books above an Hour at a Time: Then I get up and take my Violin, and walk about in my Chamber, and sing to it, or else ruminate upon what I have read, or if I have a good Companion with me, I relate it, and after a While I return to my Book again.

Eu. But tell me now, upon the Word of an honest Man; Do you feel none of the Infirmities of old Age, which are said to be a great many.

Gl. My Sleep is not so sound, nor my Memory so good, unless I fix anything deeply in it. Well, I have now acquitted myself of my Promise. I have laid open to you those magical Arts by which I have kept Myself young.

[Manners are the subject of another of the Colloquies, in which a schoolmaster addresses admonitions to a boy : —]

THE SCHOOL–MASTER'S ADMONITIONS

THE ARGUMENT.

The School-master's Instructions teach a Boy Modesty, Civility, and Manners becoming his Age, in what Posture he ought to stand while he talks to his Superiors ; concerning Habit, Discourse, and Behaviour at Table and in School.

THE SCHOOL–MASTER AND BOY.

Sch. You seem not to have been bred at Court but in a cow-stall ; you behave yourself so clownishly. A Gentleman ought to behave himself like a Gentleman. As often or whenever any one that is your Superior speaks to you, stand straight, pull off your Hat, and look neither doggedly, surlily, saucily, malapertly, nor unsettledly, but with a staid, modest, pleasant Air, in your Countenance, and a bashful Look fix'd upon the Person who speaks to you; your Feet set close one by t'other ; your Hands without Action: Don't stand titter, totter, first standing upon one Foot, and then upon another, nor playing with your Fingers, biting your Lip, scratching your head, or picking your Ears : Let your Cloaths be put on tight and neat, that your whole Dress, Air, Motion and Habit, may bespeak a modest and bashful Temper.

Bo. What if I shall try, Sir ?

Ma. Do so.

Bo. Is this right ?

Ma. Not quite.

Bo. Must I do so ?

Ma. That 's pretty well.

Bo. Must I stand so ?

Ma. Ay, that 's very well, remember that Posture ; don't be a Prittle prattle, nor Prate apace, nor be a mind-ing any Thing but what is said to you. If you are to make an Answer, do it in few Words, and to the Purpose, every now and then prefacing with some Title of Respect, and sometimes use a Title of Honour, and now and then make a Bow, especially when you have done speaking : Nor do you go away without asking Leave, or being bid to go : Now come let me see how you can practice this. How long have you been from Home ?

Bo. Almost six months.

Ma. You should have said, Sir.

Bo. Almost six months, Sir.

Ma. Don't you long to see your Mother ?

Bo. Yes, sometimes.

Ma. Have you a Mind to go to see her ?

Bo. Yes, with your Leave, Sir.

Ma. Now you should have made a Bow; that 's very well, remember to do so ; when you speak, don't speak fast, stammer, or speak in your Throat, but use your self to pronounce your Words distinctly and clearly. If you pass by any ancient Person, a Magistrate, a Minister, or Doctor, or any Person of Figure, be sure to pull off your Hat, and make your Reverence : Do the same when you pass by any sacred Place, or the Image of the Cross. When you are at a Feast, behave yourself chearfully, but always so as to remember what becomes your Age : Serve yourself last ; and if any nice Bit be offer'd you, refuse it modestly ; but if they press it upon you, take it, and thank the Person, and cutting off a Bit of it, offer the rest either to him that gave it you, or to him that sits next to you. If any Body drinks to you merrily, thank him, and drink moderately. If you don't care to drink, however, kiss the Cup. Look pleasantly upon him that speaks to you, and be sure not to speak till you are spoken to. If any Thing that is obscene be said, don't laugh at it, but keep your countenance, as though you did not understand it; don't reflect on any Body, nor take place of any Body, nor boast of any Thing of your own, nor undervalue any Thing of another Bodies. Be courteous to your Companions that are your Inferiors; traduce no Body; don't be a Blab with your Tongue, and by this means you'll get a good Character, and gain Friends without Envy. If the Entertainment shall be long, desire to be excus'd, bid much good may it do the Guests, and withdraw from the Table: See that you remember these Things.

Bo. I'll do my Endeavour, Sir. Is there any Thing else you'd have me do?

Ma. Now go to your Books.

Bo. Yes, Sir.

ROGER ASCHAM

(A. D. 1515–1568.)

ROGER ASCHAM, the accomplished scholar and teacher of Tudor times in England, tutor of Lady Jane Grey and of the Princess, afterwards Queen, Elizabeth, and author of "The Scholemaster," gave, in writing, some excellent advice to his brother-in-law (who was evidently a youth) when the latter went into the service of the Earl of Warwick, in 1559. His admonitions are partly quoted from Whitaker's "History of Richmondshire" by Mr. Furnivall, in the collection of early "bokes of nurture," etc., described on page 205. The following is taken from the latter source: —

ADVICE TO LORD WARWICK'S SERVANT.

(From Publications of the Early English Text Society, No. 32, p. 360.)

First and formost, in all your thoughts, words, and deeds, have before your eyes the feare of God; . . . love and serve your lord willingly, faithfullye, and secretlye; love and live with your fellowes honestly, quiettlye, curteouslye, that noe man have cause either to hate yow for your stubborne frowardnes, or to malice yow for your proud ungentleness, two faults which commonly yonge men soones[t] fall into in great men's service. Contemne noe poore man, mocke noe simple man, which proud fooles in cort like and love to doe; find fault with your selfe and with none other, the best waye to live honestlye and quiettly in the court. Carrye noe tales, be no common teller of newes, be not inquisitive of other menn's talke, for those that are desirous to heare what they need not, commonly be readye to babble what they shold not. Vse not to lye, for that is vnhonest; speake not everye truth, for that is vnneedfull; yea, in tyme and place a harmlesse lye is a greate deale better than a hurtfull truth. Use not dyceing nor carding; the more yow use them the lesse yow wilbe esteemed; the cunninger yow be at them the worse man yow wilbe counted. for pastime, love and learne that which your lord liketh and vseth most, whether itt be rydeing, shooteing, hunting, hawkeing, fishing, or any such exercise. Beware of secrett corners and night sitting vp, the two nurses of mischiefe, unthriftines, losse, and sicknes. Beware chiefely of ydlenes, the great pathway that leadeth directly to all evills; be diligent alwayes, be present every where in your lord's service, be at hand to call others, and be not ofte sent for your selfe; for marke this as part of your creed, that the good service of one whole yeare shall never gett soe much as the absence of one howre may lose, when your lord shall stand in need of yow to send. if yow consider alwayes that absence and negligence must needes be cause of greife and sor-rowe to your selfe, of chideing and rueing to your lord, and that dutye done diligently and presently shall gaine yow profitt, and purchase yow great praise and your lord's good countenance, yow shall ridd me of care, and wynne your selfe creditt, make me a gladd man, and your aged mother a ioyfull woman, and breed your friends great comforth. Soe I comitt and commend yow to God's mer-cifull proteccion and good guidance, who long preserve Your ever loving and affectionate brother in lawe.

R. ASKAM.

To my loveing Brother in Lawe, Mr. C. H., Servant to the Rt. Hon. the Earle of Warwick, these.

MEXICAN CODE OF MORAL PRECEPTS

(Sixteenth century.)

SOME forty years after the conquest of Mexico by Cortés, Judge Alonzo de Zurita, a Spanish official in the country, wrote a memoir on the natives, relating especially to their customs and laws, which is greatly esteemed. Among other things, he preserved some collections of rules of conduct, which he represents as being examples of instructions given by fathers to their sons, and mothers to their daughters. Two of these are quoted in Chevalier's "Mexico, Ancient and Modern," and as given below are taken from the English translation of that work (v. i. ch. 6). According to Zurita, they embody the advice of parents of the middle class — inhabitants of towns, tradesmen and artisans. "It is," says M. Chevalier, "at once a collection of moral precepts and an abridged code of what is called, in familiar language, ' polite manners for young people.' "

Prescott, in the appendix to his "History of the Conquest of Mexico," gives a similar collection of precepts addressed by a mother to her daughter, translated from Sahagun's "Historia de Nueva España."

A FATHER'S COUNSEL TO HIS SON.

(From Chevalier's "Mexico, Ancient and Modern.")

O my beloved son, created by the will of God, under the eyes of thy father and mother, and of thy relatives, like a chicken that leaves its shell and essays to fly, thou makest thy essay with difficulty. We know not till what time God will permit us to enjoy thee. Supplicate Him, my son, to protect thee, for He created thee; He is thy Father; He loves thee better than I. Address to Him thy wishes night and day; let Him be the object of thy thoughts; serve Him with love; He will be merciful to thee, and will deliver thee from all danger. Respect the image of God, and whatever is connected with Him. Pray to Him devotedly; observe the religious festivals. He who offends God will die miserable, and it will be his own fault.

Honour and salute old men. Console the poor and afflicted by thy words and thy good works.

Revere, love, and serve thy father and mother; obey them, for the son who does not so conduct himself will repent it.

Love and honour all the world, and thou wilt live in peace.

Imitate not the fools who respect neither father nor mother, and who, like the animals, listen to the counsel of no one.

Be careful, my son, not to mock the old, the infirm, the maimed, or the sinner. Be not haughty towards them; do not hate them, but humble thyself before the Lord, and tremble lest you be as unfortunate as they.

Poison no one, for thou wilt wound God in his creature; thy crime will be discovered, thou wilt suffer the punishment of it, and thou wilt die the same death.

Be upright, polite, and cause pain to no one.

Meddle not with affairs in which thou art not concerned, from the fear of displeasing and of being counted indiscreet.

Injure no one. Eschew adultery and luxury: it is a base vice, which causes the ruin of him who gives himself up to it, and offends God.

Set not bad examples.

Be modest in thy discourse; interrupt not people who are speaking; disturb them not; if they express themselves badly, if they make mistakes, content thyself with not imitating them. Keep silence when it is not thy turn to speak; and if a question is put to thee, reply with openness, without heat or falsehood. Interfere not with the interests of others, and men will pay respect to thy words. If thou keepest clear, my son, of carrying tales, of repeating jests, thou wilt keep clear of lying and of sowing discord, which is a source of confusion to him who does it.

Be not a lounger on the pavement, haunt not the streets, lose not thy time in the markets or the baths, lest the demon tempt thee and make thee his victim.

Be not affected or too studied in thy dress, for it is the mark of a little mind.

In whatever place thou mayest be, let thy looks be modest; make no grimaces; indulge not in indecent gestures: thou wilt pass for a libertine, and such things are snares of the demon. Seize no one by the hand or the clothes, for it is the mark of an indiscreet mind. Pay attention, when thou walkest, not to stop the way of any one soever.

If thou art begged to undertake a matter, and it be to tempt thee, civilly excuse thyself, though thou mightest get some advantage from it, and thou wilt be held a wise and prudent man.

Enter not nor go out before thy superiors; be careful not to take precedence of them; always leave them the place of honour, and seek not to lift thyself above any one, unless thou art raised in rank, for thou wilt be looked upon as a rude fellow. Be modest; humility merits the favour of God and the great.

Be not in a hurry in eating or drinking; and if thou art at table, offer to him who may present himself before thee, wanting to take part in thy repast; thou shalt be recompensed for it. If thou eatest in company, let it be without eagerness or gluttony; thou wilt pass for a greedy fellow. Take thy repasts with thy head bent down, and so as not to finish before the others, for fear of offending them.

If a present be made thee, however small it may be, disdain it not, and think not thou deservest more, for thou wilt not gain thereby before God or man.

Trust thyself entirely to the Lord; 't is from Him that good will come to thee, and thou knowest not when thou mayest die.

I take on myself to procure thee what is proper for thee; bear and wait patiently. If thou wishest to marry, tell me; and since thou art our child, undertake not to do it before speaking to us on the matter.

Be neither gambler nor thief, for one of those faults is the occasion of the other, and it is disgraceful. If thou keepest clear of them, thou wilt not be evil spoken of in the public squares and markets.

Take always the good part, O my son. Sow, and thou shalt reap; thou wilt live by thy labour, and consequently thou wilt be satisfied, and cherished of thy parents.

We live not in this world without much labour, we procure not easily what is necessary. I have had much trouble to rear thee, and yet I have never abandoned thee, and I have done nothing for which thou canst blush.

If thou desirest to live in tranquillity, keep clear of evil-speaking, for evil-speaking occasions quarrels.

Keep secret what thou hearest. Let it be learned from others rather than from thee; and if thou canst not avoid telling it, speak frankly, without hiding anything, even though thou believest it were well to do so.

Repeat not that of which thou hast been the witness. Be discreet, for to be a tattler is a mean vice, and if thou liest thou will certainly be punished. Keep silence; nothing is gained by talking.

If thou art sent with a message to some one that receives thee roughly, and speaks ill of him who sent thee, report not the reply given in bad temper, and let not what has been done to thee be known. If thou art asked how thou wast received, reply calmly, in mild words: conceal the ill words that were said to thee, for fear of irritating both parties, that there may be neither bloodshed nor loss of life, and that thou mayest not later have to say in sadness, " Ah, if I had never said it ! " But it will be too late, and thou wilt pass for a mischief-maker and be without excuse.

Have no relations with the wife of another; live chastely, for we exist not twice in this world. Life is short and difficult, and everything has an end.

Offend no person nor attack his honour. Make thyself worthy of the rewards God giveth to everyone as it pleases Him; receive what He shall give thee; return thanks, and if it be much, be not puffed up. Humble thyself; thy merit will be the greater, and others will have no occasion to murmur; but, on the contrary, if thou attributest to thyself what does not belong to thee, thou wilt meet with affronts and wilt offend God.

When thou art spoken to, keep thy hands and thy feet still, look not to the left or right; avoid rising, or sitting down if thou art standing; thou wilt pass for a giddy-pate or a clown.

If thou art in the service of any one, take care with zeal to render thyself useful, and to be agreeable to him; thou wilt not want necessaries, and thou wilt be everywhere well treated; if thou dost the contrary, thou wilt not be able to remain with any one.

My son, if thou refusest to hearken to the counsels of

thy father, thou wilt come to a bad end, and it will be thy own fault.

Be not proud of what God has given thee, and despise not others; thou wilt offend the Lord, who hast placed thee in an honourable position.

If thou art what thou shouldst be, thou wilt be quoted to others as a model, when it is wished they should correct themselves.

These, O my son, are the counsels given thee by a father who loves thee; observe them, and it will be well with thee.

A MOTHER'S COUNSEL TO HER DAUGHTER.

My daughter, I brought thee into the world, I have nourished and reared thee as thou shouldst be, the honour of thy father has reflected on thee. If thou dost not thy duty, thou wilt not be admitted to live with virtuous women, and no man will desire to make thee his wife.

There is no living in this world without a great deal of pain and labour; our strength exhausts itself; we must therefore serve God, that He may aid us, sustain us, and grant us health. We must be active and careful, that we may obtain what is necessary.

My beloved daughter, shun idleness and negligence; be neat and industrious; take pains with thine apartment, let order reign there, that everything may be in its place; thus thou wilt learn to do thy duty when thou art married.

Wherever thou mayest be, respect modesty. Walk not too fast, neither laughing nor looking hither and thither at the men that pass near thee; look only to thy path: thus thou wilt gain the reputation of an honest woman.

Take care to be polite, and to speak properly; and when a question is asked thee, let thy answer be short and clear.

Take care of thine household, make cloth, work; thou wilt be loved, thou wilt deserve to have necessaries to feed and clothe thee, thou wilt be happy, and thou wilt thank God for having given thee the needful talent.

Give not thyself to slumber or sloth; love not to linger in bed, or in the shade, or in the open air, for thou wilt become heedless and libertine, and thou wilt be incapacitated for living in honour and propriety. Women who yield themselves to libertinism are neither sought after nor loved.

Be thou sitting or standing, walking or working, let thy thoughts and actions, my daughter, be always praiseworthy. Fulfil thy duty, so as to obey God and thy parents.

Allow not thyself to be called twice; come forthwith to see what is wanted, so that there may not be the grief of punishing thine idleness and disobedience.

Listen attentively to the orders given thee, and answer not amiss. If thou canst not do what is ordered of thee consistently with honour, excuse thyself civilly; but lie not and deceive no one, for God seeth thee.

If thou hearest another called, and she comes not directly, hasten and see what is wanted; do that which it was wished she should do, and thou wilt be loved.

If good advice be given thee, profit by it; do not despise it, for fear of being disesteemed.

Let thy gait be neither too hurried nor immodest; thou wilt pass for a light woman.

Be charitable; have hatred and contempt for no one; shun avarice, take nothing in bad part, and be not jealous of what the good God granteth to others.

Do no wrong to another, for fear it be done unto thee; avoid evil; follow not the likings of thy heart; thou mayest be deceived and fall into vice, and thou wilt bring disgrace on thyself and on thy parents.

Shun the society of liars, idlers, gossips, and women of bad manners; they will ruin thee.

Busy thyself with thy household; go not abroad to divert thyself; lose not thy time in the market, in the squares and public baths. It is exceedingly evil, and thus females are lost and ruined, and become vicious, for so bad thoughts are nourished.

When a man seeks to address his speech to thee, hearken not to him, look not at him; keep silence, and pay no attention to him; if he follow thee, answer him not, lest thy words do but increase his passion. If thou pay no attention to him, he will cease to follow thee.

Enter not other's houses, so as to avoid being the subject of their idle talk.

If thou go to see thy parents, pay them thy respects; be not idle, take part in the work that is going on, if thou be able, and remain not to look at those who are working.

If thy parents choose thee a husband, thou must love him, listen to him, obey him, do with pleasure what he tells thee; turn not away the head when he speaks to thee; and if he says to thee anything disagreeable, endeavour to get over thy vexation. If he live on thy property, despise him not for that. Be neither sullen nor uncivil, for thou wilt offend God, and thy husband will be irritated against thee; tell him quietly what thou thinkest the proper course. Address him not in offensive terms before others, nor even when alone, for it is thou that wilt bear the shame and contempt.

If any one come to pay a visit to thy husband, receive him well and show him friendship.

Should thy husband not conduct himself properly, give him advice as to his manner of behaviour, and bid him take care of his household.

Be attentive to the labour on thy land; take care of the crop and neglect nothing.

Be not prodigal of thy property, aid thy husband in his labour; by so doing thou wilt not want necessaries, and thou wilt provide for the education of thy children.

My daughter, if thou follow my advice, thou wilt be loved and esteemed of all. In giving it to thee, I fulfil my duty as a mother; in following it, thou wilt live happy. If it be otherwise it will be thy fault; thou wilt see hereafter what will happen to thee from not having hearkened to me, and no one will be able to say that I have neglected to give thee counsels that, as a mother, I ought to have done.

SIR THOMAS WYATT

(A. D. 1503-1542.)

THE earliest of the poets belonging distinctly to the Elizabethan age was Sir Thomas Wyatt, whose poems are usually associated with those of his younger friend, Lord Henry Howard, Earl of Surrey. Wyatt was the son of Sir Henry Wyatt, of Allington, Kent; he was born at Allington Castle in 1503, and died in 1542. He was a gentleman of many accomplishments; a favorite at the court of Henry VIII.; and was employed by the king on several diplomatic missions of importance. He married the daughter of Lord Cobham, by whom he had a son, also named Thomas, who subsequently perished on the scaffold, in the reign of Queen Mary, against whom he attempted to raise a revolt. To this son Sir Thomas wrote the subjoined letters of advice, soon after the former married, which he did at the early age of fifteen. The father was then in Spain, on a mission for the king.

SIR THOMAS WYATT'S LETTERS TO HIS SON.

(From the Poetical Works of Surrey and Wyatt, vol. i.)

LETTER I.

In as much as now ye are come to some years of understanding, and that you should gather within yourself some frame of Honesty, I thought that I should not lose my labour wholly if now I did something to advertise you to take the sure foundations and stablished opinions that leadeth to Honesty.

And here, I call not Honesty that, men commonly call Honesty, as reputation for riches; for authority, or some like thing; but that Honesty, that I dare well say your grandfather, (whose soul God pardon) had rather left to me than all the lands he did leave me; that was, Wisdom, Gentleness, Soberness, desire to do Good, Friendliness to get the love of many, and Truth above all the rest. A great part to have all these things is to desire to have them. And although glory and honest name are not the very ends wherefore these things are to be followed, yet surely they must needs follow them as light followeth fire, though it were kindled for warmth.

Out of these things the chiefest and infallible ground is the dread and reverence of God, whereupon shall ensue the eschewing of the contraries of these said virtues; that is to say, ignorance, unkindness, rashness, desire of harm, unquiet enmity, hatred, many and crafty falsehood, the very root of all shame and dishonesty. I say, the only dread and reverence of God, that seeth all things, is the defence of the creeping in of all these mischiefs into you. And for my part, although I do well say there is no man that would his son better than I, yet on my faith I had rather have you lifeless, than subject to these vices.

Think and imagine always that you are in the presence of some honest man that you know; as Sir John Russell, your Father-in-law, your Uncle Parson, or some other such, and ye shall, if at any time you find a pleasure in naughty touches, remember what shame it were afore these men to do naughtily. And sure this imagination shall cause you remember, that the pleasure of a naughty deed is soon past, and the rebuke, shame, and the note thereof shall remain ever. Then, if these things ye take for vain imaginations, yet remember that it is certain, and no imagination, that ye are alway in the presence and sight of God: and though you see him not, so much is the reverence the more to be had for that He seeth, and is not seen.

Men punish with shame as greatest punishment on earth, yea! greater than death; but His punishment is, first, the withdrawing of his favour, and grace, and in leaving his hand to rule the stern to let the ship run without guide to its own destruction; and suffereth so the man that he forsaketh to run headlong as subject to all mishaps, and at last with shameful end to everlasting shame and death. Ye may see continual examples both of the one sort, and of the other; and the better, if ye mark them well that yourself are come of; and consider well your good grandfather, what things there were in him, and his end. And they that knew him noted him thus; first, and chiefly to have a great reverence of God and good opinion of godly things. Next that, there was no man more pitiful; no man more true of his word; no man faster to his friend, no man diligenter nor more circumspect, which thing, both the Kings his masters noted in him greatly. And if these things, and specially the grace of God that the fear of God always kept with him, had not been, the chances of this troublesome world that he was in had long ago overwhelmed him. This preserved him in prison from the hands of the tyrant that could find in his heart to see him racked; from two years and more prisonment in Scotland in irons and stocks; from the danger of sudden changes and commotions divers, till that well beloved of many, hated of none, in his fair age, and good reputation, godly and christianly he went to Him that loved him, for that he had always had Him in reverence.

And of myself, I may be a near example unto you of my folly and unthriftness, that hath, as I well deserved, brought me into a thousand dangers and hazards, enmities, hatreds, prisonments, despites, and indignations; but that God hath of his goodness chastised me, and not cast me clean out of his favour; which thing I can impute to nothing but to the goodness of my good father, that, I dare well say purchased with continual request of God his Grace towards me more than I regarded, or considered myself; and a little part to the small fear that I had of God in the most of my rage, and the little delight that I had in mischief. You, therefore, if ye be sure, and have God in your sleeve to call you to his grace at last, venture hardily by mine example upon naughty unthriftness, in trust of his goodness; and besides the shame, I dare lay ten to one ye shall perish in the adventure; for trust me, that my wish or desire of God for you shall not stand you in as much effect, as I think my father's did for me: we are not all accepted of Him.

Begin, therefore, betimes. Make God and goodness your foundations. Make your examples of wise and honest men: shoot at that mark: be no mocker: mocks follow them that delight therein. He shall be sure of shame that feeleth no grief in other men's shames. Have your friends in a reverence; and think unkindness to be the greatest offence, and least punished amongst men; but so much the more to be dread, for God is justiser upon that alone.

Love well, and agree with your wife; for where is noise and debate in the house there is unquiet dwelling; and much more, where it is in one bed. Frame well yourself to love and rule well and honestly your wife as your fellow, and she shall love and reverence you as her head. Such as you are unto her, such shall she be unto you. Obey and reverence your father-in-law, as you would me; and remember that long life followeth them that reverence their fathers and elders; and the blessing of God, for good agreement between the wife and husband, is fruit of many children.

Read oft this my letter, and it shall be as though I had often written to you; and think that I have herein printed a fatherly affection to you. If I may see that I have not lost my pain, mine shall be the contentation, and yours the profit; and, upon condition that you follow my advertisement, I send you God's blessing and mine, and as well come to honesty, as to increase of years.

LETTER II.

I doubt not but long ere this time my letters are come to you. I remember I wrote to you in them, that if you read them often it shall be as though I had written often to you. For all that, I cannot so content me but still to call upon you with my letters. I would not for all that, that if any thing be well warned in the other that you should leave to remember it because of this new. For it is not like with advertisements as it is with apparel that with long wearing a man casteth away, when he hath new. Honest teachings never wear; unless they wear out of his remembrance that should keep and follow them, to the shame and hurt of himself. Think not also that I have any new or change of advertisements to send you; but still it is one that I would. I have nothing to cry and call upon you for but Honesty, Honesty. It may be diversely named, but alway it tendeth to one end; and as I wrote to you last, I mean not that Honesty that the common sort calleth an honest man. Trust me, that honest man is as common a name as the name of a good fellow; that is to say, a drunkard, a tavern haunter, a rioter, a gamer, a waster. So are among the common sort all men honest men that are not known for manifest naughty knaves.

Seek not I pray thee, my Son, that Honesty which appeareth, and is not indeed. Be well assured it is no common thing, nor no common man's judgment to judge well of honesty; nor it is no common thing to come by; but so much it is the more goodly, for that it is so rare and strange.

Follow not therefore the common reputation of Honesty. If you will seem honest, be honest; or else seem as you are. Seek not the name without the thing; nor let not the name be the only mark you shoot at: that will follow though you regard it not; yea! and the more you regard it, the less. I mean not by regard it not, esteem it not; for well I wot honest name is goodly. But he that hunteth only for that, is like him that had rather seem warm than be warm, and edgeth a single coat about with a fur. Honest name is to be kept, preserved, and defended, and not to employ all a man's wit about the study of it; for that smelleth of a glorious and ambitious fool. I say, as I wrote unto you in my last letters, get the thing, and the other must of necessity follow, as the shadow followeth the thing that it is of; and even so much is the very Honesty better than the name, as the thing is better than the shadow.

The coming to this point that I would so fain have you have, is to consider a man's own self what he is, and wherefore he is; and herein let him think verily that so goodly a work as man is, for whom all other things were wrought, was not wrought but for goodly things. After a man hath gotten a will and desire to them, is first to avoid evil, and learn that point alone: "Never to do that, that within yourself you find a certain grudging against." No doubt in any thing you do, if you ask yourself, or examine the thing in yourself afore you do it, you shall find, if it be evil, a repining against it. My Son! for our Lord's love keep well that repining; suffer it not to be darked and corrupted by naughty example, as though any thing were to you excusable because other men do the same. That same repining, if it did punish as he doth judge, there were no such justicer; and of truth, so doth it punish; but not so apparently. Here however it is no small grief, of a conscience that condemneth itself; but be well assured, after this life it is a continual gnawing.

When there is a custom gotten of avoiding to do evil, then cometh a gentle courage. Be content to be idle, and to rest without doing any thing. Then too had ye need to gather an heap of good opinions and to get them perfectly, as it were on your fingers ends. Rest not greatly upon the approving of them; take them as already approved, because they were of honest men's leavings. Of them of God, there is no question; and it is no small help to them, the good opinion of moral philosophers, among whom I would Seneca [in] your study; and Epictetus, because it is little, to be ever in bosom.

These things shall lead you to know goodly [things]; which when a man knoweth and taketh pleasure in them, he is a beast that followeth not them: no, nor he cannot but follow them. But take this for conclusion and sum of all; that if God and his Grace be not the foundation, neither can ye avoid evil, nor judge well, nor do any goodly thing. Let Him be foundation of all. Will these things; desire them earnestly, and seek them at his hands, and knowledge them to come of Him, and questionless He will both give you the use and pleasure in using them, and also reward you for them that come of Him; so liberal and good is He.

I would fain see that my letters might work to frame you honest. And think that without that, I esteem nothing of you: no! not that you are my son. For I reckon it no small dishonesty to myself to have an unhonest taught child: but the fault shall not be in me. I shall do the part of a father: and if you answer not to that I look for at your hands, I shall as well study with that that I shall leave, to make such [some] honest man, as you.

LORD BURLEIGH

(A. D. 1520–1598.)

WILLIAM CECIL, Lord Burleigh, the most trusted of the ministers of Queen Elizabeth, was born at Bourn, in Lincolnshire, England, in 1520. He was educated at Cambridge; studied law; and at the early age of twenty-eight became secretary of state, under the young king, Edward VI. On the death of Edward, and the accession of Queen Mary, he resigned his office, but avoided the ensuing persecutions by conformity to the Roman Church. Queen Elizabeth came to the throne in 1558, and Cecil was at once called to her service, in which he continued until his death, in 1598. He is said to have been the one minister in whom the queen really confided, and he was practically prime minister for forty years.

The "Ten Precepts" quoted below were composed by Lord Burleigh for his son Robert, who succeeded his father as secretary of state to Queen Elizabeth; who was largely instrumental in securing to King James of Scotland the succession to the English throne, and who was raised by that sovereign to the earldom of Salisbury in 1605. The earldom of Salisbury, with the marquisate added to it in 1787, has remained in the Salisbury family to the present day.

TEN PRECEPTS BY LORD BURLEIGH.

(From "English Prose Selections;" ed. by Henry Craik, vol. i.)

SON ROBERT — The virtuous inclinations of thy matchless mother, by whose tender and godly care thy infancy was governed, together with thy education under so zealous and excellent a tutor, puts me in rather assurance than hope, that thou art not ignorant of that *summum bonum*, which is only able to make thee happy as well in thy death as life; I mean the true knowledge and worship of thy Creator and Redeemer; without which all other things are vain and miserable: so that thy youth being guided by so sufficient a teacher, I make no doubt but he will furnish thy life with divine and moral documents; yet that I may not cast off the care beseeming a parent towards his child; or that you should have cause to derive thy whole felicity and welfare rather from others than from whence thou receivedst thy breath and being; I think it fit and agreeable to the affection I bear thee, to help thee with such rules and advertisements for the squaring of thy life, as are rather gained by experience, than much reading; to the end that entering into this exorbitant age, thou mayest be the better prepared to shun those scandalous courses whereunto the world and the lack of experience may easily draw thee. And because I will not confound thy memory, I have reduced them into ten precepts; and next unto Moses' tables, if thou imprint them in thy mind, thou shalt reap the benefit, and I the content; and they are these following: —

I.

When it shall please God to bring thee to man's estate, use great providence and circumspection in choosing thy wife; for from thence will spring all thy future good or evil; and it is an action of life, like unto a stratagem of war, wherein a man can err but once. If thy estate be good, match near home and at leisure; if weak, far off and quickly. Enquire diligently of her disposition, and how her parents have been inclined in their youth; let her not be poor, how generous soever; for a man can buy nothing in the market with gentility; nor choose a base and uncomely creature altogether for wealth; for it will cause contempt in others and loathing in thee; neither make choice of a dwarf, or a fool; for by the one you shall beget a race of pigmies, the other will be thy continual disgrace, and it will yirke thee to hear her talk; for thou shalt find it, to thy great grief, that there is nothing more fulsome than a she-fool.

And touching the guiding of thy house, let thy hospitality be moderate, and according to the means of thy estate; rather plentiful than sparing, but not costly; for I never knew any man grow poor by keeping an orderly table; but some consume themselves through secret vices, and their hospitality bears the blame; but banish swinish drunkards out of thine house, which is a vice impairing health, consuming much, and makes no show. I never heard praise ascribed to the drunkard, but for the well bearing of his drink, which is better commendation for a brewer's horse or a dray man, than for either a gentleman, or a serving man. Beware thou spend not above three or four parts of thy revenues; nor above a third part of that in thy house; for the other two parts will do no more than defray thy extraordinaries, which always surmount the ordinary by much: otherwise thou shalt live like a rich beggar, in continual want: and the needy man can never live happily or contentedly; for every disaster makes him ready to mortgage or sell; and that gentleman who sells an acre of land, sells an ounce of credit, for gentility is nothing else but ancient riches; so that if the foundation shall at any time sink, the building must need follow. So much for the first precept.

II.

Bring thy children up in learning and obedience, yet without outward austerity. Praise them openly, reprehend them secretly. Give them good countenance and convenient maintenance according to thy ability, otherwise thy life will seem their bondage, and what portion thou shalt leave them at thy death, they will thank death for it, and not thee. And I am persuaded that the foolish cockering of some parents, and the overstern carriage of others, causeth more men and women to take ill courses, than their own vicious inclinations. Marry thy daughters in time, lest they marry themselves. And suffer not thy sons to pass the Alps, for they shall learn nothing there but pride, blasphemy, and atheism. And if by travel they get a few broken languages, that shall profit them nothing more than to have one meat served in divers dishes. Neither, by my consent, shalt thou train them up in wars; for he that sets up his rest to live by that profession, can hardly be an honest man or a good Christian; besides it is a science no longer in request than use; for soldiers in peace, are like chimneys in summer.

III.

Live not in the country without corn and cattle about thee; for he that putteth his hand to the purse for every expense of household, is like him that putteth water in a sieve. And what provision thou shalt want, learn to buy it at the best hand; for there is one penny saved in four, betwixt buying in thy need, and when the markets and seasons serve fittest for it. Be not served with kinsmen, or friends, or men, intreated to stay; for they expect much and do little; nor with such as are amorous, for their heads are intoxicated. And keep rather two too few, than one too many. Feed them well, and pay them with the most; and then thou mayest boldly require service at their hands.

IV.

Let thy kindred and allies be welcome to thy house and table ; grace them with thy countenance, and farther them in all honest actions ; for by this means, thou shalt so double the bond of nature, as thou shalt find them so many advocates to plead an apology for thee behind thy back ; but shake off those glow-worms, I mean parasites and sycophants, who will feed and fawn upon thee in the summer of prosperity, but in adverse storm, they will shelter thee no more than an harbour in winter.

V.

Beware of suretyship for thy best friends ; he that payeth another man's debts, seeketh his own decay; but if thou canst not otherwise choose, rather lend thy money thyself upon good bonds, although thou borrow it ; so shalt thou secure thyself, and pleasure thy friend ; neither borrow money of a neighbour or a friend, but of a stranger, where paying it, thou shalt hear no more of it, otherwise thou shalt eclipse thy credit, lose thy freedom, and yet pay as dear as to another. But in borrowing of money be precious of thy word, for he that hath care of keeping days of payment, is lord of another man's purse.

VI.

Undertake no suit against a poor man without receiving much wrong ; for besides that thou makest him thy compeer, it is a base conquest to triumph where there is small resistance ; neither attempt law against any man before thou be fully resolved that thou hast right on thy side ; and then spare not for either money or pains ; for a cause or two so followed and obtained, will free thee from suits a great part of thy life.

VII.

Be sure to keep some great man thy friend, but trouble him not with trifles; compliment him often with many, yet small gifts, and of little charge; and if thou hast cause to bestow any great gratuity, let it be something which may be daily in sight; otherwise in this ambitious age, thou shalt remain like a hop without a pole; live in obscurity, and be made a football for every insulting companion to spurn at.

VIII.

Towards thy superiors be humble, yet generous; with thine equals, familiar, yet respective; towards thine inferiors show much humanity, and some familiarity; as to bow the body, stretch forth the hand, and to uncover the head, with such like popular compliments. The first prepares thy way to advancement, the second makes thee known for a man well bred, the third gains a good report, which once got is easily kept; for right humanity takes such deep root in the minds of the multitude as they are easilier gained by unprofitable courtesies, than by churlish benefits; yet I advise thee not to affect or neglect popularity too much; seek not to be Essex; shun to be Raleigh.

IX.

Trust not any man with thy life, credit, or estate; for it is mere folly for a man to enthrall himself to his friend, as though, occasion being offered, he should not dare to become his enemy.

X.

Be not scurrilous in conversation nor satirical in thy jests; the one will make thee unwelcome to all company, the other pull on quarrels, and get thee hatred of thy best friends; for suspicious jests, when any of them savour of truth, leave a bitterness in the minds of those which are touched ; and, albeit, I have already pointed at this inclusively yet I think it necessary to leave it to thee as a special caution ; because I have seen many so prone to quip and gird, as they would rather *leese* their friend than their jest ; and if, perchance, their boiling brain yield a quaint scoff, they will travail to be delivered of it as a woman with child. These nimble fancies are but the froth of wit.

SIR HENRY SIDNEY

(A. D. 1529–1586.)

SIR HENRY SIDNEY, the father of Sir Philip Sidney, was born in 1529. "This right famous, renowned, worthy, virtuous, and heroical knight," says Holingshed, the chronicler, "by father and mother very nobly descended, was from his infancy bred and brought up in the prince's court and in nearness to his person, used familiarly even as a companion." At the age of eight, he was henchman, or page, to King Henry VIII., and later he attended constantly upon Edward VI., who died in his arms. Sir Henry married Lady Mary Dudley, daughter of the Duke of Northumberland, in 1552, and their famous son Philip, the English Bayard, was born in 1554.

When Philip had reached about the age of eleven years, and was at school in Shrewsbury, his father, then Lord Deputy of Ireland, wrote to him the letter here subjoined, which, as Mr. H. R. Fox Bourne remarks "is so indicative of the character of both father and son, so characteristic, also, of the noblest tendencies of the age, that it must be quoted entire."

A FATHER'S LETTER TO SIR PHILIP SIDNEY.

(From "A Memoir of Sir Philip Sidney," by H. R. Fox Bourne.)

Since this is my first letter that ever I did write to you, I will not that it be all empty of some advices which my natural care of you provoketh me to wish you to follow, as documents to you in this your tender age. Let your first action be the lifting up of your mind to Almighty God, by hearty prayer; and feelingly digest the words you speak in prayer, with continual meditation and thinking of Him to whom you pray, and of the matter for which you pray. And use this as an ordinary act, and at an ordinary hour; whereby the time itself shall put you in remembrance to do that which you are accustomed to do in that time. Apply your study to such hours as your discreet master doth assign you, earnestly; and the time I know he will so limit, as shall be sufficient for your learning and safe for your health. And mark the sense and the matter of that you read, as well as the words. So shall you both enrich your tongue with words, and your wit with matter; and judgment will grow as years groweth in you. Be humble and obedient to your master, for unless you frame yourself to obey others, yea, and feel in yourself what obedience is, you shall never be able to teach others how to obey you. Be courteous of gesture, and affable to all men, with diversity of reverence, according to the dignity of the person: there is nothing that winneth so much with so little cost. Use moderate diet, so as, after your meal, you may find your wit fresher and not duller, and your body more lively and not more heavy. Seldom drink wine; and yet sometimes do, lest, being enforced to drink upon the sudden, you should find yourself enflamed. Use exercise of body, yet such as is without peril of your joints or bones: it will increase your force, and enlarge your breath. Delight to be cleanly, as well in all parts of your body as in your garments: it shall make you grateful in each company, and otherwise loathsome. Give yourself to be merry; for you degenerate from your father, if you find not yourself most able in wit and body and to do anything when you be most merry: but let your mirth be ever void of scurrility and biting words to any man, for a wound given by a word is oftentimes harder to be cured than that which is given with the sword. Be you rather a hearer and bearer away of other men's talk than a beginner and procurer of speech; otherwise you shall be counted to delight to hear yourself speak. If you hear a wise sentence or an apt phrase, commit it to your memory with respect of the circumstance when you shall speak it. Let never oath be heard to come out of your mouth, nor word of ribaldry: detest it in others; so shall custom make to yourself a law against it in yourself. Be modest in each assembly; and rather be rebuked of light fellows for maiden-like shamefastness, than of your sad friends for pert boldness. Think upon every word that you will speak before you utter it, and remember how nature hath ramparted up, as it were, the tongue with teeth, lips, yea, and hair without the lips, and all betokening reins or bridles for the loose use of that member. Above all things tell no untruth; no, not in trifles: the custom of it is naughty. And let it not satisfy you that, for a time, the hearers take it for truth; for after it will be known as it is, to your shame: for there cannot be a greater reproach to a gentleman than to be accounted a liar. Study and endeavour yourself to be virtuously occupied: so shall you make such a habit of well-doing in you, that you shall not know how to do evil, though you would. Remember, my son, the noble blood you are descended of, by your mother's side; and think that only by virtuous life and good action you may be an ornament to that illustrious family; and otherwise, through vice and sloth, you shall be counted *labes generis* — one of the greatest curses that can happen to man. Well, my little Philip, this is enough for me, and too much, I fear, for you. But if I shall find that this light meal of digestion nourish anything in the weak stomach of your capacity, I will, as I find the same grow stronger, feed it with tougher food. Your loving father, so long as you live in the fear of God.

H. SIDNEY.

MONTAIGNE

(A. D. 1533–1592.)

SEIGNEUR DE MICHEL EYQUEM DE MONTAIGNE, father of all modern essayists, was a native of the department of Dordogne in southwestern France, born February 28, 1533. Carefully educated, first at home and then at Bordeaux, he was trained for the profession of the law, and took a seat as counsellor in the Parliament of Bordeaux in 1554, but resigned it in 1570, on his father's death. From that time he devoted himself mainly to travel, study, and literary pursuits. The first two books of his "Essais" were published in 1580. His death occurred in 1592.

"In Montaigne we see that new intellectual liberty of his day, not knowing how to use itself, or to take care of itself; puzzled by what it saw, and by what it had to keep to; boldly dwelling on discrepancies, but too lazy and self-willed to try to penetrate them and reconcile them. He felt the obligation, cast on men by the times in which he lived, of learning *to think*, instead of repeating other men's words; but he did not feel the greatness of the purpose for which that obligation had been cast on them. . . . Besides the keenness and good sense shown, Montaigne's thinking came to little. He broke up the ground which others after him sowed with many kinds of seed. He was a kind of imperfect Socrates, the cross-examiner of his generation, — bold, inquisitive, and shrewd, taking nothing on trust, and hating pretence, — homely, unconventional, untechnical, — with his idea right, but too careless, too selfish, and it must be added, not pure enough, not thorough enough, to give it effect; below Socrates in elevation and noble purpose, fifteen hundred years after an event which ought to have made him wiser and more serious than Socrates." — DEAN R. W. CHURCH, "The Essays of Montaigne" ("Miscellaneous Essays," i.).

MONTAIGNE'S CULTIVATION OF LIFE.

(From the " Essays of Montaigne," book iii. ch. 13.)

Of the experience I have of myself, I find enough to make me wise, if I were but a good scholar : whoever will call to mind the excess of his past anger, and to what a degree that fever transported him, will see the deformity of this passion better than in Aristotle, and conceive a more just hatred against it. Whoever will remember the hazards he has run, those that threaten him, and the light occasions that have removed him from one state to another, will by that prepare himself for future changes, and the knowledge of his condition. The life of Cæsar himself has no greater example for us than our own : both popular and imperial, it is still a life to which all human accidents may refer. Let us but listen to it, and we may apply to ourselves all that we have principal need of ; whoever shall call to memory how many and many times he has been mistaken in his own judgment, is he not a great fool if he does not ever after distrust it ? When I find myself convinced, by the reason of another, of a false opinion, I do not learn so much what he has said to me that is new, and my ignorance in this particular thing — which would be no great acquisition — as I do in general my own weakness, and the treachery of my understanding, whence I extract the reformation of the whole mass. In all my errors I do the same ; and find from this rule great utility to life. . . .

When I see both Cæsar and Alexander, in the thickest of their greatest business, so fully enjoy human and bodily pleasures, I do not say that they slackened their souls, but wound them up higher by vigour of courage, subjecting these violent employments and laborious thoughts to the ordinary use of life : wise, had they believed that the last was their ordinary employment ; the first, their extraordinary vocation. We are great fools. " He has passed his life in ease," say we : " I have done nothing to-day." What ! have you not lived ? 'T is not only the fundamental, but the most illustrious of your occupations. " Had I been put to the management of great affairs, I should have shown what I could do." Have you known how to meditate, and manage your life ? you have performed the greatest work of all : for a man to shew and set himself out, nature has no need of fortune ; she equally shews herself in all degrees, and behind a curtain, as well as without one. Have you known how to compose your manners ? You have done a great deal more than he who has composed books. Have you known how to take repose ? You have done more than he who has taken cities and empires.

The great and glorious masterpiece of man is to know how to live to purpose ; all other things, to reign, to lay up treasure, to build, are at the most but mere appendixes and little props. I take a delight to see a general of an army at the foot of a breach he intends presently to assault, giving himself up entire and free at dinner, to talk and be merry with his friends ; and Brutus, when heaven and earth were conspired against him and the Roman liberty, stealing some hour of the night from his rounds to read and abridge Polybius, as in all security. 'T is for little souls, that truckle under the weight of affairs, not to know how clearly to disengage themselves, and not to know how to lay them aside, and take them up again. . . . Grandeur of soul consists not so much in mounting and in proceeding forward, as in knowing how to govern and circumscribe itself. It takes every thing for great that is enough ; and shows its height better in loving moderate than eminent things. There is nothing so handsome and lawful as well and duly to play the man; nor science so hard as well to know how to live this life; and of all the infirmities we have, 't is the most savage to despise our being. . . .

I enjoin my soul to look upon pain and pleasure with an eye equally regular: Eodem enim vitio est effusio animi in lætitia, quo in dolore contractio, "For 't is by the same vice that we dilate ourselves in mirth, and contract in sorrow," and equally firm; but the one gaily, and the other severely, and according to what it is able, to be as careful to restrain the one as to extend the other. The judging rightly of goods brings along with it the judging soundly of evils; and pain has something not to be avoided in its tender beginnings, and pleasure has something that may be avoided in its excessive end. Plato couples them together, and will that it should be equally the office of fortitude to fight against pain, and against the immoderate and charming blandishments of pleasure: they are two fountains, from which whoever draws, when, and as much as he needs, whether city, man, or beast, is very happy. . . . Others are sensible of the sweetness of contentment and of prosperity; I feel it too as well as they, but not as it slides and passes by; a man ought to study, taste, and ruminate upon it, to render worthy thanks to Him that grants it to us. They enjoy the other pleasures as they do that of sleep, without knowing it. To the end that even sleep itself should not so stupidly escape from me, I have formerly caused myself to be disturbed in my sleep, that I might the better and more sensibly relish and savour it. I consult myself about a contentment; I do not skim, but sound it; and bend my reason, now grown perverse and ill-humoured, to entertain it. Do I find myself in calm composedness? Is there any pleasure that tickles me? I do not suffer it to dally with my senses only; I associate my soul to it too; not there to engage herself, but therein to take delight; not there to lose herself, but to be present there; and employ her on her part to view herself in this prosperous estate, to weigh, esteem, and amplify its happiness. . . .

For my part, then, I love life, and cultivate it, such as it has pleased God to bestow it upon us.

SIR WALTER RALEIGH

(A. D. 1552–1618.)

WALTER RALEIGH, soldier, statesman, explorer, colonizer, historian, poet, — the typical man of the Elizabethan age, — was born at Hayes, in South Devon, England, in 1552, the son of a poor gentleman of ancient stock. His scant schooling ended in a brief term at Oxford, and his life of adventure began at the boyish age of seventeen, when he went as a volunteer to fight under Condé and Coligny, for the Huguenots of France. From France he went fighting to the Netherlands, in aid of the Dutch against Spain, and nearly ten years pass before he is found once more in England. Then he starts with Humphrey Gilbert, his half-brother, on an exploring voyage to America, but is driven back by storms and hostile Spaniards. In 1580 he is soldiering again in Ireland; in 1582 he is winning the favor of Queen Elizabeth at the English court; in 1584 he sends out his first Virginia expedition; the next year he is knighted by the queen, and plants his unfortunate colony on Roanoke Island. In 1588 he is active and heroic in the defense of England against the Armada. The next year he is with Drake's expedition to Portugal; and afterwards with Edmund Spenser in Ireland, whence he brings the first three books of the "Faerie Queene" for presentation to Elizabeth. In 1590 he fits out a squadron and cruises with Frobisher in the West· Indies, missing the Spanish plate fleet, but capturing a rich prize at the Azores. On returning he is imprisoned in the Tower for seduction of one of the queen's maids of honor, whom he marries. Restored to favor, he enters Parliament, and acquires Sherborne Manor, where he "builds and beautifies." In 1595 he is at sea again, with an expedition which explores the Guiana coast and ascends the Orinoco, seeking Eldorado, and he publishes a narrative of his voyage. In 1596 he serves under Howard and Essex in the Cadiz expedition, and is at the taking of Fayal next year. The death of Queen Elizabeth and the accession of King James end his favor at court. Accused of complicity in the plot to raise Arabella Stuart to the throne, he is condemned to death, but remains for thirteen years a prisoner in the Tower, during which time his "History of the World" is written. Then, in 1616, he is released, to make his last ill-starred expedition to Guiana, reviving Spanish hatreds, which now pursue him to the death. King James, seeking a Spanish marriage for his son, thinks Raleigh's life a small price to pay for the good will of the court at Madrid. So Sir Walter returns to the Tower; the old sentence of 1603 is declared to be of force, and, on the 29th of October, 1618, he lays his head upon the block.

RALEIGH'S INSTRUCTIONS TO HIS SON AND TO POSTERITY.

(From his Works, vol. viii.)

CHAPTER I.

There is nothing more becoming any wise man than to make choice of friends; for by them thou shalt be judged what thou art. Let them therefore be wise and virtuous, and none of those that follow thee for gain. . . . If thy friends be of better quality than thyself, thou mayest be sure of two things: the first, that they will be more careful to keep thy counsel, because they have more to lose than thou hast; the second, they will esteem thee for thyself, and not for that which thou dost possess. . . . Let thy love therefore be to the best, so long as they do well: but take heed that thou love God, thy country, thy prince, and thine own estate, before all others, for the fancies of men change, and he that loves to-day hateth to-morrow: but let reason be thy schoolmistress, which shall ever guide thee aright.

CHAPTER II.

The next and greatest care ought to be in the choice of a wife, and the only danger therein is beauty, by which all men in all ages, wise and foolish, have been betrayed. . . .

CHAPTER III.

Take care thou be not made a fool by flatterers, for even the wisest men are abused by these. Know therefore, that flatterers are the worst kind of traitors; for they will strengthen thy imperfections, encourage thee in all evils, correct thee in nothing, but so shadow and paint all thy vices and follies as thou shalt never, by their will, discern evil from good, or vice from virtue. And because all men are apt to flatter themselves, to entertain the additions of other men's praises is most perilous. Do not therefore praise thyself, except thou wilt be counted a vainglorious fool, neither take delight in the praises of other men, except thou deserve it, and receive it from such as are worthy and honest, and will withal warn thee of thy faults. . . .

CHAPTER IV.

Be careful to avoid public disputations at feasts, or at tables among choleric or quarrelsome persons; and eschew evermore to be acquainted or familiar with ruffians. . . .

Jest not openly at those that are simple, but remember how much thou art bound to God, who hath made thee wiser. . . . Remember the divine saying; *He that keepeth his mouth keepeth his life.* Do therefore right to all men where it may profit them, and thou shalt thereby get much love; and forbear to speak evil things of men, though it be true, (if thou be not constrained,) and thereby thou shalt avoid malice and revenge.

Do not accuse any man of any crime, if it be not to save thyself, thy prince, or country; for there is nothing more dishonourable (next to treason itself) than to be an accuser. Notwithstanding, I would not have thee for any respect lose thy reputation, or endure public disgrace;

for better it were not to live, than to live a coward, if the offence proceed not from thyself; if it do, it shall be better to compound it upon good terms than to hazard thyself; for if thou overcome, thou art under the cruelty of the law; if thou art overcome, thou art dead or dishonoured. . . .

Speaking much also is a sign of vanity; for he that is lavish in words is a niggard in deeds; and as Solomon saith, *The mouth of a wise man is in his heart, the heart of a fool is in his mouth, because what he knoweth or thinketh he uttereth.* And by thy words and discourses men will judge thee: for as Socrates saith, " Such as thy words are, such will thy affections be esteemed; and such will thy deeds as thy affections, and such thy life as thy deeds." Therefore be advised what thou dost discourse of, and what thou maintainest, whether touching religion, state, or vanity; for if thou err in the first, thou shalt be accounted profane; if in the second, dangerous; if in the third, indiscreet and foolish. . . .

CHAPTER V.

Amongst all other things of the world take care of thy estate, which thou shalt ever preserve, if thou observe three things; first, that thou know what thou hast, what every thing is worth that thou hast, and to see that thou art not wasted by thy servants and officers. The second is, that thou never spend any thing before thou have it; for borrowing is the canker and death of every man's estate. The third is, that thou suffer not thyself to be wounded for other men's faults, and scourged for other men's offences, which is the surety for another; for thereby millions of men have been beggared and destroyed, paying the reckoning of other men's riot, and the charge of other men's folly and prodigality; if thou smart, smart for thine own sins; and, above all things, be not made an ass to carry the burdens of other men: if any friend desire thee to be his surety, give him a part of what thou hast to spare; if he press thee further, he is not thy friend at all, for friendship rather chooseth harm to itself than offereth it; if thou be bound for a stranger, thou art a fool: if for a merchant, thou putteth thy estate to learn to swim: if for a churchman, he hath no inheritance: if for a lawyer, he will find an evasion, by a syllable or word, to abuse thee: if for a poor man thou must pay it thyself: if for a rich man, it need not: therefore from suretyship, as from a manslayer or enchanter, bless thyself. . . .

CHAPTER VII.

Exceed not in the humour of rags and bravery, for these will soon wear out of fashion; but money in thy purse will ever be in fashion; and no man is esteemed for gay garments but by fools and women.

CHAPTER VIII.

On the other side, take heed that thou seek not riches basely, nor attain them by evil means; destroy no man for his wealth, nor take any thing from the poor, for the cry and complaint thereof will pierce the heavens. . . .

CHAPTER IX.

Take especial care that thou delight not in wine; for there never was any man that came to honour or preferment that loved it; for it transformeth a man into a beast, decayeth health, poisoneth the breath, destroyeth natural heat, brings a man's stomach to an artificial heat, deformeth the face, rotteth the teeth, and, to conclude, maketh a man contemptible, soon old, and despised of all wise and worthy men. . . .

CHAPTER X.

Now for the world, I know it too well to persuade thee to dive into the practices thereof ; rather stand upon thine own guard against all that tempt thee thereunto, or may practice upon thee in thy conscience, thy reputation, or thy purse ; resolve that no man is wise or safe, but he that is honest.

Serve God; let him be the Author of all thy actions; commend all thy endeavours to him that must either wither or prosper them ; please him with prayer, lest, if he frown, he confound all thy fortunes and labours like the drops of rain on the sandy ground. Let my experienced advice and fatherly instructions sink deep into thy heart. So God direct thee in all his ways, and fill thy heart with his grace.

JOHN LYLY

(A. D. 1554–1606.)

JOHN LYLY, born in the Weald of Kent about 1554, graduating at Oxford in 1573, and dying in London in 1606, is principally known as an author by his story of "Euphues: the Anatomy of Wit," which few people, during the last three centuries, have read, but which most readers have heard of, as giving its name to an affectedly elegant style of writing, called *euphuistic* to this day. That the book has suffered unjust contempt and neglect, and is really one of solid merit, is the opinion of many judicious critics in recent times, who have given fair attention to it. For example, the Rev. Charles Kingsley, in his romance "Westward Ho!", asks those who sneer at Lyly's "Euphues" if they have ever read it, and adds: "For if they have done so, I pity them if they have not found it, in spite of occasional tediousness and pedantry, as brave, righteous, and pious a book as man need look into; and wish for no better proof of the nobleness and virtue of the Elizabethan age than the fact that 'Euphues' and the 'Arcadia' were the two popular romances of the day. . . . Let those who have not read 'Euphues' believe that, if they could train a son after the pattern of his Ephœbus, to the great saving of their own money and his virtue, all fathers, even in these money-making days, would rise up and call them blessed."

In its own day, which fell within the great age of English literature, — the age of Shakespeare, — "Euphues" was much admired. It passed through ten editions in fifty-six years; after which it was never again published until 1868, when it appeared in Mr. Edward Arber's series of "English Reprints."

The following, from the chapter "Of the education of youth," reproduces the text given by Mr. Arber: —

EUPHUES AND HIS EPHŒBUS: OF THE EDUCATION OF YOUTH.

The sum of al wherwith I would have my Ephœbus endued, and how I would have him instructed, shal briefly appeare in this following. First, that he be of honest parents, nursed of his mother, brought up in such a place as is incorrupt, both for the ayre and manners with such a person as is undefiled, of great zeale, of profound knowledge, of absolute perfection, yat be instructed in Philosophy, whereby he may atteine learning, and have in al sciences a smacke, whereby he may readily dispute of any thing. That his body be kept in his pure strength by honest exercise, his wit and memory by diligent study.

That he abandon al allurements of vice, and continually encline to vertue, which if it shall as it may come to passe, then do I hope that if ever Platoes common weale shal flourish, that my Ephœbus shall bee a citizen, yat if Aristotle fined any happy man it wil be my childe, if Tully confesse any to be an absolute Orator, it will be my young youth. I am heere therefore gentlemen to exhort you, that with all industry you apply your minds to the study of Philosophy, that as you professe your selves students, so you may be students, that as you disdain not the name of a scholler, so you wil not be found voyd of the duety of schollers, let not your mindes be caryed away with vaine delights, as with travailing into farre and strange countries wher you shal see more wickednesse then learn vertue and wit. Neither with costly attyre of the newe cut, the Dutch hat, the French hose, the Spanish rapier, ye Italian hilt, and I know not what?

Cast not your eyes on the beauty of women, least ye cast away your hearts with folly, let not that fond love, wherewith youth fatteth himself as fatte as a foole infect you, for as a sinewe being cut though it be healed, there wil always remaine a scarre, or as fine lynnen stayned with blacke ynke, though it bee washed never so often, will have an yron Mowle: so the mind once mangled or maymed with love, though it be never so well cured with reason, or cooled by wisedome, yet there wil appeare a scarre, by the which one may gesse the minde hath ben perced, and a blemmish whereby one may judge the heart hath ben stayned.

Refraine from dicing, which was the only cause that Pyreus was striken to the heart, and from dauncing which was the meanes that lost John Baptists heade; I am not he that will disallowe honest recreation, although I detest the abuses, I speake boldely unto you bicause I myself know you: what Athens hath ben, what Athens is, what Athens shal be, I can gesse. Let not every Inne and ale-house in Athens be as it were your chamber, frequent not those ordinary tables wher either for the desire of delicate cates, or the meetinge of youthfull companions, yee both spend your money vainely and your time idly, imitate him in life whom ye [you seeme to] honour for his learning. Aristotle who was never seen in the company of those that idly bestowed their time.

There is nothing more swifter than time, nothing more sweeter: wee have not as Seneca saith little time to live, but we leese muche, neither have we a short life by Nature, but we make it shorter by naughtynesse, our life is long if we know how to use it. Follow Appelles that cunning and wise Painter, which would let no day passe over his head, without a lyne, without some labour. It was pretely sayde of Hesiodas, lette us endeavour by reason to excell beastes, seeinge beasts by nature excell men. . . . Doth not the Lyon for strength, the Turtle for love, the Ante for labour excell man? Doth not the

Eagle see cleerer, the Vulter smel better, the Mowle heare lyghtlyer? Let us therefore endeavour to excell in vertue, seeing in qualyties of ye body we are inferiour to beastes. And heere I am most earnestly to exhort you to modesty in your behaviour, to duetye to your elders, to dylligence in your studyes. . . . Frame therefore your lyves to such integritie, your studyes to atteininge of such perfection, that neither the might of the stronge, neyther the mallyce of the weake, neither the swifte reportes of the ignoraunt be able to spotte you wyth dishonestie, or note you of ungodlynesse. The greatest harme that you can doe unto the envious, is to doo well, the greatest corasive that you can give unto the ignoraunte, is to prosper in knowledge, the greatest comforte that you can bestowe on your parents is to lyve well and learne well, the greatest commoditie that you can yeelde unto your Countrey, is with wisedome to bestowe that talent, that by grace was given you.

And here I cannot choose but give you that counsel that an olde man in Naples gave mee most wisely, although I had then neither grace to followe it, neyther will to give eare to it, desiring you not to reject it bicause I did once dispise it. It was this [thus] as I can remember word for word.

Descende into your owne consciences, consider with your selves the great difference between staring and starke blynde, witte and wisedome, love and lust: Be merry but with modestie, be sober but not too sullen: be valiaunt, but not too venterous: let your attire be comely, but not too costly: your dyet wholesome, but not excessive: use pastime as the word importeth, to passe ye time in honest recreation: mistrust no man without cause, neither be ye credulous without proofe: be not lyght to follow every mans opinion, neither obstinate to stand in your owne conceipts : serve God, feare God, love God, and God will blesse you, as either your hearts can wish, or your friends desire.

This was his grave and godly advise, whose counsel I would have you all to follow.

LORD BACON

(A. D. 1561–1626.)

FRANCIS BACON, who received the title of Baron Verulam in 1618, and that of Viscount St. Albans in 1621, but who is commonly called Lord Bacon, was born in London in 1561. His father was Sir Nicholas Bacon, who held the great seal of England during the first twenty years of the reign of Elizabeth. He studied at Trinity College, Cambridge, and at Gray's Inn; was attached for a time to the English embassy in France; was admitted to the bar in 1582; entered Parliament two years later; became solicitor-general in 1607, attorney-general in 1613, lord-keeper (his father's office) in 1617, and lord chancellor in 1618. He was removed from the latter office, on a charge of receiving bribes, in 1621. His great work, on method in scientific investigation, the "Novum Organum," was published in 1620. His "Essays," which are the most popular of his writings, had first appeared more than twenty years previously.

Macaulay's estimate of Bacon, in his famous essay reviewing Montagu's edition of Bacon's works, commends itself to most minds as just. Of his genius and his philosophy he says: "What we most admire is the vast capacity of that intellect which, without effort, takes in at once all the domains of science — all the past, the present, and the future, all the errors of two thousand years, all the encouraging signs of the passing times, all the bright hopes of the coming age. Cowley, who was among the most ardent, and not among the least discerning followers of the new philosophy, has, in one of his finest poems, compared Bacon to Moses standing on Mount Pisgah. It is to Bacon, we think, as he appears in the first book of the ' Novum Organum,' that the comparison applies with peculiar felicity. There we see the great law-giver looking round from his lonely elevation on an infinite expanse; behind him a wilderness of dreary sands and bitter waters in which successive generations have sojourned, always moving, yet never advancing, reaping no harvest and building no abiding city; before him a goodly land, — a land of promise, a land flowing with milk and honey. While the multitude below saw only the flat, sterile desert in which they had so long wandered, bounded on every side by a near horizon, or diversified only by some deceitful mirage, he was gazing, from a far higher stand, on a far lovelier country — following with his eye the long course of fertilizing rivers, through ample pastures, and under the bridges of great capitals — measuring the distances of marts and havens, and portioning out all those wealthy regions from Dan to Beersheba." But on the character of Lord Bacon, the grave judgment pronounced by Macaulay is as follows: "The moral qualities of Bacon were not of a high order. We do not say that he was a bad man. He was not inhuman or tyrannical. He bore with meekness his high civil honors, and the far higher honors gained by his intellect. He was very seldom, if ever, provoked into treating any person with malignity and insolence. No man more readily held up the left cheek to those who had smitten the right. No man was more expert at the soft answer which turneth away wrath. He was never accused of intemperance in his pleasures. His even temper, his flowing courtesy, the general respectability of his demeanor, made a favorable impression on those who saw him in situations which do not severely try the principles. His faults were — we write it with pain — coldness of heart and meanness of spirit. He seems to have been incapable of feeling strong affection, of facing great dangers, of making great sacrifices. His desires were set on things below."

LORD BACON'S PRECEPTS OF THE DOCTRINE OF ADVANCEMENT IN LIFE.

(From "The Advancement of Learning," book viii.)

The things necessary for the acquisition of fortune, are neither fewer nor less difficult nor lighter than those to obtain virtue; and it is as hard and severe a thing to be a true politician, as to be truly moral. But the handling hereof concerns learning greatly, both in honour and substance. . . . Not however that learning admires or esteems this architecture of fortune otherwise than as an inferior work. For no man's fortune can be an end worthy of the gift of being that has been given him by God ; and often the worthiest men abandon their fortunes willingly, that they may have leisure for higher pursuits. But nevertheless, fortune as an instrument of virtue and merit deserves its own speculation and doctrine. To this doctrine are attached certain precepts, some summary, and some scattered or various ; whereof the former relate to the just knowledge of ourselves and others. Let the first precept then (on which the knowledge of others turns) be set down as this : that we obtain (as far as we can) that window which Momus required ; who seeing in the frame of man's heart such angles and recesses found fault that there was not a window to look into its mysterious and tortuous windings. This window we shall obtain by carefully procuring good information of the particular persons with whom we have to deal. . . .

Next to the knowledge of others comes the knowledge of self. And here, we must use even greater care in gaining good and accurate information touching ourselves, than touching others ; since the oracle " know thyself " is not only a rule of universal wisdom, but has a special place in politics. . . . Men ought therefore to take an accurate and impartial survey of their own abilities, virtues, and helps ; and again, of their wants, inabilities, and impediments ; making the account in such a manner that the former are always estimated rather more, and the latter rather less than they really are. From this examination they should frame the following considerations.

First, to consider how their natural and moral constitution sort with the general state of the times ; which if they find agreeable and consonant, then in all things to give themselves more scope and liberty, and indulge their dispositions; but if there be anything differing and discordant, then in the whole course of their life to be more close, retired, and reserved. . . .

Secondly, to consider how their nature sorts with the professions and courses of life which are in use and repute, and whereof they have to make election; so that if their profession is not already determined, they may make choice of that which is most fit and agreeable to their disposition; but if they have already entered on a path of life for which they are not naturally suited, that they may leave it the first opportunity, and adopt a fresh profession. . . .

Thirdly, to consider how they sort with their equals and rivals, whom they are like to have as competitors in their fortune; and to take that course of life wherein there is the greatest scarcity of distinguished men, and they themselves are likely to be most eminent. . . .

Fourthly, to consider their own nature and disposition in the choice of their friends and dependences. For different natures require different kinds of friends: to some is suited such as are solemn and silent; to others such as are bold and arrogant, and so on. . . .

Fifthly, to take especial heed how they guide themselves by examples, and not vainly to endeavour to frame themselves upon other men's models; as if what is open to others must needs be open to them, not at all reflecting how far the nature and character of their models may differ from their own. . . .

But it is not enough for a man only to know himself; for he should consider also of the best way to set himself forth to advantage; to disclose and reveal himself; and lastly, to turn and shape himself according to occasion. Now for the first we see nothing more usual than for the

worse man to make the better external show.   It is therefore no unimportant attribute of prudence in a man to be
able to set forth to advantage before others, with grace
and skill, his virtues, fortunes, and merits (which may be
done without arrogance or breeding disgust) ; and again,
to cover artificially his weaknesses, defects, misfortunes,
and disgraces. . . .

And so much for the two summary precepts of this
Architecture of Fortune ; whereof the scattered precepts
are numerous, but I will select a few for example's sake.

The first precept is that the carpenter of fortune should
make a good use and a right application of his rule ; that
is, that he should accustom his mind to judge of the proportion and value of all things, as they conduce more or
less to his fortune and ends, and that he do this substantially, not superficially. . . .

A second precept is to beware of being carried by an
excess of magnanimity and confidence to things beyond our
strength, and not to row against the stream.   It is excellent counsel regarding men's fortunes, " Be ruled by the
Fates and the Gods ; " for we ought to look round and
observe where things lie open to us, and where they are
closed and obstructed, where they are difficult and where
easy, that we may not waste our strength on things to
which convenient access is forbidden. . . .

The third precept seems to be somewhat repugnant to
the former two, though not so if rightly understood.
The nature of it is this, that we should not always wait
for occasions, but sometimes challenge and induce them ;
and it is that to which Demosthenes alludes in high terms,
" In the same manner as it is a received principle that the
general should lead the army, so should wise men lead
affairs, causing things to be done which they think good,
and not themselves waiting upon events." . . .

A fourth precept is to undertake nothing which of necessity takes up a great quantity of time, but to have this sound ever ringing in your ears, " time is flying, time which cannot be retrieved." . . .

A fifth precept is to a certain degree to imitate nature, which does nothing in vain ; no very difficult task, if a man will skilfully mix and interlace his several kinds of business. For in every particular action a man ought so to direct and prepare his mind, and should have one intention so underlying and subordinate to another, that if he cannot obtain his wishes in the best degree, he may yet be satisfied if he succeed in a second, or even a third ; and if he cannot obtain them all in that particular, then he may turn the labour spent in it to some other end besides the one intended. . . .

A sixth precept is not to engage oneself too peremptorily in anything, though at first sight it seem not liable to accident; but ever to have either a window open to fly out at, or a secret way to retire by. . . .

A seventh precept is that ancient precept of Bias, not construed to any point of perfidiousness, but only to caution and moderation, " Love as if you were sometime to hate, and hate as if you were sometime to love ; " for it utterly betrays and destroys all utility, for men to embark themselves too far in unfortunate friendships, troublesome and turbulent quarrels, or foolish and childish jealousies and emulations.

These will suffice for an example of the doctrine of advancement in life.

ESSEX'S LETTER OF ADVICE TO THE EARL OF RUTLAND.

The following letter of advice to the Earl of Rutland on his travels, though attributed to the Earl of Essex, and undoubtedly sent and received in his name, is believed by Mr. James Spedding, Bacon's biographer, to show unmistakable signs of the latter's hand. The style and much of the matter bears a close resemblance to the early writings of Bacon, especially to the "Advancement of Learning." "We have direct evidence," says Mr. Spedding, "that, a few years later, Essex would sometimes employ Bacon to draw up letters for him about his own most personal affairs, — letters which he was himself to sign." It would have been most natural, then, in Mr. Spedding's opinion, for Bacon to make a draft of such a letter of advice as Essex wished to write to his cousin, and it is probable that Essex did not transcribe it literally, but altered and added to it, as many passages are in his own characteristic style.

The following is Mr. Spedding's version of the letter obtained by collation of three MSS. in the Harleian Collection, and the printed copy.

LETTER OF ADVICE TO THE EARL OF RUTLAND ON HIS TRAVELS.

Your Lordship hath many friends who have more leisure to think and more sufficiency to counsel than myself; yet doth my love to you dedicate these few free hours to study of you and your intended course; in which study if I find out nothing but that which you have from others, yet I shall perhaps confirm the opinion of wiser than myself.

Your Lordship's purpose is to travel, and your study must be what use to make of your travel. The question is ordinary, and there is to it an ordinary answer; that is, your Lordship shall see the beauty of many cities, know the manners of the people of many countries, and learn the language of many nations. Some of these may serve for ornaments, and all of them for delights; but your Lordship must look further than these; for the greatest ornament is the inward beauty of the mind, and when you have known as great variety of delight as the world will afford, you will confess that the greatest delight is *sentire te indies fieri meliorem ;* to feel that you do every day become more worthy; therefore your Lordship's end and scope should be that which in moral philosophy we call *cultum animi*, the tilling and manuring of your own mind. The gifts or excellencies of the mind are the same as those are of the body; Beauty, Health, and Strength. Beauty of the mind is showed in graceful and acceptable forms, and sweetness of behaviour; and they that have that gift cause those to whom they deny anything to go better contented away, than men of contrary disposition do them to whom they grant. Health consisteth in an unmovable constancy and a freedom from passions, which are indeed the sicknesses of the mind. Strength of mind is that active power which maketh us perform good things and great things, as well as health and even temper of mind keeps from those that are evil and base. All these three are to be sought for, though the greatest part of men have none of them; some have one and lack the other two ; a few attain to have two of them and lack the third ; and almost none have all.

The first way to attain experience of forms or behaviour, is to make the mind itself expert. For behaviour is but a garment, and it is easy to make a comely garment for a body that is itself well-proportioned, whereas a deformed body can never be so helped by tailor's art but the counterfeit will appear; and in the form of our mind it is a true rule, that a man may mend his faults with as little labour as cover them.

The second way is by imitation, and to that end good choice is to be made of those with whom you converse; therefore your Lordship should affect their company whom you find to be worthiest, and not partially think them most worthy whom you affect.

To attain to health of mind, we must use the same

means that we do for the health of our bodies; that is, to take observation what diseases we are aptest to fall into, and to provide against them, for physic hath not more medicines against the diseases of the body, than reason hath preservatives against the passions of the mind. The Stoics were of opinion that there was no way to attain to this even temper of the mind but to be senseless, and so they sold their goods to ransom themselves from their evils; but not only Divinity, our schoolmistress, doth teach us the effect of grace, but even Philosophy, her handmaid, doth condemn our want of care and industry if we do not win very much upon ourselves. To prove which I will only use one instance : there is nothing in nature more general or more strong than the fear of death, and to a natural man there is nothing seems more impos- sible than to resolve against death. But both martyrs for religion, heathen for glory, some for love of their country, others for affection to one special person, have encoun- tered death without fear, and suffered it without show of alteration ; and therefore, if many have conquered pas- sion's chiefest and strongest fortress, it is lack of under- taking in him that getteth not an absolute victory. To set down the ways how a man may attain to the active power mentioned in this place (I mean strength of mind), is much harder than to give rules in the other two; for behaviour or good form may be gotten by education, and health or even temper of mind by observation. But if there be not in nature some partner to this active strength, it can never be obtained by any industry; for the virtues which are proper unto it are liberality or mag- nificence, and fortitude or magnanimity ; and some are by nature so covetous or cowardly, as it is as much in vain to seek to enlarge or inflame their minds, as to go about to plow the rocks. But where these active virtues are but budding, they must be ripened by clearness of judgment and custom of well-doing. Clearness of judgment makes men liberal, for it teacheth men to esteem of the goods of fortune not for themselves, for so they are but jailors to them, but for their use, for so they are lords over them; and it makes us to know that it is *beatius dare quam accipere*, the one being a badge of sovereignty, the other of subjection. Also it leadeth us to fortitude, for it teacheth us that we should not too much prize life which we cannot keep, nor fear death which we cannot shun; that he which dies nobly doth live for ever, and he that lives in fear doth die continually; that pain and danger be great only by opinion, and that in truth nothing is fearful but fear itself; that custom makes the thing used natural as it were to the user. I shall not need to prove these two things, since we see by experience it holds true in all things, but yet those that give with judgment are not only encouraged to be liberal by the return of thankfulness from those to whom they give, but find in the very exercise of that virtue a delight to do good. And if custom be strong to confirm any one virtue more than another, it is the virtue of fortitude, for it makes us triumph over the fear which we have conquered, and anew to challenge danger which happily we have encountered, and hold more dear the reputation of honour which we have increased.

I have hitherto set down what desire or wish I would have your Lordship to take into your mind, that is to make yourself an expert man, and what are the general helps which all men may use which have the said desire; I will now move your Lordship to consider what helps your travel may give you.

First, when you see infinite variety of behaviour and manners of men, you may choose and imitate the best;

when you see new delights which you never knew, and have passions stirred in you which before you never felt, you shall both know what disease your mind is aptest to fall into, and what the things are that breed the disease; when you come into armies, or places where you shall see anything of the wars (as I would wish you to see them before your return), you shall both confirm your natural courage, and be made more fit for true fortitude, which is not given to man by nature, but must grow out of discourse of reason; and lastly, in your travel you shall have great help to attain to knowledge, which is not only the excellentest thing in man, but the very excellency of man.

In manners or behaviour, your Lordship must not be caught with novelty, which is pleasing to young men; nor infected with custom, which makes us keep our own ill graces, and participate of those we see every day; nor given to affection (a general fault of most of our English travellers), which is both displeasing and ridiculous.

In discovering your passions and meeting with them, give not way to yourself nor dispense with yourself in little, though resolving to conquer yourself in great; for the same stream that may be stopped with one man's hand at the spring head, may drown whole armies of men when it hath run long. In your being in the wars, think it better at the first to do a great deal too much than anything too little; for a young man's, especially a stranger's, first actions are looked upon, and reputation once gotten is easily kept, but an evil impression conceived at the first is not quickly removed.

The last thing that I am to speak of, but the first that you are to seek, is conceived knowledge. To praise knowledge, or to persuade your Lordship to the love of it, I shall not need to use many words; I will only say, that

where that wants the man is void of all good; without it
there can be no fortitude, for all other darings come of
fury, and fury is a passion, and passions ever turn into
their contraries; and therefore the most furious men,
when their first blaze is spent, be commonly the most
fearful; without it there can be no liberality, for giving
is but want of audacity to deny, or of discretion to prize;
without it there can be no justice, for giving to a man
that which is his own is but chance, or want of a corrupter
or seducer; without it there can be no constancy or
patience, for suffering is but dulness or senselessness;
without it there can be no temperance, for we shall restrain ourselves from good as well as from evil, for that
they that cannot discern cannot elect or choose; nay without it there can be no true religion, all other devotion being
but blind zeal, which is as strong in heresy as in truth.
To reckon up all parts of knowledge, and to show the way
to attain to every part, is a work too great for me at any
time, and too long to discourse at this; therefore I will
only speak of such knowledge as your Lordship should
have desire to seek, and shall have means to compass. I
forbear also to speak of divine knowledge, which must
direct your faith, both because I find my own constancy
insufficiency, and also because I hope your Lordship doth
still nourish the seeds of religion, which during your education at Cambridge were sown in you. I will only say
this; as the irresolute man can never perform any action
well, so he that is not resolved in soul and conscience, can
never be resolute in anything else. But that civil knowledge, which will make you do well by yourself, and do
good unto others, must be sought by study, by conference,
and by observation. Before I persuade your Lordship to
study, I must look to answer an argument drawn from the
nobility of all places of the world, which now is utterly

unlearned, if it be not some very few; and an authority
of an English proverb, made in despite of learning, that
the greatest clerks are not the wisest men. The first I
answer that this want of learning hath been in good countries ruined by civil wars, or in states corrupted through
wealth or too great length of peace. In the one sort men's
wits were employed in their necessary defence, in the
other drowned in the study of *artes luxuriæ*. But in all
flourishing states learning hath ever flourished. If it
seem strange that I account no state flourishing but that
which hath neither civil wars nor too long peace, I answer,
that politic bodies are like our natural bodies, and must
as well have some exercise to spend their humours, as to
be kept from too violent or continual outrages which
spend their best spirits. The proverb I take to be made
in that age when the nobility of England brought up their
sons but as they entered their whelps, and thought them
wise enough if they could chase their deer; and I answer
it with another proverb made by a wise man, *Scientia
non habet inimicum præter ignorantem*. All men that
live are drawn either by book or example, and in books
your Lordship shall find (in what course soever you pro-
pound to yourself) rules prescribed by the wisest men, and
examples left by the wisest men that have lived before
us. Therefore knowledge is to be sought by your private
study; and opportunity you shall have to study, if you do
not often remove from place to place, but stay some time
and reside in the best. In the course of your study and
choice of your books, you must first seek to have the
grounds of learning, which are the liberal arts; for without them you shall neither gather other knowledge easily,
nor make use of that you have; and then use studies
of delight but sometimes for recreation, and neither drown
yourself in them, nor omit those studies whereof you

are to have continual use. Above all other books be
conversant in the Histories, for they will best instruct you
in matter moral, military, and politic, by which and in
which you must ripen and settle your judgment. In your
study you are to seek two things : the first to conceive or
understand ; the second to lay up or remember ; for as
the philosopher saith, *discere est tanquam recordari*. To
help you to conceive, you may do well in those things
which you are to read to draw yourself to read with somebody that may give you help, and to that end you must
either carry over with you some good general scholar, or
make some abode in the universities abroad, where you
may hear the professors in every art. To help you to
remember, you must use writing, or meditation, or both ;
by writing I mean making of notes and abridgments of
that which you would remember. I make conference the
second help to knowledge in order, though I have found
it the first and greatest in profiting, and I have so placed
them because he that hath not studied knows not what to
doubt nor what to ask ; but when the little I had learned
had taught me to find out mine own emptiness, I profited
more by some expert man in half a day's conference, than
by myself in a month's study. To profit much by conference, you must first choose to confer with expert men, I
mean expert in that which you desire to know ; next with
many, for expert men will be of diverse and contrary
opinions, and every one will make his own probable, so as
if you hear but one you shall know in all questions but
one opinion ; whereas by hearing many, you shall, by seeing the reasons of one, confute the reasons of the other,
and be able to judge of the truth. Besides, there is no
one man that is expert in all things, but every great
scholar is expert in some one, so as your wit shall be whet-
ted with conversing with many great wits, and you shall

have the cream and quintessence of every one of theirs. In conference be neither superstitious nor believing all you hear (what opinion soever you have of the man that delivereth it), nor too desirous to contradict. For of the first grows a facility to be led into all kind of error; since you shall ever think that he that knows all that you know, and somewhat more, hath infinite knowledge, because you cannot sound or measure it. Of the second grows such a carping humour, as you shall without reason censure all men, and want reason to censure yourself. I do conclude this point of conference with this advice, that your Lordship shall rather go a hundred miles out of the way to speak with a wise man, than five to see a fair town.

The third way to attain knowledge is observation, and not long life or seeing much; because, as he that rides a way often, and takes no care of marks or notes to direct him if he come the same again, or to make him know where he is if he come unto it, shall never prove a good guide; so he that lives long and sees much, but observes nothing, shall never prove a wise man. The use of observation is in noting the coherence of causes and effects, counsels and successes, and the proportion and likeness between nature and nature, force and force, action and action, state and state, time past and time present. The philosopher did think that all knowledge doth much depend on the knowledge of causes; as he said, *id demum scimus cujus causam scimus;* and therefore a private man cannot prove so great a soldier as he that commands an army, nor so great a *politique* as he that rules a state, because the one sees only the events and knows not the causes, the other makes the causes that govern the events. The observation of proportion or likeness between one person or one thing and another, makes nothing without example, nor nothing new: and although *exempla illus-trant non probant*, examples may make things plain that are proved, but prove not themselves; yet when circumstances agree, and proportion is kept, that which is probable in one case is probable in a thousand, and that which is reason once is reason ever.

SHAKESPEARE

(A. D. 1564–1616.)

THE supreme poet, not of the English race alone, but of all mankind, William Shakespeare, was born at Stratford-on-Avon, in Warwickshire, England, on a day in April, 1564. The precise day is not known; but the baptism of the child, which no doubt followed birth quickly, is registered April 24th. His parents were of a modest station in English middle-class society, and it is improbable that he received more than a quite moderate education; but his genius demanded little from schools. Says James Russell Lowell: "Shakespeare was doubly fortunate. Saxon by the father and Norman by the mother, he was a representative Englishman. A country boy, he learned first the rough and ready English of his rustic mates, who knew how to make nice verbs and adjectives courtesy to their needs. Going up to London, he acquired the *lingua aulica* precisely at the happiest moment, just as it was becoming, in the strictest sense of the word, modern. . . . Shakespeare . . . found a language already to a certain extent established, but not yet fetlocked by dictionary and grammar mongers. . . . What kind of culture Shakespeare had is uncertain; how much he had is disputed; that he had as much as he wanted, and of whatever kind he wanted, must be clear to whoever considers the question."

About 1585 Shakespeare went from Stratford to London, and obtained some kind of employment in connection with a theatre, which led to his becoming, first, an actor, and then a writer of plays. His earliest original work as a dramatist, the comedy of "Love's Labor Lost," was produced on the stage in 1589, when Shakespeare was twenty-five years old. This was nearly at the middle point of his life; for he died in April, 1616, at just the completion of his fifty-second year. The greatest of his works, the tragedy of "Hamlet," was produced about 1601. His last play, "King Henry VIII." (of which he is believed to be the author only in part), was produced in 1612 or 1613.

THE ADVICE OF POLONIUS TO LAERTES.

(From "Hamlet," Act I., Scene 3.)

There, my blessing with you!
And these few precepts in thy memory:
See thou character. Give thy thoughts no tongue,
Nor any unproportion'd thought his act.
Be thou familiar, but by no means vulgar.
The friends thou hast, and their adoption tried,
Grapple them to thy soul with hoops of steel;
But do not dull thy palm with entertainment
Of each new-hatch'd, unfledg'd comrade. Beware
Of entrance to a quarrel: but being in,
Bear 't that the opposed may beware of thee.
Give every man thine ear, but few thy voice:
Take each man's censure, but reserve thy judgment.
Costly thy habit as thy purse can buy,
But not express'd in fancy; rich, not gaudy:
For the apparel oft proclaims the man;
And they in France of the best rank and station
Are most select and generous, chief in that.
Neither a borrower nor a lender be:
For loan oft loses both itself and friend;
And borrowing dulls the edge of husbandry.
This above all, — To thine ownself be true;
And it must follow, as the night the day,
Thou canst not then be false to any man.
Farewell; my blessing season this in thee!

SIR HENRY WOTTON

(A. D. 1568–1639.)

SIR HENRY WOTTON, one of the minor poets of the Elizabethan age in England, was busied during most of his life in diplomatic and other public employments, and had but stolen hours to give to literature. He was a man of fine accomplishments, and, having become reduced in fortune, was appointed provost of Eton College in 1625. He died in 1639, at the age of seventy-one. His life was written by his friend, Isaac Walton.

THE HAPPY LIFE.

(By Sir Henry Wotton.)

How happy is he born and taught
　　That serveth not another's will —
Whose armor is his honest thought,
　　And simple truth his utmost skill!

Whose passions not his masters are,
　　Whose soul is still prepared for death —
Untied unto the worldly care
　　Of public fame or private breath!

Who envies none that chance doth raise,
　　Or vice; who never understood
How deepest wounds are given by praise;
　　Nor rules of state, but rules of good;

Who hath his life from rumors freed,
　　Whose conscience is his strong retreat;

Whose state can neither flatterers feed,
　Nor ruin make oppressors great;

Who God doth late and early pray
　More of His grace than gifts to lend;
And entertains the harmless day
　With a religious book or friend.

This man is freed from servile bands
　Of hope to rise, or fear to fall —
Lord of himself, though not of lands;
　And, having nothing, yet hath all.

BALTHASAR GRACIAN

(A. D. 1584–1658.)

BALTHASAR GRACIAN, a Spanish Jesuit, was born at Cala-
tayud, Aragon, in 1584, and died at Tarragona in 1658.
He was widely known once as a writer of maxims; but has received little notice from the present generation. Schopenhauer
esteemed him highly, and a translation of some three hundred
of Gracian's aphorisms was found among his papers after his
death. In Schopenhauer's opinion, Gracian's book is unique.
"It teaches," he says, "the art which all would fain practise,
and is therefore a book for every one; but it is especially
fitted to be the manual of those who live in the great world,
and peculiarly of young people who wish to prosper in the
world. . . . It is a book for constant use as occasion serves
— in short, to be a companion for life."

In the "Fortnightly Review" for April, 1877, Sir Mount-
stuart E. Grant Duff drew attention to the neglected sayings
of Gracian, translating a considerable number of them. The
precepts in the selection given below are from this source.
Recently, Mr. Joseph Jacobs has published a more complete
translation.

SELECTIONS FROM THE MAXIMS OF BALTHASAR GRACIAN.

(From translations by Sir M. E. Grant Duff, in the "Fortnightly
Review," April, 1877.)

Leave off the game with fortune while you are in luck.
— That is what all the best players do. A fine retreat is
worth just as much as a gallant attack. Let a man bring
his deeds, when there are a great many and enough of
them, into safety. Felicity which lasts very long was ever
suspicious. . . .

Have friends. — It is the second existence. Every friend is good and wise for his friend, and among them all gets well managed. . . .

Live with those from whom you can learn. Let friendly intercourse be a school of knowledge, and conversation a teaching that may fashion the mind. — Make teachers of your friends, and let the profit of learning and the pleasure of conversation interpenetrate one another. . . .

Be common in nothing, above all not in taste. . . .

Never open the door to an evil, however small, for other and greater ones will creep in after it from their ambush. . . .

Think with the few, and speak with the many.

Overcome your antipathies.

Be able to wait. — . . . First be master of yourself if you would be master of others. Only through the spaces of time do we come to the centre of opportunity. . . . He spake a great word who said, Time and I against any two.

Work with good instruments. — Some are anxious that the keenness and subtlety of their wits should be conspicuous through the meanness of their instruments, — a perilous satisfaction which deserves a punishment from Fate. . . .

Understand the art of refusing. — . . . The No of some people is more esteemed than the Yes of others, for a gilded No satisfies more than a dry Yes. . . .

Do not be unsociable. — In the most populous places live the true wild beasts.

Choose a heroic ideal, but rather to emulate than to imitate.

Do not always be jesting. — . . . Many people win themselves a reputation for being witty fellows, at the cost of their credit for being sensible. . . .

Drain nothing to the dregs, neither good nor evil.

Have a stomach able to digest great mouthsful of fortune.

Don't be a bore. — The man of one occupation and one way of speaking is tiresome. Brevity is fascinating, and better suited for business. . . . What is well said is soon said.

Never speak of yourself. — Either you will praise yourself, which is vanity, or blame yourself, which is poverty of spirit.

Accustom yourselves to the faults in the dispositions of those with whom you live, as you do to ugly faces.

Do not make a business of what is no business. . . .

Be without affectation. — . . . Do not, however, out of fear of affectation, fall into it by affecting to be unaffected.

Do not, in trying to escape from the trite, become paradoxical.

Look into the inside of things. — They are usually very different from what they seem. . . .

Do not believe, and do not love, lightly.

Let your friends be the friends of your deliberate choice.

Know your pet faults. — . . . Even the most perfect man does not escape them, and lives with them either as a wife or as a mistress.

Know how to take your own part. — . . . In great dangers there is no better companion than a bold heart. . . .

Be an honourable opponent. — . . . Be able to boast that, if gallantry and generosity were lost out of the world, men might look for and find them in your breast.

Know how to choose well. — It is the most important thing in life. It needs good taste and a most accurate judgment, for neither study nor natural intelligence is enough. Without choice there is no perfection. . . .

Keep always something behind in store. — . . . Even in one's knowledge there should be a force in reserve.

Do not get into a contest with one who has nothing to lose.

Have something left to wish for, so as not to be unhappy from very happiness. — . . . If there is nothing to desire, there is everything to fear.

Do not turn one piece of stupidity into two. — It is very common in remedying one to commit four others.

Know how to divide your life prudently: not as chance would have it, but with foresight and choice. . . .

Know how to ask. — There are some people in dealing with whom nothing is so difficult, and some in dealing with whom nothing is so easy.

Do not belong wholly to yourself nor wholly to other people. . . .

Do not despise an evil because it is small; they never come alone, but are linked together just like happiness. . . .

Know how to do good to people a little at a time and often.

Be able to forget; it is more a piece of good fortune than an art.

Have no days of carelessness. — Destiny loves to play tricks, and will pile chance on chance to take us unawares.

In one word be a saint. — So is all said at once. Virtue is the common bond of all perfections, and the centre of all felicities.

FRANCIS QUARLES

(A. D. 1592-1644.)

FRANCIS QUARLES, religious poet and moralist, was born at Rumford, in the English county of Essex, in 1592, and died in 1644. He was educated at Cambridge, and studied law at Lincoln's Inn. For a time he filled the post of cup-bearer to Elizabeth, Queen of Bohemia (the unfortunate daughter of King James I., of England). Later, he was secretary to Archbishop Ussher, and afterwards chronologer to the city of London. He espoused the cause of Charles I., and was so harassed by the opposite party, who injured his property and plundered him of his books and rare manu-scripts, that his death was attributed to the affliction and ill-health caused by these disasters. The favorite works of Quarles, in his own day and since, were the "Divine Em-blems," published in 1635, and the "Enchiridion," which appeared in 1641. Mr. Sidney Lee, who writes of Quarles in the "Dictionary of National Biography," says: "In his own day he found very few admirers among persons of liter-ary cultivation, and critics of a later age treated his literary pretensions with contempt. Anthony à Wood sneered at him as ' an old puritanical poet, . . . the sometimes darling of our plebeian judgment.' Phillips, in his ' Theatrum Poeta-rum ' (1675), wrote that his verses ' have been ever, and still are, in wonderful veneration among the vulgar.' Pope, who criticised his ' Emblems ' in detail in a letter to Atter-bury, denounces the book in the ' Dunciad ' (bk. i., 11, 139–40) as one

> ' Where the pictures for the page atone,
> And Quarles is saved by beauties not his own.'

Horace Walpole wrote that ' Milton was forced to wait till the world had done admiring Quarles.' But Quarles is not quite so contemptible as his seventeenth-and-eighteenth-cen-tury critics assumed. Most of his verse is diffuse and dull;

he abounds in fantastic, tortuous, and irrational conceits, and he often sinks into ludicrous bathos; but there is no volume of his verse which is not illumined by occasional flashes of poetic fire. Charles Lamb was undecided whether to prefer him to Wither, and finally reached the conclusion that Quarles was the wittier writer, although Wither ' lays more hold of the heart' (' Letters,' ed. Ainger, i. 95). Pope deemed Wither a better poet but a less honest man. Quarles's most distinguished admirer of the present century was the American writer, H. D. Thoreau, who asserted, not unjustly, that ' he uses language sometimes as greatly as Shakespeare' (' Letters,' 1865)."

SELECTIONS FROM QUARLES'S "ENCHIRIDION."

If thou desire not to be too poore, desire not to be too rich: he is rich, not that possesses much, but he that covets no more: and he is poore, not that enjoyes little, but he that wants too much : the contented minde wants nothing which it hath not: the covetous mind wants not onely what it hath not, but likewise what it hath.

If thou hast any businesse of consequence in agitation, let thy care be reasonable, and seasonable : continuall standing bent weakens the bow: too hasty drawing breaks it. Put off thy cares with thy cloathes : so shall thy rest strengthen thy labour; and so shall thy labour sweeten thy rest.

With three sorts of men enter no serious friendship: the ingratefull man ; the multiloquious man ; the coward: the first cannot prize thy favours ; the second cannot keep thy counsell ; the third dare not vindicate thy honour.

If thou desire the time should not passe too fast, use not too much pastime : thy life in jollity blazes like a tapour in the wind : the blast of honour wastes it, the heat of pleasure melts it ; if thou labour in a painful calling, thou shalt be lesse sensible of the flux of time, and sweetlier satisfied at the time of death.

Reade not bookes alone, but men, and amongst them chiefly thy selfe : if thou find any thing questionable there, use the commentary of a severe friend, rather than the glosse of a sweetlipt flatterer : there is more profit in a distastefull truth, than deceitfull sweetnesse.

If thou desire to take the best advantage of thy selfe (especially in matters where the fancy is most imployed) keep temperate diet, use moderate exercise, observe seasonable and set houres for rest ; let the end of thy first sleep raise thee from thy repose : then hath thy body the best temper ; then hath thy soule the least incumberance.

If thou art rich, strive to command thy mony, lest she command thee : if thou know how to use her, she is thy servant : if not, thou art her slave.

So use prosperity, that adversity may not abuse thee : if in the one, security admits no feares ; in the other, despaire will afford no hopes : he that in prosperity can foretell a danger, can in adversity foresee deliverance.

Be not too greedy in desiring riches, nor too eager in seeking them : nor too covetous in keeping them ; nor too passionate in losing them.

In the commission of evill, feare no man so much as thy own selfe : another is but one witnesse against thee : thou art a thousand : another thou mayst avoid, but thy selfe thou canst not.

In thy apparell avoyd singularity, profusenesse and gaudinesse ; be not too early in the fashion ; nor too late : decency is the halfe way betweene affection and neglect : the body is the shell of the soule ; apparell is the huske of that shell ; the huske often tels you what the kirnell is.

Let thy recreation be manly, moderate, seasonable, lawfull ; if thy life be sedentary, more tending to the exercise of thy body ; if active, more to the refreshing of thy mind ; the use of recreation is to strengthen thy labour, and sweeten thy rest.

Bee not censorious, for thou know'st not whom thou judgest; it is a more dextrous errour to speak well of an evill man than ill of a good man.

Hath any wronged thee? be bravely reveng'd: sleight it, and the work's begun; forgive it, and 't is finisht: he is below himselfe that is not above an injury.

When thy hand hath done a good act, aske thy heart if it be well done: the matter of a good action is the deed done; the forme of a good action is the manner of the doing: in the first, another hath the comfort, and thou the glory; in the other, thou hast the comfort, and God the glory: that deed is ill done wherein God is no sharer.

Gaze not on beauty too much, lest it blast thee; nor too long, lest it blind thee; nor too near, lest it burne thee: if thou like it, it deceives thee; if thou love it, it disturbs thee: if thou lust after it, it destroyes thee; if vertue accompany it, it is the heart's paradise; if vice associate it, it is the soule's purgatory: it is the wise man's bonefire, and the foole's furnace.

If thou wouldst have a good servant, let thy servant find a wise master.

Use law and physicke only for necessity; they that use them otherwise, abuse themselves into weake bodies, and light purses: they are good remedies, bad businesses, and worse recreations.

Take no pleasure in the death of a creature; if it be harmlesse or uselesse, destroy it not: if usefull, or harmefull destroy it mercifully: he that mercifully made his creatures for thy sake, expects thy mercy upon them for his sake.

Give not thy tongue too great a liberty, lest it take thee prisoner: A word unspoken is, like the sword in thy scabberd, thine; if vented, thy sword is in another's hand: if thou desire to be held wise, be so wise as to hold thy tongue.

Seest thou good dayes? prepare for evill times: No summer but hath his winter. He never reaped comfort in adversity, that sowed it not in prosperity.

Demeane thy selfe more warily in thy study, than in the street. If thy publique actions have a hundred witnesses, thy private have a thousand. The multitude lookes but upon thy actions: thy conscience lookes into them.

Of all vices take heed of drunkennesse. Other vices make their owne way; this makes way for all vices.

If thou seest any thing in thy selfe, which may make thee proud, look a little further, and thou shalt find enough to humble thee.

If thou be ignorant, endeavour to get knowledge, lest thou be beaten with stripes: if thou hast attained knowledge, put it in practice, lest thou be beaten with many stripes.

So behave thy selfe in thy course of life, as at a banquet. Take what is offer'd with modest thankfulnesse: and expect what is not as yet offer'd with hopefull patience; let not thy rude appetite presse thee.

FRANCIS OSBORNE

(A. D. 1593–1658.)

FRANCIS OSBORNE, from whose "Advice to a Son" the following injunctions are selected, was an English gentleman of ancient family, born in the later years of the reign of Queen Elizabeth, who lived through the period of the Civil War, the Commonwealth, and the Protectorate, nearly until the Restoration, adopting the Parliamentary side, in opposition to his relatives. He was the author of a number of writings, among which the "Advice" received most attention. Throughout the eighteenth century it seems to have been a book that was considerably known and read. It is mentioned by Pepys, by Swift, and by Dr. Johnson. Boswell liked it; but Johnson dismissed it with a contemptuous fling. "Were a man to write so now," said the Doctor, "the boys would throw stones at him."

As late as 1826, we find Henry Crabb Robinson, in his "Diary," saying: "Read the first part of Osborne's 'Advice to his Son,' — a book Wordsworth gave to Monkhouse, and which, therefore, I supposed to be a favorite. But I found, on inquiry, that Wordsworth likes only detached remarks, for Osborne is a mere counsellor of selfish prudence and caution."

So recently as 1896, a new edition, "with an introduction and notes by his Honour, Judge Edward Abbott Parry," was published in London. Judge Parry speaks of the book with the affection of one who "has spent many hours in its company and got to love the good in it and ceased to be amazed at the evil, as though it were an old friend."

His fondness is not likely to be shared by many at the present day; for there are few kernels of wisdom or wit to be picked out of much chaff in it; while the tone and the style are equally uninspiring.

SELECTIONS FROM FRANCIS OSBORNE'S "ADVICE TO A SON."

A few books well studied, and thoroughly digested, nourish the understanding more than hundreds but gargled in the mouth. . . .

Follow not the tedious practice of such as seek Wisdom only in Learning. . . .

The way to elegancy of style is to employ your pen upon every errand; and the more trivial and dry it is, the more brains must be allowed for sauce. . . .

Wear your clothes neat, exceeding rather than coming short of others of like fortune. . . .

Never buy but with ready money; and be drawn rather to fix where you find things cheap and good, than for friendship or acquaintance. . . . If you get nothing else by going from one shop to another, you shall gain experience. . . .

Such as are betrayed by their easy nature, to be ordinary security for their friends, leave so little to themselves, as their liberty remains ever after arbitrary at the will of others. . . .

Honesty treats with the world upon such vast disadvantage, that a pen is often as useful to defend you as a sword, by making writing the witness of your contracts. . . .

Beware . . . of thinking yourself wiser or greater than you are. Pride brake the angels in Heaven, and spoils all heads we find cracked here. . . .

Shun pride and baseness, as tutors to contempt, the first of others, the latter of yourself. . . .

To whisper with another, in company of your betters, is uncivil, and the more eminent the person is, the greater suspicion it raiseth. . . .

When you speak to any (especially of quality) look them full in the face; other gestures bewraying want of breeding, confidence, or honesty. . . .

Impudence is no virtue, yet able to beggar them all; being for the most part in good plight when the rest starve. . . .

Beware what company you keep, since example prevails more than precept. . . .

Let your wit rather serve you for a buckler to defend yourself, by a handsome reply, than the sword to wound others. . . .

Be not the trumpet of your own charity, or vices; for by the one you disoblige the receiver as well as lose your reward; and by the other you alarm the censures of men.

RENÉ DESCARTES

(A. D. 1596-1649.)

RENÉ DESCARTES, the father of modern philosophy, was a native of Touraine, in France, born in 1596, of an ancient and excellent family. When eight years old, he was placed in the Jesuit college of La Fléche, in Anjou, where he remained for eight and a half years. The result of his studies was so to disgust him with the emptiness of the knowledge he had acquired that he refused to continue them. He remained two years at home, and was then sent by his father to Paris, where he plunged for a time into the gayeties and dissipations of the capital. But he soon tired of so unsatisfactory a life, and shut himself up for two years, concealed from all his friends, in a small Parisian house, where he devoted himself to mathematical studies and philosophical meditations. His retreat having been discovered at last, he was drawn from it, and put into the army. As the French were engaged at the time in no wars, he sought active service as a volunteer, first in Holland, under Prince Maurice of Nassau, against the Spaniards, and afterwards, at the beginning of the Thirty Years' War, in the army of the Emperor Ferdinand. While in Germany, during the winter of 1619-20, he was quartered in the town of Neuberg, on the Danube, and there, becoming absorbed again in meditations, he conceived the idea which he afterwards worked out in his famous philosophical "Method." It was based on four rules: 1. Never to receive anything as true which did not show itself to be clearly so. 2. To divide all difficulties into as many parcels as possible, for distinct examination. 3. To proceed orderly in thought, from the simplest matters to the more complicated. 4. To make such complete enumerations and general reviews as to be sure to omit nothing. At the same time, he framed for himself what he called a provisional set of maxims of life and conduct. These are given below.

Soon after his winter at Neuberg, Descartes quitted the army. He then travelled for a time, before settling himself again, as he did, for several years, in Paris. In 1629 he went to Holland and resided mostly in that country for twenty years. Invited to Stockholm in 1649, by Queen Christina of Sweden, he died there a few months later.

His "Discours de la Méthode," which gave a new direction to modern thought, was published in 1637, during his stay in Holland. It is on this that his fame principally rests, though he was author of other treatises, mathematical in the main.

PROVISIONAL RULES OF DESCARTES.

When one has resolved to rebuild his house from the foundation, it is not enough to knock the old structure down, collect stones and timber, call in an architect or make a plan for oneself: one must also, and indeed first, seek out some commodious lodging to dwell in till the new house is habitable. To this business I therefore forthwith addressed myself, and presently laid down my provisional system of conduct, which consisted of the following three or four maxims: —

First, I would conform to the laws and customs of my country, holding fast by the religion which by God's grace had been taught me in childhood, and in other matters regulating myself by the customs of those about me, giving the preference always to such as lie midway betwixt either extreme. . . .

My second maxim was, when I had once made up my mind, to go stoutly through with it. If you lose yourself in a wood, the best course is to take some one path and march in a straight line. If this does not carry you where you want to go to, it will at any rate sooner or later lead you out of the wood.

My third, to aim at conquering rather my desires than

my fortune ; reflecting that what I fail to attain after I have done my best must be regarded as simply impossible, and no more to be lamented over than that my body is not so hard as steel, or that I have not the convenience of wings.

Finally, for an occupation, without disputing the tastes of others, I myself will go on as before ; that is to say, I will employ my life in cultivating my reason, and advancing all I can in the knowledge of truth, using the method I have prescribed to myself.

SIR THOMAS BROWNE

(A. D. 1605–1682.)

THOMAS BROWNE, physician and author, was born in London, October 19, 1605. He received his education at Oxford, Montpellier, Padua, and Leyden. In 1637 he settled at Norwich, where he died, on his birthday, October 19, 1682. He had been knighted by King Charles II., eleven years before his death. His most famous work, "Religio Medici," was published in 1643. "Pseudodoxia Epidemica, or Inquiry into Vulgar Errors," appeared in 1646, and "Hydriotaphia, or Urn Burial," in 1658. His "Christian Morals" was not published until after his death. It is an expansion of a "Letter to a Friend" written previously, and was probably laid aside by the author for some careful revision. Neither his thought nor his style are represented at their best in it.

Mr. Saintsbury says of Sir Thomas Browne's writings: "The work of this country doctor is for personal savour, for strangeness, and for delight, one of the most notable things in English literature. . . . His manner is exactly proportioned to his matter; his exotic and unfamiliar vocabulary to the strangeness and novelty of his thoughts. He can never be really popular; but for the meditative reading of instructed persons he is perhaps the most delightful of English prosemen."

SELECTIONS FROM SIR THOMAS BROWNE'S "LETTER TO A FRIEND."

Tread softly and circumspectly in this funambulous track and narrow path of goodness; pursue virtue virtuously; be sober and temperate, not to preserve your body in a sufficiency to wanton ends, not to spare your purse, not to be free from the infamy of common transgressors that way, and thereby to balance or palliate obscurer and closer vices, nor simply to enjoy health, by all which you may leaven good actions, and render virtues disputable ; but, in one word, that you may truly serve God, which, every sickness will tell you, you cannot well do without health. . . . Sit not down in the popular seats and common level of virtues, but endeavour to make them heroical. Offer not only peace-offerings but holocausts unto God. To serve him singly to serve ourselves, were too partial a piece of piety, nor likely to place us in the highest mansions of glory.

He that is chaste and continent, not to impair his strength, or terrified by contagion, will hardly be heroically virtuous. . . .

Be charitable before wealth makes thee covetous, and lose not the glory of the mite. If riches increase, let thy mind hold pace with them ; and think it not enough to be liberal, but munificent. Though a cup of cold water from some hand may not be without its reward, yet stick not thou for wine and oil for the wounds of the distressed ; and treat the poor as our Saviour did the multitude, to the relics of some baskets.

Trust not to the omnipotency of gold, or say unto it, Thou art my confidence ; kiss not thy hand when thou beholdest that terrestrial sun, nor bore thy ear unto its servitude. A slave unto Mammon makes no servant unto God. Covetousness cracks the sinews of faith, numbs the apprehension of any thing above sense, and, only affected with the certainty of things present, makes a peradventure of things to come ; lives but unto one world, nor hopes but fears another ; makes our own death sweet unto others, bitter unto ourselves ; gives a dry funeral, scenical mourning, and no wet eyes at the grave.

If avarice be thy vice, yet make it not thy punishment; miserable men commiserate not themselves, bowelless unto themselves and merciless unto their own bowels. Let the fruition of things bless the possession of them, and take no satisfaction in dying but living rich. For since thy good works, not thy goods, will follow thee ; since riches are an appurtenance of life, and no dead man is rich; to famish in plenty, and live poorly to die rich, were a multiplying improvement in madness, and use upon use in folly.

Persons lightly dipped, not grained in generous honesty, are but pale in goodness, and faint-hued in sincerity; but be thou what thou virtuously art, and let not the ocean wash away thy tincture. . . . Since few or none prove eminently virtuous but from some advantageous foundations in their temper and natural inclinations, study thyself betimes, and early find what nature bids thee to be, or tells thee what thou mayest be. They who thus timely descend into themselves, cultivating the good seeds which nature hath set in them, and improving their prevalent inclinations to perfection, become not shrubs, but cedars in their generation; and to be in the form of the best of the bad, or the worst of the good, will be no satisfaction unto them.

Let not the law of thy country be the " non ultra " of thy honesty, nor think that always good enough which the law will make good. Narrow not the law of charity, equity, mercy ; join gospel righteousness with legal right ; be not a mere Gamaliel in the faith, but let the Sermon on the Mount be thy Targum unto the law of Sinai.

Make not the consequences of virtue the ends thereof ; be not beneficent for a name or cymbal of applause, nor exact and punctual in commerce for the advantages of trust and credit which attend the reputation of just and true dealing; for such rewards, though unsought for, plain virtue will bring with her, whom all men honour, though they pursue not. . . .

Owe not thy humility unto humiliation by adversity, but look humbly down in that state when others look upward upon thee. Be patient in the age of pride and days of will and impatiency, when men live but by intervals of reason, under the sovereignty of humour and passion, when it is in the power of every one to transform thee out of thyself, and put thee into the short madness. If you cannot imitate Job, yet come not short of Socrates and those patient Pagans, who tired the tongues of their enemies while they perceived they spat their malice at brazen walls and statues.

Let age, not envy, draw wrinkles on thy cheeks; be content to be envied, but envy not. Emulation may be plausible, and indignation allowable; but admit no treaty with that passion, which no circumstance can make good. . . .

Look humbly upon thy virtues, and though thou art rich in some, yet think thyself poor and naked without that crowning grace, which thinketh no evil, which envieth not, which beareth, believeth, hopeth, endureth all things. With these sure graces, while busy tongues are crying out for a drop of cold water, mutes may be in happiness, and sing the Trisagium in heaven.

Let not the sun in Capricorn go down upon thy wrath, but write thy wrongs in water; draw the curtain of night upon injuries; shut them up in the tower of oblivion, and let them be as though they had not been. Forgive thine enemies totally, and without any reserve of hope that, however, God will revenge thee.

Be substantially great in thyself, and more than thou appearest unto others; and let the world be deceived in thee, as they are in the lights of heaven. Hang early plummets upon the heels of pride, and let ambition have but an epicycle or narrow circuit in thee. Measure not thyself by thy morning shadow, but by the extent of thy grave : and reckon thyself above the earth by the line thou must be contented with under it. . . .

Give no quarter unto those vices which are of thine inward family, and having a root in thy temper, plead a right and property in thee. Examine well thy complexional inclinations. Raise early batteries against those strong-holds built upon the rock of nature, and make this a great part of the militia of thy life. . . .

If length of days be thy portion, make it not thy expectation. Reckon not upon long life, but live always beyond thy account. He that so often surviveth his expectation, lives many lives, and will hardly complain of the shortness of his days. Time past is gone like a shadow; make times to come present; conceive that near which may be far off; approximate thy last times by present apprehensions of them; live like a neighbour unto death, and think there is but little to come. And since there is something in us that must still live on, join both lives together; unite them in thy thoughts and actions, and live in one but for the other. He who thus ordereth the purposes of this life, will never be far from the next, and is in some manner already in it, by a happy conformity and close apprehension of it.

FROM "CHRISTIAN MORALS," BY SIR THOMAS BROWNE.

Comply with some humours, bear with others, but serve none. Civil complacency consists with decent honesty; flattery is a juggler, and no kin unto sincerity. But while thou maintainest the plain path, and scornest to flatter others, fall not into self-adulation, and become not thine own parasite. Be deaf unto thyself, and be not betrayed at home. Self-credulity, pride, and levity lead unto self-idolatry. . . .

Let not fortune, which hath no name in scripture, have any in thy divinity. Let providence, not chance, have the honour of thy acknowledgments, and be thy Œdipus in contingencies. Mark well the paths and winding ways thereof; but be not too wise in the construction, or sudden in the application. . . . Leave future occurrences to their uncertainties, think that which is present thy own; and, since 't is easier to foretel an eclipse than a foul day at some distance, look for little regular below. Attend with patience the uncertainty of things, and what lieth yet unexerted in the chaos of futurity. The uncertainty and ignorance of things to come, makes the world new unto us by unexpected emergencies. . . .

Though a contented mind enlargeth the dimension of little things; and unto some it is wealth enough not to be poor; and others are well content, if they be but rich enough to be honest, and to give every man his due: yet fall not into that obsolete affectation of bravery, to throw away thy money, and to reject all honours or honourable stations in this courtly and splendid world. Old generosity is superannuated, and such contempt of the world out of date. . . .

When thou lookest upon the imperfections of others, allow one eye for what is laudable in them, and the balance they have from some excellency, which may render them considerable. . . .

Since virtuous actions have their own trumpets, and, without any noise from thyself, will have their resound abroad; busy not thy best member in the encomium of thyself. Praise is a debt we owe unto the virtues of others, and due unto our own from all, whom malice hath not made mutes, or envy struck dumb.

THOMAS FULLER

(A. D. 1608–1661.)

THOMAS FULLER, born at Aldwinkle, Northamptonshire, in 1608, having entered Queen's College, Cambridge, at the early age of twelve years, became a popular preacher when he was twenty, and began very shortly to publish his writings. His "Holy and Profane State" appeared in 1642, and passed rapidly through four editions. It consists of two parts, the former presenting examples for imitation, and the latter their opposites. The "Holy State" contains rules for the religious guidance of the individual in every relation of life, as the husband, father, soldier, and divine. The few of these which bear on conduct in the simply moral view are quoted below.

SELECTIONS FROM "THE HOLY STATE."

Of Company. A desert is better than a debauched companion. For the wildness of the place is but uncheerful, whilst the wildness of bad persons is also infectious. Better therefore ride alone than have a thief's company. And such is a wicked man, who will rob thee of precious time, if he doth no more mischief. . . .

If thou beest cast into bad company, like Hercules, thou must sleep with thy club in thine hand, and stand on thy guard. I mean, if against thy will the tempest of an unexpected occasion drives thee amongst such rocks; then be thou like the river Dee in Merionethshire in Wales, which running through Pimble meer remains entire, and mingles not her streams with the waters of the lake. Though with them, be not of them; keep civil communion with them, but separate from their sins. And if against thy will thou fallest amongst wicked men, know to thy comfort thou art still in thy calling, and therefore in God's keeping, who, on thy prayers, will preserve thee.

The company he keeps is the comment, by help whereof men expound the most close and mystical man; understanding him for one of the same religion, life, and manners with his associates. And though perchance he be not such a one, 't is just he should be counted so for conversing with them. . . .

To affect always to be the best of the company, argues a base disposition. Gold always worn in the same purse with silver loses both of the color and weight; and so to converse always with inferiors degrades a man of his worth. . . .

It is excellent for one to have a library of scholars, especially if they be plain to be read. I mean of a communicative nature, whose discourses are as full as fluent, and their judgments as right as their tongues ready: such men's talk shall be thy lectures. . . .

Of Anger. Anger is one of the sinews of the soul: he that wants it hath a maimed mind, and with Jacob, sinew-shrunk in the hollow of his thigh, must needs halt. Nor is it good to converse with such as cannot be angry, and with the Caspian Sea, never ebb nor flow. This anger is either heavenly, when one is offended for God; or hellish, when offended with God and goodness; or earthly, in temporal matters: which earthly anger (whereof we treat) may also be hellish, if for no cause, no great cause, too hot, or too long.

Be not angry with any without a cause. If thou beest, thou must not only, as the proverb saith, be appeased without amends (having neither cost nor damage given thee), but, as our Saviour saith, "be in danger of the judgment."

Be not mortally angry with any for a venial fault. He will make a strange combustion in the state of his soul, who at the landing of every cock-boat sets the beacons on fire. To be angry for every toy debases the worth of thy anger; for he who will be angry for anything, will be angry for nothing.

Let not thy anger be so hot, but that the most torrid zone thereof may be habitable. Fright not people from thy presence with the terror of thy intolerable impatience. Some men, like a tiled house, are long before they take fire, but once on flame there is no coming near to quench them.

Take heed of doing irrevocable acts in thy passion; as the revealing of secrets, which makes thee a bankrupt for society ever after: neither do such things which once are done forever, so that no bemoaning can amend them. Samson's hair grew again, but not his eyes: time may restore some losses, others are never to be repaired. . . .

Of Recreation. Recreation is a second creation, when weariness hath almost annihilated one's spirits. It is the breathing of the soul, which otherwise would be stifled with continual business. We may trespass in them, if using such as are forbidden by the lawyer as against the statutes; physician, as against health; divine, as against conscience. Be well satisfied in thy conscience of the lawfulness of the recreation thou usest. . . .

Spill not the morning (the quintessence of the day) in recreations. For sleep itself is a recreation; add not therefore sauce to sauce; and he cannot properly have any title to be refreshed, who was not first faint. Pastime, like wine, is poison in the morning. It is then good husbandry to sow the head, which hath lain fallow all night, with some serious work. Chiefly, intrench not on the Lord's day, to use unlawful sports; this were to spare thine own flock, and to shear God's lamb.

Let thy recreations be ingenious, and bear proportion with thine age. If thou sayest with Paul, " When I was a child I did as a child," say also with him, " But when I was a man I put away childish things." Wear also the child's coat, if thou usest his sports. . . .

Refresh that part of thyself which is most wearied. If thy life be sedentary, exercise thy body; if stirring and active, recreate thy mind. But take heed of cozening thy mind, in setting it to do a double task under pretence of giving it a play-day, as in the labyrinth of chess, and other tedious and studious games. . . .

Choke not thy soul with immoderate pouring in the cordial of pleasures. The creation lasted but six days of the first week : profane they whose recreation lasts seven days every week.

LA ROCHEFOUCAULD

(A. D. 1613–1680.)

"ROCHEFOUCAULD," says Mr. Andrew Lang, in his "Letters on Literature," "was so clever that he was often duped, first by the general honest dulness of mankind, and then by his own acuteness. He thought he saw more than he did see, and he said even more than he thought he saw. If the true motive of all our actions is self-love, or vanity, no man is a better proof of the truth than the great maxim-maker. His self-love took the shape of a brilliancy that is sometimes false. He is tricked out in paste for diamonds, now and then, like a vain, provincial beauty at a ball. ' A clever man would frequently be much at a loss,' he says, ' in stupid company.' One has seen this embarrassment of a wit in a company of dullards. It is Rochefoucauld's own position in this world of men and women. We are all, in the mass, dullards compared with his cleverness, and so he fails to understand us, is much at a loss among us. ' People only praise others in hopes of being praised in turn,' he says. Mankind is not such a company of ' log-rollers ' as he avers. . . . The Duke is his own best critic after all, when he says: ' The greatest fault of a penetrating wit is going beyond the mark.' Beyond the mark he frequently goes." He might have said with equal truth that the greatest fault of a critical looker-on at life is falling short of the mark; and in that, too, he would have touched his own weaknesses. He watched the world too shrewdly, too narrowly, not with a large enough vision, for real truth-seeking. His place is not among the men of wisdom, but where Mr. Lang has put him, among the men of cleverness and wit.

He was of the old French nobility — Duke de la Rochefoucauld and Prince of Marcillac; born at Paris in 1613, and dying in 1680. His "Maxims" were first published in 1665; the earliest English translation of them in 1698.

Besides these apothegms, he published "Mémoires sur la Regence d'Anne d'Austriche."

SELECTIONS FROM A TRANSLATION OF THE "SENTENCES ET MAXIMES MORALES" OF THE DUKE DE LA ROCHEFOUCAULD.

The passions have an injustice and an interest of their own, which renders it dangerous to obey them, and we ought to mistrust them even when they appear most reasonable.

It requires greater virtues to support good than bad fortune.

We often make a parade of passions, even of the most criminal; but envy is a timid and shameful passion which we never dare to avow.

Jealousy is in some sort just and reasonable, since it only has for its object the preservation of a good which belongs, or which we fancy belongs, to ourselves, while envy, on the contrary, is a madness which cannot endure the good of others.

We have more power than will; and it is often by way of excuse to ourselves that we fancy things are impossible.

Those who bestow too much application on trifling things, become generally incapable of great ones.

Happiness lies in the taste, and not in things ; and it is from having what we desire that we are happy — not from having what others think desirable.

We are never so happy, or so unhappy, as we imagine.

Nothing ought so much to diminish the good opinion we have of ourselves as to see that we disapprove at one time what we approve at another.

Sincerity is an opening of the heart: we find it in very

few people; and that which we generally see is nothing but a subtle dissimulation to attract the confidence of others.

The pleasure of love is in loving. We are happier in the passion we feel than in that we excite.

It is more disgraceful to distrust one's friends than to be deceived by them.

Politeness of mind consists in the conception of honorable and delicate thoughts.

If we did not flatter ourselves, the flattery of others would be very harmless.

Avarice is more opposed to economy than liberality is.

Hope, deceitful as she is, serves at least to conduct us through life by an agreeable path.

It is better to employ our minds in supporting the misfortunes which actually happen, than in anticipating those which may happen to us.

He who thinks he can find in himself the means of doing without others is much mistaken; but he who thinks that others cannot do without him is still more mistaken.

A truly virtuous man is he who prides himself upon nothing.

Hypocrisy is the homage which vice renders to virtue.

Nothing is so contagious as example; and we never do any great good or evil which does not produce its like.

Flattery is a false coin, which only derives its currency from our vanity.

Magnanimity is well enough defined by its name; nevertheless, we may say that it is the good sense of pride, and the most noble way of earning praise.

In jealousy there is more self love than love.

Envy is more irreconcilable than hatred.

Little minds are too much hurt by little things. Great minds perceive them all, and are not touched by them.

Humility is the true proof of Christian virtues; without it we retain all our faults, and they are only hidden by pride, which conceals them from others, and often from ourselves.

We should often be ashamed of our best actions if the world could see all the motives which produced them.

We have few faults which are not more excusable than the means we take to conceal them.

The truest mark of being born with great qualities is being born without envy.

We should not judge of a man's merit by his good qualities, but by the use he can make of them.

Quarrels would not last long, if the fault was only on one side.

When we cannot find contentment in ourselves, it is useless to seek it elsewhere.

LORD HALIFAX

(A. D. 1630–1695.)

OF George Savile, first Marquis of Halifax, who held a distinguished place among the wiser and better Englishmen of the age of the Restoration and the Revolution, Macaulay has written in his "History of England:" "Among the statesmen of those times Halifax was, in genius, the first. His intellect was fertile, subtle, and capacious. His polished, luminous, and animated eloquence, set off by the silver tones of his voice, was the delight of the House of Lords. His conversation overflowed with thought, fancy, and wit. His political tracts well deserved to be studied for their literary merit, and fully entitled him to a place among English classics. . . . He always saw passing events, not in the point of view in which they commonly appear to one who bears a part in them, but in the point of view in which, after the lapse of many years, they appear to the philosophic historian. . . . His understanding was keen, skeptical, inexhaustibly fertile in distinctions and objections; his taste refined; his sense of the ludicrous exquisite; his temper placid and forgiving, but fastidious, and by no means prone either to malevolence or to enthusiastic admiration."

Recently, for the first time, the writings of Lord Halifax have been published in a collected form, edited with ability by Miss H. C. Foxcroft, who had written previously, in the "English Historical Review," of the need of an edition that would make them better known. In the article referred to, she describes the "Moral and Miscellaneous Maxims" as being "sagacious and brilliant, shrewd, incisive, forcible, flavoured with a cynicism which is never after all very bitter," and as embodying the comments of "a keen and not unkindly observer, whose experience had been scarcely calculated to induce a very exalted opinion of average human nature." Of the "Advice to a Daughter," from which some passages are quoted, she wrote: "Addison mentions it among the contents of Leonora's library, and we suspect that, till the close of the eighteenth century, it was the most popular manual for the benefit of young girls. It is certainly the most entertaining, since its pages are as remarkable for their wit and vivacity as for their strong good sense. His admonitions, though addressed to the sex in whose education external graces have ever played so prominent and so natural a part, show hardly a trace of the foppery — intellectual, social, and moral — to which the virile understanding of Lord Chesterfield so often stooped. Nor can they be reproached with the laxity which has been made a charge against the celebrated 'Letters.' Lord Halifax had lived upon terms of intimacy with the most respected women of his time — with Catharine of Braganza, with Rachel, Lady Russell, with 'Sacharissa,' Lady Sunderland — and his standard of womanly decorum was high to the verge of prudery."

SELECTIONS FROM LORD HALIFAX'S "MORAL THOUGHTS AND REFLECTIONS."

(From "Life and Works of Sir George Savile, Bart., First Marquis of Halifax," by H. C. Foxcroft.)

Popularity is a crime from the moment it is sought; it is only a virtue where men have it whether they will or no.

An honest man must lose so many occasions of getting, that the world will hardly allow him the character of an able one.

There is, however, more wit requisite to be an honest man than there is to be a knave.

There is no such thing as a venial sin against morality, no such thing as a small knavery; he that carries a small crime easily, will carry it on when it grows to be an ox. . . .

Mistaken kindness is little less dangerous than premeditated malice.

There is so much danger in talking, that a man strictly wise can hardly be called a sociable creature.

Hope is generally a wrong guide, though it is very good company by the way. . . .

There can be no entire disappointment to a wise man, because he maketh it a cause of succeeding another time. . . .

Where ill-nature is not predominant, anger will be short-breathed; it cannot hold out a long course. . . .

There is a dignity in good sense that is offended and defaced by anger.

The defending an ill thing is more criminal than the doing it, because it wanteth the excuse of its not being premeditated.

There is hardly any man so strict as not to vary a little from truth when he is to make an excuse.

Not telling all the truth is hiding it, and that is comforting or abetting a lie.

Malice is a greater magnifying glass than kindness.

Anger may have some excuse for being blind, but malice none; for malice hath time to look before it.

Malice may be sometimes out of breath, envy never. A man may make peace with hatred, but never with envy.

If men considered how many things there are that riches cannot buy, they would not be so fond of them. The things to be bought with money are such as least deserve the giving a price for them.

Great reading, without applying it, is like corn heaped that is not stirred; it groweth musty.

There must be a nice diet observed to keep friendship from falling sick; nay, there is more skill necessary to keep a friend than there is to reclaim an enemy.

Wise venturing is the most commendable part of human prudence. It is the upper story of prudence, whereas perpetual caution is a kind of underground wisdom that doth not care to see the light.

To desire what belongeth to another man is misprision of robbery.

A difficulty raiseth the spirits of a great man; he hath a mind to wrestle with it, and give it a fall. A man's mind must be very low, if the difficulty doth not make a part of his pleasure. The pride of compassing may more than compare with the pleasure of enjoying.

It is a piece of arrogance to dare to be drunk, because a man showeth himself without a veil.

Good manners is such a part of good sense that they cannot be divided; but that which a fool calleth good breeding is the most unmannerly thing in the world. Right good manners require so much sense that there is hardly any such thing in the world.

He that can be quite indifferent when he seeth another man injured, hath a lukewarm honesty that a wise man will not depend upon.

Half the truth is often as arrant a lie as can be made.

A man who is master of patience is master of everything else.

A man that doth not use his reason is a tame beast; a man that abuses it is a wild one.

Misspending a man's time is a kind of self-homicide; it is making life to be of no use.

PASSAGES FROM LORD HALIFAX'S "ADVICE TO A DAUGHTER."

(From "Life and Works of Sir George Savile, Bart., First Marquis of Halifax," by H. C. Foxcroft.)

I must tell you that no respect is lasting but that which is produced by our being in some degree useful to those that pay it; where that faileth, the homage and the reverence go along with it, and fly to others where something may be expected in exchange for them. And upon this principle the respects even of the children and the servants will not stay with one that doth not think them worth their care, and the old housekeeper shall make a better figure in the family than the lady with all her fine clothes, if she wilfully relinquish her title to the government; therefore take heed of carrying your good breeding to such a height as to be good for nothing, and to be proud of it. . . . No age ever erected altars to insignificant gods, they all had some quality applied to them to draw worship from mankind; this maketh it the more unreasonable for a lady to expect to be considered and at the same time resolve not to deserve it. Good looks alone will not do. . . .

You are to have as strict a guard upon yourself amongst your children as if you were amongst your enemies; they are apt to make wrong inferences, to take encouragement from half words, and misapply what you may say or do, so as either to lessen their duty or to extend their liberty farther than is convenient. Let them be more in awe of your kindness than of your power. . . .

Your servants are in the next place to be considered; and you must remember not to fall in the mistake of thinking, that because they receive wages, and are so much inferior to you, therefore they are below your care to know how to manage them. It would be as good reason for a master workman to despise the wheels of his engine because they are made of wood. These are the wheels of your family. . . . Besides, the inequality which is between you must not cause you to forget that Nature maketh no such distinction, but that servants may be looked upon as humble friends, and that returns of kindness and good usage are as much due to such of them as deserve it, as their service is due to us when we require it. A foolish haughtiness in the style of speaking, or in the manner of commanding them, is in itself very undecent. . . .

You are never to neglect the duty of the present hour, to do another thing which, though it may be better in itself, is not to be unseasonably preferred. . . .

I must not forget one of the greatest articles belonging to a family, which is the expense. It must not be such as by failing either in the time or measure of it may rather draw censure than gain applause. If it was well examined, there is more money given to be laughed at than for anything in the world, though the purchasers do not think so. . . . The art of laying out money wisely is not attained to without a great deal of thought. . . .

In your clothes avoid too much gaudiness; do not value yourself upon an embroidered gown; and remember that a reasonable word, or an obliging look, will gain you more respect than all your fine trappings. . . . Fix it in your thoughts, as an unchangeable maxim, that nothing is truly fine but what is fit. . . .

Remember that children and fools want every thing, because they want wit to distinguish; and, therefore, there is no stronger evidence of a crazy understanding than the making too large a catalogue of things necessary, when in truth there are so very few things that have a right to be placed in it. . . .

I must in a particular manner recommend to you a strict care in the choice of your friendships. . . . The violent intimacies, when once broken, of which they scarce ever fail, make such a noise; the bag of secrets untied, they fly about like birds let loose from a cage, and become the entertainment of the town. . . . Do not lay out your friendships too lavishly at first, since it will, like other things, be so much the sooner spent; neither let be of too quick a growth. . . .

Avoid being the first in fixing a hard censure; let it be confirmed by the general voice before you give in to it; neither are you then to give sentence like a magistrate, or as if you had a special authority to bestow a good or ill name at your discretion. . . .

You are to consider that the invisible thing called a *Good Name* is made up of the breath of numbers that speak well of you; so that if, by a disobliging word, you silence the meanest, the gale will be the less strong which is to bear up your esteem. . . .

I must with more than ordinary earnestness give you caution against vanity, it being the fault to which your sex seemeth to be the most inclined; and since affectation, for the most part, attendeth it, I do not know how to divide them. . . . The first may be called the root of self-love, the other the fruit; vanity is never at its full growth till it spreadeth into affectation, and then it is complete. . . . Vanity maketh a woman tainted with it so topful of herself that she spilleth it upon the company. . . .

After having said this against vanity, I do not intend to apply the same censure to pride well placed and rightly defined. It is an ambiguous word; one kind of it is as much a virtue as the other is a vice; but we are naturally so apt to choose the worst that it is become dangerous to commend the best side of it. . . . A pride that raiseth a little anger to be outdone in anything that is good will have so good an effect that it is very hard to allow it to be a fault. . . .

Diversions are the most properly to be applied to ease and relieve those who are oppressed by being too much employed ; those that are idle have no need of them, and yet they above all others give themselves up to them. To unbend our thoughts when they are too much stretched by our cares is not more natural than it is necessary, but to turn our whole life into a holiday is not only ridiculous but destroyeth pleasure instead of promoting it. The mind, like the body, is tired by being always in one posture ; too serious breaketh it, and too diverting looseneth it. It is variety that giveth the relish.

JOHN LOCKE

(A. D. 1632–1704.)

JOHN LOCKE, the English philosopher, born at Pensford, near Bristol, in 1632, was educated at Westminster school and at Christ Church, Oxford. After taking his degree he had a taste of diplomatic life, being appointed secretary to the ambassador to Germany. He was offered diplomatic service in Spain, but declined, and returned to Oxford, where he studied medicine.

While in Oxford, Locke formed the habit of writing down, for his own eye, such thoughts as occurred to him on subjects of special interest. In his old age he wrote to his friend Molyneux: "I have often had experience that a man cannot well judge of his own notions till either by setting them down in paper or in discoursing them to a friend, he has drawn them out and, as it were, spread them fairly before himself."

The following, under the head of "Thus I think," was probably written early, and illustrates Locke's theory of life. It is given by his first biographer, Lord King.

THUS I THINK.

(From the "Life of John Locke," edited by Lord King, vol. ii.)

It is a man's proper business to seek happiness and avoid misery.

Happiness consists in what delights and contents the mind; misery, in what disturbs, discomposes, or torments it.

I will therefore make it my business to seek satisfaction and delight, and avoid uneasiness and disquiet; to have as much of the one, and as little of the other, as may be.

But here I must have a care I mistake not; for if I prefer a short pleasure to a lasting one, it is plain I cross my own happiness.

Let me then see wherein consists the most lasting pleasures of this life; and that, as far as I can observe, is in these things:

1st. Health, — without which no sensual pleasure can have any relish.

2nd. Reputation, — for that I find every body is pleased with, and the want of it is a constant torment.

3rd. Knowledge, — for the little knowledge I have, I find I would not sell at any rate, nor part with for any other pleasure.

4th. Doing good, — for I find the well-cooked meat I eat to-day does now no more delight me, nay, I am diseased after a full meal. The perfumes I smelt yesterday now no more affect me with any pleasure; but the good turn I did yesterday, a year, seven years since, continues still to please and delight me as often as I reflect on it.

5th. The expectation of eternal and incomprehensible happiness in another world is that also which carries a constant pleasure with it.

If, then, I will faithfully pursue that happiness I propose to myself, whatever pleasure offers itself to me, I must carefully look that it cross not any of those five great and constant pleasures above mentioned. For example, the fruit I see tempts me with the taste of it that I love, but if it endanger my health, I part with a constant and lasting for a very short and transient pleasure, and so foolishly make myself unhappy, and am not true to my own interest.

Hunting, plays, and other innocent diversions delight

me : if I make use of them to refresh myself after study and business, they preserve my health, restore the vigour of my mind, and increase my pleasure ; but if I spend all, or the greatest part of my time in them, they hinder my improvement in knowledge and useful arts, they blast my credit, and give me up to the uneasy state of shame, ignorance, and contempt, in which I cannot but be very unhappy. Drinking, gaming, and vicious delights will do me this mischief, not. only by wasting my time, but by a positive efficacy endanger my health, impair my parts, imprint ill habits, lessen my esteem, and leave a constant lasting torment on my conscience ; therefore all vicious and unlawful pleasures I will always avoid, because such a mastery of my passions will afford me a constant pleasure greater than any such enjoyments ; and also deliver me from the certain evil of several kinds, that by indulging myself in a present temptation I shall certainly afterwards suffer.

All innocent diversions and delights as far as they will contribute to my health, and consist with my improvement, condition, and my other more solid pleasures of knowledge and reputation, I will enjoy, but no farther, and this I will carefully watch and examine, that I may not be deceived by the flattery of a present pleasure to lose a greater.

WILLIAM PENN

(A. D. 1644–1718.)

THE founder of Pennsylvania, William Penn, was the son of a British admiral, Sir William Penn, and was bred in the aristocratic circles of the English court. London was the place of his birth, which occurred on the 14th of October, 1644, in the midst of the Civil War. He reached manhood soon after the Restoration, with every prospect of a career that should be gilded by the sunshine of royal favor. But in 1668 he made what seemed to be a choice of worldly ruin, by embracing the religious doctrines of the despised and persecuted sect of Friends, or Quakers. The suffering which he shared with his fellows in the humble society of George Fox led Penn to interest himself in American colonization. He first became one of the proprietors of West Jersey, and assisted in establishing Quaker settlements in that province; but in 1681 he acquired in his own name a more princely domain. For payment of a debt due his father he procured from the king a proprietary grant of the great territory now covered by the State of Pennsylvania. Furthermore, the next year, he joined with other Friends in the purchase of the province of East Jersey from the trustees of Sir George Carteret. Not content with the title to Pennsylvania derived from the English king, Penn entered into personal treaty with the Indians and purchased their territorial rights. Twice during his lifetime, in 1682–84 and 1699–1701, he visited his province, remaining in all some four years. He died in England on the 30th of July, 1718.

In the "Life of Penn," which he prepared for the second series of the "Library of American Biography," Mr. George E. Ellis classes him with "the very few of the innocently great of the earth." "He pursued," says Mr. Ellis, "exalted aims, drawn from the most advanced attainments of the age in which he lived, and anticipating the light of an after time. Three great principles controlled his mind and cheered his heart; reverence for God, love for man, and confidence in freedom. . . . Penn excelled in the best of human qualities. He was free from vice. His natural powers were of a high order; his acquired advantages were large and various, embracing bodily strength, learning, wisdom, and discretion, as the furniture of his mind, with the richest and most attractive graces of the heart. As a writer he used few images, but employed a wide compass of language. He makes constant references to the Scriptures, but always quotes them in their natural sense, with no forced applications. . . . They who conceive of Penn as a sanctimonious and rigid zealot, with a stiffened countenance, a formal garb, and a frowning look cast upon the innocent pleasures and good things of life, would go wide of the truth. He was quite a gentleman in his dress and manner of life, in his furniture and equipage. He loved manly sports; he could hunt and angle. Dean Swift says, that he ' talked very agreeably and with great spirit.' "

Penn wrote clearly and eloquently, from a full mind and a full heart, and he wrote much, chiefly in the way of religious appeal and encouragement, or in explanation of the beliefs of the Society of Friends. But among his published writings there are two which come within the range of the gleanings made for this collection. One of these, first published in 1693, under the title of "Fruits of Solitude," gave great delight to Robert Louis Stevenson, when he came upon it a few years ago. At San Francisco, Stevenson had picked up a Philadelphia reprint of the little book, and some time afterwards he sent it to a friend, with this note written in it: "If ever in all my ' human conduct ' I have done a better thing to any fellow creature than handing on to you this sweet, dignified, and wholesome book, I know I shall hear of it on the last day. To write a book like this were impossible; at least one can hand it on — with a wrench — one to another. My wife cries out and my own heart misgives me, but still here it is. . . . Even the copy was dear to me, printed in the colony that Penn established, and carried in my pocket all about the San Francisco streets, read in street cars and ferry-boats, when I was sick unto death, and found in all times and places a peaceful and sweet companion." — "Letters of Stevenson," vol. i. p. 232.

Possibly the meditations first ripened epigrammatically in these "Fruits of Solitude" were simply reconsidered and broadened out in the "Advice to his Children," which Penn published in 1699. The same spirit, with something more of religious warmth in it, is carried to the latter, and the essence of the teaching is the same. It is a far finer and purer teaching of righteousness for its own sake than was at all common in the age to which William Penn belonged.

SELECTED "REFLECTIONS AND MAXIMS RELATING TO THE CONDUCT OF LIFE."

(From William Penn's "Fruits of Solitude.")

Lend not beyond thy ability, nor refuse to lend out of thy ability; especially when it will help others more than it can hurt thee.

Frugality is good, if liberality be joined with it. The first, is leaving off superfluous expenses; the last, bestowing them to the benefit of others that need. The first without the last, begins covetousness; the last without the first, begins prodigality: both together make an excellent temper.

Hospitality is good, if the poorer sort are the subjects of our bounty; else too near a superfluity.

Love labour: for if thou dost not want it for food, thou mayest for physic.

The receipts of cookery are swelled to a volume; but a good stomach excels them all; to which nothing contributes more, than industry and temperance.

"Let nothing be lost," said our Saviour: but that is lost that is misused.

Choose thy clothes by thine own eyes, not another's. If thou art clean and warm, it is sufficient; for more doth but rob the poor, and please the wanton.

Never marry but for love: but see that thou lovest what is lovely.

He that minds a body and not a soul, has not the better part of that relation; and will consequently want the noblest comfort of a married life.

Between a man and his wife, nothing ought to rule but love. Authority is for children and servants; yet not without sweetness.

Choose a friend as thou dost a wife, " till death separate you."

Be not easily acquainted : lest, finding reason to cool, thou makest an enemy, instead of a good neighbour.

Be reserved, but not sour; grave, but not formal; bold, but not rash; humble, but not servile; patient, not insensible; constant, not obstinate; cheerful, not light; rather sweet, than familiar; familiar, than intimate; and intimate with very few, and upon very good grounds.

If thou hast done an injury to another, rather own it, than defend it. One way thou gainest forgiveness; the other, thou doublest the wrong and reckoning.

If thou thinkest twice, before thou speakest once, thou wilt speak twice the better for it.

Better say nothing, than not to the purpose.

In all debates, let truth be thy aim ; not victory, or an unjust interest : and endeavour to gain, rather than to expose, thy antagonist.

Truth often suffers more by the heat of its defenders, than from the arguments of its opposers.

It is wise not to seek a secret ; and honest, not to reveal one.

Only trust thyself, and another shall not betray thee.

Openness has the mischief, though not the malice, of treachery.

It is not enough that a thing be right, if it be not fit to

be done. If not prudent, though just, it is not advisable. He that loses by getting, had better lose than get.

Knowledge is the treasure, but judgment the treasurer, of a wise man.

He that has more knowledge than judgment, is made for another man's use, more than his own.

Where judgment has wit to express it, there is the best orator.

If thou wouldst be obeyed, being a father, being a son, be obedient.

It were endless to dispute upon everything that is disputable.

Rarely promise. But, if lawful, constantly perform.

Be not fancifully jealous; for that is foolish: as, to be reasonably so, is wise.

If we would amend the world, we should mend ourselves; and teach our children to be, not what we are, but what they should be.

It is not how we leave our children, but what we leave them.

Patience and diligence, like faith, remove mountains.

Never give out while there is hope: but hope not beyond reason; for that shows more desire than judgment.

Do good with what thou hast, or it will do thee no good.

Seek not to be rich, but happy. The one lies in bags, the other in content; which wealth can never give.

If thou wouldst be happy, bring thy mind to thy condition, and have an indifferency for more than what is sufficient.

Have but little to do, and do it thyself: and do to others as thou wouldst have them do to thee: so, thou canst not fail of temporal felicity.

A man, like a watch, is to be valued for his goings.

He that prefers him upon other accounts, bows to an idol.

We should not be troubled for what we cannot help: but if it was our fault, let it be so no more. Amendment is repentance, if not reparation.

Virtue is not secure against envy. Men will lessen, what they will not imitate.

Dislike what deserves it, but never hate: for that is of the nature of malice.

Not to be provoked, is best: but if moved, never correct till the fume is spent: for every stroke our fury strikes, is sure to hit ourselves at last.

They that censure, should practice: or else, let them heave the first stone, and the last too.

Nothing needs a trick, but a trick; sincerity loathes one.

Passion is a sort of fever in the mind, which ever leaves weaker than it found us.

But being intermitting, to be sure it is curable with care.

Be not provoked by injuries, to commit them.

Tempt no man; lest thou fall for it.

Opportunities should never be lost, because they can hardly be regained.

Affect not to be seen, and men will less see thy weakness.

We have a call to do good, as often as we have the power and occasion.

Do what good thou canst unknown; and be not vain of what ought rather to be felt than seen.

SELECTIONS FROM THE ADVICE OF WILLIAM PENN TO HIS CHILDREN.

Fear God; show it in desire, refraining and doing; keep the inward watch, keep a clear soul and a light heart. Mind an inward sense upon doing any thing. When you read the Scripture, remark the notablest places, as your spirits are most touched and affected, in a common-place book, with that sense or opening which you receive; for they come not by study or in the will of man, no more than the Scripture did; and they may be lost by carelessness and over-growing thoughts, and businesses of this life; so in perusing any other good or profitable book, yet rather meditate than read much. For the spirit of a man knows the things of a man, and with that spirit, by observation of the tempers and actions of men you see in the world, and looking into your own spirits, and meditating thereupon, you will have a deep and strong judgment of men and things. For from what may be, what should be, and what is most probable or likely to be, you can hardly miss in your judgment of human affairs; and you have a better spirit than your own in reserve for a time of need, to pass the final judgment in important matters.

In conversation, mark well what others say or do, and hide your own mind, at least till last, and then open it as sparingly as the matter will let you. A just observance and reflection upon men and things give wisdom; those are the great books of learning seldom read. The laborious bee draws honey from every flower. Be always on your watch, but chiefly in company; then be sure to have your wits about you, and your armor on; speak last and little, but to the point; interrupt none; anticipate none. Read Prov. x. 8, 13. Be quick to hear, slow to speak

(Prov. xvii. 27).   It gives time to understand, and ripens an answer.   Affect not words, but matter, and chiefly to be pertinent and plain.   Truest eloquence is plainest, and brief speaking (I mean brevity and clearness to make yourselves easily understood by everybody, and in as few words as the matter will admit of) is the best.

Prefer the aged, the virtuous, and the knowing, and choose those that excel for your company and friendship, but despise not others.

Return no answer to anger, unless with much meekness, which often turns it away; but rarely make replies, less rejoinders, for that adds fuel to the fire. . . . Silence to passion, prejudice, and mockery, is the best answer, and often conquers what resistance inflames. . . .

Cast up your incomes and live on half — if you can, one-third — reserving the rest for casualties, charities, portions.

Be plain in clothes, furniture, and food, but clean, and then the coarser the better; the rest is folly and a snare. Therefore next to sin, avoid daintiness and choiceness about your persons and houses; for if it be not an evil in itself, it is a temptation to it, and may be accounted a nest for sin to brood in.

Be sure to draw your affairs into as narrow a compass as you can, and in method and proportion, time and other requisites proper for them.

Have very few acquaintances, and fewer intimates, but of the best in their kind.

Keep your own secrets, and do not covet others; but if trusted, never reveal them unless mischievous to somebody; nor then, before warning to the party to desist and repent.   Prov. xi. 13, xxv. 9, 10.

Trust no man with the main chance, and avoid to be trusted.

Make few resolutions, but keep them strictly.

Prefer elders and strangers on all occasions; be rather last than first in conveniency and respect, but first in all virtues. . . .

Above all, remember your Creator; remember yourselves and your families, when you have them, in the youthful time and forepart of your life; for good methods and habits obtained then will make you easy and happy the rest of your days. Every estate has its snare: Youth and middle age, pleasure and ambition; old age, avarice; remember, I tell you, that man is a slave where either prevails. Beware of the pernicious lusts of the eye, and the flesh, and the pride of life (1 John ii. 15, 16, 17), which are not of the Father, but of the world. Get higher and nobler objects for your immortal part, oh, my dear children! and be not tied to things without you; for then you can never have the true and free enjoyment of yourselves to better things; no more than a slave in Algiers has of his house or family in London. Be free; live at home — in yourselves, I mean — where lie greater treasures hid than in the Indies. The pomp, honor, and luxury of the world are the cheats, and the unthinking and inconsiderate are taken by them. But the retired man is upon higher ground, he sees and is aware of the trick, contemns the folly, and bemoans the deluded.

Choose God's trades before men's; Adam was a gardener, Cain a ploughman, and Abel a grazier or shepherd. These began with the world, and have least of snare, and most of use. When Cain became a murderer, as a witty man said, he turned a builder of cities, and quitted his husbandry. Mechanics, as handicrafts, are also commendable, but they are but a second brood, and younger brothers. . . .

Have but few books, but let them be well chosen and

well read, whether of religious or civil subjects. Shun fantastic opinions; measure both religion and learning by practice; reduce all to that, for that brings a real benefit to you; the rest is a thief and a snare. And indeed, reading many books is but a taking off the mind too much from meditation. Reading yourselves and nature, in the dealings and conduct of men, is the truest human wisdom. The spirit of a man knows the things of man, and more true knowledge comes by meditation and just reflection than by reading; for much reading is an oppression of the mind, and extinguishes the natural candle, which is the reason of so many senseless scholars in the world.

Do not that which you blame in another. Do not that to another which you would not that another should do to you; but above all, do not that in God's sight you would not man should see you do.

And that you may order all things profitably, divide your day: such a share of time for your retirement and worship of God; such a proportion for your business, in which remember to ply that first which is first to be done; so much time for yourselves, be it for study, walking, visit, etc.; in this, be first, and let your friends know it, and you will cut off many impertinences and interruptions, and save a treasure of time to yourselves, which people most unaccountably lavish away. And to be more exact (for much lies in this), keep a short journal of your time, though a day require but a line; many advantages flow from it. . . .

Avoid discontented persons, unless to inform or reprove them. Abhor detraction, the sin of fallen angels and the worst of fallen men.

Excuse faults in others, own them in yourselves, and forgive them against yourselves, as you would have your heavenly Father and Judge forgive you. Read Prov. xvii. 9, and Matt. vi. 14, 15. Christ returns and dwells upon that passage of his prayer above all the rest — forgiveness — the hardest lesson to man, that of all other creatures most needs it. . . .

Love silence, even in the mind; for thoughts are to that, as words to the body, troublesome; much speaking, as much thinking, spends; and in many thoughts, as well as words, there is sin. True silence is the rest of the mind, and is to the spirit what sleep is to the body, nourishment and refreshment. It is a great virtue; it covers folly, keeps secrets, avoids disputes, and prevents sin. See Job xiii. 5; Prov. x. 19, xii. 13, xiii. 3, xvii. 28, xviii. 6, 7.

The wisdom of nations lies in their Proverbs, which are brief and pithy; collect and learn them, they are notable measures and directions for human life; you have much in little; they save time in speaking, and upon occasion may be the fullest and safest answers.

Never meddle with other folks' business, and less with the public, unless called to the one by the parties concerned, in which move cautiously and uprightly, and required to the other by the Lord in a testimony for his name and truth, remembering that old, but most true and excellent proverb: *Bene qui latuit, bene vixit.* He lives happily that lives hiddenly or privately, for he lives quietly. It is a treasure to them that have it; study it, get it, keep it; too many miss it that might have it; the world knows not the value of it; it doubles man's life by giving him twice the time to himself that a large acquaintance or much business will allow him.

Have a care of resentment, or taking things amiss, a natural, ready, and most dangerous passion; but be apter to remit than resent, it is more Christian and wise. For as softness often conquers, where rough opposition fortifies, so resentment, seldom knowing any bounds, makes many times greater faults than it finds; for some people have out-resented their wrong so far that they made themselves faultier by it, by which they cancel the debt through a boundless passion, overthrow their interest and advantage, and become debtor to the offender.

Rejoice not at the calamity of any, though they be your enemies (Prov. xvii. 5; xxiv. 17).

Envy none; it is God that maketh rich and poor, great and small, high and low (Psalm xxxvii. 1; Prov. iii. 31; xxiii. 17; xxiv. 1; 1 Chron. xxii. 11, 12; Psalm cvii. 40, 41). . . .

Beware of jealousy, except it be godly, for it devours love and friendship; it breaks fellowship and destroys the peace of the mind. It is a groundless and evil surmise.

Be not too credulous. Read Prov. xiv. 15. Caution is a medium; I recommend it. . . .

Meddle not with government; seldom speak of it; let others say or do as they please, but read such books of law as relate to the office of a justice, a coroner, sheriff, and constable; also the "Doctor and Student"; some book of clerkship, and a treatise of wills, to enable you about your own private business only, or a poor neighbor's. For it is a charge I leave with you and yours, meddle not with the public, neither business nor money; but understand how to avoid it, and defend yourselves, upon occasion, against it. For much knowledge brings sorrow, and much doings more. Therefore know God, know yourselves; love home, know your own business and mind it, and you have more time and peace than your neighbors.

If you incline to marry, then marry your inclination rather than your interest; I mean what you love, rather than what is rich. But love for virtue, temper, education, and person, before wealth or quality, and be sure you are beloved again. In all which, be not hasty, but serious; lay it before the Lord, proceed in his fear, and be you well advised. And when married, according to the way of God's people, used among Friends, out of whom only choose, strictly keep covenant; avoid occasion of misunderstanding, allow for weaknesses, and variety of constitution and disposition, and take care of showing the least disgust or misunderstanding to others, especially your children. Never lie down with any displeasure in your minds, but avoid occasion of dispute and offence; overlook and cover failings. Seek the Lord for one another; wait upon him together, morning and evening, in his holy fear, which will renew and confirm your love and covenant; give way to nothing that would in the least violate it; use all means of true endearment, that you may recommend and please one another; remembering your relation and union is the figure of Christ to his church; therefore, let the authority of love only bear sway your whole life.

If God give you children, love them with wisdom, correct them with affection; never strike in passion, and suit the correction to their age as well as fault. Convince them of their error before you chastise them, and try them; if they show remorse before severity, never use that but in case of obstinacy or impenitency. Punish them more by their understandings than the rod, and show them the folly, shame, and undutifulness of their faults, rather with a grieved than an angry countenance, and you will sooner affect their natures, and with a nobler sense, than a servile and rude chastisement can produce. . . . There should be the greatest care imaginable, what impressions are given to children; that method which earliest awakens their understandings to love, duty, sobriety, just and honorable things, is to be preferred. Education is the stamp parents give their children; they pass for that they breed them. . . . The world is in nothing more wanting and reprovable, both in precept and example; they do with their children as with their souls — put them out at livery for so much a year. They will trust their estates or shops with none but themselves; but for their souls and posterity they have less solicitude. But do you rear your children yourselves; I mean as to their morals, and be their bishops and teachers in the principles of conversation. . . .

Be humble; it becomes a creature, a depending and borrowed being that lives not of itself, but breathes in another's air, with another's breath, and is accountable for every moment of time, and can call nothing its own, but is absolutely a tenant at will of the great Lord of heaven and earth. And of this excellent quality you cannot be wanting, if you dwell in the holy fear of the omnipresent and all-seeing God. . . .

From humility springs meekness. Of all the rare qualities of wisdom, learning, valor, etc., with which Moses was endued, he was dominated by his meekness: This gave the rest a lustre they must otherwise have wanted. The difference is not great between these excellent graces, yet the Scripture observes some. God will teach the humble his way, and guide the meek in judgment. It seems to be humility perfectly digested, and from a virtue become a nature. . . .

Patience is an effect of a meek spirit, and flows from it; it is a bearing and suffering disposition; not choleric or soon moved to wrath, or vindictive; but ready to hear and endure, too, rather than be swift and hasty in judgment or action. . . .

Show mercy whenever it is in your power; that is, forgive, pity, and help, for so it signifies. Mercy is one of the attributes of God (Gen. xix. 19; Exod. xx. 6; Psalm lxxxvi. 15; Jer. iii. 12). It is exalted in Scripture above all his works, and is a noble part of his image in man. God hath recommended it (Hos. xii. 6). Keep mercy and judgment, and wait on the Lord. God hath shown it to man, and made it his duty (Mic. vi. 8). . . .

Charity is a near neighbor to mercy. It is generally taken to consist in this, not to be censorious, and to relieve the poor. For the first, remember you must be judged (Matt. vii. 1). And for the last, remember you are but stewards. Judge not, therefore, lest you be judged. Be clear yourselves before you fling the stone. Get the beam out of your own eye; it is humbling doctrine, but safe. Judge, therefore, at your own peril; see it be righteous judgment, as you will answer it to the Great Judge. This part of charity also excludes whisperings, backbiting, tale-bearing, evil surmising, most pernicious follies and evils — of which beware. Read 1 Cor. xiii. For the other part of charity, relieving the poor, it is a debt you owe to God: You have all you have or may enjoy, with the rent-charge upon it. . . .

Liberality or bounty is a noble quality in man, entertained of few, yet praised of all; but the covetous dislike it, because it reproaches their sordidness. In this she differs from Charity, that she has sometimes other objects, and exceeds in proportion. For she will cast her eye on those that do not absolutely want, as well as those that do; and always outdoes necessities and services. She finds out virtue in a low degree, and exalts it. She eases their burden that labor hard to live. . . .

Justice or Righteousness is another attribute of God (Deut. xxxii. 4; Psalm ix. 7, 8; v. 8; Dan. ix. 7), of large extent in the life and duty of man. Be just, therefore, in all things, to all; to God as your Creator, render to him that which is his, your hearts. . . . Render also to Cæsar that which is his, lawful subjection; not for fear only, but conscience' sake. To parents a filial love and obedience. To one another, natural affection. To all people, in doing as you would be done by. Hurt no man's name or person. Covet no man's property in any sort. . . .

Integrity is a great and commendable virtue. A man of integrity is a true man, a bold man, and a steady man; he is to be trusted and relied upon. No bribes can corrupt him, no fear daunt him; his word is slow in coming, but sure. He shines brightest in the fire, and his friend hears of him most when he most needs him. His courage grows with danger, and conquers opposition by constancy. As he cannot be flattered or frighted into that he dislikes, so he hates flattery and temporizing in others. He runs with truth, and not with the times; with right, and not with might. His rule is straight; soon seen, but seldom followed. . . .

Gratitude or thankfulness is another virtue of great lustre, and so esteemed with God and all good men. It is an owning of benefits received to their honor and service that confer them. It is, indeed, a noble sort of justice, and might, in a sense, be referred as a branch to that head; with this difference, though, that since benefits exceed justice, the tie is greater to be grateful than to be just; and consequently there is something baser and more reproachful in ingratitude than injustice. . . .

Diligence is another virtue useful and laudable among men. It is a discreet and understanding application of one's self to business; and avoids the extremes of idleness and drudgery. It gives great advantages to men; it loses no time, it conquers difficulties, recovers disappointments, gives dispatch, supplies want of parts ; and is that to them which a pond is to a spring ; though it has no water of itself, it will keep what it gets, and is never dry. . . . It belongs to you throughout your whole man ; be no more sauntering in your minds than in your bodies. And if you would have the full benefit of this virtue, do not balk it by a confused mind. Shun diversions ; think only of the present business, till that be done. Be busy to purpose ; for a busy man and a man of business are two different things. Lay your matters right, and diligence succeeds them, else pains are lost. How laborious are some to no purpose ! Consider your end well ; suit your means to it, and then diligently employ them, and you arrive where you would be, with God's blessing. . . .

Frugality is a virtue, too, and not of little use in life ; the better way to be rich, for it has less toil and temptation. It is proverbial, a penny saved is a penny got. It has a significant moral ; for this way of getting is more in your own power, and less subject to hazard, as well as snares, free of envy, void of suits, and is beforehand with calamities. For many get that cannot keep, and for want of frugality spend what they get, and so come to want what they have spent. But have a care of the extreme. . . . As I would have you liberal but not prodigal, and diligent but not drudging, so I would have you frugal but not sordid. . . .

Temperance I most earnestly recommend to you throughout the whole course of your lives. It is numbered amongst the fruits of the spirit (Gal. v. 23), and is a great and requisite virtue. Properly and strictly speaking, it refers to diet, but, in general, may be considered as having relation to all the affections and practices of men. . . . Bound your desires, teach your will subjection, take Christ for your example as well as guide. It was he that led and taught a life and faith in Providence, and told his disciples the danger of the cares and pleasures of this world; they choked the seed of the kingdom, stifled and extinguished virtue in the soul, and rendered man barren of good fruit. His sermon upon the mount is one continued, divine authority in favor of an universal temperance.

FÉNELON

(A. D. 1651–1715.)

FRANÇOIS DE SALIGNAC DE LA MOTHE FÉNELON, one of
the saintliest and most liberal-minded of French divines, was
born on the 6th of August, 1651, at the Château de Fénelon,
in Dordogne, southwestern France. He received holy orders
about 1675; became preceptor of the sons of the Dauphin in
1689, was admitted to the French Academy in 1693, and
made Archbishop of Cambray in 1695. His most celebrated
work, "Les Aventures de Télémaque," was composed for his
royal pupils, but not published until 1699. In close friendship with Madame Guyon and in sympathy with her doctrines, he was denounced as a heretic by Bossuet, and compelled to recant. His purity of character was conspicuous
in the corrupted France of his day, and his personal influence
upon the better spirits of the time was very great. He died
at Cambray on the 7th of January, 1715.

"Seldom has a purer mind tabernacled in flesh. He pro-
fessed to believe in an infallible church; but he listened
habitually to the voice of God within him, and speaks of this
in language so strong as to have given the Quakers some plea
for ranking him among themselves. . . . His works have
the great charm of coming fresh from the soul. He wrote
from experience, and hence, though he often speaks a language which must seem almost a foreign one to men of the
world, yet he always speaks in a tone of reality. . . .
Fénelon saw far into the human heart and especially into the
lurkings of self-love. He looked with a piercing eye through
the disguises of sin. But he knew sin, not, as most men
do, by bitter experience of its power, so much as by his knowledge and experience of virtue. Deformity was revealed to
him by his refined perception and intense love of moral
beauty. The light which he carried with him into the dark
corners of the human heart, and by which he laid open its

most hidden guilt, was that of celestial goodness. Hence, though the severest of censors, he is the most pitying. Not a tone of asperity escapes him." — Dr. WILLIAM E. CHANNING, "Remarks on the Character and Writings of Fénelon" ("Works," v. i.).

FÉNELON'S "RULES FOR A CHRISTIAN LIFE."

(From "Letters to Men," No. xviii.)

I. Be stedfast in your religious exercises; that is, in reading, daily meditation, regular confession, and communion.

II. Let your meditation always be systematic, and suited to your needs, with a view to mental humility and the repression of bodily sensuality.

III. Let your reading have a practical bearing, and tend to the correction of your faults. Apply all you read to yourself.

IV. Be careful as to the society you frequent habitually, and be specially on your guard as to the women with whom you are intimate.

V. Avoid harsh judgments of others, and let the recollection of your own faults hinder you from fastidiousness and censoriousness.

VI. Accustom yourself to withhold judgment in all things on which you are not obliged to pronounce. The habit of judging hastily, especially in an adverse sense, fosters rash judgments, presumption, a harsh, malicious criticism, reliance on self, and contempt for the opinions of others, all of which are out of keeping with the interior life, in which gentleness and humility are needful.

VII. Shun the dissipation which sudden fancies always involve. Such an *engouement*, to begin with, is too engrossing: it absorbs and chokes the inner life; then something else takes its place, and life is spent in a succession of such fancies. When an *engouement* is in its first stage, let it cool down, and pray over it; then when somewhat abated, use it moderately, and so far as will not harm you.

VIII. Never seek to change your position out of anxiety, depression, a false shame, or the itching desire to be somebody (*de faire un personnage*). All the states of life which you have not tried have their thorns and snares and weariness, only you do not see them from without. "Sufficient unto the day is the evil thereof. To-morrow will take care for the things of itself." For to-day think only of to-day.

MASSILLON

(A. D. 1663–1742.)

JEAN BAPTISTE MASSILLON, one of the most eminent pulpit orators of France, was a native of Provence, born at Hyères, in 1663. Educated by the fathers of the Congregation of the Oratory, he entered that order in 1681, and was engaged for some years in teaching. His success as a lecturer drew him to the pulpit, where he acquired great fame. In 1717 he was made bishop of Clermont, and in 1719 he was elected a member of the Academy. He died at Clermont in 1742. The works left by him are mostly sermons, which are among the classics of French religious literature. The passages subjoined are from a volume of translated selections from Massillon's writings.

THE USE OF TIME.

(From Selections from the Works of Jean Baptiste Massillon.)

The cause of all the evils, which reign amongst men, is the improper use they make of time. Some pass their lives in supine indolence, useless to their country, their fellow citizens, and themselves; others, in a tumult of human affairs and occupations: the former seem to exist but for the enjoyment of an unworthy repose, and to divest themselves of that listlessness by their diversions, which accompanies them everywhere; the latter, as if here only to agitate themselves incessantly with cares, which will disengage them from themselves. It appears, that time is a common enemy, against which all men conspire; all their lives are but a deplorable attention to make away with it, and the happiest appear to be those who succeed the best, in whatever way they find the pleasantest, either in frivolous pleasures, or in serious occupations, that can beguile them of their days and moments. Time, that precious deposit, which the Lord has confided to us, thus becomes a wearisome burden; yet we fear being deprived of it, as the last evil that can happen to us. It is a treasure that we would retain eternally, and yet can hardly endure it on our hands.

We should look upon a man as deranged, who in succeeding to an immense inheritance, dissipated it carelessly, making no other use of it, either to raise himself from obscurity to places and dignities, or to secure himself against the reverses of fortune. Time is this precious treasure we have inherited from our births, which the Lord, in his gracious mercy, has left in our hands, to make the best use of. It is not to raise us to frivolous honours and human greatness, alas! all this passes, and is too vile to be the price of time, which is itself the price of eternity! It is to place us by Jesus Christ, in the highest heavens. . . .

There is not a day, an hour, a moment, which, put to profitable use, might not gain us heaven! We ought, therefore, to regret the loss of one day, a thousand times more acutely, than the loss of a great fortune; nevertheless, time, that ought to be so precious, encumbers us; our life is but a continual contrivance to lose it, and in spite of all our attempts to get rid of it, there is always some left we know not what to do with; we consider our time as of the least consequence upon earth. Our offices we reserve for our friends, our benefits, for our inferiors; our property, for our relations and children; our credit and favour, for ourselves; our praises, for those who appear worthy of them; but our time we give to all the world! we expose it, I may say, a prey to every man! they even gratify in relieving us from an incumbrance, we are seeking incessantly to get rid of. Thus, the gift of God, the most valuable blessing of his clemency, and the price of eternity, becomes the embarrassment and heaviest oppression of our lives.

DEAN SWIFT

(A. D. 1667–1745.)

SAYS Mr. Gosse, in his "History of Eighteenth Century [English] Literature:" "Jonathan Swift, ' the great Irish patriot,' had nothing Irish about him except the accident of being born in Dublin. His father was a Herefordshire man, and his mother was a Leicestershire woman. The elder Jonathan Swift was made steward to the Society of the King's Inns, Dublin, in 1666, and there died about a year afterwards. Some months later his widow bore him a post-humous son, the 30th of November, 1667, and this was the famous writer." Swift's mother was a relative of Sir William Temple, and found a patron for her son in that much esteemed gentleman. He entered the Church, but remained in Sir William's service and in his household during most of the time for ten years.

Swift's literary career may be said to have begun in 1696 or 1697, when the "Tale of a Tub," one of the most remarkable of his satires, and "The Battle of the Books," scarcely inferior to it, were written. "Gulliver's Travels," the most famous of his works, did not appear until 1726, though he had probably been engaged upon it for some years.

The great satirist was never distinguished for good manners; yet he wrote a treatise on that subject, in which the fundamental principles of politeness are pithily set forth. Some passages from it are subjoined.

DEAN SWIFT ON GOOD MANNERS.

Good manners is the art of making those people easy with whom we converse.

Whoever makes the fewest persons uneasy is the best bred in the company.

As the best law is founded upon reason, so are the best manners. And as some lawyers have introduced unreasonable things into common law, so likewise many teachers have introduced absurd things into common good manners.

Pride, ill nature, and want of sense, are the three great sources of ill manners; without some one of these defects, no man will behave himself ill for want of experience, or of what, in the language of fools, is called knowing the world.

I defy any one to assign an incident wherein reason will not direct us what to say or do in company, if we are not misled by pride or ill nature.

Therefore I insist that good sense is the principal foundation of good manners; but because the former is a gift which very few among mankind are possessed of, therefore all the civilized nations of the world have agreed upon fixing some rules upon common behaviour, best suited to their general customs or fancies, as a kind of artificial good sense, to supply the defects of reason. . . .

As the common forms of good manners were intended for regulating the conduct of those who have weak understandings; so they have been corrupted by the persons for whose use they were contrived. For these people have fallen into a needless and endless way of multiplying ceremonies, which have been extremely troublesome to those who practise them, and are insupportable to everybody else: insomuch that wise men are often more uneasy at the over-civility of these refiners, than they could possibly be in the conversation of peasants or mechanics.

There is a pedantry in manners, as in all arts and sciences: and sometimes in trades. Pedantry is properly the over-rating of any kind of knowledge we pretend to.

And if that kind of knowledge be a trifle in itself, the pedantry is the greater. . . .

A necessary part of good manners, is a punctual observance of time at our own dwellings, or those of others, or at third places; whether upon matter of civility, business, or diversion. . . . If you duly observe time for the service of another, it doubles the obligation; if upon your own account, it would be manifest folly, as well as ingratitude, to neglect it; if both are concerned, to make your equal or inferior attend on you to his own disadvantage, is pride and injustice.

Ignorance of forms cannot properly be styled ill manners; because forms are subject to frequent changes; and consequently, being not founded upon reason, are beneath a wise man's regard. Besides, they vary in every country; and after a short period of time, very frequently in the same. . . .

Among the many impertinencies that superficial young men bring with them from abroad, this bigotry of forms is one of the principal, and more predominant than the rest; who look upon them not only as if they were matters capable of admitting of choice, but even as points of importance; and are therefore zealous on all occasions to introduce and propagate the new forms and fashions they have brought back with them; so that, usually speaking, the worst bred person in company is a young traveller just returned from abroad.

ADDISON

(A. D. 1672–1719.)

JOSEPH ADDISON was born on the 1st of May, 1672. He was the eldest son of Lancelot Addison, at the time of his birth rector of Milston, near Amesbury, in Wiltshire, and afterwards Dean of Lichfield. He was in school at Amesbury, Salisbury, Lichfield, and finally at the Charter House, from which he passed into Queen's College, Oxford. He formed, however, a more permanent connection with Magdalen College, which elected him, in 1698, to a fellowship that he retained until 1711. The influence of Lord Halifax, whose acquaintance he made at an early period, had much to do with the shaping of his life, diverting him from the Church and devoting him to literature. The same potent influence procured for him a pension of £300 a year, in 1699, which placed him at his ease. He travelled on the continent for three years, from 1700 to 1703. In 1706 he entered public office, under the Whig ministry of the day, as under-secretary of state, and he continued in public employments during much of the remainder of his life, becoming secretary of state in 1717. In the previous year he had married the Countess of Warwick. He died at Holland House in 1719, at the early age of forty-seven.

The most important work of Addison was done in connection with "The Spectator," a daily periodical, purely literary in character, but with high moral aims, which Addison and Steele conducted jointly during most of the two years 1711 and 1712. It is with reference especially to his delightful essays in "The Spectator" that Macaulay speaks of Addison as "the great satirist who alone knew how to use ridicule without abusing it; who, without inflicting a wound, effected a great social reform, and who reconciled wit and virtue, after a long and disastrous separation, during which wit had been led astray by profligacy, and virtue by fanaticism." "To estimate Addison at his real value," says Mr. Courthorpe, one of his latest biographers, "we must regard him as the chief architect of Public Opinion in the eighteenth century. . . . The work of Addison consisted in building up a public opinion which, in spite of its durable solidity, seems, like the great Gothic cathedrals, to absorb into itself the individuality of the architect. A vigorous effort of thought is required to perceive how strong this individuality must have been. We have to reflect on the ease with which, even in these days, when the foundations of all authority are called in question, we form judgments on questions of morals, breeding, and taste, and then to dwell in imagination on the state of conflict in all matters religious, moral, and artistic, which prevailed in the period between the Restoration and the succession of the House of Hanover. To whom do we owe the comparative harmony we enjoy? Undoubtedly to the authors of 'The Spectator,' and first among these by universal consent to Addison."

METHODS FOR FILLING UP EMPTY SPACES OF LIFE.

(From "The Spectator," Nos. 93-94, June 16, 18, 1711.)

If we divide the life of most men into twenty parts, we shall find that at least nineteen of them are mere gaps and chasms, which are neither filled with pleasure nor business. I do not however include in this calculation the life of those men who are in a perpetual hurry of affairs, but of those only who are not always engaged in scenes of action; and I hope I shall not do an unacceptable piece of service to these persons, if I point out to them certain methods for the filling up their empty spaces of life. The methods I shall propose to them are as follow.

The first is the exercise of virtue, in the most general acceptation of the word. That particular scheme which comprehends the social virtues, may give employment to the most industrious temper, and find a man in business more than the most active station in life. To advise the ignorant, relieve the needy, comfort the afflicted, are duties that fall in our way almost every day of our lives. A man has frequent opportunities of mitigating the fierceness of a party; of doing justice to the character of a deserving man; of softening the envious, quieting the angry, and rectifying the prejudiced; which are all of them employments suited to a reasonable nature, and bring great satisfaction to the person who can busy himself in them with discretion.

There is another kind of virtue that may find employment for those retired hours in which we are altogether left to ourselves, and destitute of company and conversation; I mean that intercourse and communication which every reasonable creature ought to maintain with the great Author of his being. The man who lives under an habitual sense of the divine presence keeps up a perpetual cheerfulness of temper, and enjoys every moment the satisfaction of thinking himself in company with his dearest and best of friends. The time never lies heavy upon him; it is impossible for him to be alone. . . .

I have here only considered the necessity of a man's being virtuous, that he may have something to do; but if we consider further, that the exercise of virtue is not only an amusement for the time it lasts, but that its influence extends to those parts of our existence which lie beyond the grave, and that our whole eternity is to take its colour from those hours which we here employ in virtue or in vice, the argument redoubles upon us, for putting in practice this method of passing away our time.

When a man has but a little stock to improve, and has opportunities of turning it all to good account, what shall we think of him if he suffers nineteen parts of it to lie dead, and perhaps employs even the twentieth to his ruin or disadvantage? But because the mind cannot be always in its fervours, nor strained up to a pitch of virtue, it is necessary to find out proper employments for it in its relaxations.

The next method therefore that I would propose to fill up our time, should be useful and innocent diversions. I must confess I think it is below reasonable creatures to be altogether conversant in such diversions as are merely innocent, and have nothing else to recommend them, but that there is no hurt in them. Whether any kind of gaming has even thus much to say for itself, I shall not determine; but I think it very wonderful to see persons of the best sense passing away a dozen hours together in shuffling and dividing a pack of cards, with no other conversation but what is made up of a few game phrases, and no other ideas but those of black or red spots ranged together in different figures. Would not a man laugh to hear any one of this species complaining that life is short?

The stage might be made a perpetual source of the most noble and useful entertainments, were it under proper regulations.

But the mind never unbends itself so agreeably as in the conversation of a well-chosen friend. There is indeed no blessing of life that is in any way comparable to the enjoyment of a discreet and virtuous friend. It eases and unloads the mind, clears and improves the understanding, engenders thoughts and knowledge, animates virtue and good resolutions, soothes and allays the passions, and finds employment for most of the vacant hours of life.

Next to such an intimacy with a particular person, one would endeavour after a more general conversation with such as are able to entertain and improve those with whom they converse, which are qualifications that seldom go asunder.

There are many other useful amusements of life which one would endeavour to multiply, that one might on all occasions have recourse to something, rather than suffer the mind to lie idle, or run adrift with any passions that chance to rise in it.

A man that has a taste of music, painting, or architecture, is like one that has another sense, when compared with such as have no relish of those arts. The florist, the planter, the gardener, the husbandman, when they are only as accomplishments to the man of fortune, are great reliefs to a country life, and many ways useful to those who are possessed of them.

But of all the diversions of life, there is none so proper to fill up its empty spaces as the reading of useful and entertaining authors. . . .

The hours of a wise man are lengthened by his ideas, as those of a fool are by his passions. The time of the one is long, because he does not know what to do with it; so is that of the other, because he distinguishes every moment of it with useful or amusing thoughts; or, in other words, because the one is always wishing it away, and the other always enjoying it.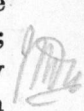

How different is the view of past life, in the man who is grown old in knowledge and wisdom, from that of him who is grown old in ignorance and folly! The latter is like the owner of a barren country, that fills his eye with the prospect of naked hills and plains, which produce nothing either profitable or ornamental; the other beholds a beautiful and spacious landscape divided into delightful gardens, green meadows, fruitful fields, and can scarce cast his eye on a single spot of his possessions, that is not covered with some beautiful plant or flower.

KING STANISLAUS OF POLAND

(A. D. 1677–1766.)

STANISLAUS LESZCZYNSKI, or Leszinski, son of a Grand Treasurer of Poland, was elected to the throne of that country, in 1705, through the influence of Charles XII. of Sweden, and lost his kingship four years later, after Charles's defeat at Pultowa. He was called again to the throne in 1733, and stepped down from it again in 1735, retaining the title, and being invested, in 1737, with the duchies of Lorraine and Bar. His daughter was married to Louis XV. of France, and he enjoyed the favor of the French court. He gained some distinction, too, as a man of letters in France, being, indeed, better fitted for a studious and literary life than for public affairs. A collection of his writings was published in 1765 — the year before his death — under the title of "Works of the Benevolent Philosopher." He is said to have realized quite consistently in his own character the ideal philosopher whose qualities are described in one of his works. "The true philosopher," he wrote, "is exempt from prejudices; he must know how to estimate the great conditions of life at no more than their worth, and its lower conditions at no less than they are. He must enjoy pleasures without being their slave, riches without being dependent on them, honors without pride and without display. He must be always the same, in every state of fortune; he must be always tranquil; he must love order, and put it into all that he does."

TRAITS OF MORAL COURAGE IN EVERY-DAY LIFE.

(By Stanislaus, King of Poland.)

Have the courage to discharge a debt, while you have the money in your pocket.

Have the courage to do without that which you do not need, however much you may admire it.

Have the courage to speak your mind when it is necessary that you should do so, and to hold your tongue when it is better that you should be silent.

Have the courage to speak to a friend in a "seedy" coat, even in the street, and when a rich one is nigh; the effort is less than many people take it to be, and the act is worthy a king.

Have the courage to set down every penny you spend, and add it up weekly.

Have the courage to pass your host's lackey at the door, without giving him a shilling, when you know you cannot afford it, and, what is more, that the man has not earned it.

Have the courage to own that you are poor, and you disarm poverty of its sharpest sting.

Have the courage to laugh at your personal defects, and the world will be deprived of that pleasure, by being reminded of their own.

Have the courage to admit that you have been in the wrong, and you will remove the fact from the mind of others, putting a desirable impression in the place of an unfavorable one.

Have the courage to adhere to a first resolution, when you cannot change it for a better, and to abandon it at the eleventh hour, upon conviction.

Have the courage to acknowledge your age to a day, and to compare it with the average life of man. Have the courage to make a will, and what is more, a just one.

Have the courage to face a difficulty, lest it kick you harder than you bargain for: difficulties, like thieves, often disappear at a glance.

Have the courage to avoid accommodation bills, however badly you want money; and to decline pecuniary assistance from your dearest friend.

Have the courage to shut your eyes at the prospect of large profits, and to be content with small ones.

Have the courage to tell a man why you will not lend him your money; he will respect you more than if you tell him you can't.

Have the courage to " cut " the most agreeable acquaintance you possess, when he convinces you that he lacks principle; " a friend should bear with a friend's infirmities " — not his vices.

Have the courage to show your preference for honesty, in whatever guise it appears; and your contempt for vice, surrounded by attractions.

Have the courage to give occasionally that which you can ill afford to spare; giving what you do not want nor value neither brings nor deserves thanks in return; who is grateful for a drink of water from another's overflowing well, however delicious the draught?

Have the courage to wear your old garments till you can pay for new ones.

Have the courage to obey your Maker, at the risk of being ridiculed by man.

Have the courage to wear thick boots in winter, and to insist upon your wife and daughter doing the like.

Have the courage to acknowledge ignorance of any kind; every body will immediately doubt you, and give you more credit than any false pretensions could secure.

Have the courage to prefer propriety to fashion — one is but the abuse of the other.

Have the courage to listen to your wife, when you should do so, and not to listen when you should not.

Have the courage to provide a frugal dinner for a friend whom you " delight to honor;" when you cannot afford wine, offer him porter; the importance of most things is that which we ourselves attach to them.

Have the courage to ask a visitor to excuse you when his presence interferes with your convenience.

Have the courage to throw your snuff-box into the fire or the melting-pot; to pass a tobacconist's shop; and to decline the use of a friend's box, or even one pinch.

Have the courage to be independent if you can, and act independently when you may.

CHESTERFIELD

(A. D. 1694–1773.)

PHILIP DORMER STANHOPE, fourth Earl of Chesterfield, celebrated in his day as an orator and a politician, but still more as a polished man of the eighteenth century English world, — its glass of fashion and its mould of form, — is made known to posterity mainly by the "Letters to his Son," which were published after his death. The son was a lout, with whose manners he was concerned, rather than with his morals, and these letters were written principally to that end. While showing a polite deference to some ethical principles, the immorality of the advice given in other directions is rank, even for the first half of the eighteenth century. But the fund of worldly wisdom in the "Letters" has rarely been excelled. Dr. Johnson thought that, with the immorality taken out, they ought to be put into the hands of every gentleman. On the other hand, the French critic, Taine, says of Chesterfield and his letters: "He wishes to polish his son, to give him a French air, to add to solid diplomatic knowledge and large views of ambition an engaging, lively, and frivolous manner. This outward polish, which at Paris is of the true color, is here but a shocking veneer. This transplanted politeness is a lie, this vivacity is senselessness, this worldly education seems fitted only to make actors and rogues."

Chesterfield was born in London in 1694, and died in 1773.

CHESTERFIELDIAN MAXIMS.

(From Lord Chesterfield's "Letters to his Son.")

If a fool knows a secret, he tells it because he is a fool; if a knave knows one, he tells it wherever it is his interest to tell it. But women, and young men, are very apt to tell what secrets they know, from the vanity of having been trusted. Trust none of these, whenever you can help it. . . .

In your friendships, and in your enmities, let your confidence and your hostilities have certain bounds: make not the former dangerous, nor the latter irreconcilable. There are strange vicissitudes in business!

Smooth your way to the head, through the heart. The way of reason is a good one; but it is commonly something longer, and perhaps not so sure. . . .

A man's own good breeding is his best security against other people's ill manners.

Good breeding carries along with it a dignity, that is respected by the most petulant. Ill breeding invites and authorizes the familiarity of the most timid. No man ever said a pert thing to the Duke of Marlborough. No man ever said a civil one (though many a flattering one) to Sir Robert Walpole. . . .

Knowledge may give weight, but accomplishments only give lustre; and many more people see than weigh.

Most arts require long study and application; but the most useful art of all, that of pleasing, requires only the desire. . . .

It is very difficult to fix the particular point of economy; the best error of the two is on the parsimonious side. That may be corrected, the other cannot. . . .

Take care always to form your establishment so much within your income, as to leave a sufficient fund for unexpected contingencies, and a prudent liberality. There is hardly a year, in any man's life, in which a small sum of ready money may not be employed to great advantage.

PRECEPTS SELECTED FROM "THE ECONOMY OF HUMAN LIFE."

(Attributed to Chesterfield.)

In 1750 there was published at London a little book entitled "The Economy of Human Life," containing a collection of maxims which purported to be "from an Indian manuscript, written by an ancient Brahmin." It excited no little interest, and the authorship of the work was attributed to Lord Chesterfield, without denial on his part. Not long after its publication, a spurious second part appeared, which the anonymous author of the original found it necessary to disown, by public advertisement. Altogether, the book made a good deal of stir, and successive editions of it have been published, nearly, if not quite, down to the present day. That Chesterfield was the author, does not seem to have been questioned until after the death of the publisher, Dodsley. It was then said that Dodsley wrote "The Economy of Human Life," and that Chesterfield permitted his name to be connected with it by rumor, in order to promote the sale, for Dodsley's benefit. There seems to be, however, no good reason for doubting that the book is really Chesterfield's. The question is discussed in volume ten of the First Series of "Notes and Queries," pages 8, 74, and 318.

The following is a selection from the precepts of the pseudo-"Brahmin."

The first step towards being wise, is to know that thou art ignorant; and if thou wouldst not be esteemed foolish in the judgment of others, cast off the folly of being wise in thine own conceit.

Since the days that are past are gone for ever, and those that are to come may not come to thee; it behoveth thee, O man! to employ the present time, without regretting the loss of that which is past, or too much depending on that which is to come.

Endeavour to be first in thy calling, whatever it be;

neither let any one go before you in well-doing; nevertheless, do not envy the merits of another, but improve thine own talents.

Of much speaking cometh repentance, but in silence is safety.

A talkative man is a nuisance to society; the ear is sick of his babbling, the torrent of his words overwhelmeth conversation.

Avarice is the parent of evil deeds; but frugality is the sure guardian of our virtues.

From the experience of others, do thou learn wisdom: and from their failings, correct thine own faults.

Trust no man until thou hast tried him; yet mistrust not without reason; it is uncharitable.

Use not to-day what to-morrow may want; neither leave that to hazard, which foresight may provide for, or care prevent.

The fool is not always unfortunate, nor the wise man always successful; yet never had a fool thorough enjoyment, never was a wise man wholly unhappy.

A noble spirit disdaineth the malice of fortune; his greatness of soul is not cast down.

If thou sufferest not the allurements of fortune to rob thee of justice, or temperance, or charity, or modesty, even riches themselves shall not make thee unhappy.

If thou believest a thing impossible, thy despondency shall make it so; but he that persevereth, shall overcome all difficulties.

Let not thy mirth be so extravagant as to intoxicate thy mind, nor thy sorrow so heavy as to depress thy heart.

Indulge not thyself in the passion of anger; it is whetting a sword to wound thine own breast or murder thy friend.

A fool is provoked with insolent speeches, but a wise man laugheth them to scorn.

Consider how few things are worthy of anger, and thou wilt wonder that any but fools should be in wrath.

He who pitieth another recommendeth himself.

Let not the rich . . . presume on his riches, nor the poor despond in his poverty; for the providence of God dispenseth happiness to them both, and the distribution thereof is more equally made than the fool can believe.

Thy food, thy clothing, thy convenience of habitation; thy protection from the injuries, thy enjoyments of the comforts and pleasures of life; all these thou owest to the assistance of others, and couldst not enjoy but in the bands of society.

It is thy duty therefore to be a friend to mankind, as it is thy interest that man should be friendly to thee.

JONATHAN EDWARDS

(A. D. 1703–1758.)

JONATHAN EDWARDS, the New England metaphysician and divine, was born on the 5th of October, 1703, at East Windsor, Conn., where his father ministered to the church. His mother was the daughter of a minister at Northampton, Mass. At thirteen years of age he entered Yale College; at seventeen he graduated. Four years later he became a tutor at Yale. In 1727 he was settled as pastor of the church at Northampton, where he married and remained until 1750. Differences then arose between the congregation and himself on the subject of admissions to the communion table, and he withdrew to become a missionary among the Indians. Shortly afterwards he produced his famous treatise on "The Freedom of the Will." In 1757 he was chosen President of Princeton College, in New Jersey, but enjoyed the congenial office no longer than a year. His death occurred on the 22d of March, 1758.

"He is not only the greatest of all the thinkers that America has produced, but also the highest speculative genius of the eighteenth century. . . . Take him all in all, in the beauty of his character, in the elevation of his thought, his claim to stand amid the great thinkers of the world is indisputable. In England here we have just [1896] been making welcome the new edition of Bishop Butler's works, — edited by the statesman who in his retirement shows his undiminished vigour and reveals his lifelong interest in theology, — and I have been comparing Butler's answer to Tindal with Edwards's, with the result that I am forced to confess that, while the rigour and vigour of inexorable logic and the strength which comes from a concentration due to the careful exclusion of all irrelevant matter are with Butler, the elevation, the insight, the oversight, the feeling of the magnitude of the problem, and the forecast of the lines along which the ultimate answer must move, are all with Edwards." — A. M. FAIRBAIRN, D. D., "Jonathan Edwards" ("Prophets of the Christian Faith"), ch. 9.

RESOLUTIONS OF JONATHAN EDWARDS.

(From Dwight's " Life of President Edwards.")

Being sensible that I am unable to do anything without God's help, I do humbly entreat him by his grace, to enable me to keep these Resolutions, so far as they are agreeable to his will, for Christ's sake.

Remember to read over these Resolutions once a week.

1. *Resolved*, That *I will do whatsoever* I think to be most to the glory of God and my own good, profit and pleasure, in the whole of my duration; without any consideration of the time, whether now, or never so many myriads of ages hence. Resolved to do, whatever I think to be my *duty*, and most for the good and advantage of mankind in general. Resolved, so to do, whatever *difficulties* I meet with, how many soever, and how great soever.

2. *Resolved*, To be continually endeavouring to find out some *new contrivance*, and invention, to promote the forementioned things.

3. *Resolved*, If ever I shall fall and grow dull, so as to neglect to keep any part of these Resolutions, to repent of all I can remember, when I come to myself again.

4. *Resolved*, Never *to do* any manner of thing, whether in soul or body, less or more, but what tends to the glory of God, nor *be*, nor *suffer* it, if I can possibly avoid it.

5. *Resolved*, Never to lose one moment of time, but to improve it in the most profitable way I possibly can.

6. *Resolved*, To live with all my might, while I do live.

7. *Resolved*, Never to do any thing, which I should be afraid to do, if it were the last hour of my life.

8. *Resolved*, To act, in all respects, both speaking and doing, as if nobody had been so vile as I, and as if I had committed the same sins, or had the same infirmities or failings as others ; and that I will let the knowledge of their failings promote nothing but shame in myself, and prove only an occasion of my confessing my own sins and misery to God. *Vid. July* 30.

9. *Resolved*, To think much, on all occasions, of my own dying, and of the common circumstances which attend death.

10. *Resolved*, When I feel pain, to think of the pains of Martyrdom, and of Hell.

11. *Resolved*, When I think of any Theorem in divinity to be solved, immediately to do what I can towards solving it, if circumstances do not hinder.

12. *Resolved*, If I take delight in it as a gratification of pride, or vanity, or on any such account, immediately to throw it by.

13. *Resolved*, To be endeavouring to find out fit objects of charity and liberality.

14. *Resolved*, Never to do any thing out of Revenge.

15. *Resolved*, Never to suffer the least motions of anger towards irrational beings.

16. *Resolved*, Never to speak evil of any one, so that it shall tend to his dishonour, more or less, upon no account except for some real good.

17. *Resolved*, That I will live so, as I shall wish I had done when I come to die.

18. *Resolved*, To live so, at all times, as I think is best in my most devout frames, and when I have the clearest notions of the things of the Gospel, and another world.

19. *Resolved*, Never to do any thing, which I should

be afraid to do, if I expected it would not be above an hour, before I should hear the last trump.

20. *Resolved*, To maintain the strictest temperance, in eating and drinking.

21. *Resolved*, Never to do any thing, which, if I should see in another, I should count a just occasion to despise him for, or to think any way the more meanly of him.

22. *Resolved*, To endeavour to obtain for myself as much happiness, in the other world, as I possibly can, with all the power, might, vigour, and vehemence, yea violence, I am capable of, or can bring myself to exert, in any way that can be thought of.

23. *Resolved*, Frequently to take some deliberate action, which seems most unlikely to be done, for the glory of God, and trace it back to the original intention, designs and ends of it ; and if I find it not to be for God's glory, to repute it as a breach of the fourth Resolution.

24. *Resolved*, Whenever I do any conspicuously evil action, to trace it back, till I come to the original cause ; and then, both carefully endeavour to do so no more, and to fight and pray with all my might against the original of it.

25. *Resolved*, To examine carefully and constantly, what that one thing in me is, which causes me in the least to doubt of the love of God ; and to direct all my forces against it.

26. *Resolved*, To cast away such things, as I find do abate my assurance.

27. *Resolved*, Never wilfully to omit any thing, except the omission be for the glory of God ; and frequently to examine my omissions.

28. *Resolved*, To study the Scriptures so steadily, constantly and frequently, as that I may find, and plainly perceive myself to grow in the knowledge of the same.

29. *Resolved*, Never to count that a prayer, nor to let that pass as a prayer, nor that as a petition of a prayer, which is so made, that I cannot hope that God will answer it; nor that as a confession, which I cannot hope God will accept.

30. *Resolved*, To strive, every week, to be brought higher in Religion, and to a higher exercise of grace, than I was the week before.

31. *Resolved*, Never to say any thing at all against any body, but when it is perfectly agreeable to the highest degree of christian honour, and of love to mankind, agreeable to the lowest humility, and sense of my own faults and failings, and agreeable to the Golden Rule; often, when I have said any thing against any one, to bring it to, and try it strictly by the test of this Resolution.

32. *Resolved*, To be strictly and firmly faithful to my trust, that that, in Prov. xx. 6, *A faithful man, who can find?* may not be partly fulfilled in me.

33. *Resolved*, To do, always, what I can towards making, maintaining and preserving peace, when it can be done without an over-balancing detriment in other respects. *Dec.* 26, 1722.

34. *Resolved*, In narrations, never to speak any thing but the pure and simple verity.

35. *Resolved*, Whenever I so much question whether I have done my duty, as that my quiet and calm is thereby disturbed, to set it down, and also how the question was resolved. *Dec.* 18, 1722.

36. *Resolved*, Never to speak evil of any, except I have some particular good call to it. *Dec.* 19, 1722.

37. *Resolved*, To enquire every night, as I am going to bed, Wherein I have been negligent, — What sin I have committed, — and wherein I have denied myself; — also,

at the end of every week, month and year.   *Dec.* 22 *and* 26, 1722.

38. *Resolved*, Never to utter any thing that is sportive, or matter of laughter, on a Lord's day.   *Sabbath evening, Dec.* 23, 1722.

. 39. *Resolved*, Never to do any thing, of which I so much question the lawfulness, as that I intend, at the same time, to consider and examine afterwards, whether it be lawful or not; unless I as much question the lawfulness of the omission.

40. *Resolved*, To enquire every night, before I go to bed, whether I have acted in the best way I possibly could, with respect to eating and drinking.   *Jan.* 7, 1723.

41. *Resolved*, To ask myself, at the end of every day, week, month and year, wherein I could possibly, in any respect, have done better.   *Jan.* 11, 1723.

42. *Resolved*, Frequently to renew the dedication of myself to God, which was made at my baptism, which I solemnly renewed, when I was received into the communion of the church, and which I have solemnly re-made this 12th day of January, 1723.

43. *Resolved*, Never, hence forward, till I die, to act as if I were any way my own, but entirely and altogether God's. . . . *Jan.* 12, 1723.

44. *Resolved*, That no other end but religion, shall have any influence at all on any of my actions ; and that no action shall be, in the least circumstance, any otherwise than the religious end will carry it.   *Jan.* 12, 1723.

45. *Resolved*, Never to allow any pleasure or grief, joy or sorrow, nor any affection at all, nor any degree of affection, nor any circumstance relating to it, but what helps Religion.   *Jan.* 12 *and* 13, 1723.

46. *Resolved*, Never to allow the least measure of any fretting or uneasiness at my father or mother.   *Resolved*,

To suffer no effects of it, so much as in the least alteration of speech, or motion of my eye ; and to be especially
careful of it with respect to any of our family.

47. *Resolved*, To endeavour, to my utmost, to deny
whatever is not most agreeable to a good and universally
sweet and benevolent, quiet, peaceable, contented and
easy, compassionate and generous, humble and meek, submissive and obliging, diligent and industrious, charitable
and even, patient, moderate, forgiving and sincere, temper ;
and to do at all times, what such a temper would lead me
to ; and to examine strictly, at the end of every week,
whether I have so done. *Sabbath morning, May* 5,
1723.

48. *Resolved*, Constantly, with the utmost niceness
and diligence, and the strictest scrutiny, to be looking
into the state of my soul that I may know whether I have
truly an interest in Christ or not ; that when I come to
die, I may not have any negligence respecting this, to repent of. *May* 26, 1723.

49. *Resolved*, That this never shall be, if I can
help it.

50. *Resolved*, That I will act so, as I think I shall
judge would have been best, and most prudent, when I
come into the future world. *July* 5, 1723.

51. *Resolved*, That I will act so, in every respect, as I
think I shall wish I had done, if I should at last be
damned. *July* 8, 1723.

52. I frequently hear persons in old age, say how they
would live, if they were to live their lives over again :
Resolved, That I will live just so, as I can think I shall
wish I had done, supposing I live to old age. *July* 8,
1723.

53. *Resolved*, To improve every opportunity, when I
am in the best and happiest frame of mind, to cast and

venture my soul on the Lord Jesus Christ, to trust and confide in him, and consecrate myself wholly to him; that from this I may have assurance of my safety, knowing that I confide in my Redeemer. *July* 8, 1723.

54. *Resolved,* Whenever I hear any thing spoken in commendation of any person, if I think it would be praiseworthy in me, that I will endeavour to imitate it. *July* 8, 1723.

55. *Resolved,* To endeavour, to my utmost, so to act, as I can think I should do, if I had already seen the happiness of Heaven, and Hell torments. *July* 8, 1723.

56. *Resolved,* Never to give over, nor in the least to slacken, my fight with my corruptions, however unsuccessful I may be.

57. *Resolved,* When I fear misfortunes and adversity, to examine whether I have done my duty, and resolve to do it, and let the event be just as Providence orders it. I will, as far as I can, be concerned about nothing but my duty, and my sin. *June* 9, *and July* 13, 1723.

58. *Resolved,* Not only to refrain from an air of dislike, fretfulness, and anger in conversation, but to exhibit an air of love, cheerfulness and benignity. *May* 27, *and July* 13, 1723.

59. *Resolved,* When I am most conscious of provocations to ill-nature and anger, that I will strive most to feel and act good-naturedly; yea, at such times, to manifest good-nature, though I think that in other respects it would be disadvantageous, and so as would be imprudent at other times. *May* 12, *July* 11, *and July* 13.

60. *Resolved,* Whenever my feelings begin to appear in the least out of order, when I am conscious of the least uneasiness within, or the least irregularity without, I will then subject myself to the strictest examination. *July* 4, *and* 13, 1723.

61. *Resolved*, That I will not give way to that listlessness which I find unbends and relaxes my mind from being fully and fixedly set on religion, whatever excuse I may have for it — that what my listlessness inclines me to do, is best to be done, etc. *May* 21, *and July* 13, 1723.

62. *Resolved*, Never to do any thing but my duty, and then according to Eph. vi. 6–8, to do it willingly and cheerfully, as unto the Lord, and not to man ; knowing that whatever good thing any man doth, the same shall he receive of the Lord. *June* 25, *and July* 13, 1723.

63. On the supposition, that there never was to be but one individual in the world, at any one time, who was properly a complete christian, in all respects of a right stamp, having christianity always shining in its true lustre, and appearing excellent and lovely, from whatever part and under whatever character viewed: *Resolved*, To act just as I would do, if I strove with all my might to be that one, who should live in my time. *Jan.* 14, *and July* 13, 1723.

64. *Resolved*, When I find those ' *groanings which cannot be uttered*,' of which the Apostle speaks, and those ' *breakings of soul* for the longing it hath,' of which the Psalmist speaks, Psalm cxix. 20, That I will promote them to the utmost of my power, and that I will not be weary of earnestly endeavouring to vent my desires, nor of the repetitions of such earnestness. *July* 23, *and Aug.* 10, 1723.

65. *Resolved*, Very much to exercise myself in this, all my life long, viz. With the greatest openness, of which I am capable, to declare my ways to God, and lay open my soul to him, all my sins, temptations, difficulties, sorrows, fears, hopes, desires, and every thing, and every circumstance, according to Dr. Manton's Sermon on the 119th Psalm. *July* 26, *and Aug.* 10, 1723.

66. *Resolved*, That I will endeavour always to keep a benign aspect, and air of acting and speaking in all places, and in all companies, except it should so happen that duty requires otherwise.

67. *Resolved*, After afflictions, to enquire, what I am the better for them; What good I have got by them; and, What I might have got by them.

68. *Resolved*, To confess frankly to myself all that which I find in myself, either infirmity or sin; and, if it be what concerns religion, also to confess the whole case to God, and implore needed help. *July* 23, *and Aug.* 10, 1723.

69. *Resolved*, Always to do that, which I shall wish I had done when I see others do it. *Aug.* 11, 1723.

70. Let there be something of benevolence, in all that I speak. *Aug.* 17, 1723.

BENJAMIN FRANKLIN

(A. D. 1706–1790.)

"HE was born in Boston, on the 17th of January, 1706. Thence he ran away in the autumn of 1723, and in October found himself a new home in Philadelphia, where he made his first meal in the street one Sunday morning from a draught of Delaware River water and a pennyworth of bread, giving twopence worth to a poor woman. Such was his first breakfast and his earliest charity in his adopted state. Here he worked as a journeyman printer. Deceived by Keith, the Governor of Pennsylvania, he went to England, landing there the 24th of December, 1724. He followed his trade in London for about two years. He returned to Philadelphia on the 11th of October, 1726, and resumed his business as printer, entering also into politics; or, rather, I should say, he became a statesman, for he was never a politician, but a statesman from the beginning, who never solicited an office, nor used any indirection to retain one when it was in his possession. As agent for Pennsylvania, he again went to England in October, 1757, and returned to Philadelphia in November, 1762. But he went back to England in December, 1764, as agent for several colonies, and returned thence, 5th of May, 1775. He was sent as minister to France by the revolted colonies in 1776, whence, on September 14, 1785, he returned to Philadelphia, which he never left again. He was President, or what we should now call Governor, of Pennsylvania, from October, 1785, to October, 1788, and was also a member of the Federal Convention, which made the Constitution of the United States. He died on the 17th April, 1790, aged eighty-four years and three months, and his body lies buried at Philadelphia, in the corner of the churchyard, close to the Quaker meeting-house. . . . He had an intellect of a very high order, — inventive, capacious, many-sided, retentive. His life covers nearly the whole of the eighteenth century. Ten years he was the contemporary of Leibnitz, twenty-one of Sir Isaac Newton. He was sixty-three years old when Alexander Humboldt and Cuvier were born. He embraced Voltaire. His orbit was intersected by that of Berkeley, Montesquieu, Hume, Kant, Priestley, Adam Smith. But in the eighty-four years to which his life extended, I find no mind which, on the whole, seems so great. I mean so generally able, various, original, and strong. Others were quite superior to him in specialties of intellect, — metaphysical, mathematical, and poetical. Many surpassed him in wide learning, of literature, or science, and in careful and exact culture; but none equalled him in general largeness of power, and great variety and strength of mind. In an age of encyclopædias, his was the most encyclopædic head in all Christendom. In the century of revolution, his was the most revolutionary and constructive intellect. He had no nonsense, was never eccentric." — THEODORE PARKER in "Historic Americans."

FRANKLIN'S PLAN FOR ACQUIRING HABITS OF VIRTUE.

(From his Autobiography.)

It was about this time [1730] I conceiv'd the bold and arduous project of arriving at moral perfection. I wish'd to live without committing any fault at any time; I would conquer all that either natural inclination, custom, or company might lead me into. As I knew, or thought I knew, what was right and wrong, I did not see why I might not always do the one and avoid the other. But I soon found I had undertaken a task of more difficulty than I had imagined. While my care was employ'd in guarding against one fault, I was often surprised by another; habit took the advantage of inattention; inclination was sometimes too strong for reason. I concluded, at length, that the mere speculative conviction that it was our interest to be completely virtuous, was not sufficient to prevent our slipping; and that the contrary habits must be broken, and good ones acquired and established, before we can have any dependence on a steady, uniform rectitude of conduct. For this purpose I therefore contrived the following method.

In the various enumerations of the moral virtues I had met with in my reading, I found the catalogue more or less numerous, as different writers included more or fewer ideas under the same name. Temperance, for example, was by some confined to eating and drinking, while by others it was extended to mean the moderating every other pleasure, appetite, inclination, or passion, bodily or mental, even to our avarice and ambition. I propos'd to myself, for the sake of clearness, to use rather more names, with fewer ideas annex'd to each, than a few names with more ideas; and I included under thirteen names of virtues all that at that time occurr'd to me as necessary or desirable, and annexed to each a short precept, which fully express'd the extent I gave to its meaning.

These names of virtues, with their precepts were:

1. TEMPERANCE.

Eat not to dulness; drink not to elevation.

2. SILENCE.

Speak not but what may benefit others or yourself; avoid trifling conversation.

3. ORDER.

Let all your things have their places; let each part of your business have its time.

4. RESOLUTION.

Resolve to perform what you ought; perform without fail what you resolve.

5. FRUGALITY.

Make no expense but to do good to others or yourself; *i. e.* waste nothing.

6. INDUSTRY.

Lose no time; be always employed in something useful; cut off all unnecessary actions.

7. SINCERITY.

Use no hurtful deceit; think innocently and justly; and, if you speak, speak accordingly.

8. JUSTICE.

Wrong none by doing injuries, or omitting the benefits that are your duty.

9. MODERATION.

Avoid extreams; forbear resenting injuries so much as you think they deserve.

10. CLEANLINESS.

Tolerate no uncleanliness in body, cloaths, or habitation.

11. TRANQUILLITY.

Be not disturbed at trifles, or at accidents common or unavoidable.

12. CHASTITY.

Rarely use venery but for health or offspring, never to dulness, weakness, or the injury of your own or another's peace or reputation.

13. HUMILITY.

Imitate Jesus and Socrates.

My intention being to acquire the *habitude* of all these virtues, I judg'd it would be well not to distract my attention by attempting the whole at once, but to fix it on one of them at a time; and, when I should be master of that, then to proceed to another, and so on, till I should have gone thro' the thirteen; and, as the previous acquisition of some might facilitate the acquisition of certain others, I arrang'd them with that view, as they stand above. Temperance first, as it tends to procure that coolness and clearness of head, which is so necessary where constant vigilance was to be kept up, and guard maintained against the unremitting attraction of ancient habits, and the force of perpetual temptations. This being acquir'd and establish'd, Silence would be more easy; and my desire being to gain knowledge at the same time that I improv'd in virtue, and considering that in conversation it was obtain'd rather by the use of the ears than of the tongue, and therefore wishing to break a habit I was getting into of prattling, punning, and joking, which only made me acceptable to trifling company, I gave Silence the second place. This and the next, Order, I expected would allow me more time for attending to my project and my studies. Resolution, once become habitual, would keep me firm in my endeavors to obtain all the subsequent virtues; Frugality and Industry freeing me from my remaining debt, and producing affluence and independence, would make more easy the practice of Sincerity and Justice, etc., etc. Conceiving then, that agreeably to the advice of Pythagoras in his Golden Verses, daily examination would be necessary, I contrived the following method for conducting that examination. I made a little book, in which I allotted a page for each of the virtues. I rul'd each page with red ink, so as to have seven columns, one for each day of the week, marking each column with a letter for the day. I cross'd these columns with thirteen red lines, marking the beginning of each line with the first letter of one of the virtues, on which line, and in its proper column, I might mark, by a little black spot, every fault I found upon examination to have been committed respecting that virtue upon that day.

TEMPERANCE.

EAT NOT TO DULNESS.
DRINK NOT TO ELEVATION.

	S.	M.	T.	W.	T.	F.	S.
T.							
S.	*	*		*		*	
O.	**	*	*		*	*	*
R.			*			*	
F.		*			*		
I.			*				
S.							
J.							
M.							
C.							
T.							
C.							
H.							

I determined to give a week's strict attention to each of the virtues successively. Thus, in the first week, my great guard was to avoid every the least offence against Temperance, leaving the other virtues to their ordinary chance, only marking every evening the faults of the day. Thus, if in the first week I could keep my first line, marked T, clear of spots, I suppos'd the habit of that virtue so much strengthen'd, and its opposite weaken'd, that I might venture extending my attention to include the next, and for the following week keep both lines clear of spots. Proceeding thus to the last, I could go thro' a course compleat in thirteen weeks, and four courses in a year. And like him who, having a garden to weed, does not attempt to eradicate all the bad herbs at once, which would exceed his reach and his strength, but works on one of the beds at a time, and, having accomplish'd the first, proceeds to a second, so I should have, I hoped, the encouraging pleasure of seeing on my pages the progress I made in virtue, by clearing successively my lines of their spots, till in the end, by a number of courses, I should be happy in viewing a clean book, after a thirteen weeks' daily examination.

This my little book had for its motto these lines from Addison's *Cato*:

> "Here will I hold. If there's a power above us
> (And that there is, all nature cries aloud
> Thro' all her works), He must delight in virtue;
> And that which he delights in must be happy."

Another from Cicero,

"O vitæ Philosophia dux! O virtutum indagatrix expultrix-que vitiorum! Unus dies, bene et ex præceptis tuis actus, peccanti immortaliti est anteponendus."

Another from the Proverbs of Solomon, speaking of wisdom or virtue:

" Length of days is in her right hand, and in her left hand riches and honour. Her ways are ways of pleasantness, and all her paths are peace." iii. 16, 17.

And conceiving God to be the fountain of wisdom, I thought it right and necessary to solicit his assistance for obtaining it; to this end I formed the following little prayer, which was prefix'd to my tables of examination, for daily use.

" *O powerful Goodness! bountiful Father! merciful Guide! Increase in me that wisdom which discovers my truest interest. Strengthen my resolutions to perform what that wisdom dictates. Accept my kind offices to thy other children as the only return in my power for thy continual favours to me.*"

I used also sometimes a little prayer which I took from Thomson's Poems, viz. :

> " Father of light and life, thou Good Supreme !
> O teach me what is good ; teach me Thyself !
> Save me from folly, vanity, and vice,
> From every low pursuit ; and fill my soul
> With knowledge, conscious peace, and virtue pure ;
> Sacred, substantial, never-fading bliss ! "

The precept of Order requiring that *every part of my business should have its allotted time*, one page in my little book contain'd the following scheme of employment for the twenty-four hours of a natural day.

The Morning.
Question. What good shall I do this day?

{ 5, 6, 7 } Rise, wash, and address *Powerful Goodness!* Contrive day's business, and take the resolution of the day; prosecute the present study, and breakfast.

{ 8, 9, 10, 11 } Work.

Noon.	12, 1	Read, or overlook my accounts, and dine.
	2, 3, 4, 5	Work.
Evening. *Question.* What good have I done to-day?	6, 7, 8, 9	Put things in their places. Supper. Music or diversion, or conversation. Examination of the day.
Night.	10, 11, 12, 1, 2, 3, 4	Sleep.

I enter'd upon the execution of this plan for self-examination, and continu'd it with occasional intermissions for some time. I was surpris'd to find myself so much fuller of faults than I had imagined; but I had the satisfaction of seeing them diminish. To avoid the trouble of renewing now and then my little book, which, by scraping out the marks on the paper of old faults to make room for new ones in a new course, became full of holes, I transferr'd my tables and precepts to the ivory leaves of a memorandum book, on which the lines were drawn with red ink, that made a durable stain, and on those lines I mark'd my faults with a black-lead pencil, which marks I could easily wipe out with a wet sponge. After a while I went thro' one course only in a year, and afterward only one in several years, till at length I omitted them entirely, being employ'd in voyages and business abroad, with a multiplicity of affairs that interfered; but I always carried my little book with me.

My scheme of ORDER gave me the most trouble. . . . In truth, I found myself incorrigible with respect to Order ; and now I am grown old, and my memory bad, I feel very sensibly the want of it. But, on the whole, tho' I never arrived at the perfection I had been so ambitious of obtaining, but fell far short of it, yet I was, by the endeavour, a better and a happier man than I otherwise should have been if I had not attempted it ; as those who aim at perfect writing by imitating the engraved copies, tho' they never reach the wish'd-for excellence of those copies, their hand is mended by the endeavour, and is tolerable while it continues fair and legible.

It may be well my posterity should be informed that to this little artifice, with the blessing of God, their ancestor ow'd the constant felicity of his life, down to his 79th year, in which this is written. What reverses may attend the remainder is in the hand of Providence ; but, if they arrive, the reflection on past happiness enjoy'd ought to help his bearing them with more resignation. To Temperance he ascribes his long-continued health, and what is still left to him of a good constitution ; to Industry and Frugality, the early easiness of his circumstances and acquisition of his fortune, with all that knowledge that enabled him to be a useful citizen, and obtained for him some degree of reputation among the learned ; to Sincerity and Justice, the confidence of his country, and the honorable employs it conferred upon him ; and to the joint influence of the whole mass of the virtues, even in the imperfect state he was able to acquire them, all that evenness of temper, and that cheerfulness in conversation, which makes his company still sought for, and agreeable even to his younger acquaintance. I hope, therefore, that some of my descendants may follow the example and reap the benefit.

LORD CHATHAM

(A. D. 1708–1778.)

WILLIAM PITT, the Elder, called "the Great Commoner"
until he gave up that highest of titles to become the Earl
of Chatham, was the son of Robert Pitt, of Boconnock, Corn-
wall. He was born at Westminster, November 15, 1708;
entered Parliament in 1735; was made Paymaster-General
in 1746, and attained a place in the cabinet in 1756, as
Secretary of State. From that time until 1761, though not
premier in name, he was the master-mind in the English
government, controlling and directing the Seven Years' War,
with brilliant results of colonial conquest and commercial
expansion. He resigned office in 1761; returned to the
ministry in 1766 as premier, and accepted a peerage, as
Viscount Pitt and Earl of Chatham. Ill health compelled
his resignation again in 1768. He had opposed the policy
pursued by the government toward the American colonies,
and he continued to do so with strenuous eloquence after they
were driven to revolt; but his last speech in the House of
Lords was made in protest against proposals of peace with
France which involved a recognition of the independence of
the colonies. He sank in a swoon while speaking, and died
four days afterwards, on the 11th of May, 1778.

"Pitt had," says Mr. Lecky, in his "History of England
in the Eighteenth Century," "every quality that was required for a great popular leader. His splendid eloquence,
his disinterestedness, his position outside the charmed circle
of aristocratic connections, the popular cast and tendency of
his politics, filled the people with admiration, and their
enthusiasm was by no means diminished by the pride with
which, relying on their favour, he encountered every aristocratic cabal, or by the insatiable ambition which was the
most conspicuous element of his character. His pride was
indeed of that kind which is the guardian of many virtues,

and his ambition was indissolubly linked with the greatness of his country. Beyond all other statesmen of the eighteenth century he understood and sympathized with the feelings of the English people, and recognized the great unrepresented forces of the nation, and amid all the variations of his career his love of freedom never faltered, and a burning, passionate patriotism remained the guiding principle of his life. The qualities of a great popular leader are, however, by no means his only title to our admiration. It is his peculiar merit, that while no statesman of his time rested more entirely upon popular favour, or enjoyed it more largely, or valued it more highly, very few risked it so boldly in a righteous cause. . . .

"Great disinterestedness, great courage, and great patriotism, united with an intense love of liberty, with splendid talents, and with splendid success, were sufficient to overbalance and sometimes to conceal faults that would have ruined an inferior man. No impartial judge, indeed, who considers the career of Pitt, can fail to admit that it was disfigured by the grossest inconsistencies. . . . He was . . . singularly theatrical and affected. His speeches owed much of their charm to the most consummate acting, and he carried his histrionic turn into every sphere in which he moved. . . . His letters — whether he was addressing a minister on affairs of state, or exhorting his young nephew to guard against the ungracefulness of laughter — were tumid, formal, and affected. . . . It is said of him that in his family circle he delighted in reading out the tragedies of Shakespeare, which he did with great pathos and power; but whenever he came to any light or comic parts, he immediately stopped and gave the book to some member of his family to read. This anecdote is characteristic of his whole life. He never unbent. He was always acting a part, always self-conscious, always aiming at a false and unreal dignity. These faults increased with age."

LETTERS OF THE EARL OF CHATHAM TO HIS NEPHEW, THOMAS PITT, FROM BATH, JANUARY, 1754.

(From the "Correspondence of the Earl of Chatham.")

You are already possessed of the true clue to guide you through this dangerous and perplexing part of your life's journey, the years of education; and upon which, the complexion of all the rest of your days will infallibly depend: I say, you have the true clue to guide you, in the maxim you lay down in your letter to me; namely, that the use of learning is, to render a man more wise and virtuous, not merely to make him more learned. *Macte tuâ virtute.* Go on, my dear boy, by this golden rule, and you cannot fail to become every thing your generous heart prompts you to wish to be, and that mine most affectionately wishes for you.

There is but one danger in your way; and that is, perhaps, natural enough to your age — the love of pleasure, or the fear of close application and laborious diligence. With the last, there is nothing you may not conquer; and the first is sure to conquer and enslave whoever does not strenuously and generously resist the first allurements of it, lest by small indulgences, he fall under the yoke of irresistible habit. " *Vitanda est improba siren, Desidia,*" I desire may be affixed to the curtains of your bed, and to the walls of your chambers. If you do not rise early, you never can make any progress worth talking of; and another rule is, if you do not set apart your hours of reading, and never suffer yourself or any one else to break in upon them, your days will slip through your hands unprofitably and frivolously; unpraised by all you wish to please, and really unenjoyable to yourself. Be assured, whatever you take from pleasure, amusements, or indolence, for these first few years of your life, will re-pay you a hundred fold, in the pleasures, honours, and advantages of all the remainder of your days. . . ,

As to your companions, let this be your rule : — . . . be sure to associate with men much older than yourself; scholars whenever you can, but always with men of de-cent and honourable lives. As their age and learning, superior both to your own, must necessarily, in good sense, and in the view of acquiring knowledge from them, entitle them to all deference, and submission of your own lights to theirs, you will particularly practise that first and greatest rule for pleasing in conversation, as well as for drawing instruction and improvement from the com-pany of one's superiors in age and knowledge, namely, to be a patient, attentive, and well-bred hearer, and to an-swer with modesty ; to deliver your own opinions sparingly and with proper diffidence ; and if you are forced to de-sire farther information or explanation upon a point, to do it with proper apologies for the trouble you give ; or if obliged to differ, to do it with all possible candour, and an unprejudiced desire to find and ascertain truth, with an entire indifference to the side on which that truth is to be found.

There is likewise a particular attention required to con-tradict with good manners ; such as, begging pardon, beg-ging leave to doubt, and such like phrases. Pythagoras enjoined his scholars an absolute silence for a long noviti-ate. I am far from approving such a taciturnity; but I highly recommend the end and intent of Pythagoras's in-junction, which is, to dedicate the first parts of life more to hear and learn, in order to collect materials, out of which to form opinions founded on proper lights and well-examined sound principles, than to be presuming, prompt, and flippant in hazarding one's own slight crude notions of things, and thereby exposing the nakedness and emptiness of the mind — like a house opened to company, before it is fitted either with necessaries, or any ornaments for their reception and entertainment.

And not only will this disgrace follow from such temerity and presumption, but a more serious danger is sure to ensue, that is, the embracing errors for truths, prejudices for principles; and when that is once done (no matter how vainly and weakly), the adhering perhaps to false and dangerous notions, only because one has declared for them, and submitting, for life, the understanding and conscience to a yoke of base and servile prejudices, vainly taken up and obstinately retained. . . .

As to your manner of behaving towards those unhappy young gentlemen you describe, let it be manly and easy: decline their parties with civility; retort their raillery with raillery, always tempered with good breeding: if they banter your regularity, order, decency, and love of study, banter in return their neglect of them, and venture to own frankly, that you came to Cambridge to learn what you can, not to follow what they are pleased to call pleasure. In short, let your external behaviour to them be as full of politeness and ease, as your inward estimation of them is full of pity, mixed with contempt.

I come now to the part of the advice I have to offer to you, which most nearly concerns your welfare, and upon which every good and honourable purpose of your life will assuredly turn; I mean the keeping up in your heart the true sentiments of religion. If you are not right towards God, you can never be so towards man: the noblest sentiment of the human breast is here brought to the test. Is gratitude in the number of a man's virtues? if it be, the highest benefactor demands the warmest returns of gratitude, love and praise. . . .

Hold fast, therefore, by this sheet-anchor of happiness, religion : you will often want it in the times of most danger ; the storms and tempests of life. Cherish true religion as preciously as you will fly with abhorrence and contempt superstition and enthusiasm. The first is the perfection and glory of the human nature ; the two last the deprivation and disgrace of it. . . .

I will now, my dear nephew, say a few things to you upon a matter where you have surprisingly little to learn, considering you have seen nothing but Boconnock; I mean behaviour. Behaviour is of infinite advantage or prejudice to a man, as he happens to have formed it to a graceful, noble, engaging, and proper manner, or to a vulgar, coarse, ill-bred, or awkward and ungenteel one. Behaviour, though an external thing, which seems rather to belong to the body than to the mind, is certainly founded in considerable virtues ; though I have known instances of good men, with something very revolting and offensive in their manner of behaviour, especially when they have the misfortune to be naturally very awkward and ungenteel, and which their mistaken friends have helped to confirm them in, by telling them that they were above such trifles as being genteel, dancing, fencing, riding, and doing all manly exercises, with grace and vigour : as if the body, because inferior, were not a part of the composition of man ; and the proper, easy, ready, and graceful use of himself, both in mind and limb, did not go to make up the character of an accomplished man. . . .

As to the carriage of your person, be particularly careful, as you are tall and thin, not to get a habit of stooping ; nothing has so poor a look. Above all things, avoid contracting any peculiar gesticulations of the body, or movements of the muscles of the face. It is rare to see in any one a graceful laughter ; it is generally better to smile than laugh out, especially to contract a habit of laughing at small or no jokes. Sometimes it would be affectation, or worse, mere moroseness, not to laugh heartily, when the truly ridiculous circumstances of an incident, or the true pleasantry and wit of a thing call for and justify it; but the trick of laughing frivolously is by all means to be avoided — *risu inepto, res ineptior nulla est.*

Now as to politeness; many have attempted definitions of it. I believe it is best to be known by description; definition not being able to comprise it. I would, however, venture to call it *benevolence in trifles,* or the preference of others to ourselves in little daily, hourly, occurrences in the commerce of life. A better place, a more commodious seat, priority in being helped at table, &c., what is it, but sacrificing ourselves in such trifles to the convenience and pleasure of others? And this constitutes true politeness. It is a perpetual attention (by habit it grows easy and natural to us) to the little wants of those we are with, by which we either prevent or remove them. Bowing, ceremonious, formal compliments, stiff civilities, will never be politeness; that must be easy, natural, unstudied, manly, noble. And what will give this, but a mind benevolent, and perpetually attentive to exert that amiable disposition in trifles towards all you converse and live with. Benevolence in greater matters takes a higher name, and is the queen of virtues. Nothing is so incompatible with politeness as any trick of absence of mind.

I would trouble you with a word or two more upon some branches of behaviour, which have a more serious moral obligation in them than those of mere politeness, which are equally important in the eye of the world. I mean a proper behaviour, adapted to the respective relations we stand in, towards the different ranks of superiors, equals, and inferiors. Let your behaviour towards superiors, in dignity, age, learning, or any distinguished excellence, be full of respect, deference, and modesty: towards equals, nothing becomes a man so well as well-bred ease, polite freedom, generous frankness, manly spirit, always tempered with gentleness and sweetness of manner, noble sincerity, candour, and openness of heart, qualified and restrained within the bounds of discretion and prudence, and ever limited by a sacred regard to secrecy in all things intrusted to it, and an inviolable attachment to your word. To inferiors, gentleness, condescension, and affability, is the only dignity. Towards servants, never accustom yourself to rough and passionate language. When they are good, we should consider them as *humiles amici*, as fellow Christians, *ut conservi;* and when they are bad, pity, admonish, and part with them if incorrigible. On all occasions beware, my dear child, of anger, that demon, that destroyer of our peace: —

> " Ira furor brevis est, animum rege, qui nisi paret,
> Imperat : hunc frenis, hunc tu compesce catenâ."

> " Anger's a shorter madness of the mind :
> Subdue the tyrant, and in fetters bind."
> > *Francis's Horace.*

COWPER

(A. D. 1731–1800.)

"WILLIAM COWPER," says Mr. Goldwin Smith, "came of the Whig nobility of the robe. His great-uncle, after whom he was named, was the Whig Lord Chancellor of Anne and George I. His grandfather was that Spencer Cowper, judge of the Common Pleas, for love of whom the pretty Quakeress drowned herself, and who, by the rancour of party, was indicted for her murder. His father, the Rev. John Cowper, D. D., was chaplain to George II. His mother was a Donne, of the race of the poet, and descended by several lines from Henry III. A Whig and a gentleman he was by birth, a Whig and a gentleman he remained to the end. He was born on the 15th November (old style), 1731, in his father's rectory of Berkhampsted. From nature he received, with a large measure of the gifts of genius, a still larger measure of its painful sensibilities. . . . For the battle of life he was totally unfit. His judgment in its healthy state was, even on practical questions, sound enough, as his letters abundantly prove; but his sensibility not only rendered him incapable of wrestling with a rough world, but kept him always on the verge of madness, and frequently plunged him into it. To the malady which threw him out of active life we owe not the meanest of English poets."

In Mr. Smith's view, "Cowper is the most important English poet of the period between Pope and the illustrious group headed by Wordsworth, Byron, and Shelley, which arose out of the intellectual ferment of the European Revolution. As a reformer of poetry, who called it back from conventionality to nature, and at the same time as the teacher of a new school of sentiment which acted as a solvent upon the existing moral and social system, he may perhaps himself be numbered among the precursors of the Revolution, though he was certainly the mildest of them all."

Cowper's most important poem, "The Task," was published in 1785, fifteen years before his death, which occurred in 1800.

THE HAPPY MAN.

(From "The Task," by William Cowper, book vi.)

He is the happy man, whose life even now
Shows somewhat of that happier life to come;
Who doomed to an obscure but tranquil state
Is pleased with it, and were he free to choose,
Would make his fate his choice; whom peace, the fruit
Of virtue, and whom virtue, fruit of faith,
Prepare for happiness; bespeak him one
Content indeed to sojourn while he must
Below the skies, but having there his home.
The world o'erlooks him in her busy search
Of objects more illustrious in her view;
And occupied as earnestly as she,
Though more sublimely, he o'erlooks the world.
She scorns his pleasures, for she knows them not;
He seeks not hers, for he has proved them vain.
He cannot skim the ground like summer birds
Pursuing gilded flies, and such he deems
Her honours, her emoluments, her joys.
Therefore in contemplation is his bliss,
Whose power is such, that whom she lifts from earth
She makes familiar with a heaven unseen,
And shows him glories yet to be reveal'd.
Not slothful he, though seeming unemployed,
And censured oft as useless.   Stillest streams
Oft water fairest meadows, and the bird
That flutters least is longest on the wing.
Ask him indeed what trophies he has raised,
Or what achievements of immortal fame

He purposes, and he shall answer — none.
His warfare is within.   There unfatigued
His fervent spirit labours.   There he fights,
And there obtains fresh triumphs o'er himself,
And never-withering wreaths, compared with which
The laurels that a Cæsar reaps are weeds.
Perhaps the self-approving haughty world,
(That as she sweeps him with her whistling silks
Scarce deigns to notice him, or if she see
Deems him a cypher in the works of God,)
Receives advantage from his noiseless hours
Of which she little dreams.   Perhaps she owes
Her sunshine and her rain, her blooming spring
And plenteous harvest, to the prayer he makes,
When Isaac-like, the solitary saint
Walks forth to meditate at eventide,
And think on her, who thinks not for herself.
Forgive him then, thou bustler in concerns
Of little worth, and idler in the best,
If author of no mischief and some good,
He seek his proper happiness by means
That may advance, but cannot hinder thine.
Nor, though he tread the secret path of life,
Engage no notice, and enjoy much ease,
Account him an incumbrance on the state,
Receiving benefits, and rendering none.
His sphere though humble, if that humble sphere
Shine with his fair example, and though small
His influence, if that influence all be spent
In soothing sorrow and in quenching strife,
In aiding helpless indigence, in works
From which at least a grateful few derive
Some taste of comfort in a world of woe,
Then let the supercilious great confess

He serves his country ; recompenses well
The state beneath the shadow of whose vine
He sits secure, and in the scale of life
Holds no ignoble, though a slighted place.
The man whose virtues are more felt than seen,
Must drop indeed the hope of public praise ;
But he may boast what few that win it can,
That if his country stand not by his skill,
At least his follies have not wrought her fall.
Polite refinement offers him in vain
Her golden tube, through which a sensual world
Draws gross impurity, and likes it well,
The neat conveyance hiding all the offence.
Not that he peevishly rejects a mode
Because that world adopts it : if it bear
The stamp and clear impression of good sense,
And be not costly more than of true worth,
He puts it on, and for decorum sake
Can wear it even as gracefully as she.
She judges of refinement by the eye,
He by the test of conscience, and a heart
Not soon deceived ; aware that what is base
No polish can make sterling, and that vice
Though well perfumed and elegantly dress'd,
Like an unburned carcase trick'd with flowers,
Is but a garnish'd nuisance, fitter far
For cleanly riddance than for fair attire.
So life glides smoothly and by stealth away,
More golden than that age of fabled gold
Renown'd in ancient song ; not vex'd with care
Or stained with guilt, beneficent, approved
Of God and man, and peaceful in its end.

WASHINGTON

(A. D. 1732–1799.)

GEORGE WASHINGTON, the great leader of the American struggle for national independence, and first President of the republic of the United States, was born in Westmoreland County, Virginia, on the 22d of February (N. S.), 1732, and died at Mount Vernon, Virginia, on the 14th of December, 1799. He won reputation as a soldier in the French and Indian War, 1754–58, and, on the outbreak of the War of Independence, was appointed commander-in-chief of the Continental forces, June 15th, 1775. He resigned his commission at the close of the war, in 1783, and retired to his estate at Mount Vernon; but was called forth again in 1787, to serve his country in a civil capacity, first as the presiding officer of the convention which framed the constitution of the federal republic of the United States of America, and then to become the chief magistrate of the nation so constituted.

Of the two letters copied below, addressing advice to his nephews on the plan and conduct of their lives, the first was written a short time before his retirement from the army; the second just after his election to the presidency, and on the eve of his inauguration. It is characteristic of the nobility of his nature that he should have been thoughtful of his young kinsmen at such times.

Appended to these excellent letters are some precepts selected from what are often spoken of as " Washington's Rules of Civility." The rules in question are found in a manuscript book, now preserved in the State Archives at Washington, which Washington used as a boy, for various purposes. It was formerly supposed that the young Virginian had either composed these rules, or collected them from different sources; and that belief gave more importance to them than they possess in themselves. Mr. Moncure D. Conway has discovered their source in an old French book on Behavior, originally prepared for the pupils of the College of La Fleche, as long ago as 1595, but which passed through many later editions and translations. Washington received them, without doubt, from the Rev. James Marye, a French gentleman, whose school he attended, at Fredericksburg, in 1745. He probably wrote them in his book from the teacher's dictation, making many boyish mistakes in spelling, punctuation, and otherwise, all of which are reproduced in the exact text published by Mr. Conway. The selection given here is from that text. It includes only a few of the more permanently valuable among the one hundred and ten rules in Washington's manuscript. There are not many of the remainder that have much significance at the present day. Generally their subject is Manners, not Morals.

GEORGE WASHINGTON TO HIS NEPHEW, BUSHROD WASHINGTON.

NEWBURG, 15 January, 1783.

. . . Let the object, which carried you to Philadelphia, be always before your Eyes. Remember, that it is not the mere study of the Law, but to become eminent in the profession of it, which is to yield honor and profit. The first was your choice; let the second be your ambition, and that dissipation is incompatible with both; that the Company, in which you will improve most, will be least expensive to you; and yet I am not such a Stoic as to suppose that you will, or to think it right that you should, always be in Company with senators and philosophers; but of the young and juvenile kind let me advise you to be choice. It is easy to make acquaintances, but very difficult to shake them off, however irksome and unprofitable they are found, after we have once committed ourselves to them. The indiscretions and scrapes, which very often they involuntarily lead one into, prove equally distressing and disgraceful.

Be courteous to all, but intimate with few; and let those few be well tried before you give them your confidence. True friendship is a plant of slow growth, and must undergo and withstand the shocks of adversity before it is entitled to the appellation.

Let your heart feel for the afflictions and distresses of every one, and let your hand give in proportion to your purse; remembering always the estimation of the widow's mite, but, that it is not every one who asketh that deserveth charity; all, however, are worthy of the inquiry, or the deserving may suffer.

Do not conceive that fine clothes make fine men any more than fine feathers make fine Birds. A plain genteel dress is more admired, and obtains more credit than lace and embroidery, in the Eyes of the judicious and sensible.

The last thing, which I shall mention, is first in importance; and that is, to avoid Gaming. This is a vice which is productive of every possible evil; equally injurious to the morals and health of its votaries. It is the child of avarice, the brother of iniquity, and father of mischief.

TO GEORGE STEPTOE WASHINGTON.

MOUNT VERNON, 23 March, 1789.

Dear George,

As it is probable I shall soon be under the necessity of quitting this place, and entering once more into the bustle of public life, in conformity to the voice of my Country and the earnest entreaties of my friends, however contrary it is to my own desires or inclinations; I think it incumbent on me as your Uncle and friend, to give you some advisory hints, which if properly attended to, will, I conceive, be found very useful to you in regulating your conduct and giving you respectability not only at present but through every period of life. You have now arrived to that age when you must quit the trifling amusements of a boy, and assume the more dignified manners of a man.

At this crisis your conduct will attract the notice of those who are about you; and as the first impressions are generally the most lasting; your doings now may mark the leading traits of your character through life. It is, therefore, absolutely necessary, if you mean to make any figure upon the stage, that you should take the first steps right. What these steps are and what general line is to be pursued to lay the foundation of an honorable and happy progress, is the part of age and experience to point out. This I shall do, as far as in my power with the utmost chearfulness; and, I trust, that your own good sense will shew you the necessity of following it. The first and great object with you at present is to acquire, by industry and application, such knowledge as your situation enables you to obtain, as will be useful to you in life. In doing this two other important objects will be gained besides the acquisition of knowledge — namely a habit of industry, and a disrelish of that profusion of money and dissipation of time which are ever attendant upon idleness. I do not mean by a close application to your studies that you should never enter into those amusements which are suited to your age and station. They may be made to go hand in hand with each other, and used in their proper seasons, will ever be found to be a mutual assistance to each other. But what amusements are to be taken, and when, is the great matter to be attended to — your own judgement, with the advice of your real friends who may have an opportunity of a personal intercourse with you can point out the particular manner in which you may best spend your moments of relaxation, much better than I can at a distance. — One thing, however, I would strongly impress upon you, viz: that when you have leisure, to go into company; that it should always be of the best kind that the place you are in will afford; by this means you will be constantly improving your manners and cultivating your mind while you are relaxing from your books; and good company will always be found much less expensive than bad. You cannot offer, as an excuse for not using it, that you cannot gain admission there, or that you have not a proper attention paid you in it, this is an apology made only by those whose manners are disgusting, or whose character is exceptionable; neither of which, I hope, will ever be said of you. I cannot enjoin too strongly upon you a due observance of economy and frugality: As you well know yourself, the present state of your property and finances will not admit of any unnecessary expense. The article of clothing is now one of the chief expenses, you will incur; and in this, I fear, you are not so economical as you should be. Decency and cleanliness will always be the first object in the dress of a judicious and sensible man. A conformity to the prevailing fashion in a certain degree is necessary — but it does not follow from thence that a man should always get a new coat, or other clothes, upon every trifling change in the mode, when perhaps he has two or three very good ones by him. A person who is anxious to be a leader of the fashion, or one of the first to follow it, will certainly appear in the eyes of judicious men, to have nothing better than a frequent c[h]ange of dress to recommend him to notice. I would always wish you to appear sufficiently decent to entitle you to admission into any company, where you may be, — but I cannot too strongly enjoin it upon you — and your own knowledge must convince you of the truth of it — that you should be as little expensive in this respect as you properly can — You should always keep some clothes to wear to church, or on particular occasions, which should not be worn every day. This can be done without any additional expense; for whenever it is necessary to get new clothes, those which have been kept for particular occasions, will then come in as every day ones, unless they should be of a superior quality to the new. What I have said with respect to clothes will apply perhaps more pointedly to Lawrence than to you, — and as you are much older than he is, and more capable of judging of the propriety of what I have here observed, you must pay attention to him, in this respect, and see that he does not wear his clothes improperly or extravagantly. Much more might be said to you, as a young man, upon the necessity of paying due attention to the moral virtues, — but this may, perhaps, more properly be the subject of a future letter when you are about to enter into the world. . . .

Your affectionate friend and Uncle.

SELECTIONS FROM GEORGE WASHINGTON'S RULES OF CIVILITY.

Be no Flatterer, neither Play with any that delights not to be Playd Withal.

Reproach none for the Infirmities of Nature, nor Delight to Put them that have in mind thereof.

Shew not yourself glad at the misfortune of another though he were your enemy.

When you see a Crime punished, you may be inwardly pleased; but always shew Pity to the Suffering Offender.

Superfluous Complements and all Affectation of Ceremony are to be avoided, yet where due they are not to be neglected.

Do not express Joy before one sick or in pain for that contrary Passion will aggravate his Misery.

When a man does all he can though it Succeeds not well blame not him that did it.

Take all Admonitions thankfully in what Time or Place Soever given but afterwards not being culpable take a Time or Place Convenient to let him Know it that gave them.

Wherein you reprove Another be unblameable yourself; for example is more prevalent than Precepts.

Be not hasty to believe flying Reports to the Disparagement of any.

In your Apparel be Modest and endeavour to accommodate Nature, rather than to procure Admiration; Keep to the Fashion of your equals.

Associate yourself with Men of good Quality if you Esteem your own Reputation; for 't is better to be alone than in bad Company.

Let your Conversation be without Malice or Envy, for 't is a Sign of a Tractable and Commendable Nature: & in all Causes of Passion admit Reason to Govern.

Be not immodest in urging your Friends to Discover a Secret.

A Man ought not to value himself of his Atchievements or rare Qualities, his Riches, Titles Virtue or Kindred; but he need not speak meanly of himself.

Break not a Jest where none take pleasure in Mirth; Laugh not aloud, nor at all without Occasion, deride no man's misfortune, though there seem to be some cause.

Speak not injurious Words neither in Jest nor Earnest; scoff at none although they give Occasion.

Detract not from others neither be excessive in Commending.

If two contend together take not the part of either unconstrained, and be not obstinate in your Opinion, in Things indifferent be of the major side.

Reprehend not the imperfections of others for that belongs to Parents Masters and Superiors.

Gaze not at the marks or blemishes of Others and ask not how they came. What you may Speak in Secret to your Friend deliver not before others.

Think before you speak pronounce not imperfectly nor bring out your Words too hastily but orderly and Distinctly.

Be not Curious to Know the Affairs of Others neither approach to those that Speak in Private.

Undertake not what you cannot Perform but be Carefull to Keep your Promise.

In Disputes, be not so desirous to Overcome as not to give Liberty to each one to deliver his Opinion.

Speak not Evil of the absent for it is unjust.

When you Speak of God or his Attributes, let it be Seriously & with words of Reverence. Honour & obey your Natural Parents altho they be Poor.

Let your Recreations be Manfull not Sinfull.

Labour to Keep alive in your Breast that little Spark of Celestial fire called Conscience.

JEFFERSON

(A. D. 1743-1826.)

THOMAS JEFFERSON, third President of the United States of America, and author of the famous "Declaration," under which the independence of the "States" had been assumed, was born in Albemarle County, Virginia, on the 13th of April, 1743. He was a student at William and Mary College, and studied law in Williamsburg. After eight years of successful practice at the bar, he entered public life, and his professional career was practically at an end. He was successively a member of the Virginia House of Burgesses, a member of the Continental Congress, Governor of Virginia, Plenipotentiary to France (1784–1789), Secretary of State in President Washington's cabinet, Vice President of the United States, and President of the United States for two consecutive terms. He retired to private life in 1809, and died at his residence, Monticello, on the 4th of July, 1826, — the fiftieth anniversary of the signing of the Declaration of Independence, — almost simultaneously with the death of his contemporary and friend, John Adams, which occurred on the same day.

The character of Jefferson and his rank in American history are described admirably, in a few words, by Dr. John Fiske, in his "History of the American Revolution:" "His temper," says Dr. Fiske, "was exceedingly placid, and his disposition was sweet and sympathetic. He was deeply interested in all the generous theories of the eighteenth century concerning the rights of man and the perfectibility of human nature; and, like most of the contemporary philosophers whom he admired, he was a sturdy foe to intolerance and priestcraft. He was in his way a much more profound thinker than Hamilton, though he had not such a constructive genius as the latter; as a political leader he was superior to any other man of his age; and his warm sympathies, his almost feminine tact, his mastery of the dominant political ideas of the time, and, above all, his unbounded faith in the common sense of the people and in their essential rectitude of purpose, served to give him one of the greatest and most commanding positions ever held by any personage in American history."

JEFFERSON'S LETTER TO THOMAS JEFFERSON RANDOLPH.

(From "The Writings of Thomas Jefferson," ed. by H. A. Washington, v. 5.)

WASHINGTON, November 24, 1808.

MY DEAR JEFFERSON, —

Your situation, thrown at such a distance from us, and alone, cannot but give us all great anxieties for you. As much has been secured for you, by your particular position and the acquaintance to which you have been recommended, as could be done towards shielding you from the dangers which surround you. But thrown on a wide world, among entire strangers, without a friend or guardian to advise, so young too, and with so little experience of mankind, your dangers are great, and still your safety must rest on yourself. A determination never to do what is wrong, prudence and good humor, will go far towards securing to you the estimation of the world. When I recollect that at fourteen years of age, the whole care and direction of myself was thrown on myself entirely, without a relation or friend qualified to advise or guide me, and recollect the various sorts of bad company with which I associated from time to time, I am astonished I did not turn off with some of them, and become as worthless to society as they were. I had the good fortune to become acquainted very early with some characters of very high standing, and to feel the incessant wish that I could ever become what they were. Under temptations and difficulties, I would ask myself what would Dr. Small, Mr. Wythe, Peyton Randolph do in this situation? What course in it will insure me their approbation? I am certain that this mode of deciding on my conduct, tended more to correctness than any reasoning powers I possessed. Knowing the even and dignified line they pursued, I could never doubt for a moment which of two courses would be in character for them. Whereas, seeking the same object through a process of moral reasoning, and with the jaundiced eye of youth, I should often have erred. From the circumstances of my position, I was often thrown into the society of horse racers, card players, fox hunters, scientific and professional men, and of dignified men; and many a time have I asked myself, in the enthusiastic moment of the death of a fox, the victory of a favorite horse, the issue of a question eloquently argued at the bar, or in the great council of the nation, well, which of these kinds of reputation should I prefer? That of a horse jockey? a fox hunter? an orator? or the honest advocate of my country's rights? Be assured, my dear Jefferson, that these little returns into ourselves, this self-catechising habit, is not trifling nor useless, but leads to the prudent selection and steady pursuit of what is right.

I have mentioned good humor as one of the preservatives of our peace and tranquillity. It is among the most effectual, and its effect is so well imitated and aided, artificially, by politeness, that this also becomes an acquisition of first rate value. In truth, politeness is artificial good humor, it covers the natural want of it, and ends by rendering habitual a substitute nearly equivalent to the real virtue. It is the practice of sacrificing to those whom we meet in society, all the little conveniences and preferences which will gratify them, and deprive us of nothing worth a moment's consideration; it is the giving a pleasing and flattering turn to our expressions, which will conciliate others, and make them pleased with us as well as themselves. How cheap a price for the good will of another! When this is in return for a rude thing said by another, it brings him to his senses, it mortifies and corrects him in the most salutary way, and places him at the feet of your good nature, in the eyes of the company. But in stating prudential rules for our government in society, I must not omit the important one of never entering into dispute or argument with another. I never saw an instance of one of two disputants convincing the other by argument. I have seen many, on their getting warm, becoming rude, and shooting one another. Conviction is the effect of our own dispassionate reasoning, either in solitude, or weighing within ourselves, dispassionately, what we hear from others, standing uncommitted in argument ourselves. It was one of the rules which, above all others, made Dr. Franklin the most amiable of men in society, "never to contradict anybody." If he was urged to announce an opinion, he did it rather by asking questions, as if for information, or by suggesting doubts. When I hear another express an opinion which is not mine, I say to myself, he has a right to his opinion, as I to mine; why should I question it? His error does me no injury, and shall I become a Don Quixotte, to bring all men by force of argument to one opinion? If a fact be misstated, it is probable he is gratified by a belief of it, and I have no right to deprive him of the gratification. If he wants information, he will ask it, and then I will give it in measured terms; but if he still believes his own story, and shows a desire to dispute the fact with me, I hear him and say nothing. It is his affair, not mine, if he prefers error. There are two classes of disputants most frequently to be met with among us. The first is of young students, just entered the threshold of science, with a first view of its outlines, not yet filled up with the details and modifications which a further progress would bring to their knowledge. The other consists of the ill-tempered and rude men in society, who have taken up a passion for politics. (Good humor and politeness never introduce into mixed society, a question on which they foresee there will be a difference of opinion.) From both of those classes of disputants, my dear Jefferson, keep aloof, as you would from the infected subjects of yellow fever or pestilence. Consider yourself, when with them, as among the patients of Bedlam, needing medical, more than moral counsel. Be a listener only, keep within yourself, and endeavor to establish with yourself the habit of silence, especially on politics. . . . Look steadily to the pursuits which have carried you to Philadelphia, be very select in the society you attach yourself to, avoid taverns, drinkers, smokers, idlers, and dissipated persons generally; for it is with such that broils and contentions arise; and you will find your path more easy and tranquil. The limits of my paper warn me that it is time for me to close with my affectionate adieu.

JEFFERSON'S LETTER TO THOMAS JEFFERSON SMITH.

(From "The Domestic Life of Thomas Jefferson," by Sarah N. Randolph.

A friend and admirer of Jefferson's, who had named a son after him, requested that he would write a letter of advice for his young namesake. Jefferson accordingly wrote the following beautiful note to be kept for him until the young child came to years of understanding:

To Thomas Jefferson Smith.

This letter will, to you, be as one from the dead. The writer will be in the grave before you can weigh its counsels. Your affectionate and excellent father has requested that I would address to you something which might possibly have a favorable influence on the course of life you have to run; and I too, as a namesake, feel an interest in that course. Few words will be necessary, with good dispositions on your part. Adore God. Reverence and cherish your parents. Love your neighbor as yourself, and your country more than yourself. Be just. Be true. Murmur not at the ways of Providence. So shall the life into which you have entered, be the portal to one of eternal and ineffable bliss. And if to the dead it is permitted to care for the things of this world, every action of your life will be under my regard. Farewell.

MONTICELLO, February 21st, 1825.

The Portrait of a Good Man by the most sublime of Poets, for your Imitation.[1]

Lord, who's the happy man that may to thy blest courts
        repair;
Not stranger-like to visit them, but to inhabit there?

'T is he whose every thought and deed by rules of virtue
        moves;
Whose generous tongue disdains to speak the thing his
        heart disproves;

Who never did a slander forge, his neighbor's fame to
        wound;
Nor hearken to a false report by malice whispered round;

[1] Paraphrase of Psalm xv.

Who vice in all its pomp and power, can treat with just
    neglect ;
And piety, though clothed in rags, religiously respect;

Who to his plighted vows and trust has ever firmly
    stood ;
And though he promise to his loss, he makes his promise
    good ;

Whose soul in usury disdains his treasure to employ;
Whom no rewards can ever bribe the guiltless to destroy ;

The man who, by this steady course, has happiness in-
    sured,
When earth's foundations shake, shall stand by Providence
    secured.

*A Decalogue of Canons for Observation in Practical
Life.*

1. Never put off till to-morrow what you can do to-
day.

2. Never trouble another for what you can do yourself.

3. Never spend your money before you have it.

4. Never buy what you do not want because it is
cheap ; it will be dear to you.

5. Pride costs us more than hunger, thirst, and cold.

6. We never repent of having eaten too little.

7. Nothing is troublesome that we do willingly.

8. How much pain have cost us the evils which have
never happened !

9. Take things always by their smooth handle.

10. When angry, count ten before you speak ; if very
angry, an hundred.

GOETHE

(A. D. 1749–1832.)

JOHANN WOLFGANG VON GOETHE, the greatest of German poets, was born at Frankfort-on-the-Main on the 28th of August, 1749. His family was one of comparative wealth and good social position. He was educated for the law, but gave it little attention in practice, devoting himself to literature from his youth. In 1775, on the invitation of the Duke of Saxe-Weimar, he fixed his residence at Weimar, which became, through his influence, the literary capital of Germany. He was made privy councillor and president of the ducal chamber. His earliest tragedy, "Götz von Berlichingen," was produced in 1773; his youthful novel, "The Sorrows of Young Werther" was written in 1774. His greater work in prose fiction, "Wilhelm Meister's Lehrjahre," was begun in 1777 and finished in 1796. His greatest dramatic work, the tragedy of "Faust," was under his pen for nearly sixty years, from 1772, when some of its scenes were sketched, until 1831. The first part of the drama was published in 1808; the second only a few months before his death, which occurred at Weimar on the 22d of March, 1832.

"Goethe is a perfect Solomon for proverbs; they pour from him in floods. He has such an abundance of them to communicate that he is often at a loss where to find room for them, and puts them recklessly into the mouths of personages who cannot reasonably be credited with such a rare talent for generalization. . . . He is a sage as truly as he is a poet, and never, unless in Shakespeare, has such another combination of the generalizing with the imaginative faculty been witnessed. But when we examine his wisdom, we find that it is much more than a mere instinctive habit of observation combined with an unrivalled power of expression. His sentences are not mere detached fragments, or momentary

flashes, of insight. They are the coherent aphorisms of a
sort of practical philosophy. He is not merely a sage, he
is even a philosopher. . . . He is a philosopher in a higher
degree than any other literary man, and has produced a
deeper impression than any literary man upon thinkers and
students. Though in the modern sense we hesitate to call
him a philosopher, yet in the old sense, and in the highest
sense of the name, few of the recognized philosophers have
nearly so good a title to it as he. For to him philosophy
is not merely a study, but a life; it is not summed up in
thinking and classifying and constructing systems, but extends to all departments of activity. And it would be difficult to name the philosopher who has devoted himself with
more methodical seriousness than Goethe to the problem of
leading, and then of teaching, the best and most desirable
kind of life. He conceives the problem in its largest possible
extent. From prudential maxims in the style of Johnson,
he rises to more general precepts on the choice of a vocation,
pouring out a fund of wisdom peculiarly his own on the mistakes men make about their own aptitudes; then he dwells
more particularly on the life of the artist, a subject till then
scarcely noticed by moralists, but treated by Goethe with the
greatest comprehensiveness; then he rises to morality and
religion. On all subjects alike he is serious; on all subjects
perfectly unfettered. He has the advantage of a vast experience, for he has practised many arts, tasted almost every
literature, informed himself about every science." — J. R.
SEELEY, "Goethe reviewed after Sixty Years," ch. 3.

GOETHE'S MAXIMS AND REFLECTIONS.

(Selected from " Maxims and Reflections from the German of
Goethe ; " " Fraser's Magazine," March, 1876.)

All that is wise has been thought already; we must try,
however, to think it again.

How shall you learn to know yourself? — Not by contemplation, but action. Strive to do your duty, and you
will soon discover what stuff you are made of.

But what is your duty? — To fulfil the claims of the day.

Let the active able man deserve and expect: —

From the Great — grace;
From the Powerful — favour;
From the Good and Active — help;
From the Multitude — liking;
From the Individual — love.

Every one must think in his own way; for he will always discover some sort of truth or approximation to truth which helps him through his life. But he must not let himself drift along; he must exercise self-control; it beseems not man to allow himself to be ruled by mere instinct.

Unlimited activity of whatever kind must at last end in bankruptcy.

What we plan, what we undertake, should already be so clearly mapped out and so beautiful in its proportions that the World by interfering could only mar it. We should thus be in an advantageous position to adjust what might have got out of joint, and to replace what had been destroyed.

A great mistake: to hold oneself too high and rate oneself too cheap.

We are only really alive when we enjoy the goodwill of others.

"One must do more when one is old than when one was young."

Even the fulfilment of duty leaves a sense of being indebted, because we are never thoroughly satisfied with ourselves.

In contemplation, as well as in action, we must distinguish between what is attainable and what is not: failing this, we can accomplish little either in life or knowledge.

Errors are not of much consequence in youth, but we must guard against dragging them with us into our old age.

Superannuated errors are fusty, unprofitable lumber.

Let memory fail so long as you can rely on your judgment at a moment's notice.

I should say the happiest man is he who can link the end of his life with its commencement.

(Selected from "Maxims and Reflections of Goethe," translated by Thomas Bailey Saunders.)

One need only grow old to become gentler in one's judgments. I see no fault committed which I could not have committed myself.

It is much easier to recognize error than to find truth ; for error lies on the surface and may be overcome ; but truth lies in the depths, and to search for it is not given to every one.

Ingratitude is always a kind of weakness. I have never known men of ability to be ungrateful.

There are people who make no mistakes because they never wish to do anything worth doing.

If a man knows where to get good advice, it is as though he could supply it himself.

In the world people take a man at his own estimate ; but he must estimate himself at something. Disagreeableness is more easily tolerated than insignificance.

A man's manners are the mirror in which he shows his portrait.

There is a politeness of the heart, and it is allied to love. It produces the most agreeable politeness of outward demeanour.

It is not enough to know, we must also apply; it is not enough to will, we must also do.

Perfection is the measure of heaven, and the wish to be perfect the measure of man.

It is not worth while to do anything for the world that we have with us, as the existing order may in a moment pass away. It is for the past and the future that we must work : for the past, to acknowledge its merits ; for the future, to try to increase its value.

Let every man ask himself with which of his faculties he can and will somehow influence his age.

Let no one think that people have waited for him as for the Saviour.

Character in matters great and small consists in a man steadily pursuing the things of which he feels himself capable.

(Selected from "The Wisdom of Goethe," by John Stuart Blackie.)

Who is the happiest person ? — he whose nature asks for nothing that the world does not wish and use.

Wouldst thou be a happy liver,
Let the past be past for ever !
Fret not, when prigs and pedants bore you ;
Enjoy the good that's set before you ;
But chiefly hate no man ; the rest
Leave thou to God, who knows what 's best.

Live with the world whoso has nerve
To make the world his purpose serve ;
But if you leave your lofty level
To do the world's vile command,

You were as well to let the devil
Keep all your gear in hand.

Use well the moment; what the hour
Brings for thy use is in thy power;
And what thou best canst understand,
Is just the thing lies nearest to thy hand.
Art thou little, do that little well, and for thy comfort
        know,
The biggest man can do his biggest work no better than
        just so.

Wouldst thou live well in the land,
Take two wallets in thy hand,
This to gather what you find,
That to give with willing mind;
Just as princes when they travel,
With heavy hand lay on the charges,
And then from overflowing founts
Of Royal bounty make a largess!

Like the star
That shines afar,
Without haste
And without rest,
Let each man wheel with steady sway,
Round the task that rules the day,
And do his best!

JOSEPH JOUBERT

(A. D. 1754–1824.)

JOSEPH JOUBERT was born at Montignac, in Perigord, France, in 1754. He began the study of law, but abandoned it to enter the College of the Fathers of the Christian Doctrine, at Toulouse, where he remained for some years, both teaching and studying. He then removed to Paris, and continued to live a studious life, his home becoming one of the most attractive centres of the best society of the time. Nothing that he wrote was published until several years after his death, which occurred in 1824. A volume of his much esteemed aphorisms was then given to the world, under the editorship of Châteaubriand. It is from a partial translation of these "Pensées," or "Thoughts," as they were entitled, that the selection given below is borrowed. A more complete publication of Joubert's writings, including his correspondence, was made in France in 1842.

SELECTIONS FROM THE PENSÉES OF JOUBERT.

(Translated by Henry Atwell.)

The passions must be purified. They may all become innocent if well directed and controlled. Hatred itself may be a praiseworthy emotion if provoked in us by a lively love of good.

If you are poor, distinguish yourself by your virtues; if rich, by your good deeds.

Be saving; but not at the cost of all liberality. Have the soul of a king, and the hand of a wise economist.

Living requires but little life; doing requires much.

We should always keep open and free a corner of our

head in which to make room for the opinions of our friends. Let us have heart and head hospitality.

It is better to debate a question without settling it, than to settle it without debate.

Politeness is a sort of guard which covers the rough edges of our character, and prevents their wounding others. We should never throw it off, even in our conflicts with coarse people.

Consult the ancients, listen to the aged. He is far from wise who has but his own wisdom, and but indifferently learned who possesses but his own knowledge.

To think what we do not feel is to lie to one's-self. Whatever we think should be thought by our whole being, soul and body.

Men must either be the slaves of duty or of force.

Order is the co-ordination of the means to the end, of the parts to the whole, of the whole to its destination, of action to duty, of a work to its model, of recompense to merit.

Order is to arrangement what the soul is to the body, and what mind is to matter. Arrangement without order is a body without a soul.

Imitate time. It destroys slowly. It undermines, wears, loosens, separates. It does not uproot.

Let us bear well in mind that education does not consist merely in adorning the memory and enlightening the understanding. Its main business should be to direct the will.

ROBERT BURNS

(A. D. 1759–1796.)

IN some important matters of morals, Robert Burns was better fitted to be a teacher by warning example than by precept, as he himself tacitly confesses in the last couplet of the verses subjoined. But there was a fine true quality in his nature, at the bottom, which imparts perfect genuineness to the good advice contained in this "Epistle to a Young Friend," and assures us of the sincerity with which it was given. The "Epistle" was written in 1786, the year in which his first volume of poems was published, at Kilmarnock, and in which he first visited Edinburgh. He wrote it just before fame came to him, and when he was undoubtedly at his best, in every way. The date and the sentiment of the little poem lend great interest to it in connection with the life of Burns. He was but twenty-seven years old when he wrote it; for he was born at Alloway, near Ayr, Scotland, in 1759. He lived but ten years after writing it, dying at Dumfries in 1796.

BURNS' EPISTLE TO A YOUNG FRIEND.

I lang hae thought, my youthfu' friend,
    A something to have sent you,
Tho' it should serve nae ither end
    Than just a kind memento.
But how the subject-theme may gang,
    Let time and chance determine;
Perhaps it may turn out a sang;
    Perhaps, turn out a sermon.

Ye 'll try the world soon, my lad;
  And, Andrew dear, believe me,
Ye 'll find mankind an unco [1] squad,
  And muckle they may grieve ye:
For care and trouble set your thought,
  Ev'n when your end 's attainèd;
And a' your views may come to nought,
  Where ev'ry nerve is strainèd.

I 'll no say, men are villains a';
  The real, harden'd wicked,
Wha hae nae check but human law,
  Are to a few restricket;
But och! mankind are unco [2] weak,
  An' little to be trusted;
If SELF the wavering balance shake,
  It 's rarely right adjusted!

Yet they wha fa' in fortune's strife,
  Their fate we shouldna censure;
For still, th' important end of life
  They equally may answer:
A man may hae an honest heart,
  Tho' poortith [3] hourly stare him;
A man may tak a neibor's part,
  Yet hae nae cash to spare him.

Ay free, aff han', your story tell,
  When wi' a bosom crony;
But still keep something to yoursel
  Ye scarcely tell to ony:
Conceal yoursel as weel 's ye can
  Frae critical dissection;

---

[1] Strange.   [2] Uncommonly.   [3] Poverty.

But keek [1] thro' ev'ry other man,
　Wi' sharpen'd, sly inspection.

The sacred lowe [2] o' weel-plac'd love,
　Luxuriantly indulge it;
But never tempt th' illicit rove,
　Tho' naething should divulge it:
I waive the quantum o' the sin,
　The hazard of concealing;
But och! it hardens a' within,
　And petrifies the feeling!

To catch dame Fortune's golden smile,
　Assiduous wait upon her;
And gather gear by ev'ry wile
　That's justify'd by honor;
Not for to hide it in a hedge,
　Nor for a train attendant;
But for the glorious privilege
　Of being independent.

The fear o' hell's a hangman's whip,
　To haud [3] the wretch in order;
But where ye feel your honor grip,
　Let that ay be your border:
Its slightest touches, instant pause —
　Debar a' side-pretences;
And resolutely keep its laws,
　Uncaring consequences.

The great Creator to revere
　Must sure become the creature;
But still the preaching cant forbear,
　And ev'n the rigid feature:

[1] Peer keenly.　　　　[2] Flame.　　　　[3] Hold, keep.

Yet ne'er with wits profane to range,
  Be complaisance extended;
An atheist laugh 's a poor exchange
  For Deity offended!

When ranting round in pleasure's ring,
  Religion may be blinded;
Or if she gie [1] a random sting,
  It may be little minded;
But when on life we 're tempest-driv'n —
  A conscience but [2] a canker —
A correspondence fix'd wi' Heaven,
  Is sure a noble anchor.

Adieu, dear, amiable youth!
  Your heart can ne'er be wanting!
May prudence, fortitude, and truth,
  Erect your brow undaunting!
In ploughman phrase, " God send you speed,"
  Still daily to grow wiser;
And may ye better reck the rede [3]
  Than ever did th' adviser!

[1] Give.   [2] Without.   [3] Attend to the counsel.

JEAN PAUL FRIEDRICH RICHTER

(A. D. 1763–1825.)

"RICHTER," writes Carlyle, whose thought and style were profoundly influenced by him, "was born at Wonsiedel in Baireuth, in the year 1763; and as his birthday fell on the 21st of March, it was sometimes wittily said that he and the Spring were born together. . . . Destiny, he seems to think, made another witticism on him; the word *Richter* being appellative as well as proper, in the German tongue, where it signifies *Judge*. His Christian name, Jean Paul, which long passed for some freak of his own, and a pseudonym, he seems to have derived honestly enough from his maternal grandfather, Johann Paul Kuhn, a substantial clothmaker in Hof; only translating the German *Johann* into the French *Jean*. The Richters, for at least two generations, had been schoolmasters, or very subaltern churchmen, distinguished for their poverty and their piety; the grandfather, it appears, is still remembered in his little circle as a man of quite remarkable innocence and holiness. . . . The father, who at this time occupied the humble post of *Tertius* (Underschoolmaster) and Organist at Wonsiedel, was shortly afterwards appointed Clergyman in the hamlet of Jodiz; and thence, in the course of years, transferred to Schwarzenbach on the Saale." The removal to Schwarzenbach occurred in the thirteenth year of Jean Paul. Three years later the father died, leaving his family in poverty and debt. Nevertheless, suffering infinite hardships, Paul struggled through the Hof Gymnasium and through Leipzig University, and entered his career of authorship at nineteen, when he produced the satirical sketches which he called "Grönländische Prozesse" (Greenland Lawsuits). "He lived as the young ravens; he was often in danger of starving. ' The prisoner's allowance,' says he, ' is bread and water; but I had only the latter.' . . . Richter does not anywhere appear to have faltered in his progress; for a moment to have lost heart, or even to have lost good humour." In 1784 he rejoined his mother, who had taken up her residence at Hof, and the family, sometimes including several brothers, lived in a single apartment. It was not till 1788 that he could find a publisher for his next book, the "Selection from the Papers of the Devil," and then few readers. "It appears that the 'Unsichtbare Loge' (Invisible Lodge) sent forth from the Hof spinning establishment in 1793, was the first of his works that obtained any decisive favour. . . . With the appearance of 'Hesperus,' another wondrous novel, which proceeded from the same 'single apartment,' in 1796, the siege may be said to have terminated by storm." In 1797 the mother died, and in the following year Richter married, settling himself shortly afterwards at Weimar, where he lived for several years "in high favour with whatever was most illustrious in that city. . . .

"'Titan,' one of his chief romances (published at Berlin in 1800), was written during his abode at Weimar; so likewise the 'Flegeljahre' (Wild Oats); and the Eulogy of 'Charlotte Corday.' . . . Richter's other novels published prior to this period are the 'Invisible Lodge;' the 'Siebenkas' (or Flower, Fruit, and Thorn Pieces); the 'Life of Quintus Fixlein;' the 'Jubalsenior' (Parson in Jubilee): 'Jean Paul's Letters and Future History,' the 'Déjeuner in Kuchschnappel,' the 'Biographical Recreations under the Cranium of a Giantess,' scarcely belonging to this species. The novels published afterwards are the 'Leben Fibels' (Life of Fibel); 'Katzenbergers Badereise' (Katzenberger's Journey to the Bath); 'Schmelzles Reise nach Flätz' (Schmelzle's Journey to Flätz); the 'Comet,' named also 'Nicholaus Margraf.' . . .

"We hope many will agree with us in honouring Richter, such as he was; and, 'in spite of his hundred real, and his ten thousand seeming faults,' discern under this wondrous guise the spirit of a true Poet and Philosopher. A Poet, and among the highest of his time we must reckon him, though he wrote no verses; a Philosopher, though he promulgated no systems: for, on the whole, that 'Divine Idea of the World' stood in clear, ethereal light before his mind; he recognized the Invisible, even under the mean forms of these days, and with a high, strong, not uninspired heart, strove to represent it in the Visible, and publish tidings of it to his fellowmen." — THOMAS CARLYLE, "Jean Paul Friedrich Richter again" ("Miscellanies," v. iii.).

In the fictitious "Life of Quintus Fixlein," Jean Paul, himself one of the characters and the narrator of the story, notes down the following Rules of Life, for his own guidance and that of his friends: —

QUINTUS FIXLEIN'S RULES OF LIFE.

(From Richter's "Life of Quintus Fixlein," translated by Thomas Carlyle.)

Little joys refresh us constantly like house-bread, and never bring disgust; and great ones, like sugar-bread, briefly, and then bring it.

Trifles we should let, not plague us only, but also gratify us; we should seize not their poison-bags only, but their honey-bags also; and if flies often buzz about our room, we should, like Domitian, amuse ourselves with flies, or like a certain still living Elector, feed them.

For *civic* life and its micrologies, for which the parson has a natural taste, we must acquire an artificial one; must learn to love without esteeming it; learn, far as it ranks beneath *human* life, to enjoy it like another twig of this human life, as poetically as we do the pictures of it in romances. The loftiest mortal loves and seeks the *same sort* of things with the meanest; only from higher grounds and by higher paths. Be every minute, Man, a full life to thee!

Despise anxiety and wishing, the Future and the Past!

If the *Second-pointer* can be no road-pointer into an Eden for thy soul, the *Month-pointer* will still less be so, for thou livest not from month to month, but from second to second! Enjoy thy Existence more than thy Manner of Existence, and let the dearest object of thy Consciousness be this Consciousness itself!

Make not the Present a means of thy Future; for this Future is nothing but a coming Present; and the Present, which thou despisest, was once a Future which thou desiredest!

Stake in no lotteries, — keep at home, — give and accept no pompous entertainments, — travel not abroad every year!

Conceal not from thyself, by long plans, thy household goods, thy chamber, thy acquaintance.

Despise Life, that thou mayst enjoy it!

Inspect the neighborhood of thy life; every shelf, every nook of thy abode; and nestling in, quarter thyself in the farthest and most domestic winding of thy snail-house!

Look upon a capital but as a collection of villages, a village as some blind-alley of a capital; fame as the talk of neighbors at the street-door; a library as a learned conversation, joy as a second, sorrow as a minute, life as a day; and three things as all in all: God, Creation, Virtue!

WORDSWORTH

(A. D. 1770–1850.)

WILLIAM WORDSWORTH, one of the greatest of English poets, was born at Cockermouth, in Cumberland, England, on the 7th of April, 1770. His father, John Wordsworth, was law-agent of Sir James Lowther, afterwards Earl of Lonsdale. The future poet was educated, first at a school in Hawkshead, and then at St. John's College, Cambridge. He travelled and lived during several years in France and elsewhere on the Continent; and, after several changes of English residence, settled with his devoted sister Dorothy in the Westmoreland Lake Country, where the remainder of his life was passed in meditation and poetical composition. He married happily in 1802. In 1843, on the death of his friend Southey, he was appointed Poet Laureate. His death occurred in 1850.

The noble poem quoted below, entitled "The Happy Warrior," was inspired by the death of Lord Nelson, in 1805, following the loss, in that same year, of the poet's brother, John Wordsworth, captain of an East Indiaman, whose ship was sunk by an incompetent pilot. He drew a blended portrait, joining the two heroic memories in one grand ideal. He "had recourse," says Mr. F. W. H. Myers, "to the character of his own brother John for the qualities in which the great Admiral appeared to him to have been deficient. . . . And surely these two natures taken together make the perfect Englishman. Nor is there any portrait fitter than that of ' The Happy Warrior ' to go forth to all lands as representing the English character at its height — a figure not ill-matching with ' Plutarch's men.' For indeed this short poem is itself a manual of greatness; there is a Roman majesty in its simple and weighty speech."

CHARACTER OF THE HAPPY WARRIOR.

(By William Wordsworth.)

Who is the happy warrior?   Who is he
Whom every man in arms should wish to be?
— It is the generous spirit, who, when brought
Among the tasks of real life, hath wrought
Upon the plan that pleased his childish thought:
Whose high endeavours are an inward light
That make the path before him always bright;
Who, with a natural instinct to discern
What knowledge can perform, is diligent to learn;
Abides by this resolve, and stops not there,
But makes his moral being his prime care;
Who, doom'd to go in company with pain,
And fear, and bloodshed, miserable train!
Turns his necessity to glorious gain;
In face of these doth exercise a power
Which is our human nature's highest dower;
Controls them and subdues, transmutes, bereaves
Of their bad influence, and their good receives;
By objects which might force the soul to abate
Her feeling, render'd more compassionate;
Is placable — because occasions rise
So often that demand such sacrifice;
More skilful in self-knowledge, even more pure
As tempted more; more able to endure,
As more exposed to suffering and distress
Thence, also, more alive to tenderness.
— 'T is he whose law is reason; who depends
Upon that law as on the best of friends;
Whence, in a state where men are tempted still
To evil for a guard against worse ill,

And what in quality or act is best
Doth seldom on a right foundation rest,
He fixes good on good alone, and owes
To virtue every triumph that he knows;
— Who, if he rise to station of command,
Rises by open means; and there will stand
On honourable terms, or else retire
And in himself possess his own desire;
Who comprehends his trust, and to the same
Keeps faithful with a singleness of aim;
And therefore does not stoop, nor lie in wait
For wealth, or honours, or for worldly state;
Whom they must follow; on whose head must fall,
Like showers of manna, if they come at all;
Whose powers shed round him in the common strife,
Or mild concerns of ordinary life,
A constant influence, a peculiar grace;
But who, if he be call'd upon to face
Some awful moment to which Heaven has join'd
Great issues, good or bad for human kind,
Is happy as a lover; and attired
With sudden brightness, like a man inspired;
And through the heat of conflict, keeps the law
In calmness made, and sees what he foresaw;
Or if an unexpected call succeed,
Come when it will, is equal to the need:
— He who, though thus endued as with a sense
And faculty for storm and turbulence,
Is yet a soul whose master bias leans
To homefelt pleasures and to gentle scenes;
Sweet images! which, wheresoe'er he be,
Are at his heart; and such fidelity
It is his darling passion to approve;
More brave for this, that he hath much to love:

'T is, finally, the man, who, lifted high,
Conspicuous object in a nation's eye,
Or left unthought of in obscurity, —
Who with a toward or untoward lot,
Prosperous or adverse, to his wish or not,
Plays, in the many games of life, that one
Where what he most doth value must be won ;
Whom neither shape of danger can dismay,
Nor thought of tender happiness betray ;
Who, not content that former worth stand fast,
Looks forward, persevering to the last,
From well to better, daily self-surpass'd :
Who, whether praise of him must walk the earth,
For ever, and to noble deeds give birth,
Or he must go to dust without his fame,
And leave a dead, unprofitable name,
Finds comfort in himself and in his cause ;
And, while the mortal mist is gathering, draws
His breath in confidence of Heaven's applause :
This is the happy warrior ; this is he
Whom every man in arms should wish to be.

ZSCHOKKE

(A. D. 1771–1848.)

JOHANN HEINRICH DANIEL ZSCHOKKE, celebrated as an author, as a teacher, and as a public-spirited citizen, was born at Magdeburg, Germany, in 1771; but settled in Switzerland in 1796, and became a citizen of that republic. He was a voluminous writer, his collected works filling forty volumes, including ten volumes of tales, many of them much admired, besides religious, historical, and economic writings. The most noted of Zschokke's books is the "Stunden der Andacht," translated into English under the title "Meditations on Life, Death, and Eternity," from which the counsel given hereunder is quoted. Its author died in 1848.

ON THE OVERCOMING OF FAULTS.

(From "Meditations on Life, Death, and Eternity," by Zschokke, translated by Frederica Rowan.)

When a man intends to sketch out a plan of some great and important undertaking relative to worldly matters, he first weighs and examines calmly and carefully what means will be most likely to help him to achieve his object; considers the circumstances amid which he will have to act; measures the extent of his own powers in respect of the undertaking; and even calculates the obstacles which he may possibly have to encounter, and ponders beforehand on the best means of overcoming them. . . . Dost thou think that the elevating, perfecting, and sanctifying of thy soul require less effort and reflection than the increase of thy revenue, or of the consideration in which thou art held by the world? . . .

Do not begin by making a solemn promise to God that thou wilt at once become a holier being, and that thou wilt conquer all thy faults and all thy passions; for experience ought to have taught thee ere this, that thou wilt be unable to fulfill this rash promise.

On the contrary, ask thyself first: Wherein am I most faulty? Which are the defects in my character which more especially lead me to commit unjust acts? And which is the one among these defects which is most injurious to myself and to others? Thou wilt never have any difficulty in discovering these faults, for thy conscience, that is to say, the sacred though faint voice of thy spirit which is yearning for perfection, will aid thee in detecting them.

Then inquire further: Whence comes this defect? Is it owing to my early education? Or is it a consequence of the power of outward things over me? Or the effect of my temperament? Or is it, perhaps, caused by a still more deep-seated or concealed passion, or the result of some bad habit indulged in till it has become, as it were, second nature?

And when thou hast thus fathomed the cause from which thy principal defect springs, then consider the circumstances amidst which thou livest, and the character of the persons by whom thou art surrounded; reflect earnestly upon what would be the most effective means of preventing these from calling forth this fault in you, and of rendering it innoxious to them and to thee. To do this, it is not sufficient to make an impulsive resolution. Thou must take a calm and deliberate survey of all the means that may be available for conquering the fault, whether it arise from thy education, thy temperament, or from habit.

Probably thou mayst not succeed in getting the better of it for some days, or even weeks or months. The evil tendency will, no doubt, often assail thee anew ; but thou wilt nevertheless be able to keep it in check and gradually to conquer it, if, each time it stirs within thee, thou wilt recall to mind thy noble resolve, and say to thyself : " Now is the time to show strength of mind, and to exercise power over my lower nature." Avoid everything that is likely to tempt thee and to make thee forget thyself; but when thou canst not do so, then exert thyself to the utmost to master thy feelings, and to act in such manner that thou needst not be ashamed even were the whole world to witness thy conduct. But never place thyself in the way of temptation in order to test thy strength. They who expose themselves to temptation are sure, sooner or later, to succumb. The only means of destroying our evil tendencies and of conquering our weaknesses, is by never rousing them. If they are never called into activity, our faults at last die out of themselves.

Do not attempt too much at once. First conquer the greatest obstacles in thy way to perfection, afterwards the others will be the more easily subdued. Attack thine enemies singly, if thou wouldst be victor. To wage war against all, at one and the same time, might prove too much for thy strength, and might end in robbing thee of all energy and hope.

In like manner, it is easier, in daily life, to keep a strict guard over thyself, when thou hast only one enemy, though it be the strongest, and the greatest, to observe and to combat. This will allow thee to concentrate thy strength, which must, on the contrary, be divided, if thou undertakest ever to keep carefully before thy mind every precept of Christianity, and anxiously to weigh and to test thy every thought and word. To carry out such an attempt exceeds the measure of human strength.

Be without guile, take men as they are, and let thy intercourse with them be simple and straightforward, without always weighing and calculating results; but never for one moment lose sight of thy chief enemy, thy besetting sin.

MADAME SWETCHINE

(A. D. 1782–1859.)

MADAME SWETCHINE — Sophie Soymonoff in her maidenhood — was of high Russian birth, and lived for a time the life of the Russian court, as maid of honor to the Empress Marie, unhappy wife of the Czar Paul I. At the bidding of her parents she married General Swetchine, who was many years her senior in age and with whom she had few tastes or interests in common; but he gained her esteem and she lived with him not unhappily until he died, in 1850, at the age of ninety-two. In 1816 they changed their residence to Paris, and there she became the central spirit of a social circle both morally and intellectually distinguished. She had already withdrawn herself from the Greek Church to join the Roman, and was, by her nature, sincerely devout. Her piety, however, had no ascetic taint. She enjoyed society, and, according to the French phrase, "established a salon," which was famous for its charm. Its doors were open to her guests from three o'clock in the afternoon until six, and from nine in the evening until midnight. After that hour, it appears, she gave some time to noting such thoughts as are quoted in the selections that follow. Yet she rose before sunrise, and spent early hours in attending church and visiting the poor.

Madame Swetchine lived to the ripe age of seventy-seven years, dying in 1859. During her life she published nothing. Only her friends had known of the Thoughts she had written down in her meditative hours. After her death they were given to the world, and the world is richer for the gift.

SELECTIONS FROM THE "AIRELLES" AND "THOUGHTS" OF MADAME SWETCHINE.

(From the "Writings of Madame Swetchine," translated by H. W. Preston.)

Those who have suffered much are like those who know many languages: they have learned to understand and be understood by all.

Let us desire no more intellect than is requisite for perfect goodness, and that is no small degree; for goodness consists in a knowledge of all the needs of others, and all the means of supplying them which exist within ourselves.

Let us resist the opinion of the world fearlessly, provided only that our self-respect grows in proportion to our indifference.

Our vanity is the constant enemy of our dignity.

Providence has willed that all the virtues should originate in actual wants, and all the vices in factitious ones.

It is by doing right that we arrive at just principles of action.

He who has never denied himself for the sake of giving, has but glanced at the joys of charity. We owe our superfluity; and, to be happy in the performance of our duty, we must exceed it.

How can that gift leave a trace, which has left no void?

"Is not life useful when it is happy?" asks the egotist. "Is it not sufficiently happy when it is useful?" asks the good man.

Let us exceed our appointed duties, and keep within our lawful pleasures.

Repentance is accepted remorse.

Let us not fail to scatter along our pathway the seeds

of kindness and sympathy. Some of them will doubtless perish; but if one only lives, it will perfume our steps and rejoice our eyes.

There is nothing at all in life, except what we put there.

It is a mercy to the rich that there are poor. Alms is but the material life of the latter: it is, at least in a degree, the spiritual life of the former.

There are not good things enough in life to indemnify us for the neglect of a single duty.

There is a transcendent power in example. We reform others unconsciously when we walk uprightly.

We are rich only through what we give, and poor only through what we refuse.

The best advice on the art of being happy is about as easy to follow as advice to be well when one is sick.

To do nothing is not always to lose one's time. To do what we do carelessly, is to lose it inevitably. It is weariness without profit.

We forgive too little — forget too much.

Youth should be a savings-bank.

There are two ways of attaining an important end, — force and perseverance. Force falls to the lot only of the privileged few, but austere and sustained perseverance can be practised by the most insignificant.

SCHOPENHAUER

(A. D. 1788–1860.)

ARTHUR SCHOPENHAUER, who is called the philosopher of Pessimism, was born at Dantzic, before it became a Prussian city, on the 22d of February, 1788, and died at Frankfort-on-the-Main, in September, 1860. His father was a wealthy merchant, of Dutch descent, — a man of superior character and education, whose memory was held in reverence by the son, though he died while the latter was a youth. His mother was a woman of talent, but so different from himself in disposition that they lived apart, by common agreement, after the father's death. "As long as you are what you are," wrote his mother to him when he was nineteen, "I would rather bring any sacrifice than consent to live with you. Your eternal quibbles, your laments over the stupid world and human misery give me bad nights and unpleasant dreams." Thus early he had acquired the view of the world and of human life which inspired his pessimistic philosophy. According to his own statement, he had fully matured his philosophical system before he was twenty-seven. At thirty he had finished the work in which it is mainly set forth. This, of which the translated title is "The World as Will and as Idea," drew little attention for many years; but Schopenhauer lived to see it rank with the greatest productions of German thought. Its influence on the deeper thinking of the world — and perhaps quite as much in the minds that reject its fundamental doctrine as in the minds that accept it —has been of steady growth to the present day.

But his principal work is by no means the sole source of the influence which Schopenhauer has caused to be felt. He wrote on Ethics and on Art, especially on Music, not only with profound originality and suggestiveness, but with a charm of imagination and wit, and with a deftness of literary touch, which are unique in the writings of German philosophers.   Of his ethical doctrines, a remarkably comprehensive summary is contained in a few sentences that we will quote from Miss Helen Zimmer's little book entitled "Arthur Schopenhauer: His   Life   and   Philosophy."   "Schopenhauer's ethics," says Miss Zimmer, "are implied in the leading principle of his system.   Everything hinges upon the affirmation or negation of ' the Will to live.' . . . All wrongdoing is in the last analysis resolvable into contempt for the rights of others, into pursuit of one's own advantage, in affirmation of ' the Will to live' at their expense.   In its coarsest form this implies the commission of crimes of violence punishable by the legislator, but between these and the most refined forms of egotism the difference is merely one of degree. Right moral action can spring only from the recognition of the essential evil of the phenomenal world, and the deliberate resolve to reduce it to a minimum.   The secret of this lies in one word, abnegation.   ' The Will to live ' comprehends self-assertion in every form and shape, and as every charitable action involves the denial of self in some respect, it follows that Schopenhauer's morality is in the main equivalent to the inculcation of universal philanthropy. . . . It will be at once apparent that in its practical ethical aspect Schopenhauer's teaching differs in nothing from Buddhism. The reference of all existence to egotistic desire, the conclusion that as such it must be essentially evil, the further corollary that the road to the extinction of sorrow can only lie through the extinction of desire, and that this can only be attained by the mortification of every passion; these are the very commonplaces of Buddhistic teaching.   The spirit in which they are urged is indeed very different.   No two things can be much more dissimilar than Schopenhauer's angry invective and Buddha's mild persuasiveness; nor perhaps is the whole body of his ethical doctrine so expressive as Buddha's matchless definition of virtue: ' The agreement of the Will with the Conscience.'   Substantially, however, the accordance is perfect."

The practical inculcations to which his doctrines led are exemplified in the following maxims, culled from a translation of the first and second parts of Schopenhauer's "Aphorismen zur Lebensweisheit."

SELECTED PASSAGES FROM SCHOPENHAUER'S "APH-ORISMS ON THE WISDOM OF LIFE."

(From a translation by T. Bailey Saunders, M. A., published by Messrs. Swan Sonnenschein & Co., in two parts, respectively entitled "The Wisdom of Life" and "Counsels and Maxims.")

What a man has in himself is . . . the chief element in his happiness. . . .

What a man is, and so what he has in his own person, is always the chief thing to consider; for his individuality accompanies him always and everywhere, and gives its color to all his experiences. . . .

The man who is cheerful and merry has always a good reason for being so, — the fact, namely, that he is so. . . . Nothing contributes so little to cheerfulness as riches, or so much as health. . . .

The most general survey shows us that the two foes of happiness are pain and boredom. We may go further, and say that in the degree in which we are fortunate enough to get away from the one, we approach the other. Life presents, in fact, a more or less violent oscillation between the two. . . . Needy surroundings and poverty produce pain; while, if a man is more than well off he is bored. . . . Nothing is so good a protection . . . as inward wealth, the wealth of the mind, because the greater it grows the less room it leaves for boredom.

Ordinary people think merely how they shall *spend* their time; a man of intellect tries to *use* it.

The conclusion we come to is that the man whom nature has endowed with intellectual wealth is the happiest. . . . The man of inner wealth wants nothing from outside but the negative gift of undisturbed leisure, to develop and mature his intellectual faculties, that is, to enjoy his wealth; in short he wants permission to be himself, his whole life long, every day and every hour. . . .

The value we set upon the opinion of others, and our constant endeavour in respect of it, are each quite out of proportion to any result we may reasonably hope to attain; so that this attention to other people's attitude may be regarded as a kind of universal mania which every one inherits. In all we do, almost the first thing we think about is, what will people say; and nearly half the troubles and bothers of life may be traced to our anxiety on this score. . . .

Honour is, on its objective side, other people's opinion of what we are worth; on its subjective side, it is the respect we pay to this opinion. From the latter point of view, to be a man of honour is to exercise what is often a very wholesome, but by no means a purely moral influence. . . .

The ultimate foundation of honour is the conviction that moral character is unalterable: a single bad action implies that future actions of the same kind will, under similar circumstances, also be bad. . . .

Fame is something which must be won; honour, only something which must not be lost. The absence of fame is obscurity, which is only a negative; but loss of honour is shame, which is a positive quality. . . .

The first and foremost rule for the wise conduct of life seems to me to be contained in a view to which Aristotle parenthetically refers in the Nichomachean Ethics: . . . not pleasure, but freedom from pain, is what the wise man will aim at. . . .

A man who desires to make up the book of his life and determine where the balance of happiness lies, must put down in his accounts, not the pleasures which he has enjoyed, but the evils which he has escaped. . . . To live happily only means to live less unhappily — to live a tolerable life. There is no doubt that life is given us, not to be enjoyed, but to be overcome — to be got over. . . .

The fool rushes after the pleasures of life and finds himself their dupe; the wise man avoids its evils. . . .

The safest way of not being very miserable is not to expect to be very happy. . . .

To estimate a man's condition in regard to happiness, it is necessary to ask, not what things please him, but what things trouble him; and the more trivial these things are in themselves, the happier the man will be. . . .

Another important element in the wise conduct of life is to preserve a proper proportion between our thought for the present and our thought for the future; in order not to spoil the one by paying over-great attention to the other. Many live too much in the present — frivolous people, I mean; others too much in the future, ever anxious and full of care. . . .

Peace of mind is impossible without a considerable amount of solitude. . . . Let me advise you . . . to form the habit of taking some of your solitude with you into society, to learn to be to some extent alone even though you are in company. . . . Society is . . . like a fire — the wise man warming himself at a proper distance from it. . . .

Envy is natural to man; and still it is at once a vice and a source of misery. We should treat it as the enemy of our happiness, and stifle it like an evil thought. This is the advice given by Seneca; as he well puts it, we shall be pleased with what we have if we avoid the self-torture of comparing our own lot with some other and happier one. . . .

We should . . . open our eyes wide to all [the] enormity [of our faults], in order that we may firmly resolve to avoid them in time to come. . . .

We should sometimes try to look upon our possessions in the light in which they would appear if we had lost them. . . . It is usually only when we have lost them that we begin to find out their value. . . .

Self-control may not appear so very difficult if we consider that every man has to submit to a great deal of very severe control on the part of his surroundings. . . . A little self-control at the right moment may prevent much subsequent compulsion at the hands of others. . . .

Activity! — doing something, if possible creating something, at any rate learning something — how fortunate it is that men cannot exist without that! A man wants to use his strength, to see, if he can, what effect it will produce; and he will get the most complete satisfaction of this desire if he can make or construct something — be it a book or a basket. . . .

If you have to live amongst men, you must allow every one the right to exist in accordance with the character he has, whatever it turns out to be; and all you should strive to do is to make use of this character in such a way as its kind and nature permit, rather than to hope for any alteration in it, or to condemn it offhand for what it is. This is the true sense of the maxim — " Live and let live.". . .

No man can see over his own height. . . . You cannot see in another man any more than you have in yourself. . . .

He who can see truly in the midst of general infatuation is like a man whose watch keeps good time, when all clocks in the town in which he lives are wrong. He alone knows the right time; but what use is that to him? for every one goes by the clocks which speak false. . . .

A man shows his character just in the way in which he deals with trifles, — for then he is off his guard. . . .

To observe and blame faults in another is a very suitable way of becoming conscious of one's own. We require a looking glass for the due dressing of our morals. . . .

Politeness is like a counter — an avowedly false coin, with which it is foolish to be stingy. . . .

Politeness is to human nature what warmth is to wax. . . .

If you want your judgment to be accepted, express it coolly and without passion.

Money is never spent to so much advantage as when you have been cheated out of it; for at one stroke you have purchased prudence.

THOMAS CARLYLE

(A. D. 1795–1881.)

THOMAS CARLYLE was born at Ecclefechan, Dumfriesshire, Scotland, December 4, 1795. His parents were in humble life, but he won his way through Edinburgh University, and supported himself by teaching and writing until his pen found continuous employment. He married Miss Jane Baillie Welsh in 1826, and removed from Edinburgh to Craigenputtoch in 1828. In 1834 he went to London and settled his residence at Chelsea, in Cheyne Row, where he lived until his death, which occurred on the 4th of February, 1881. His "Life of Schiller" was first published in the "London Magazine" in 1823–24, and in book form in 1825; his translation of Goethe's "Wilhelm Meister" in 1824; "Sartor Resartus" in "Fraser's Magazine," in 1833–34; the "French Revolution" in 1837; "Chartism" in 1839; "Heroes and Hero-worship" in 1841; "Past and Present" in 1843; "Oliver Cromwell's Letters and Speeches" in 1845; "Latter-day Pamphlets" in 1850; "Life of John Stirling" in 1851; "History of Friedrich II., called the Great," in 1858–65.

CARLYLE'S VIEW OF LIFE.

(From "Sartor Resartus," ch. ix.)

'The whim we have of Happiness is somewhat thus. By certain valuations, and averages, of our own striking, we come upon some sort of average terrestrial lot; this we fancy belongs to us by nature, and of indefeasible right. It is simple payment of our wages, of our deserts; requires neither thanks nor complaint; only such *overplus* as there may be do we account Happiness; any *deficit* again is Misery. Now consider that we have the valuation of our own deserts ourselves, and what a fund of Self-conceit there is in each of us, — do you wonder that the balance should so often dip the wrong way, and many a Blockhead cry : See there, what a payment ; was ever worthy gentleman so used ! — I tell thee, Blockhead, it all comes of thy Vanity ; of what thou *fanciest* those same deserts of thine to be. Fancy that thou deservest to be hanged (as is most likely), thou wilt feel it happiness to be only shot : fancy that thou deservest to be hanged in a hair-halter, it will be a luxury to die in hemp.'

'So true is it, what I then said, that *the Fraction of Life can be increased in value not so much by increasing your Numerator as by lessening your Denominator*. Nay, unless my Algebra deceive me, *Unity* itself divided by *Zero* will give *Infinity*. Make thy claim of wages a zero, then ; thou hast the world under thy feet. Well did the Wisest of our time write : " It is only with Renunciation (Entsagen) that Life, properly speaking, can be said to begin." '

'I asked myself : What is this that, ever since earliest years, thou hast been fretting and fuming, and lamenting and self-tormenting, on account of ? Say it in a word : is it not because thou art not HAPPY ? Because the THOU (sweet gentleman) is not sufficiently honoured, nourished, soft-bedded, and lovingly cared-for ? Foolish soul ! What Act of Legislature was there that *thou* shouldst be Happy ? A little while ago thou hadst no right to *be* at all. What if thou wert born and predestined not to be Happy, but to be Unhappy ! Art thou nothing other than a Vulture, then, that fliest through the Universe seeking after somewhat to *eat* ; and shrieking dolefully because carrion enough is not given thee ? Close thy *Byron* ; open thy *Goethe*.'

'*Es leuchtet mir ein*, I see a glimpse of it ! ' cries he

[Professor Teufelsdröckh] elsewhere: 'there is in man a HIGHER than Love of Happiness: he can do without Happiness, and instead thereof find Blessedness! Was it not to preach-forth this same HIGHER that sages and martyrs, the Poet and the Priest, in all times, have spoken and suffered; bearing testimony, through life and through death, of the Godlike that is in Man, and how in the Godlike only has he Strength and Freedom? Which God-inspired Doctrine art thou also honoured to be taught; O Heavens! and broken with manifold merciful Afflictions, even till thou become contrite, and learn it! O, thank thy Destiny for these; thankfully bear what yet remain: thou hadst need of them; the Self in thee needed to be annihilated. By benignant fever-paroxysms is Life root-ing out the deep-seated chronic Disease, and triumphs over Death. On the roaring billows of Time, thou art not engulfed, but borne aloft into the azure of Eternity. Love not Pleasure; love God. This is the EVERLASTING YEA, wherein all contradiction is solved: wherein whoso walks and works, it is well with him.' . . .

'To me, in this our life,' says the Professor, 'which is an internecine warfare with the Time-spirit, other warfare seems questionable. Hast thou in any way a Contention with thy brother, I advise thee, think well what the mean-ing thereof is. If thou gauge it to the bottom, it is simply this: "Fellow, see! thou art taking more than thy share of Happiness in the world, something from *my* share: which, by the Heavens, thou shalt not; nay, I will fight thee rather." — Alas, and the whole lot to be divided is such a beggarly matter, truly a "feast of shells," for the substance has been spilled out: not enough to quench one Appetite; and the collective human species clutching at them! — Can we not, in all such cases, rather say, "Take it, thou too-ravenous individual; take that pitiful additional fraction of a share, which I reckoned mine, but which thou so wantest; take it with a blessing: would to Heaven I had enough for thee!" If Fichte's *Wissenschaftslehre* be, "to a certain extent, Applied Christianity," surely to a still greater extent, so is this. We have not here a Whole Duty of Man, yet a Half Duty, namely the Passive half: could we but do it, as we can demonstrate it!'

'But indeed Conviction, were it never so excellent, is worthless till it convert itself into Conduct. Nay properly Conviction is not possible till then; inasmuch as all Speculation is by nature endless, formless, a vortex amid vortices: only by a felt indubitable certainty of Experience does it find any centre to revolve round, and so fashion itself into a system. Most true is it, as a wise man teaches us, that "Doubt of any sort cannot be removed except by Action." On which ground, too, let him who gropes painfully in darkness or uncertain light, and prays vehemently that the dawn may ripen into day, lay this other precept well to heart, which to me was of invaluable service: "*Do the Duty which lies nearest thee*," which thou knowest to be a Duty! Thy second Duty will already have become clearer.'

'May we not say, however, that the hour of Spiritual Enfranchisement is even this: When your Ideal World, wherein the whole man has been dimly struggling and inexpressibly languishing to work, becomes revealed, and thrown open; and you discover, with amazement enough, like the Lothario in *Wilhelm Meister*, that your "America is here or nowhere"? The Situation that has not its Duty, its Ideal, was never yet occupied by man. Yes here, in this poor, miserable, hampered, despicable Actual, wherein thou even now standest, here or nowhere is thy Ideal: work it out therefrom; and working, believe, live, be free. Fool! the Ideal is in thyself, the impediment too is in thyself: thy Condition is but the stuff thou art to shape that same Ideal out of: what matters whether such stuff be of this sort or that, so the Form thou give it be heroic, be poetic? O thou that pinest in the imprisonment of the Actual, and criest bitterly to the gods for a kingdom wherein to rule and create, know this of a truth: the thing thou seekest is already with thee, "here or nowhere," couldst thou only see!'

'But it is with man's Soul as it was with Nature: the beginning of Creation is — Light. Till the eye have vision, the whole members are in bonds. Divine moment, when over the tempest-tost Soul, as once over the wild-weltering Chaos, it is spoken: Let there be Light! Ever to the greatest that has felt such moment, is it not miraculous and God-announcing; even as, under simpler figures, to the simplest and least? The mad primeval Discord is hushed; the rudely-jumbled conflicting elements bind themselves into separate Firmaments: deep silent rock-foundations are built beneath; and the skyey vault with its everlasting Luminaries above: instead of a dark wasteful Chaos, we have a blooming, fertile, heaven-encompassed World.'

'I too could now say to myself: Be no longer a Chaos, but a World, or even Worldkin. Produce! Produce! Were it but the pitifulest infinitesimal fraction of a Product, produce it, in God's name! 'T is the utmost thou hast in thee: out with it, then. Up, up! Whatsoever thy hand findeth to do, do it with thy whole might. Work while it is called To-day; for the Night cometh, wherein no man can work.'

LACORDAIRE

(A. D. 1802–1861.)

JEAN BAPTISTE HENRI LACORDAIRE, born near Dijon, France, May 12, 1802, was first a student of law, but turned from law to theology in 1824. He was ordained a priest in 1827, and became after some time a famous preacher at Notre Dame de Paris. His published conferences or sermons and funeral orations are greatly admired specimens of pulpit eloquence. He joined the Dominican Order of monks in 1840, and was elected to the French Academy in 1860, — a year before his death, which occurred on the 22d of November, 1861.

"This man — brilliant, ready, supple, adroit, meteor-like, diamond-like — has supplied his countrymen with a career on which they may exhaust their vocabulary of antithesis. He combined two types — the rigid mediævalist and the modern demagogue. He was an orator and an ascetic. He was a haughty priest and a champion of the democracy. He was a confessor of nuns and a writer in Liberal journals. He was a brilliant, polished, cultivated Parisian in a shaven head and a white habit. He practised the austerities of the monastic life; but 'Brother Henri Domenic Lacordaire, of the Friars' Preachers,' was the friend of Montalembert and the correspondent of Guizot. He instinctively recognized these contrasted aspects of his character. 'I hope to live and die,' he said, 'a penitent Catholic and an impenitent Liberal.'" — J. SKELTON, "Essays in History and Biography."

THE FOUR CARDINAL VIRTUES.

(From "The Moral Life," by Père Lacordaire ; translated by H. D. Langdon.)

The ancients decided, and we have not altered their decision, that there exist four fundamental virtues to which all the others return as to their natural trunk. We call them cardinal virtues, and we still range them, from respect for logic as much as consideration for antiquity, in the same order in which they placed them. The first is prudence. It is at the beginning of all the others, because it embraces human things in their most general point of view. . . .

Justice comes after prudence to forbid whatever is unjust, that is to say, whatever is against the right of a man. . . .

Temperance is the third cardinal virtue. It is moderation in desires and wants, especially in what concerns the life of the senses ; food, sleep, movement, repose, outer pleasures. By temperance, man limits himself to what is good for him ; he makes of his body a being obedient to the truth of his nature, obedient also to the law of justice. . . .

Thus the prudence of the magistrate, the justice of the honest man, the temperance of the sage, these are the first virtues, and as it were the first lines which constitute moral rectitude. This done, much is done : nevertheless this is not yet enough ; moral rectitude exists, moral greatness is absent, the man is worthy of esteem, but not of admiration. . . . Virtue being the highest thing in man, there should be in it, besides prudence, justice, and temperance, which do not suffice to his greatness, another virtue, a supreme virtue which gives to him the majesty of what is august, the splendor of character. . . .

We must have that last virtue which crowns the others by raising them to the dignity of martyrdom, the virtue which Rome called force — FORTITUDE, and the Greeks by the very name of Rome; for Rome in the Greek language, signifies strength; a prophetic name given by Providence to that city which it had destined to govern the world by the empire of right and the empire of character.

LACORDAIRE TO YOUNG MEN.

("Letters to Young Men," translated by Rev. James Trenor.)

Spend a fair share of every day upon the serious occupations of your state, and look upon this work as one of your first duties, and as the personal accomplishment of that sentence passed by God upon our first father. *In the sweat of thy brow shalt thou eat thy bread.*

As to the lawful pleasures of the mind, the heart, or the senses, indulge in them with gratitude and moderation, drawing up sometimes in order to punish yourself, without waiting to be forced to do so by necessity.

Bear constantly in mind that we have two great vices to beat down and destroy, pride and sensuality; and two great virtues to acquire, humility and penance.

Raise from time to time your heart to God, and think upon the painful passion of our Lord, in order to neutralize by the contemplation of his mangled and bleeding body the involuntary impression produced upon you by the objects you are condemned to see.

Choose some poor person, and relieve him regularly according to your means, and look upon him as *Jesus Christ Himself*, visit him, talk to him, and if you have courage enough, kiss his clothes or his feet sometimes.

Fasten yourself in spirit to His cross, hand yourself

over to the executioner: to dwell upon the thought of chastisement, and undergo it mentally, is a suffering in itself. The martyrs had immolated themselves a hundred times in their hearts before they were sacrificed in reality.

Think too of the number of slaves and poor who get scarcely anything but a little bad bread moistened with their tears and even with their blood.

Endeavor to be good, amiable, simple in your dealings with every one, and do not consider the life of a Christian as necessarily one of moroseness and melancholy. Saint Paul is continually saying to the faithful, *rejoice!* The real Christian is filled with interior joy even in the midst of sufferings: he bears his cross good-humoredly; martyrdom and opprobrium don't affect his spirits; he offers his body to be afflicted as Providence sees fit without losing his serenity; he turns into roses chains, hunger, thirst, rags, fire, scourges, the sword, death. He loves and is loved, what more does he need?

EMERSON

(A. D. 1803–1882.)

RALPH WALDO EMERSON was born in Boston, Massachusetts, on the 25th of May, 1803. After graduating from Harvard College in 1821, he taught school for five years, and then entered the ministry, to which he had seemed to be dedicated by a long line of reverend ancestors on one or the other side. In 1829 he became the colleague of the Rev. Henry Ware, in pastoral charge of the Second Unitarian Church, at Boston. Three years later, after preaching a sermon in which he made known a change of views with regard to the Lord's Supper, he resigned his charge and withdrew from the pulpit. His first visit to England was made that year, and his acquaintance and life-long correspondence with Carlyle began. After returning to America, he took up the calling of a public lecturer, and most of the now classic essays which he gave to the world during the remainder of his life were first prepared for reading on the lyceum platform. The first collection of his "Essays" was published in 1841, the second in 1844, and a volume of his poems in 1846.

The influence of Emerson on thoughtful minds soon made itself felt, in England as well as in his own country, and when he went abroad a second time, in 1847, he found many admirers awaiting him. In 1850 he published the course of lectures entitled "Representative Men." His "English Traits" was published in 1856; "The Conduct of Life" in 1860; "Society and Solitude" in 1869, and "May-Day and other Poems" the same year. These were his principal writings.

Mr. Emerson's residence in Concord began in 1835, and he lived there until his death, which occurred on the 27th of April, 1882.

"We have not in Emerson a great poet, a great writer, a great philosophy-maker. His relation to us is not that of one of those personages; yet it is a relation of, I think, even superior importance. His relation to us is more like that of the Roman Emperor Marcus Aurelius. Marcus Aurelius is not a great writer, a great philosophy-maker, he is the friend and aider of those who would live in the spirit. Emerson is the same. He is the friend and aider of those who would live in the spirit. All the points in thinking which are necessary for this purpose he takes; but he does not combine them into a system, or present them as a regular philosophy. Combined in a system by a man with the requisite talent for this kind of thing, they would be less useful than as Emerson gives them to us. . . . As Wordsworth's poetry is, in my judgment, the most important work done in verse, in our language, during the present century, so Emerson's 'Essays' are, I think, the most important work done in prose." — MATTHEW ARNOLD, "Discourses in America."

PASSAGES FROM "THE CONDUCT OF LIFE."

If now in this connection of discourse, we should venture on laying down the first obvious rules of life, I will not here repeat the first rule of economy, already propounded once and again, that every man shall maintain himself, — but I will say, get health. No labor, pains, temperance, poverty, nor exercise, that can gain it, must be grudged. For sickness is a cannibal which eats up all the life and youth it can lay hold of, and absorbs its own sons and daughters. I figure it as a pale, wailing, distracted phantom, absolutely selfish, heedless of what is good and great, attentive to its sensations, losing its soul, and afflicting other souls with meanness and mopings, and with ministration to its voracity of trifles. Dr. Johnson said severely, "Every man is a rascal as soon as he is sick." Drop the cant, and treat it sanely. In dealing with the drunken, we do not affect to be drunk. We must treat the sick with the same firmness, giving them, of course, every aid — but withholding ourselves. . . .

'T is a Dutch proverb, that "paint costs nothing," such are its preserving qualities in damp climates. Well, sunshine costs less, yet is finer pigment. And so of cheerfulness, or a good temper, the more it is spent, the more of it remains. The latent heat of an ounce of wood or stone is inexhaustible. You may rub the same chip of pine to the point of kindling, a hundred times; and the power of happiness of any soul is not to be computed or drained. It is observed that a depression of spirits develops the germs of a plague in individuals and nations. . . .

Genial manners are good, and power of accommodation to any circumstance, but the high prize of life, the crowning fortune of a man is to be born with a bias to some pursuit, which finds him in employment and happiness, — whether it be to make baskets, or broadswords, or canals, or statutes, or songs. I doubt not this was the meaning of Socrates, when he pronounced artists the only truly wise, as being actually, not apparently so. . . .

The uses of travel are occasional, and short; but the best fruit it finds, when it finds it, is conversation; and this is a main function of life. What a difference in the hospitality of minds! Inestimable is he to whom we can say what we cannot say to ourselves. Others are involuntarily hurtful to us, and bereave us of the power of thought, impound and imprison us. As, when there is sympathy, there needs but one wise man in a company, and all are wise, — so a blockhead makes a blockhead of his companion. Wonderful power to benumb possesses this brother. When he comes into the office or public room, the society dissolves; one after another slips out, and the apartment is at his disposal. What is incurable but a frivolous habit?

Ask what is best in our experience, and we shall say, a few pieces of plain-dealing with wise people. Our conversation once and again has apprised us that we belong to better circles than we have yet beheld; that a mental power invites us, whose generalizations are more worth for joy and for effect than anything that is now called philosophy or literature. In excited conversation, we have glimpses of the Universe, hints of power native to the soul, far-darting lights and shadows of an Andes landscape, such as we can hardly attain in lone meditation. Here are oracles sometimes profusely given, to which the memory goes back in barren hours.

Add the consent of will and temperament, and there exists the covenant of friendship. Our chief want in life, is, somebody who shall make us do what we can. This is the service of a friend. With him we are easily great. There is a sublime attraction in him to whatever virtue is in us. How he flings wide the doors of existence! . . . And yet we do not provide for the greatest good of life. We take care of our health; we lay up money; we make our roof tight, and our clothing sufficient; but who provides wisely that he shall not be wanting in the best property of all, — friends? We know that all our training is to fit us for this, and we do not take the step towards it. How long shall we sit and wait for these benefactors?

It makes no difference, in looking back five years, how you have been dieted or dressed; whether you have been lodged on the first floor or the attic; whether you have had gardens and baths, good cattle and horses, have been carried in a neat equipage, or in a ridiculous truck: these things are forgotten so quickly, and leave no effect. But it counts much whether we have had good companions, in that time — almost as much as what we have been doing. . . . But we live with people on other platforms; we live with dependents, not only with the young whom we are to teach all we know, and clothe with the advantages we have earned, but also with those who serve us directly, and for money. Yet the old rules hold good. Let not the tie be mercenary, though the service is measured by money. Make yourself necessary to somebody. Do not make life hard to any.

. . . But why multiply these topics, and their illustrations, which are endless? Life brings to each his task, and, whatever art you select, algebra, planting, architecture, poems, commerce, politics, — all are attainable, even to the miraculous triumphs, on the same terms, of selecting that for which you are apt; begin at the beginning, proceed in order, step by step. 'T is as easy to twist iron anchors and braid cannons, as to braid straw, to boil granite as to boil water, if you take all the steps in order. Wherever there is failure, there is some giddiness, some superstition about luck, some step omitted, which Nature never pardons. The happy conditions of life may be had on the same terms. Their attraction for you is the pledge that they are within your reach. Our prayers are prophets. There must be fidelity, and there must be adherence. How respectable the life that clings to its objects! Youthful aspirations are fine things, your theories and plans of life are fair and commendable: — but will you stick? Not one, I fear, in that Common full of people, or, in a thousand, but one: and when you tax them with treachery, and remind them of their high resolutions, they have forgotten that they made a vow. The individuals are fugitive, and in the act of becoming something else, and irresponsible. The race is great, the ideal fair, but the men whiffling and unsure. The hero is he who is immovably centred. The main difference between people seems to be, that one man can come under obligations on which you can rely, — is obligable; and another is not.

As he has not a law within him, there's nothing to tie him to.

'T is inevitable to name particulars of virtue, and of condition, and to exaggerate them. But all rests at last on that integrity which dwarfs talent, and can spare it.

THOREAU

(A. D. 1817–1862.)

HENRY DAVID THOREAU, the neighbor and friend of Ralph Waldo Emerson, was born in the famous town of Concord, Massachusetts, in 1817. At twenty years of age he graduated from Harvard College, and was a teacher at Concord and on Staten Island for five or six years. In later life, he engaged to some extent in land-surveying, and also employed himself in the making of lead-pencils, of which his father had been a manufacturer; but he reduced "business" to the smallest share possible in his life, minimizing his wants, making them simple, and devoting the most of his time to nature-study, meditation, and writing. From July, 1845, until September, 1847, he made his dwelling in a cabin that he had constructed on Walden Pond, near Concord, of which experiment in simple and undistracted living he gave a charming account in his book entitled "Walden." From one of the chapters of that book the passages quoted below are taken.

The moral quality of Thoreau's character is described by his friend and biographer, William Ellery Channing, in the words following: "The high moral impulse never deserted him, and he resolved early to 'read no book, take no walk, undertake no enterprise, but such as he could endure to give an account of to himself; and live thus deliberately for the most part.' In our estimate of his character, the moral qualities form the basis: for himself, rigidly enjoined; if in another, he could overlook delinquency. Truth before all things; in your daily life, integrity before all things; in all your thoughts, your faintest breath, the austerest purity, the utmost fulfilling of the interior law; faith in friends, and an iron and flinty pursuit of right, which nothing can tease or purchase out of us."

The death of Thoreau occurred in 1862.

ON THE MAKING OF LIFE DELIBERATE AND SIMPLE.

(From "Walden," by Henry D. Thoreau.)

I know of no more encouraging fact than the unquestionable ability of man to elevate his life by a conscious endeavor. It is something to be able to paint a particular picture, or to carve a statue, and so to make a few objects beautiful; but it is far more glorious to carve and paint the very atmosphere and medium through which we look, which morally we can do. To affect the quality of the day, that is the highest of arts. Every man is tasked to make his life, even in its details, worthy of the contemplation of his most elevated and critical hour. If we refused, or rather used up, such paltry information as we get, the oracles would distinctly inform us how this might be done.

I went to the woods because I wished to live deliberately, to front only the essential facts of life, and see if I could not learn what it had to teach, and not, when I came to die, discover that I had not lived. I did not wish to live what was not life, living is so dear; nor did I wish to practise resignation, unless it was quite necessary. I wanted to live deep and suck out all the marrow of life, to live so sturdily and Spartan-like as to put to rout all that was not life, to cut a broad swath and shave close, to drive life into a corner, and reduce it to its lowest terms, and, if it proved to be mean, why then to get the whole and genuine meanness of it, and publish its meanness to the world; or if it were sublime, to know it by experience, and be able to give a true account of it in my next excursion. For most men, it appears to me, are in a strange uncertainty about it, whether it is of the devil or of God, and have somewhat hastily concluded that it is the chief end of man here to " glorify God and enjoy him forever."

Still we live meanly, like ants; though the fable tells us that we were long ago changed into men; like pygmies we fight with cranes; it is error upon error, and clout upon clout, and our best virtue has for its occasion a superfluous and evitable wretchedness. Our life is frittered away by detail. An honest man has hardly need to count more than his ten fingers, or in extreme cases he may add his ten toes, and lump the rest. Simplicity, simplicity, simplicity! I say, let your affairs be as two or three, and not a hundred or a thousand; instead of a million count half a dozen, and keep your accounts on your thumb nail. In the midst of this chopping sea of civilized life, such are the clouds and storms and quicksands and thousand-and-one items to be allowed for, that a man has to live, if he would not founder and go to the bottom and not make his port at all, by dead reckoning, and he must be a great calculator indeed who succeeds. Simplify, simplify. Instead of three meals a day, if it be necessary eat but one; instead of a hundred dishes, five; and reduce other things in proportion. Our life is like a German Confederacy, made up of petty states, with its boundary forever fluctuating, so that even a German cannot tell you how it is bounded at any moment. The nation itself, with all its so called internal improvements, which by the way, are all external and superficial, is just such an unwieldy and overgrown establishment, cluttered with furniture and tripped up by its own traps, ruined by luxury and heedless expense, by want of calculation and a worthy aim, as the million households in the land; and the only cure for it as for them is in a rigid economy, a stern and more than Spartan simplicity of life and eleva-

tion of purpose.   It lives too fast.   Men think that it is
essential that the *Nation* have commerce, and export ice,
and talk through a telegraph, and ride thirty miles an
hour, without a doubt, whether *they* do or not; but
whether we should live like baboons or like men, is a
little uncertain. . . .

Why should we live with such hurry and waste of life?
We are determined to be starved before we are hungry.
Men say that a stitch in time saves nine, and so they take
a thousand stitches to-day to save nine to-morrow.   As
for *work*, we have n't any of any consequence.   We have
the Saint Vitus' dance, and cannot possibly keep our
heads still. . . . Hardly a man takes a half hour's nap
after dinner, but when he wakes he holds up his head and
asks, "What's the news?" as if the rest of mankind had
stood his sentinels. . . .

To a philosopher all *news*, as it is called, is gossip, and
they who edit and read it are old women over their tea.
Yet not a few are greedy after this gossip. . . .

If we respected only what is inevitable and has a right
to be, music and poetry would resound along the streets.
When we are unhurried and wise, we perceive that only
great and worthy things have any permanent and absolute
existence, — that petty fears and petty pleasures are but
the shadow of the reality.   This is always exhilarating
and sublime.   By closing the eyes and slumbering, and
consenting to be deceived by shows, men establish and
confirm their daily life of routine and habit every where,
which still is built on purely illusory foundations.   Children, who play life, discern its true law and relations
more clearly than men, who fail to live it worthily, but
who think that they are wiser by experience, that is, by
failure. . . .

Time is but the stream I go a-fishing in.   I drink at

it ; but while I drink I see the sandy bottom and detect how shallow it is.   Its thin current slides away, but eternity remains.   I would drink deeper ; fish in the sky, whose bottom is pebbly with stars.   I cannot count one. I know not the first letter of the alphabet.   I have always been regretting that I was not as wise as the day I was born.   The intellect is a cleaver ; it discerns and rifts its way into the secret of things.   I do not wish to be any more busy with my hands than is necessary.   My head is hands and feet.   I feel all my best faculties concentrated in it.   My instinct tells me that my head is an organ for burrowing, as some creatures use their snout and fore-paws, and with it I would mine and burrow my way through these hills.   I think that the richest vein is somewhere hereabouts ; so by the divining rod and thin rising vapors I judge ; and here I will begin to mine.

INDEX OF SUBJECTS AND SOURCES

ACARA, the, 65.

Accomplishments : Knowledge may give weight, accomplishments only lustre ; but more people see than weigh (Chesterfield), 361.

Achievement. See Doing.

Addison, Joseph. On methods for filling up empty spaces of life, 352.

Admonition. See Reproof.

Adornment, personal. See Dress.

Adultery. See Chastity.

Adversity. See Prosperity, Lot in life, Fortune, Disappointment.

Advice. See Counsel.

Affectation : Do not, out of fear of affectation, fall into it (Gracian), 286.

Afflictions : Resolved, after afflictions, to inquire what I am the better for them (Edwards), 374 ; those who have suffered much are like those who know many languages (Swetchine), 437. See, also, Sorrow, Prosperity.

Age. See Youth.

Agitation. See Calmness.

Ahikar, the story of, 103.

Almsgiving. See Giving.

Altruistic sentiment. See Benevolence, Considerateness, Giving, Kindness, Mercy, Love, Filial duty, Elders, Neighbors.

Ambition. See Honors, worldly.

Amiability. See Geniality.

Amusement. See Pleasure.

Anger. — Wrath. — Resentment. — Irritability. — Ill-temper. — Ill-humor : If thou findest a disputant while he is hot . . . do not get into a passion with him. . . . Be not of an irritable temper (Ptahhotep), 33, 36; A soft answer turneth away wrath (Proverbs), 54; He that is slow to anger is of great understanding (Proverbs) 54 ; Anger resteth in the bosom of fools (Ecclesiastes), 60 ; With an angry man be never angry. . . . Abstinence from anger included in the tenfold summary of duty (Manu), 70 ; Our anger to command (Periander), 76 ; He who holds back rising anger like a rolling chariot, I call a real driver . . . . Overcome anger by love. . . . Do not yield to anger (Dhammapada), 84 ; Anger is foreign from Divinity (Pythagoras), 90 ; Vanquish an angry man by gentleness. . . . Never meet an angry man with anger (Maha-bharata), 95, 96 ; Study to remove resentments and angry feelings. . . . The superior man, when angry, thinks of the difficulties his anger may involve (Confucius), 101, 102 ; To be angry at the right time, &c., not easy (Aristotle), 110, 111 ; Envy and wrath shorten the life (Ecclesiasticus), 124; One who is angry with his brother shall be in danger of the judgment (Jesus), 131 ; Not he who gives ill-language or a blow affronts, but the principle which represents these things as affronting (Epictetus), 152 ; A man when he practices wrath becomes forgetful of his duties (Spirit of Wisdom), 164; Many man for anger beateth himself with his own staff (La Tour), 191 ; Beware of wrath (Wyclif), 197 ; When wrath takes possession wisdom takes to flight (Thomas à Kempis), 203 ; Be slack and slow to ire (Rhodes), 207 ; Whoever will call to mind the excess of his past anger will see the deformity of the passion (Montaigne), 249 ; Anger is one of the sinews of the soul. . . . To be angry for every toy debases the worth of thy anger (Fuller), 306, 307 ; There is a dignity in good sense that is offended by anger (Halifax), 315 ; Every stroke our fury strikes is sure to hit ourselves. . . . Return no answer to anger, unless with meekness. . . . Be apter to remit than resent (Penn), 331, 334; Quieting the angry is an employment suited to a reasonable nature (Addison), 353; Consider how few things are worthy of anger (Chesterfield), 364; Resolved never to suffer the least anger towards irrational beings (Edwards), 367; Forbear resenting injuries so much as you think they deserve (Franklin), 378; Beware of anger, that demon, that destroyer of our peace (Chatham), 392; When angry count ten before you speak (Jefferson), 411. *See, also,* Good nature.

Animals, treatment of : A righteous man regardeth the life of his beast (Proverbs), 53; Take no pleasure in the death of a creature (Quarles), 291.

Annoyances: Escape from and forget (Ptah-hotep), 38; Trifles we should let not plague us only, but also gratify us (Richter), 426.

Antoninus, Marcus Aurelius. Selections from the "Thoughts," 157.

Anxiety: He that observeth the wind shall not sow. . . . Carefulness bringeth age (Ecclesiasticus), 62, 124; Be not anxious for your life. . . . Be not anxious for the morrow. . . . Sufficient unto the day is the evil thereof (Jesus), 134, 135; Let not future things disturb thee, etc. (Marcus Aurelius), 160; He that is anxious . . . decay results to his body and soul (Spirit of Wisdom), 164; I let reason do that for me which, after a little, time would do (Erasmus), 214; Whoever will remember the hazards he has run will prepare himself for future changes (Montaigne), 249; Let thy care be reasonable, and seasonable. . . . Put off thy care with thy clothes (Quarles), 289; Leave future occurrences to their uncertainties (Browne), 304; Better to employ our minds in supporting misfortunes which actually happen, &c. (La Rochefoucauld), 311; We should not be troubled for what we cannot help (Penn), 329; For to-day think only of to-day (Fénelon), 344; How much pain have cost us the evils that never happened (Jefferson), 411; Despise anxiety and wishing (Richter), 426; Preserve a proper proportion between thought for the present and thought for the future (Scho-

penhauer), 443. *See, also,* Trust, Prudence.

Apparel. *See* Dress.

Aristotle : Moral philosophy, 13; Injunctions for the keeping of "the mean," 108.

Art. *See* Taste.

Ascham, Roger. Advice to his brother-in-law, 219.

Asking : Know how to ask (Gracian), 287.

Attire. *See* Dress.

Authority, respect for (Ptah-hotep), 34.

Avarice. — Hoarding. — Miserliness. — Greed: Let us dwell free from greed (Dhammapada), 83; Be watchful lest thy mind . . . be to sordid avarice inclined (Pythagoras), 89; Whatever I possess, I will neither hoard nor squander (Seneca), 141; Shun avarice (Mexican precept), 227; Clearness of judgment makes men liberal, for it teacheth, &c. (Essex-Bacon), 273, 275; If avarice be thy vice, make it not thy punishment (Browne), 301; Avarice is more opposed to economy than liberality is (La Rochefoucauld), 311; Avarice, the snare of old age (Penn), 332; Avarice is the parent of evil deeds (Chesterfield), 363. *See, also,* Expenditure, Giving.

"Babees Book," the, 205.

Backbiting. *See* Slander.

Bacon, Francis. Precepts of the doctrine of advancement in life, 265; Essex's letter of advice to the Earl of Rutland, 269.

Bad humor. *See* Anger.

Beatitudes, Buddhist, 79.

Benevolence. — Helpfulness. — Pity. — Kindness: Withhold not good (Proverbs), 49; High-minded men delight in doing good, without a thought of their own interest. . . . Enjoy the prosperity of others (Maha-bharata), 96, 79; Add not more trouble to a heart that is vexed (Ecclesiasticus), 115; Reject not the supplication of the afflicted. . . . Deliver him that suffereth wrong. . . . Be a father unto the fatherless. . . . Be not slow to visit the sick. . . . Mourn with them that mourn. . . . Is not a word better than a gift ? (Ecclesiasticus), 115, 118, 120; I will so live as to remember that I was born for others (Seneca), 141; Be not ashamed to be helped (Marcus Aurelius), 160; The expenditure of charity and benevolence is profit (Maimonides), 169; Concern for the welfare of mankind a primary principle of wisdom (Welsh Triad), 171; Be gentle and compassionate towards the poor, the unfortunate, &c. (St. Louis), 174; Live a rightful life, doing the works of mercy (Wyclif), 196; Be useful to all, for such is piety (Thomas à Kempis), 203; Think unkindness to be the greatest offence, and least punished amongst men (Wyatt), 233; Do not belong wholly to yourself nor wholly to others. . . . Know how to do good to people a little at a time and often (Gracian), 287; Mistaken kindness is little less dangerous than malice (Halifax), 314; We have a call to do good as often as we have the power and the occasion (Penn), 329; To relieve the needy and comfort the afflicted are almost daily duties (Addison), 353; He who pitieth another recommendeth himself (Chesterfield), 364; Resolved to do whatever I think to be most for the good of mankind. . . . Let there be something of benevolence in all that I speak (Edwards), 366, 374; Benevolence is the queen of virtues (Chatham), 391; Reproach none for the infirmities of nature (Washington), 402; Take two wallets in thy hand: this to gather what you find, that to give with willing mind (Goethe), 417; A man may tak a neibor's part, yet hae na cash to spare him (Burns), 421; Make yourself necessary to somebody. Do not make life hard to any (Emerson), 459. See, also, Giving, Neighbors.

Best, the. See Good.

Bias, saying of, 76.

Blame. See Censure, Justice.

Boasting. See Vanity.

Bodily care. — Health. — Exercise: For health and welfare prudently provide (Pythagoras), 88; Health above all gold (Ecclesiasticus), 123; It is a mark of want of genius to spend much time in things relating to the body (Epictetus), 153; The perfection of the body precedes the perfection of the soul (Maimonides), 165; Use exercise of body, yet such as is without peril. . . . Delight to be cleanly (Sidney), 246; To take the best advantage of thyself, keep temperate diet, &c. (Quarles), 290; Refresh that part of thyself which is most wearied (Fuller), 308; Be plain in clothes, furniture, and food, but clean (Penn), 331; Have courage to wear thick boots in winter (Stanislaus), 358; Tolerate no uncleanliness (Franklin), 378; Unlimited activity must end in bankruptcy (Goethe), 414; No labor, pains, temperance, poverty, nor exercise that can gain health must be grudged (Emerson), 456. See, also, Temperance, Pleasure.

" Boke of Nurture," Hugh Rhodes's, 205.

Books: Of making many books there is no end (Ecclesiastes), 63; Mark the sense and the matter of that you read (Sidney), 246; All men that live are drawn either by book or example (Essex-Bacon), 276; Read not books alone, but men, chiefly thyself (Quarles), 289; A few books well studied, &c. (Osborne), 294; Great reading, without applying, is like corn heaped, that is not stirred (Halifax), 315; In perusing any good book, rather meditate than read much. . . . Have few books, well chosen and well read (Penn), 330, 332, 333; Apply all you read to yourself (Fénelon), 343; Of all the diversions of life, there are none so proper, &c. (Addison), 355; If you do not set apart your hours of reading, your days will slip unprofitably (Chatham), 387; Look upon a library as a learned conversation (Richter), 427. See, also, Education.

Boorishness. See Courtesy.

Borrowing. — Lending: He that borroweth till no man will lend him, let him go where no man knoweth him (Rhodes), 208, 209; Neither borrow of a neighbor or a friend. . . . In borrowing be precious of thy word (Burleigh), 242; Borrowing is the canker and death of a man's estate (Raleigh), 256; Neither a borrower nor a lender be (Shakespeare), 281; Lend not beyond thy ability, nor refuse, &c.(Penn), 326; Have courage to avoid accommodation bills (Stanislaus), 357. See, also, Debt, Expenditure, Honesty.

Bountifulness. See Giving.

Browne, Sir Thomas. Selections from a letter to a friend, and from " Christian Morals," 299, 303.

Buddhism, 77; Eight precepts and ten commandments of, 78. Beatitudes of, 79.

Burleigh, William Cecil, Lord. Ten precepts, 238.

Burns, Robert. Epistle to a Young Friend, 420.

Business. See Occupation.

Calling. *See* Occupation.

Calmness. *See* Self-control, Equanimity.

Candor. *See* Sincerity.

Carefulness. *See* Prudence.

Carlyle, Thomas. On Happiness, 29, 30, 446.

Caution. *See* Prudence.

Censure. — Blame. — Criticism : Blame not before thou hast examined (Ecclesiasticus), 120 ; Judge not that ye be not judged (Jesus), 135 ; If a person speaks ill of you do not make excuses but answer, " He doth not know my other faults " . . . . If you act rightly, why fear those who censure you wrongly (Epictetus), 152, 153 ; Look carefully into your own faults and you will find little leisure to weigh others (Thomas à Kempis), 203 ; Take the evil judgments of evil persons as true praise (Rhodes), 206 ; I find no fault with what any man purposes to do or does (Erasmus), 212 ; Find fault with yourself and with none other (Ascham), 219 ; Take each man's censure, but reserve thy judgment (Shakespeare), 281 ; Accustom yourself to the faults of those with whom you live as you do to ugly faces (Gracian), 286 ; Think thyself poor and naked without that crowning grace which thinketh no evil, &c. . . . When thou lookest upon the imperfections of others, allow one eye for what is laudable (Browne), 302, 304 ; Avoid being first in fixing a hard censure (Halifax), 319 ; They that censure should practice (Penn), 329 ; Let recollection of your own faults hinder you from fastidiousness and censoriousness (Fénelon), 343 ; I will let knowledge of the failings of others promote nothing but shame in myself (Edwards), 367 ; I see no fault committed which I could not have commited myself (Goethe), 415. *See, also,* Justice.

Ceremony : Superfluous compliments and affectations of ceremony to be avoided, yet where due not to be neglected (Washington), 402, 403.

Character : Character consists in a man steadily pursuing the things of which he thinks himself capable (Goethe), 416.

Charity (of the purse) : *See* Giving, Benevolence.

Charity (of the spirit) : Ever keep charity (Wyclif), 198. *See, also,* Censure, Justice, Magnanimity, Pride.

Chastity. — Purity. — Lust. — Licentious-

ness. — Adultery : Keep from making advances to a woman (Ptah-hotep), 36 ; Thou shalt not commit adultery (Decalogue), 42 ; Warnings against " the strange woman " (Proverbs), 50 ; Included in the tenfold summary of duty (Manu), 70 ; One should refrain from unlawful sexual intercourse (Buddha), 78 ; The superior man guards against lust (Confucius), 102 ; Keep thine eye from immodest glances (Ahikar), 104 ; Give not thyself to a light woman. . . . Meet not with a harlot. . . . Go not after thy lusts (Ecclesiasticus), 118, 119, 121 ; Lust arises from a mistake about what is good (Cicero), 127 ; Blessed are the pure in heart. . . . One that looketh on a woman to lust after her hath committed adultery in his heart (Jesus), 17, 130, 131 ; Commit no lustfulness (Spirit of Wisdom), 164 ; He that preserves purity in soul and body is like God's angels(Thomas à Kempis), 203 ; Put a bridle and a measure to thy concupiscence (Rhodes), 206 ; Eschew adultery. . . . It is a base vice (Mexican precept), 222, 225 ; Cast not your eyes on the beauty of women (Lyly), 260 ; Gaze not on beauty too much, &c. (Quarles), 291; Rarely use venery (Franklin), 378; Never tempt th' illicit rove. . . . It hardens a' within (Burns), 422 ; We have two great vices to beat down, pride and sensuality (Lacordaire), 453. *See, also,* Modesty, Ribaldry, Marriage.

Chatham, Lord. Letters to his nephew, 387.

Cheating. *See* Honesty.

Cheerfulness : Of countenance (Ptah-hotep), 39; He that is of a cheerful heart hath a continual feast (Proverbs), 54 ; Nothing contributes so little to cheerfulness as riches, or so much as health (Schopenhauer), 441 ; The more of cheerfulness is spent, the more of it remains (Emerson), 457. *See, also,* Good nature.

Chesterfield, Earl of. Maxims from " Letters to his Son," and precepts from " The Economy of Human Life," 360, 362.

Children, training of. *See* Parental duty.

Chilo, saying of, 76.

Choice. *See* Discrimination.

Christianity and Morals, 17–19.

Cicero, on the good that makes life happy, 127.

Civility. *See* Courtesy.

Cleanliness. *See* Bodily care.

Cleobolus, saying of, 76.

Clothing. *See* Dress.

Commandments: The ten Mosaic, 41; Further Mosaic, 44; The ten of Manu (tenfold summary of duty), 70; The ten Buddhistic, 78, 79. *See, also*, Religious injunctions.

Companions: Walk with wise men . . . the companion of fools shall smart (Proverbs), 53; There is no companionship with a fool (Dhammapada), 82; He that toucheth pitch shall be defiled (Ecclesiasticus), 120; Beware of associating with the wanton. . . . Be found among respectable and learned men (Maimonides), 166; Flee and avoid the society of the wicked (St. Louis), 175; Make the acquaintance of wise men (Mediæval precept), 179; Flee the company and counsel of proud men, &c. . . . Draw to you good and virtuous men (Suffolk), 201; Shun the society of liars, idlers, gossips (Mexican precept), 228; Affect their company whom you find to be worthiest (Essex-Bacon), 271; Do not dull thy palm with entertainment of each new-hatch'd, unfledg'd comrade (Shakespeare), 281; A desert is better than a debauched companion. . . . It is excellent to have a library of scholars (Fuller), 305, 306; Be not easily acquainted . . . intimate with few. . . . Prefer the aged, the virtuous, and the knowing (Penn), 327, 331; Be specially on guard as to the women with whom you are intimate (Fénelon), 343; Associate with men much older than yourself (Chatham), 388; The company in which you will improve most will be the least expensive to you. . . . It is easy to make acquaintances, but difficult to shake them off (Washington), 398, 401, 403; Be very select in the society you attach yourself to (Jefferson), 409; Learn to be to some extent alone even though you are in company (Schopenhauer), 443; It makes no difference in looking back five years how you have been dieted or dressed; . . . but it counts much whether we have had good companions (Emerson), 458. *See, also*, Friendship.

Complaining. — Fault - finding. — Grumbling: Grumble not (Ptah-hotep), 36.

Condescension: Towards thine inferiors show much humanity, and some familiarity (Burleigh), 243.

Confidence. *See* Trust.

Conformity: I would conform to the laws and customs of my country (Descartes), 297.

Confucius, maxims and analects of, 10, 99.

Conscience: The gods see the sinful, and the omniscient spirit within their breasts. . . . The soul is its own witness. . . . Grieve thou not thy soul. . . . The great Divinity who dwells within thy breast (Manu), 66, 67; Do nothing because of public opinion, but everything because of conscience (Seneca), 141; Never do that that within yourself you find a certain grudging against (Wyatt), 235; There is nothing more troublesome than a guilty conscience (Erasmus), 214; Happy is he . . . whose conscience is his strong retreat (Wotton), 282; In the commission of evil fear no man so much as thyself. . . . The multitude looks but upon thy actions; thy conscience looks into them (Quarles), 290, 292; That little spark of celestial fire called conscience (Washington), 404; A conscience but [without] a canker is sure a noble anchor (Burns), 423. *See, also*, Soul.

Considerateness for others: Wound not another, though provoked. . . . Utter no word to pain (Manu), 65.

Consistency: To change opinion is as consistent with freedom as to persist in error (Marcus Aurelius), 161.

Constancy. *See* Patience.

Contention. — Dissension. — Strife. — Quarrelling. — Disputation: Be not angry with a disputant, nor discourteous (Ptah-hotep), 33, 34, 39; The Lord hateth him that soweth discord among brethren. . . . Go not forth hastily to strive. . . . Where there is no whisperer contention ceaseth (Proverbs), 51, 56, 57; He who has given up both victory and defeat is happy. . . . Victory breeds hatred (Dhammapada), 83; Cultivate peace and concord (Confucius), 100; The superior man guards against quarrelsomeness (Confucius), 102; Abstain from strife (Ecclesiasticus), 122; Blessed are the peacemakers. . . . Agree with thine adversary quickly. . . . Resist not him that is evil (Jesus), 131, 132; with a malicious man carry on no conflict. . . . With a foolish man make no dispute (Spirit of Wisdom), 164; Quarrelsomeness and petulance waste the body, the soul, and the property (Maimonides), 168 ; God will not love him who loves to look at fighting (Welsh Triad), 171, 172 ; Do not quarrel with your neighbor, and avoid disputing with him (Mediæval precept), 178 ; Who that seeketh riot gladly, he meeteth therewith (La Tour), 191 ; Stir all to love true peace and charity ; suffer no men to be at dissension (Wyclif), 195 ; Beware of entrance to a quarrel ; but being in, &c. (Shakespeare), 281 ; Quarrels would not last long if fault was on one side (La Rochefoucauld), 312 ; In all debates let truth be thy aim, not victory. . . . It were endless to dispute upon everything disputable (Penn), 327, 328 ; Resolved to do always what I can towards making peace (Edwards), 369 ; Peace, the fruit of virtue, and . . . virtue, fruit of faith, prepare for happiness (Cowper), 394 ; In disputes be not so desirous to overcome as not to give liberty, &c. (Washington), 404 ; I never saw an instance of one of two disputants convincing the other (Jefferson), 408.

Contentment. — Resignation Contentment is the root of happiness. . . . Included in the tenfold summary of duty (Manu), 67, 70 ; Contentment the greatest blessing (Buddha), 80 ; Happy the man, &c. (Martial-Pope), 145 ; Require not things to happen as you wish, but wish them to happen as they do. . . . Never say of anything, " I have lost it," but, " I have restored it " (Epictetus), 151; Love the art which thou hast learned and be content with it. . . . Think not so much of what thou hast not as of what thou hast (Marcus Aurelius), 159, 161 ; I consult myself about a contentment ; I do not skim, but sound it. . . . A man ought to study, taste, and ruminate upon it (Montaigne), 251; He is rich, not that possesses much, but that covets no more (Quarles), 289 ; A contented mind enlargeth the dimension of little things (Browne), 304 ; When we cannot find contentment in ourselves, it is useless to seek it (La Rochefoucauld), 312; Avoid discontented persons, unless to inform or reprove them (Penn), 333 ; All the states of life which you have not tried have their thorns, &c. (Fénelon), 344 ; Murmur not at the ways of Providence (Jefferson), 410 ; Enjoy the good that 's set before thee (Goethe), 416. See, also, Lot in life, Simplicity.

Contradiction. See Disputation.

Conversation, courtesy in (Ptah-hotep), 39; Buddhistic command against vain conversation, 79 ; Conversation is a main function of life (Emerson), 457.

Correction : He is in the way of life that heedeth correction (Proverbs), 52.

Counsel. — Advice : In the multitude of counsellors there is safety (Proverbs), 52 ; He . . . is good that to the wiser friend his docile reason can submissive bend (Hesiod), 72 ; Do nothing without advice, and when done repent not (Ecclesiasticus), 124; Act by the advice of good and honorable men (St. Louis) 176; Never follow your own wit in nowise (Suffolk), 201 ; If advice be given thee, profit by it (Mexican precept), 227 ; If a man knows where to get good advice, it is as though he could supply it himself (Goethe), 415 ; He is far from wise who has but his own wisdom (Joubert), 419.

Courage : Habits of courage are spoiled by excess and defect (Aristotle), 109; Better not to live than to live a coward (Raleigh), 256 ; Be valiant, but not too venturous (Lyly), 262 ; In dangers there is no better companion than a bold heart (Gracian), 286 ; Traits of moral courage in every-day life (Stanislaus), 356.

Courtesy.— Politeness.— Civility. — Rudeness : Better a compliment to that which displeases than rudeness. . . . Treat a disputant with courtesy. . . . Answer him not in a crushing manner (Ptah-hotep), 36, 39 ; Exhibit yielding courtesy. . . . The superior man is anxious that his demeanor be respectful (Confucius), 101, 102 ; Jest not with a rude man (Ecclesiasticus), 119 ; Salute all people. . . . Be courteous and spend freely (Mediæval precept), 178, 179 ; Humility and courtesy overcometh all proud hearts (La Tour), 189; There is nothing that winneth so much with so little cost (Sidney), 246 ; Civil complacency consists with decent honesty (Browne), 303 ; Politeness of mind is in honorable and delicate thoughts (La Rochefoucauld), 311; Politeness I would venture to call benevolence in trifles (Chatham), 391; Politeness is artificial good humor (Jefferson), 407 ; There is a politeness of the heart, allied to love (Goethe), 415 ; Politeness is a guard which covers rough edges of character and prevents their wounding others (Joubert), 419; Politeness is to human nature what warmth is to wax (Schopenhauer), 445. *See, also,* Manners.

Covetousness: Thou shalt not covet, &c. (Decalogue), 43; Buddhistic command against, 79; The superior man guards against covetousness (Confucius), 102; Form no covetous desire, that the benefit of the world may not be tasteless (Spirit of Wisdom), 164; Covetousness cracks the sinews of faith, &c. (Browne), 300; To desire what belongs to another is misprision of robbery (Halifax), 316; Covet no man's property in any sort (Penn), 339.

Cowley, Abraham. Translation from Martial, 144.

Cowper, William. Description of The Happy Man, from "The Task," 394.

Credulity. *See* Trust.

Criticism. *See* Censure.

Cruelty: Thou shalt not put a stumbling block before the blind (Leviticus), 45; He that is cruel troubleth his own flesh (Proverbs), 52. *See, also,* Mercy, and Animals, treatment of.

Curiosity: I never am curious to pry in the privacies of other men (Erasmus), 212; Be not curious to know the affairs of others (Washington), 404.

Cursing: Blessings give for curses (Manu), 65.

Dancing: Abstain from (Buddhist commandments), 78.

Death: The day of death better than the day of birth. . . . There is no work . . . in the grave (Ecclesiastes), 59, 61; Virtue alone stays by [one] at the tomb. . . . Long not for death, nor hanker after life (Manu), 68, 70; Look to the end of life (Solon), 76; Death does not see him who looks down on the world (Dhammapada), 83; Look upon death or upon a comedy with the same expression (Seneca), 141; Death is not terrible; the terror consists in our notion of death (Epictetus), 151; No man loses any other life than that which he now lives. . . . The present is the same to all. . . . It is one of the acts of life, this by which we die (Marcus Aurelius), 158, 160; To live in fear of death may possibly shorten life, but never make it longer (Erasmus), 214; We should not too much prize life which we cannot keep, nor fear death which we cannot shun (Essex-Bacon), 273; Happy is he . . . whose soul is still prepared for death (Wotton), 282; Live like a neighbor unto death (Browne), 303. *See, also,* Life.

Debt: Salt and lead not heavier than debt (Ahikar), 105; If you owe anything, pay it willingly (Mediæval precept), 178; He that oweth much and hath nought, may be sorry, &c. (Rhodes), 208; Have the courage to discharge a debt while you have money (Stanislaus), 356; Never spend your money before you have it (Jefferson), 411. *See, also,* Borrowing, Honesty, Expenditure.

Decalogue: The Buddhistic, 78, 79; The Hindu: Tenfold summary of duty, 70; The Mosaic, 4, 41.

Decalogue of canons for practical life (Jefferson), 411.

Deceit. *See* Falsehood, Hypocrisy.

Deeds. *See* Doing.

Deference. *See* Filial Duty, Elders, Authority, Honor.

Deliberation. *See* Prudence.

Dependents, treatment of (Ptah-hotep), 37.

Descartes, René, the provisional rules of, 297.

Designing. *See* Malice.

Desirable. *See* Good.

Desire: Desire is not extinguished by enjoyment (Manu), 67; Right desire in the heart, the greatest blessing (Buddha), 79; If you desire things not in our own power you must be disappointed (Epictetus), 150; Have something left to wish for (Gracian), 287; Children and fools want everything (Halifax), 318.

Detraction. *See* Slander.

Dhammapada, selections from the, 82.

Diligence. *See* Industry.

Disappointment: There can be no entire disappointment to a wise man (Halifax), 315. *See, also,* Prosperity.

Discord. *See* Contention.

Discrimination. — Choice: To choose well is the most important thing in life (Gracian), 286.

Disdain. *See* Pride.

Dishonesty. *See* Honesty.

Disputation. *See* Contention.

Dissension. *See* Contention.

Dissimulation. *See* Falsehood, Hypocrisy.

Distrust. *See* Trust.

Diversions. *See* Pleasure.

Divorce. *See* Marriage.

Dogmatism : The prudent man affirms not lightly what is doubtful (Thomas à Kempis), 203.

Doing. — Deeds. — Achievement. — Performance : Divinity does not principally esteem the tongue, but the deeds. . . . Perform great things, promising nothing great (Pythagoras), 90, 93 ; We should not judge a man's merit by his good qualities, but by the use he can make of them (La Rochefoucauld), 312 ; The pride of compassing may more than compare with the pleasure of enjoying (Halifax), 316 ; A man, like a watch, is to be valued for his goings (Penn), 328, It is not enough to know, we must apply ; not enough to will, we must do (Goethe), 416 ; Living requires little life ; doing requires much (Joubert), 418 ; It is by doing right that we arrive at just principles (Swetchine), 437 ; A man wants to use his strength, to see, if he can, what effect it will produce (Schopenhauer), 444 ; Conviction, were it never so excellent, is worthless till it convert itself into conduct. . . . Produce ! produce ! were it but the pitifullest infinitesimal fraction of a product, produce it (Carlyle), 449, 450. *See, also,* Firmness.

Drama. *See* Stage.

Dress. — Personal adornment : One should not wear garlands or use perfumes (Buddha), 78 ; Be not too studied in dress ; it is the mark of a little mind (Mexican precept), 223 ; Rags and bravery will soon wear out of fashion ; but money in thy purse will ever be in fashion (Raleigh), 257 ; Let attire be comely, not too costly (Lyly), 262 ; The apparel oft proclaims the man (Shakespeare), 281 ; In apparel, avoid singularity, profuseness, and gaudiness (Quarles), 290 ; Wear your clothes neat, &c. (Osborne), 294 ; Nothing is truly fine but what is fit (Halifax), 318 ; Choose thy clothes by thine own eyes (Penn), 326, 331 ; Do not conceive that fine clothes make fine men (Washington), 399, 401, 402, 403.

Drunkenness. *See* Temperance.

Duplicity. *See* Sincerity.

Duty : Let no one forget his own duty for the sake of another's (Dhammapada), 83 ; Let it make no difference to thee whether cold or warm, if thou art doing thy duty (Marcus Aurelius), 160 ; Resolved to do whatever I think to be my duty (Edwards), 366, 373 ; What is your duty ? To fulfil the claims of the day. . . . Art thou little, do that little well. . . . Like the star. . . let each man wheel with steady sway round the task that rules the day, and do his best (Goethe), 414, 417 ; Men must either be the slaves of duty or of force (Joubert), 419 ; Let us exceed our appointed duties. . . . There are not good things enough in life to indemnify us for the neglect of a duty (Swetchine), 437, 438 ; Do the duty which lies nearest thee (Carlyle), 449 ; *See, also,* Fidelity, Filial duty, Elders, Political duty, Religious injunctions.

Early rising. *See* Sleep.

Earnestness. — Seriousness. — Gravity. — Thoughtlessness. — Frivolity : Those who are in earnest do not die (Dhammapada), 82 ; Do every act of thy life as if it were the last (Marcus Aurelius), 158.

Ecclesiastes, selections from, 7, 58.

Ecclesiasticus, selections from, 113.

Economy. *See* Expenditure.

Economy of Human Life, selections from The, 362.

Education. — Teaching. — Learning : Be not arrogant because of learning (Ptahhotep) 33 ; Of making many books there is no end, and much study is a weariness (Ecclesiastes), 63 ; Much insight and education the greatest blessing (Buddha), 79 ; Make much of the colleges and seminaries. . . . Instruct sons and younger brothers (Confucius), 101 ; Hast thou children ? instruct them (Ecclesiasticus), 118 ; Men exist for one another ; teach them then, or bear with them (Marcus Aurelius), 161 ; Men learn when they teach (Rhodes), 208 ; Study the greatest pleasure of life. Make it a diversion, not a toil (Erasmus), 215 ; In study seek two things : first to conceive or understand ; second to lay up or remember (Essex-Bacon), 277 ; To advise the ignorant is one of the duties that fall in our way almost daily (Addison), 353 ; The main business of education should be to direct the will (Joubert), 419. *See, also,* Books, Knowledge, Teachableness, Edwards, Jonathan, the resolutions of, 366.

Effrontery. — Impudence. — Impertinence : Impudence is no virtue, yet able to beggar them all (Osborne), 295.

Eighteenth century, moral characteristics of, 27–29.

Elders, conduct towards : Treat not with disrespect thy father, mother, teacher, elder brother (Manu), 65 ; Honor and salute old men. . . . Be careful not to mock the old (Mexican precept), 222 ; Prefer elders and strangers (Penn), 332.

Emerson, Ralph Waldo : Passages from "The Conduct of Life," 456.

Enchiridion of Epictetus, 15, 16, 149.

Enchiridion of Quarles, 289.

Enjoyment. See Pleasure.

Enmity : If thine enemy be hungry, &c. (Proverbs), 56 ; Love your enemy (Jesus), 132 ; In friendships and enmities let your confidence and your hostilities have bounds (Chesterfield), 361.

Envy : Envy is the rottenness of the bones (Proverbs), 54 ; Provoke not envy (Pythagoras), 89 ; Envy and wrath shorten the life (Ecclesiasticus), 124 ; Bear no envy, that life may not be tasteless (Spirit of Wisdom), 164 ; Envy always is a concomitant of a pompous felicity (Erasmus), 211 ; Be not jealous of what the good God granteth to others (Mexican precept), 227 ; The greatest harm you can do unto the envious is to do well (Lyly), 262 ; Happy is he . . . who envies none (Wotton), 282 ; Let age, not envy, draw wrinkles on thy cheeks (Browne), 302 ; Envy is a passion we never dare to avow. . . . Envy is more irreconcilable than hatred (La Rochefoucauld), 310, 311 ; Malice may be sometimes out of breath, envy never (Halifax), 315 ; Virtue is not secure against envy. . . . Envy none (Penn), 329, 335 ; Softening the envious is an employment suited to a reasonable nature (Addison), 353 ; We should treat envy as the enemy of our happiness (Schopenhauer), 443.

Epictetus, selections from the precepts of, 15, 16, 149.

Epicurean morality, 13–15.

Equanimity : Men are disturbed, not by things, but by the principles and notions which they form concerning things (Epictetus), 150 ; To be at peace with God is the fountain of true tranquillity (Erasmus), 214 ; Shun the dissipation which sudden fancies involve (Fénelon), 343 ; The tranquillity of the life of the happy man described (Cowper), 394 ; Be not disturbed at trifles or accidents (Franklin), 378 ; Take things always by their smooth handle (Jefferson), 411 ; Who through the heat of conflict keeps the law in calmness made (Wordsworth), 430. See, also, Self-control, Anxiety, Anger, Patience.

Equity. See Justice, Honesty.

Erasmus. "The Old Men's Dialogue," from the "Colloquies," 211.

Essex, Earl of, Letter of advice to the Earl of Rutland, 269.

Euphues and his Ephœbus, 260.

Evil. See Righteousness, Goodness, Virtue.

Evil-designing. See Malice.

Evil-speaking. See Slander.

Example : Thou mayest take examples of good conduct from a foe. . . . Something from all (Manu), 65 ; Example of good life more stirreth rude men than true preaching (Wyclif), 196 ; Edify thy neighbor by word and deed (Thomas à Kempis), 203 ; Set not bad examples (Mexican precept), 222 ; Make your examples of wise and honest men (Wyatt), 233 ; The life of Cæsar has no greater example for us than our own (Montaigne), 249 ; A man should not vainly endeavor to frame himself on other men's models (Bacon), 267 ; All men that live are drawn either by book or example (Essex-Bacon), 276 ; Example prevails more than precept (Osborne), 295 ; Nothing is so contagious as example (La Rochefoucauld), 311 ; Resolution to imitate what seems commendable in others (Edwards), 372 ; Wherein you reprove another be unblamable yourself (Washington), 403 ; Personal experience of the effect of a contemplation of good examples in character (Jefferson), 406, 407 ; We reform others unconsciously when we walk uprightly (Swetchine), 438.

Excuses : Defending an ill thing is more criminal than doing it (Halifax), 315.

Exercise. See Bodily care.

Expenditure. — Extravagance. — Squandering. — Luxury. — Frugality. — Parsimony : Seek not in needless luxury to waste (Pythagoras), 89 ; Expenditure is divided into four classes : profit, loss, disgrace, and honor (Maimonides), 169 ;

Three things corrupt the world : pride, superfluity, and indolence (Welsh Triad), 172 ; Be courteous and spend freely, and you will be more loved (Mediæval precept), 179 ; Waste not thy goods in great feasts (Wyclif), 196 ; Beware thou spend not above three or four parts of thy revenue (Burleigh), 240 ; Never spend anything before thou have it (Raleigh), 256 ; Never buy but with ready money (Osborne), 294 ; The art of laying out money wisely is not attained without thought (Halifax), 318 ; Frugality is good, if liberality be joined. . . . That is lost that is misused. . . . Cast up your income and live on half. . . . Frugality is the better way to be rich, for it has less toil and temptation (Penn), 326, 331, 340 ; Have courage to do without what you do not need ; . . . to set down every penny you spend (Stanislaus), 357 ; The best error is on the parsimonious side. . . . Frugality is the sure guardian of our virtues (Chesterfield), 363 ; Make no expense but to do good to others or yourself (Franklin), 378, 379, 384 ; I cannot enjoin too strongly a due observance of economy (Washington), 401; Never buy what you do not want because it is cheap (Jefferson), 411 ; Be saving, but not at the cost of liberality (Joubert), 418. *See, also*, Avarice, Thrift, Debt.

Extortion : Extortion maketh a wise man foolish (Ecclesiastes), 60.

Extravagance. *See* Expenditure.

Failure. *See* Success.

Faith. *See* Trust.

Faithfulness. *See* Fidelity.

Falsehood. — Truthfulness. — Lying : Thou shalt not bear false witness (Decalogue), 42 ; Nor lie one to another (Leviticus), 44 ; He that speaketh truth in his heart (Psalm), 46, 410 ; The Lord hateth a lying tongue ; . . . a false witness. . . . A righteous man hateth lying (Proverbs), 51, 53 ; Speak not agreeable falsehood. . . . Veracity included in the tenfold summary of duty (Manu), 65, 70. One should not tell lies (Buddha), 78 ; Overcome the liar by truth (Dhammapada), 84 ; Subdue untruthful men by truthfulness (Maha-bharata), 95 ; Swear not false. . . . Love the truth (Ahikar), 104, 105 ; In no wise speak against the truth. . . . Strive for the truth unto death.

. . . Use not to make any manner of lie. . . . A thief better than a man accustomed to lie (Ecclesiasticus), 115, 117, 122 ; If thou findest anything better than truth, &c., turn to it. . . . With all thy soul do justice and say the truth (Marcus Aurelius), 158, 159, 161 ; I have found no remedy for weakness of heart like the pursuit of truth and justice (Maimonides), 167 ; Stir all to love truth (Wyclif), 195 ; Proclaim the truth (Thomas à Kempis), 203 ; He that lieth till no man believe him, let him go where no man knoweth him (Rhodes), 208, 209 ; Use not to lie ; . . . speak not every truth ; . . . a harmless lie is better than a huitful truth (Ascham), 219, 220 ; Above all things, tell no untruth (Sidney), 247 ; Not telling all the truth is hiding it (Halifax), 315, 316 ; Never to speak anything but the pure and simple verity (Edwards), 369 ; Be true (Jefferson), 410 ; It is much easier to recognize error than to find truth (Goethe), 415 ; May prudence, fortitude, and truth erect your brow (Burns), 423. *See, also*, Sincerity, Promises, Hypocrisy.

Fame. — Renown. — Glory : The vulgar is a depraved judge of beautiful deeds (Pythagoras), 93 ; There is a shame which is glory. . . . Envy not the glory of a sinner (Ecclesiasticus), 115, 119 Notoriety and popular fame not to be reckoned amongst goods (Cicero), 128 ; Be a despiser of vain glory (Rhodes), 208 ; Happy is he . . . untied unto the worldly care of public fame (Wotton), 282 ; Be substantially great in thyself, and more than thou appearest (Browne), 302 ; Look upon fame as the talk of neighbors at the street door (Richter), 427. *See, also*, Honors, worldly ; Reputation.

Familiarity : Be familiar to few, equal to all (Rhodes), 207 ; Be thou familiar, but by no means vulgar (Shakespeare), 281.

Fanshawe, Sir R. Translation from Martial, 144.

Fashion : Have courage to prefer propriety to fashion (Stanislaus), 358. *See, also*, Dress.

Father, duty towards. *See* Filial duty.

Fault-finding. *See* Complaining, Censure.

Fawning. *See* Flattery.

Fear. *See* Courage.

Fellowship. *See* Neighbors.

Fénelon. Rules for a Christian life, 343.

Fickleness. See Firmness.

Fidelity. — Treachery : The perversity of the treacherous shall destroy them (Proverbs), 52 ; There is no inheritance like faithfulness (Maimonides), 168 ; Be faithful in little things (Thomas à Kempis), 203 ; Who comprehends his trust, and to the same keeps faithful (Wordsworth), 430.

Filial duty (Ptah-hotep), 39, 40 ; Honor thy father and thy mother (Decalogue), 42 ; Fear every man his mother and his father (Leviticus), 44 ; Hear the instruction of thy father, forsake not the law of thy mother (Proverbs), 48 ; By deep devotion seek thy debt to pay. . . . Treat not with disrespect (Manu), 65 ; The man of sin is he confess'd who . . . his hoary parent stings with taunting rage (Hesiod), 73, 74 ; To support father and mother, the greatest blessing (Buddha), 80 ; With lowly duty to thy parents bow (Pythagoras), 86 ; Esteem most highly filial piety (Confucius), 100 ; Honor thy father and mother. . . . Help thy father in his age (Ecclesiasticus), 114, 118 ; To thy father and mother show honor and respect (St. Louis), 176 ; Love your lady and mother, obey her commandments, believe her counsels (Suffolk), 200 ; Revere, love and serve father and mother (Mexican precept), 222 ; The greatest comfort you can bestow on parents is to live well and learn well (Lyly), 262 ; If thou wouldst be obeyed as a father, be obedient as a son (Penn), 328 ; Honor and obey your natural parents, altho' they be poor (Washington), 404 ; Reverence and cherish your parents (Jefferson), 410.

Firmness.— Steadfastness.— Resolution. — Will. — Fickleness : Not lightly from thy resolution swerve (Pythagoras), 87; Abide by the rules of life you have deliberately proposed to yourself (Epictetus), 153 ; The prudent man changes not unreasonably (Thomas à Kempis), 203 ; Be constant, but not obstinate (Rhodes), 207 ; Take some one path and march in a straight line (Descartes), 297 ; We have more power than will (La Rochefoucauld), 310 ; Have the courage to adhere to a resolution . . . and to abandon it upon conviction. . . . Have courage to face a difficulty (Stanislaus), 357 ; If

thou believest a thing impossible, thy despondency shall make it so (Chesterfield), 363 ; Resolve to perform what you ought ; perform without fail what you resolve (Franklin), 377. See, also, Stubbornness, Persuasion, Refusing, Doing.

Fitness : It is not enough that a thing be right, if it be not fit (Penn), 327.

Flattery : Have nothing to do with a treacherous flatterer (Mediæval precept), 179 ; Flatterers are the worst kind of traitors (Raleigh), 255 ; Love rather right words than flattering. . . . Let it be as painful to be praised of lewd and inhonest persons as if praised for lewd and inhonest deeds. . . . Allure not the love of any man by flattery (Rhodes), 206, 207 ; Keep some great man thy friend (Burleigh), 243 ; Happy is he . . . whose state can neither flatterers feed, nor &c. (Wotton), 283 ; Use the commentary of a severe friend, rather than the glosse of a sweetlipt flatterer (Quarles), 290 ; If we did not flatter ourselves, flattery of others would be harmless. . . . Flattery is a false coin, &c. (La Rochefoucauld), 311 ; Be no flatterer (Washington), 402. See, also, Praise.

Folly. See Fools.

Fools : As the crackling of thorns under a pot is the laughter of the fool (Ecclesiastes), 60 ; Shame shall be the promotion of fools. . . . The companion of fools shall smart (Proverbs), 50, 53 ; There is no companionship with a fool. . . . The fool becomes full of evil, even if he gathers it little by little (Dhammapada), 82, 83 ; Consult not with a fool (Ecclesiasticus), 119 ; The three laughs of a fool : at the good, at the bad, and at he knows not what (Welsh Triad), 172 ; Never had a fool thorough enjoyment (Chesterfield), 363.

Forbearance : See Magnanimity, Patience, Retaliation, Anger.

Forestalling : He that withholdeth corn, the people shall curse him (Proverbs), 53.

Forethought. See Prudence.

Forgetfulness : Be able to forget (Gracian), 287.

Forgiveness. — Pardon : Forgive . . . so shall thy sins be forgiven (Ecclesiasticus), 122 ; If ye forgive men, your heavenly Father will forgive you (Jesus), 133 ; Grant pardon before it is asked (Seneca),

142; Draw the curtain of night upon injuries (Browne), 302; Forgiveness — the hardest lesson to man (Penn), 334; We forgive too little — forget too much (Swetchine), 438.

Fortitude : If thou findest anything better than fortitude, &c., turn to it. . . . It is a shame for the soul to give way when the body does not (Marcus Aurelius), 158, 159, 160; Suffering with fortitude the accidents of life a primary principle of wisdom (Welsh Triad), 171; Clearness of judgment leadeth us to fortitude. . . . If custom be strong to confirm one virtue more than another it is fortitude (Essex-Bacon), 273; May prudence, fortitude, and truth erect your brow (Burns), 423; Fortitude, that last virtue which crowns the others (Lacordaire), 453. *See, also,* Patience, Courage.

Fortune : What man calls fortune is from God (Pythagoras), 87; Things necessary to acquisition of fortune as difficult as those for obtaining virtue. . . . No man's fortune can be an end worthy of the gift of being (Bacon), 265-266; Leave off the game with fortune while in luck (Gracian), 284; Let not fortune, which hath no name in scripture, have any in thy divinity (Browne), 304; A noble spirit disdaineth the malice of fortune (Chesterfield), 363. *See, also,* Lot in life, Prosperity.

Franklin, Benjamin. Plan for acquiring habits of virtue, 376.

Fraud. *See* Honesty.

Friendship : Make no friendship with a man that is given to anger (Proverbs), 55; Have for friends the best of men (Dhammapada), 82; Choose out the man to virtue best inclined. . . . Esteem those eminently friends who assist your soul (Pythagoras), 86, 91; If thy friend be sick, go on foot and see him (Ahikar), 104; If thou wouldst get a friend, prove him first. . . . A faithful friend is the medicine of life. . . . Change not a friend for any good. . . . Forsake not an old friend; the new is not comparable. . . . A friend cannot be known in prosperity. . . . Admonish a friend; it may be he hath not done it (Ecclesiasticus), 117, 118, 119, 120, 122; I had rather lose my money than my friend (Erasmus), 212; Nothing more becoming any wise man than to make choice of friends (Raleigh),

254; The friends thou hast, and their adoption tried, grapple them to thy soul (Shakespeare), 281; Live with those from whom you can learn. . . . Make teachers of your friends. . . . Let your friends be the friends of your deliberate choice (Gracian), 285, 286; Enter no serious friendship with the ingrateful man, the multiloquious man, the coward (Quarles), 289; There is more skill necessary to keep a friend than to reclaim an enemy. . . . Do not lay out your friendship too lavishly at first (Halifax), 315, 318, 319; Choose a friend as thou dost a wife, till death (Penn), 327; No blessing of life is comparable to the enjoyment of a discreet and virtuous friend (Addison), 354; A friend should bear with a friend's infirmities — not his vices (Stanislaus), 358; In friendships and enmities, let your confidence and your hostilities have bounds (Chesterfield), 361; Be courteous to all, but intimate with few; and let those few be well tried. . . . True friendship is a plant of slow growth (Washington) 399; Our chief want in life is somebody who shall make us do what we can (Emerson), 458. *See, also,* Companions.

Frivolity. *See* Earnestness.

Frugality. *See* Expenditure.

" Fruits of Solitude," selections from Penn's, 326.

Fuller, Thomas. Selections from " The Holy State," 305.

Gambling : Despise gambling. . . . If [a man] gaineth, he weaveth spider's webs (Maimonides), 169; Use not dicing nor carding (Ascham), 220; Be neither gambler nor thief. . . . One is the occasion of the other (Mexican precept), 224; Refrain from dicing (Lyly), 261; Gambling is a vice productive of every possible evil (Washington), 399; Stake in no lotteries (Richter), 427.

Generosity. *See* Magnanimity, Charity (of the Spirit), Benevolence, Giving.

Geniality. *See* Good nature, Anger.

Gentlemanliness. *See* Courtesy, Manners.

Gentleness : A soft answer turneth away wrath (Proverbs), 54; Do not speak harshly to anybody (Dhammapada), 83; Be gentle in works and words (Ahikar), 104; Be gentle and mild to foes (Seneca), 142; He that speaks hastily is like a snarling hound (Thomas à Kempis), 203. *See, also*, Anger.

Giving. — Almsgiving. — Bountifulness. — Stinginess. — Liberality : Leave gleanings for the poor (Leviticus), 44 ; The liberal soul shall be made fat. . . . He that hath pity upon the poor lendeth to the Lord (Proverbs), 52, 55 ; Cast thy bread on the waters. . . . Give a portion to seven (Ecclesiastes), 61 ; See that he to whom thou givest worthy be. . . . Talk not of thy gifts. . . . The merit of thy alms melts away by ostentation. . . . Bestowing gifts on strangers while kindred starve . . . is cruelty disguised (Manu), 66, 69 ; Give to the giver, but the churl pass by. Men fill the giving, not the ungiving hand. . . . Though much he give, the willing donor shall rejoice and live (Hesiod), 74 ; To bestow alms ; . . . to give help to kindred, the greatest blessing (Buddha), 80 ; Give, if thou art asked for little. . . . Overcome the greedy by liberality (Dhammapada), 84 ; Conquer a man who never gives by gifts. . . . He who is not rich and yet can give will be exalted (Maha-bharata), 95, 96 ; To give to the right person, at the right time, &c. not easy (Aristotle), 110 ; Turn not away from the needy. Give unto the good, and help not the sinner. . . . Lose thy money for thy brother and friend (Ecclesiasticus), 115, 120, 123 ; When thou doest alms sound not a trumpet (Jesus), 133 ; I have no possessions so real as those I have given to deserving people (Seneca), 141 ; Have compassion upon the needy. . . . Take care that their faces be not put to the blush on account of your gifts (Maimonides), 168 ; Give to the poor whenever you have money. . . . Be liberal in gifts (Mediæval precept), 178, 179 ; Those that give with judgment find a delight (Essex-Bacon), 273, 275 ; Be charitable before wealth makes thee covetous (Browne), 300 ; Giving what you do not want nor value neither brings nor deserves thanks (Stanislaus), 358 ; Not every one who asketh deserveth charity ; all, however, are worthy of the inquiry (Washington), 399 ; How can that gift leave a trace which has left no void (Swetchine), 437 ; Choose some poor person and relieve him regularly (Lacor-

daire), 453. *See, also*, Avarice, Benevolence.

Glory. *See* Fame.

Gluttony. *See* Temperance.

God. *See* Religious injunctions.

Goethe, Johann Wolfgang von. Selections from "Maxims and Reflections," 28, 29, 413.

Golden Rule, the : In the Maha-bharata (twice formulated), 8, 97 ; In Confucian Analects, 10, 101 ; In the sayings of Ahikar, 105 ; In the Sermon on the Mount, 17, 135.

"Golden Verses of Pythagoras," 86.

Good. — Desirable. — The Best : Esteem that eminently good which is increased to yourself when communicated to another (Pythagoras), 91 ; What is honorable alone is good (Cicero), 127, 128; The highest good is a mind which despises the accidents of fortune and takes pleasure in virtue (Seneca), 138 ; Let whatever appears best be an inviolable law (Epictetus), 153 ; Happy is he . . . who never understood . . . nor rules of state, but rules of good (Wotton), 282 ; He fixes good on good alone (Wordsworth), 430. *See, also*, Happiness.

Good name, A. *See* Reputation.

Good nature. — Geniality. — Benignity. — Moroseness. — Sullenness : Pleasant words are as an honeycomb (Proverbs), 54 ; The superior man is anxious that his countenance be benign (Confucius), 102 ; A merry heart maketh a cheerful countenance (Ecclesiasticus), 120 ; Smooth your way to the head thro' the heart. . . . The most useful art of all, that of pleasing, requires only the desire (Chesterfield), 361 ; Resolved to exhibit an air of love, cheerfulness and benignity. . . . When most conscious of provocation, to strive most to feel good-naturedly (Edwards), 372, 374 ; Good humor one of the preservatives of peace and tranquillity (Jefferson), 407.

Goodness : It is hard to be good (Aristotle), 110 ; Every good tree bringeth forth good fruit (Jesus), 136 ; No longer talk about the kind of man that a good man ought to be, but be such (Marcus Aurelius), 161 ; Reject death and evil ; choose life and good ; the option is given you (Maimonides), 165 ; Resolutions to strive for all qualities of goodness (Edwards), 366–374 ; Perfection is the measure of heaven ; the wish to be perfect the measure of man (Goethe), 416 ; Desire no more intellect than is requisite for perfect goodness (Swetchine), 437. *See, also,* Virtue, Righteousness.

Gossip. — Talebearing. — Scandal : Do not repeat extravagances of language (Ptahhotep), 37 ; Thou shalt not go up and down as a talebearer (Leviticus), 45 ; He that goeth about as a talebearer (Proverbs), 52 ; If thou hearest an evil word about any one hide it (Ahikar), 104 ; Be not called a whisperer. . . . If thou hast heard a word let it die with thee (Ecclesiasticus), 116, 121 ; Utter no ill-timed gossip (Spirit of Wisdom), 164 ; Of absent persons I either say nothing or speak with kindness (Erasmus), 212 ; Carry no tales (Ascham), 219 ; If thou keepest clear of carrying tales and repeating jests thou wilt keep clear of lying and of sowing discord (Mexican precept), 223, 224. *See, also,* Scandal, Speech.

Gracian, Balthasar, selections from the maxims of, 284.

Gratitude. — Ingratitude. — Thankfulness : I will not reckon benefits by their magnitude or number (Seneca), 141 ; Gratitude is a noble sort of justice. . . . There is something baser in ingratitude than injustice (Penn), 339 ; I have never known men of ability to be ungrateful (Goethe), 415.

Gravity. *See* Earnestness.

Greed. *See* Avarice.

Grief. *See* Sorrow.

Grumbling. *See* Complaining.

Habit. — Use. — Practice : By virtuous use thy life and manners frame (Pythagoras), 89 ; For a test of the formation of habits take the pleasure or pain which succeeds the acts (Aristotle), 109; Accustom yourself to good morals, for the nature of man dependeth upon habit (Maimonides), 165; When there is a custom gotten of avoiding to do evil, then cometh a gentle courage (Wyatt), 236 ; Make such a habit of well-doing that you shall not know how to do evil (Sidney), 247 ; Where virtues are but budding they must be ripened by clearness of judgment and custom of well-doing (Essex-Bacon), 272, 273 ; Good methods and habits obtained in youth will make you happy the rest of your days (Penn), 332 ; Plan for acquiring

habits of virtue (Franklin), 376; Importance of the habits acquired in the acquisition of knowledge (Washington), 400.

Halifax, Lord. Selections from Moral Thoughts and "Advice to a Daughter," 314, 316.

Happiness : Contentment is the root of happiness. . . . Wouldst thou be happy, be thou moderate (Manu), 67 ; Happiness is the outcome of good. . . . Let us live happily, though we call nothing our own (Dhammapada), 83 ; Seek happiness in deeds of virtue and usefulness (Mahabharata), 96 ; Tranquillity renders life happy. . . . The wise man is always happy. . . . A happy life is comprised in honesty alone. . . . Happiness compounded of good things which alone are honorable (Cicero), 127, 128 ; Rules for a happy life (Seneca), 138 ; The happy life described by Martial, 143-147 ; If thou workest at that which is before thee, . . . expecting nothing, fearing nothing, . . . thou wilt live happy. . . . Enjoy life by joining one good thing to another, not to leave the smallest interval between (Marcus Aurelius), 159, 161, 162 ; The happy life described (Wotton), 282 ; Happiness lies in the taste, and not in things. . . . We are never so happy or unhappy as we imagine (La Rochefoucauld), 310 ; The great and constant pleasures of life, not to be crossed if one faithfully seeks happiness, are in health, reputation, knowledge, doing good, and the expectation of another world (Locke), 321-323 ; If thou wouldst be happy, bring thy mind to thy condition (Penn), 328 ; Never was a wise man wholly unhappy (Chesterfield), 363 ; The happy man described (Cowper), 394 ; The happiest man is he who can link the end of his life with its commencement. . . . The happiest is he whose nature asks for nothing that the world does not wish and use (Goethe), 415, 416 ; Character of the happy warrior (Wordsworth), 429 ; Is not life sufficiently happy when it is useful (Swetchine), 437 ; What a man has in himself is the chief element in his happiness. . . . The two foes of happiness are pain and boredom. . . . The man whom nature has endowed with intellectual wealth is the happiest (Schopenhauer), 441, 443 ; There is in man a higher than love of happiness : he can do without happiness, and instead find blessedness (Carlyle), 448. *See, also,* Good, Contentment, Pleasure, Life.

Harlotry. *See* Chastity.

Hatred : Thou shalt not hate thy brother (Leviticus), 45 ; He that hideth hatred is of lying lips. . . . Better a dinner of herbs where love is than a stalled ox and hatred (Proverbs), 52, 54 ; Let us dwell free from hatred (Dhammapada), 83 ; Hate as if sometime to love (Bias), 269 ; Hatred attends upon fear (Pythagoras), 92 ; Have hatred and contempt for no one (Mexican precept), 227 ; Dislike what deserves it, but never hate (Penn), 329; Chiefly, hate no man (Goethe), 416 ; Hatred may be praiseworthy if provoked by a lively love of good (Joubert), 418.

Haughtiness. *See* Pride.

Health. *See* Bodily care.

Helpfulness. *See* Benevolence.

Hesiod, Selections from " Works and Days," 11, 71.

Hoarding. *See* Avarice.

Honesty. — Integrity. — Uprightness. — Dishonesty. — Fraud : A just weight is the Lord's delight. . . . Divers weights and measures are an abomination to the Lord. . . . It is naught, saith the buyer (Proverbs), 52, 55 ; Pay that which thou vowest (Ecclesiastes), 58 ; Ne'er give thy mind to aught but honest gain. . . . Honesty included in the tenfold summary of duty (Manu), 70 ; He that shall heaps of gold command [by fraud or rapacity], him shall the gods cast down. . . . The man of sin is he confess'd . . . who robs the orphans (Hesiod), 73 ; When the superior man sees gain to be got, he thinks of righteousness (Confucius), 102 ; Eat not bread that is not thine own. . . . Take not with a big weight and give with a little (Ahikar), 104 ; Defraud not the poor. . . . Let not thy hand be stretched to receive and shut when thou shouldst repay. . . . Be not ashamed of exactness of balance and weights (Ecclesiasticus), 114, 116, 125 ; Plunder not from the wealth of others (Spirit of Wisdom), 164 ; Keep firm to your word. . . . Disdain all cunning subterfuges. . . . Flee far from doubtful possessions (Maimonides), 167 ; The sure foundations and stablished opinions that leadeth to honesty. . . . If you will seem honest, be honest (Wyatt), 230, 235 ; Resolve that no man

is wise or safe but he that is honest (Raleigh), 258 ; Let not the law be the *non ultra* of thy honesty (Browne), 301 ; There is more wit requisite to be an honest man than to be a knave (Halifax), 314 ; A man of integrity is a true man, a bold man, and a steady man (Penn), 339; Have courage to show preference for honesty (Stanislaus), 358 ; All rests at last on that integrity which dwarfs talent, and can spare it (Emerson), 460. *See, also,* Righteousness, Sincerity, Fidelity, Falsehood, Theft, Extortion.

Honor. — Respect. — Deference. — Veneration : To honor those worthy of honor is the greatest blessing (Buddha), 79 ; Due rites perform and honors to the dead (Pythagoras), 86.

Honorable : What is honorable is the only good (Cicero), 127, 128 ; Be an honorable opponent (Gracian), 286 ; Where ye feel your honor grip, let that ay be your border (Burns), 422 ; Fame is something which must be won ; honor, only something which must not be lost (Schopenhauer), 442.

Honors, worldly : Shrink from worldly honor as from poison (Manu), 67 ; There is no nobility like that of morality (Maimonides), 168 ; Let ambition have but an epicycle or narrow circuit in thee (Browne), 303 ; The pomp, honor, and luxury of the world are cheats (Penn), 332 ; The happy man o'erlooks the world (Cowper), 394 ; Does not stoop nor lie in wait for wealth or honors, &c. (Wordsworth), 430. *See, also,* Fame.

Hope : Hope deferred maketh the heart sick (Proverbs), 53 ; Hope serves at least to conduct us thro' life by an agreeable path (La Rochefoucauld), 311 ; Hope is generally a wrong guide, though very good company (Halifax), 315 ; Hope not beyond reason (Penn), 328.

Hospitality : Be courteous to thy guest (Manu), 69 ; The man of sin is he confess'd . . . who wrongs the guest. . . . Bid to thy feast a friend ; thy foe forbear (Hesiod), 73, 74 ; Let thy hospitality be moderate ; . . . rather plentiful than sparing, but not costly (Burleigh), 240, 242 ; Hospitality is good, if the poorer sort are the subjects (Penn), 326.

Humility. — Lowliness. — Meekness : The Lord giveth grace unto the lowly. . . . With the lowly is wisdom (Proverbs),

50, 52; Reverence and lowliness, the greatest blessing (Buddha), 80; If thy doorposts be loftily built, bow thy head (Ahikar), 104; The greater thou art, the more humble thyself (Ecclesiasticus), 114; Blessed are the poor in spirit. . . . Blessed are the meek (Jesus), 130; Meekness and humility are the steps of the ladder to virtue (Maimonides), 169; Humility and courtesy overcometh all proud hearts (La Tour), 189; Live a humble life. . . . Ever keep meekness (Wyclif), 196, 198; Humility merits the favor of God (Mexican precept), 223, 225; Owe not thy humility unto humiliation by adversity. . . . Look humbly upon thy virtues (Browne), 302; Humility is the true proof of Christian virtues (La Rochefoucauld), 312; Be humble, but not servile. . . . Meekness seems to be humility perfectly digested, and from a virtue become a nature (Penn), 327, 337; Imitate Jesus Christ and Socrates (Franklin), 378; We have two great virtues to acquire, humility and penance (Lacordaire), 453. See, also, Pride.

Husband. See Marriage.

Hypocrisy; He who pretends to be what he is not commits the worst of crimes (Manu), 69; No dissimulation can be long concealed (Pythagoras), 92; Hypocrisy is the homage which vice renders to virtue (La Rochefoucauld), 311. See, also, Sincerity, Earnestness, Falsehood.

Ideals: Choose a heroic ideal, rather to emulate than imitate (Gracian), 285; Whose high endeavors are an inward light, &c. (Wordsworth), 429.

Idleness. See Industry.

Idolatry: Commandments against (Decalogue), 42; (Leviticus), 44.

Ignorance. See Knowledge.

Ill nature. — Ill temper. See Good nature, Anger.

Independence. See Self-reliance.

Indolence. See Industry.

Industry. — Diligence. — Work. — Labor. — Indolence. — Idleness: Do not spoil the time of thy activity. . . . Love for the work they accomplish transports men to God (Ptah-hotep), 35, 38; The hand of the diligent maketh rich. . . . Go to the ant, thou sluggard. . . . He that gathereth by labor shall have increase. . . . The soul of the diligent shall be

made fat. . . . A man diligent in business shall stand before kings (Proverbs), 51, 53, 56; Whatsoever thy hand findeth to do, do it with thy might. . . . In the morning sow thy seed (Ecclesiastes), 61, 62; Perform thy own appointed work unweariedly. . . . Thou canst not gather what thou dost not sow (Manu), 67, 68; On the sluggard hungry want attends. . . . Love every seemly toil (Hesiod), 73; To follow a peaceful calling, the greatest blessing (Buddha), 80; Rouse thyself! do not be idle (Dhammapada), 83; True goods never produced by indolent habits (Pythagoras), 91; Be active now, while thou art young (Maha-bharata), 97; Labor diligently at your proper callings (Confucius), 101; Hate not laborious work (Ecclesiasticus), 118; Submit to labors, however great (Seneca), 141; Labor not unwillingly (Marcus Aurelius), 158; Eat of thine own regular industry; form a portion for God and the good (Spirit of Wisdom), 164; Abhor indolence (Maimonides), 168; Three things corrupt the world: pride, superfluity, and indolence (Welsh Triad), 172; Truly and willingly do thy labor (Wyclif), 197; Be neither idle in solitude nor a babbler in public (Thomas à Kempis), 204; Beware chiefly of idleness, the great pathway to all evils (Ascham), 220; Be not a lounger on the pavement. . . . Sow and thou shalt reap. . . . We live not in this world without much labor (Mexican precept), 223, 224, 226; If thou dost not want labor for food thou mayest for physic. . . . Diligence is a discreet and understanding application of one's self to business (Penn), 326, 339; Be always employed in something useful (Edwards), 378, 379, 384; With diligence there is nothing you may not conquer (Chatham), 387; Spend a fair share of every day upon the serious occupations of your state (Lacordaire), 453; I do not wish to be any more busy with my hands than is necessary. My head is hands and feet (Thoreau), 465. See, also, Thrift, Doing, Occupation.

Ingratitude. See Gratitude.

Iniquity. See Wickedness.

Inquisitiveness. See Questioning.

Instruction. See Education, Teachableness.

Integrity. See Honesty.

Jealousy: Who is able to stand before jealousy (Proverbs), 57 ; Be not jealous over the wife of thy bosom (Ecclesiasticus), 119 ; Jealousy is in some sort just and reasonable, &c. . . . In jealousy there is more self-love than love (La Rochefoucauld), 310, 311 ; Be not fancifully jealous; to be reasonably so is wise (Penn), 328, 335.

Jefferson, Thomas, Letters to Thomas Jefferson Randolph and Thomas Jefferson Smith, 406, 410.

Jesting: Mix with sadness thy merry jests, but temperately (Rhodes), 206 ; Many win a reputation for being witty at the cost of their credit for being sensible (Gracian), 285 ; Break not a jest where none take pleasure in mirth (Washington), 403. See, also, Merriment.

Jesus : The Sermon on the Mount, 130.

Joubert, Joseph. Selections from the Pensées, 418.

Judgment. See Justice, Reason.

Justice : Of the wise man (Ptah-hotep), 39 ; Do no unrighteousness in judgment (Leviticus), 45 ; Let justice o'er thy word and deed preside. . . . Not to act unjustly is sufficient to a blessed life (Pythagoras), 87, 91 ; The man with power who forbears to use it indiscreetly will be exalted (Maha-bharata), 96 ; Be not fainthearted in judgment. . . . Blame not before thou hast examined (Ecclesiasticus), 115, 120 ; Judge not that ye be not judged (Jesus), 135 ; If thou findest anything better than justice, &c., turn to it. . . . With all thy soul do justice and say the truth (Marcus Aurelius), 158, 159, 161 ; With enemies, struggle with equity (Spirit of Wisdom), 164 ; Truth and justice are the ornaments of the soul (Maimonides), 167 ; Help the right (St. Louis), 175 ; Do right and equity to all men (Wyclif), 195 ; Without knowledge there can be no justice (Essex-Bacon), 275 ; Be just in all things, to all (Penn), 338, 339 ; Withhold judgments which you are not obliged to pronounce (Fénelon), 343 ; Doing justice to a deserving character is an employment suited to a reasonable nature (Addison), 353 ; Wrong none, by deed or omission (Franklin), 378, 379, 384 ; Be just (Jefferson), 410 ; Justice comes after prudence as a cardinal virtue (Lacordaire), 452. See, also, Censure, Oppression.

Kempis, Thomas à. See Thomas à Kempis.

Kindness. See Benevolence.

Kinship : Behave with generosity to your kindred (Confucius), 100.

Knight of La Tour-Landry, The book of the, 185.

Knowledge. — Ignorance : The fear of the Lord is the beginning of knowledge (Proverbs), 48 ; Knowledge of the noble truths, the greatest blessing (Buddha), 80 ; Bend thy serious thought to search the profitable knowledge out. . . . Beware thy meddling hand . . . beyond thy reach of knowledge. . . . The whole life of an ignorant man a disgrace (Pythagoras), 88, 92 ; Better be blind of eye than blind of mind (Ahikar), 104 ; If thou hast understanding, answer; if not, lay thy hand on thy mouth. . . . Be not ignorant of anything (Ecclesiasticus), 116 ; With an ignorant man be not a confederate (Spirit of Wisdom), 164 ; The three great ends of knowledge : duty, utility, and decorum (Welsh Triad), 172 ; Meddle with nothing you do not understand (Mediæval precept), 179 ; The prudent man speaks with reserve of what he is ignorant of (Thomas à Kempis), 203 ; Let it not be unknown nor grievous to thee that thou hast not knowledge of anything (Rhodes), 207, 208 ; Where knowledge wants, the man is void of all good (Bacon), 275-278 ; If thou hast attained knowledge, put it in practice (Quarles), 292 : Knowledge is the treasure, but judgment the treasurer (Penn), 338 ; Have the courage to acknowledge ignorance (Stanislaus), 358 ; The first step towards being wise is to know that thou art ignorant (Chesterfield), 362 ; The use of learning is to render a man wise and virtuous (Chatham), 387 ; It is much easier to recognize error than to find truth (Goethe), 415 ; See, also, Education.

Labor. See Industry.

Lacordaire, Jean Baptiste Henri. The four cardinal virtues. Advice to young men, 452, 453.

Language. See Speech.

La Rochefoucauld, Duke de. Selections from Sentences and Moral Maxims, 310.

La Tour, Geoffroy de. Instructions to his daughters, 187.

Laughter. See Merriment.

Laziness. *See* Indolence.

Learning. *See* Knowledge, Education.

Lending. *See* Borrowing.

Leviticus, Commandments from, 44.

Liberality. *See* Giving, Expenditure, Avarice.

Licentiousness. *See* Chastity.

Life : Look upon the world as a bubble (Dhammapada), 83 ; Where a man can live, there he can live well. . . . Live with the gods (Marcus Aurelius), 160 ; Each man ought to live to save himself and to help others (Wyclif), 198 ; The great and glorious masterpiece of man is to know how to live to purpose. . . . 'T is not only the fundamental, but the most illustrious of occupations. . . . There is no science so hard as well to know how to live this life (Montaigne), 250, 251 ; Our life is long if we know how to use it (Lyly), 261 ; Behave thyself in thy course of life as at a banquet (Quarles), 292 ; Reckon not upon long life, but live always beyond thy account (Browne), 303 ; If we divide the life of most men into twenty parts, we shall find at least nineteen are mere gaps and chasms (Addison), 352 ; Resolved to live with all my might while I do live (Edwards), 366 ; Enjoy thy existence more than thy manner of existence. . . . Despise life, that thou mayest enjoy it (Richter), 427 ; There is nothing at all in life except what we put there (Swetchine), 438 ; Why should we live with such hurry and waste of life ? . . . As for work, we have n't any of any consequence (Thoreau), 464. *See, also,* Lot in life, Death.

Litigation : Be fully resolved that thou hast right on thy side before attempting law (Burleigh), 242 ; Use law and physic only for necessity (Quarles), 291.

" Little Garden of Roses," Selections from the, 202.

Locke, John. Thus I think, 321.

Lot in life : Behave in life as at an entertainment, taking your share with moderation. . . . Remember that you are an actor in a drama, of such kind as the author pleases to make it (Epictetus), 151, 152 ; Adapt thyself to the things with which thy lot has been cast (Marcus Aurelius), 160 ; God knoweth what state is best for thee (Wyclif), 197. *See, also,* Contentment, Prosperity, Fortune.

Louis IX., King of France (Saint Louis). Instructions to his son, 174.

Love : Better a dinner of herbs where love is. . . . Better open rebuke than love that is hidden (Proverbs), 54, 57 ; Overcome anger by love (Dhammapada), 84 ; Love attends upon reverence (Pythagoras), 92 ; Love your enemy (Jesus), 132 ; He that no man loves, few will know (Rhodes), 209 ; Love as if some time to hate (Bias), 269 ; Do not believe and do not love lightly (Gracian), 286 ; The pleasure of love is in loving (La Rochefoucauld), 311.

Lowliness. *See* Humility.

Loyalty : Above all earthly things, be true liegeman to the king (Suffolk), 200.

Lust. *See* Chastity.

Luxury. *See* Expenditure.

Lying. *See* Falsehood.

Lyly, John, on the education of youth, 250.

Magnanimity, Towards a disputant (Ptah-hotep), 34 ; If thine enemy be hungry, &c. (Proverbs), 56 ; Thoughts of magnanimity (Marcus Aurelius), 157, 161 ; Magnanimity is the good sense of pride (La Rochefoucauld), 311 ; Show not yourself glad at the misfortune of another, though your enemy (Washington), 402. *See, also,* Charity (of the Spirit).

Maha-bharata, Selections from the, 8, 9, 95.

Maimonides, Moses ben, to his son, 165.

Malice. — Mischief-making. — Evil designing : The Lord hateth mischief-making. . . . The Lord hateth an heart that deviseth wicked imaginations. . . . He that searcheth after mischief, it shall come unto him (Proverbs), 51, 53 ; Buddhistic command against, 79 ; Life is easy for a mischief-maker (Dhammapada), 84 ; Malice is a greater magnifying glass than kindness (Halifax), 315.

Manners : Mediæval code of good manners, from " Stans Puer ad Mensam," 180 ; Instructions of a schoolmaster to a boy on gentlemanly behavior (Erasmus), 216 ; Mexican rules of polite behavior, 222–225 ; Towards superiors, equals, and inferiors (Burleigh), 243 ; Have you known how to compose your manners ? You have done more than he who has composed books (Montaigne), 250 ; In manners, be not caught with novelty

(Essex-Bacon), 274 ; Good manners is such a part of good sense that they cannot be divided (Halifax), 316 ; Pride, ill nature, and want of sense are the great sources of ill manners. . . . Good sense is the principal foundation of good manners (Swift), 349 ; One's own good breeding is best security against ill manners of others (Chesterfield), 361 ; Behavior [manners] is certainly founded in considerable virtues (Chatham), 390–392 ; A man's manners are the mirror in which he shows his portrait (Goethe), 415. See, also, Courtesy.

Manu, Selections from the Code of, 9, 64.

Marcus Aurelius, Selections from the "Thoughts" of, 16, 157.

Marriage : Love thy wife without alloy (Ptah-hotep), 37 ; Live joyfully with thy wife whom thou lovest (Ecclesiastes), 61 ; To cherish wife and child, the greatest blessing (Buddha), 80 ; Be not jealous over the wife of thy bosom (Ecclesiasticus), 119 ; One that putteth away his wife, saving for fornication, maketh her an adulteress (Jesus), 131 ; Live happily with the wife of your youthful years ; but touch not the one which is not yours (Maimonides), 170 ; Govern well thy wife, children, and household attendants (Wyclif), 196 ; Mexican injunctions to a wife, 228 ; Such as ye are unto your wife shall she be unto you (Wyatt), 233 ; From the choosing of thy wife will spring all thy future good or evil. . . . Marry thy daughters in time, lest they marry themselves (Burleigh), 239, 241 ; The only danger [in the choice of a wife] is beauty (Raleigh), 254 ; Never marry but for love ; but see that thou lovest what is lovely (Penn), 327, 335, 336 ; Have courage to listen to your wife, &c. (Stanislaus), 358.

Martial. Description of the happy life, 143–147.

Massillon. On the use of time, 345

Mean, The : Still the best (Cleobulus), 76 ; Injunctions for the keeping of the (Aristotle), 108.

Meddling : I intermeddled with no one's affairs (Erasmus), 212 ; Meddle not with affairs in which thou art not concerned (Mexican precept), 222 ; Never meddle with other folk's business. . . . Know your own business and mind it (Penn), 334, 335.

Mediæval precepts, 178.

Mediæval code of manners, 180.

Mediæval morals, 19, 20.

Meditation. See Self-communion.

Meekness. See Humility.

Mercy : The merciful man doeth good to his own soul. . . He that hath mercy on the needy honoreth his Maker (Proverbs), 52, 54 ; Blessed are the merciful (Jesus), 130 ; Stir all men to love mercy (Wyclif), 195 ; God has shown mercy to man and made it his duty (Penn), 338. See, also, Cruelty, Benevolence.

Merivale, C., Translation from Martial, 146.

Merriment, —Mirth.— Laughter : Sorrow is better than laughter. . . . As the crackling of thorns under a pot is the laughter of the fool (Ecclesiastes), 59, 60 ; Let not your laughter be much. . . . Avoid an endeavor to excite laughter (Epictetus), 152 ; Laughter is reprovable if out of measure (Rhodes), 206 ; Give yourself to be merry (Sidney), 246 ; Be merry, but with modesty ; sober, but not too sullen (Lyly), 262 ; Let not thy mirth intoxicate thy mind (Chesterfield), 363 ; It is rare to see in any one a graceful laughter (Chatham), 390. See, also, Pleasure, Jesting.

Method. See Order.

Mexican code of moral precepts, 221.

Mildness. See Gentleness.

Mind : Be vigilant in your intellectual part (Pythagoras), 90 ; Gifts or excellencies of mind the same as those of the body ; beauty, health, and strength (Essex-Bacon), 271.

Mirth. See Merriment.

Mischief-making. See Malice.

Miserliness. See Avarice.

Mistakes. See Success.

Mockery. See Ridicule.

Moderation : Wouldst thou be happy, be thou moderate (Manu), 67 ; Too much of nothing (Pittacus), 76 ; Prize moderation (Confucius), 101 ; It is the nature of moral action to be spoiled by defect and excess (Aristotle), 108 ; Be not unsatiable in any dainty thing (Ecclesiasticus), 124 ; Drain nothing to the dregs ; neither good nor evil (Gracian), 286 ; Christ's sermon on the mount is one continued divine authority in favor of an universal temperance (Penn), 340,

341; Avoid extremes (Franklin), 378. *See, also,* Temperance.

Modesty : Life is hard for a modest man (Dhammapada), 84; The most pleasing thing on earth (Ahikar), 105 ; Be modest, for it is reasonable (Thomas à Kempis), 203 ; Be modest in discourse . . . Let thy looks be modest (Mexican precept), 222, 223, 226 ; Be modest in each assembly (Sidney), 247. *See, also,* Chastity, Ribaldry.

Montaigne. On the cultivation of life, 249.

Moroseness. *See* Good nature, Anger.

Mosaic Commandments, 4, 5, 41, 44.

Mother, Duty towards a. *See* Filial Duty.

Motives : We should often be ashamed of our best actions if the world saw all the motives (La Rochefoucauld), 312.

Murder, Thou shalt do no (Decalogue), 42 ; The Lord hateth hands that shed innocent blood (Proverbs), 51 ; One should not take life (Buddha), 78 ; Poison no one (Mexican precept), 222.

Music : Abstain from (Buddhist commandments), 78.

Needy, Treatment of the : *See* Giving, Mercy, Oppression.

Neighbors. — Fellowship. — Social Relationship : Be not irritable towards thy neighbor (Ptah-hotep), 36 ; Thou shalt love thy neighbor as thyself (Leviticus), 45 ; Devise not evil against thy neighbor. . . . He that despiseth his neighbor is void of wisdom. . . . Let thy feet be seldom in thy neighbor's house, &c. (Proverbs), 49, 52, 56 ; The good neighbor is our prop and stay (Hesiod), 74 ; The golden rule of conduct towards a neighbor (Maha-bharata), 97 ; We are made for co-operation, like feet, like hands, &c. . . . . To act against one another is contrary to nature (Marcus Aurelius), 157, 158 ; Thy food, clothing, protection, &c., thou owest to the assistance of others. . . . It is thy duty therefore to be a friend to mankind (Chesterfield), 364.

Niggardliness. *See* Expenditure, Giving.

No, Saying. *See* Refusing.

Non-resistance. *See* Retaliation.

Oath, Making : He that sweareth to his own hurt (Psalm), 46, 410 ; Swear not at

all (Jesus), 132 ; Avoid swearing, if possible, altogether (Epictetus), 152.

Obedience : to authority (Ptah-hotep), 34 ; Unless you feel what obedience is you shall never teach others to obey (Sidney), 246.

Obscenity. *See* Ribaldry.

Observation : He that lives long and sees much, but observes nothing, shall never prove a wise man (Essex-Bacon), 278.

Obstinacy. *See* Stubborness, Firmness.

Occupation. — Business : Do not make a business of what is no business (Gracian), 286 ; Choose God's trades [agricultural and pastoral] before men's (Penn), 332 ; Endeavor to be first in thy calling, whatever it be (Chesterfield), 362 ; Let eminence in your profession be your ambition (Washington), 398 ; What thou best canst understand is just the thing lies nearest to thy hand (Goethe), 417 ; The high prize of life is to be born with a bias to some pursuit (Emerson), 457.

Old age : The bodily decay of age (Ptah-hotep), 32. *See, also,* Youth.

Old Men's Dialogue, The, 211.

Oldest book in the world, The, 1, 32.

Opinion : Despise not one who differs in opinion (Ptah-hotep), 34 ; Many are deceived by their own vain opinion (Ecclesiasticus), 114 ; Gather an heap of good opinions . . . as it were on your fingers' ends (Wyatt), 236 ; Be not light to follow every man's opinion, neither obstinate in your own conceit (Lyly), 262, 263 ; Think with the few, and speak with the many (Gracian), 285 ; Shun fantastic opinions (Penn), 333.

Opinion, Public : Do nothing because of public opinion, but everything because of conscience (Seneca), 141.

Opportunity : He who lets slip an opportunity finds not again the fitting time (Maha-bharata), 97 ; Observe the opportunity (Ecclesiasticus), 115 ; We should not always wait for occasions, but sometimes challenge them (Bacon), 268 ; Opportunity should never be lost, &c. (Penn), 329.

Oppression : Thou shalt not oppress thy neighbor (Leviticus), 44 ; He that oppresseth the poor reproacheth his Maker (Proverbs), 54 ; One higher than the high regardeth . . . the oppression of the poor and the violent taking away of judgment (Ecclesiastes), 59. *See, also,* Justice.

Order.—Method.—System : Never neglect the duty of the present hour to do another thing (Halifax), 318 ; Draw your affairs into as narrow a compass as you can, and in method and proportion. . . . Divide your day, &c. (Penn), 331, 333 ; Let all things have their places; each part of business its time (Franklin), 377, 379, 384 ; Order is to arrangement what soul is to body and mind to matter (Joubert), 419.

Osborne, Francis. Selections from " Advice to a Son," 294.

Ostentation of piety and good works : Do not your righteousness before men. . . . Let not thy left hand know, &c. . . . When thou prayest enter thy inner chamber (Jesus), 132, 133 ; Be a hider of virtue as other be of vice (Rhodes), 208 ; Be not the trumpet of your own charity (Osborne), 295 ; Do what good thou canst unknown (Penn), 329 ; The man whose virtues are more felt than seen (Cowper), 396.

Parental duty : Bring up a son who shall be pleasing to God. . . . Train thy son to be a teachable man (Ptah-hotep), 35, 39 ; I reckon it no small dishonesty to myself to have an unhonest taught child (Wyatt), 236; Bring thy children up in learning and obedience, yet without outward austerity (Burleigh), 240, 241 ; Euphues and his Euphœbus (Lyly), 260 ; Have as strict a guard upon yourself amongst your children as amongst your enemies (Halifax), 317 ; It is not how we leave our children, but what we leave them. . . . Love them with wisdom, correct them with affection. . . . Punish more by their understandings than the rod (Penn), 328, 336, 337. *See, also,* Education, Marriage.

Parents, Duty towards. *See* Filial duty.

Parsimony. *See* Expenditure, Avarice.

Passion. *See* Anger, Self-control.

Passions : Restrain thy passions (Manu), 66 ; It is more painful to be subservient to passions than to tyrants. . . . As many passions, so many despots (Pythagoras), 91, 92 ; Physic hath not more medicines against diseases of the body than reason hath preservatives against

passions of the mind (Essex-Bacon), 272 ; The passions have an injustice and an interest of their own (La Rochefoucauld), 310 ; Passion is a sort of fever . . . curable with care (Penn), 329 ; The passions may all become innocent if well directed (Joubert), 418. *See, also,* Self-control.

Pastime. *See* Pleasure.

Patience. — Constancy : The patient in spirit is better than the proud (Ecclesiastes), 60 ; With patience bear reviling language. . . . Included in the tenfold summary of duty (Manu), 65, 70; To be long-suffering, the greatest blessing (Buddha), 80 ; With patience bear the lot to thee assigned (Pythagoras), 87 ; Bear railing words with patience (Mahabharata), 96 ; Everything has two handles, one by which it may be borne, the other by which it cannot (Epictetus), 153 ; Ever keep patience (Wyclif), 197 ; Without knowledge there can be no constancy or patience (Essex-Bacon), 275 ; Be able to wait (Gracian), 285 ; If you cannot imitate Job, yet come not short of Socrates (Browne), 302 ; A man who is master of patience is master of everything (Halifax), 316 ; Be patient, but not insensible. . . . Patience and diligence, like faith, remove mountains. . . . Patience is an effect of a meek spirit (Penn), 327, 328, 337; Take things always by their smooth handle (Jefferson), 411 ; Imitate time ; it destroys slowly (Joubert), 419. *See, also,* Fortitude.

Peacemaking. *See* Contention.

Penance : Think not to hide thy guilt under a cloak of penance (Manu), 66.

Penitence. — Repentance : Be not ashamed to confess thy sins. . . . Reproach not a man that turneth from sin (Ecclesiasticus), 115, 119 ; Amendment is repentance (Penn), 329 ; Repentance is accepted remorse (Swetchine), 437 ; We have two great virtues to acquire, humility and penance (Lacordaire), 453.

Penn, William. Selections from his " Fruits of Solitude," and from his " Advice to his Children," 25–27, 326, 330.

Performance. *See* Doing.

Periander, saying of, 76.

Persecution : Blessed they that have been persecuted for righteousness' sake. . . . Pray for them that persecute you (Jesus), 130, 132.

Perses, advice to, 72.

Perseverance.—Persistence: Strive to complete the task commenced. . . . Seek fortune with persistency till death (Manu), 68; Force falls to the lot only of the privileged few, but perseverance can be practiced by the most insignificant (Swetchine), 438; Theories and plans of life are fair and commendable (Emerson), 459.

Personal adornment. *See* Dress.

Persuasion: Sweet persuasion wins the easy to believe (Pythagoras), 87. *See, also,* Firmness.

Petitioners: Give respectful hearing to petitioners (Ptah-hotep), 35; The man of sin is he confessed who spurns the suppliant (Hesiod), 73.

Piety. *See* Religious injunctions.

Pitt, William, Earl of Chatham, Letters to his nephew, 387.

Pittacus, saying of, 76.

Pity. *See* Benevolence, Mercy, Cruelty.

Pleasure. — Amusement. — Recreation. — Diversions: He who amuses himself all day long keeps not his fortune (Ptah-hotep), 38; He that loveth pleasure shall be a poor man (Proverbs), 55; A man hath no better thing than to eat, drink, and be merry (Ecclesiastes), 61; Abstain from dancing, music, singing and stage plays (Buddhist commandments), 78; He who lives without looking for pleasure, Mâra will not overthrow. . . . Leave the small pleasure and look to the great (Dhammapada), 82, 84; Impossible to be a lover of pleasure and a lover of Divinity (Pythagoras), 93, 94; Guard most carefully against pleasure, because we are not impartial judges of it (Aristotle), 111; He that denies himself lawful pleasures increases the surety of resisting the unlawful (Thomas à Kempis), 202; Look upon pain and pleasure with an eye equally regular (Montaigne), 251; Use pastime as the word importeth (Lyly), 262; If thou desire time should not pass too fast, use not too much pastime . . . Let recreation be manly, moderate, seasonable, lawful (Quarles), 282, 290; Spill not the morning in recreations; for sleep itself is a recreation (Fuller), 307; To turn our whole life into a holiday destroyeth pleasure (Halifax), 320; A mastery of passions will afford a constant pleasure greater than vicious enjoyments (Locke), 323; Such diversions as are merely innocent, and have nothing else to recommend them, are below reasonable creatures (Addison), 354; The love of pleasure is sure to enslave whoever does not resist the first allurements (Chatham), 387; The happy man o'erlooks the world. She scorns his pleasures, for she knows them not (Cowper), 394; What amusements are to be taken, and when, is the great matter. . . . Let your recreations be manful, not sinful (Washington), 400, 404; Little joys refresh us constantly like house-bread (Richter), 426; Not pleasure, but freedom from pain, is what the wise man will aim at (Schopenhauer), 442; Indulge in lawful pleasures of mind, heart, or senses with gratitude and moderation (Lacordaire), 453. *See, also,* Happiness, Merriment.

Pole, William de la, Duke of Suffolk. Letter to his son, 200.

Politeness. *See* Courtesy, Manners.

Political duty: Promptly pay your taxes (Confucius), 101; It is as hard to be a true politician as to be truly moral (Bacon), 265; Meddle not with government (Penn), 335; Mitigating the fierceness of party is an employment suited to a reasonable nature (Addison), 353; Love your neighbor as yourself, and your country more (Jefferson), 410.

Polonius to Laertes, 281.

Poor, Treatment of the. *See* Giving, Benevolence, Mercy, Oppression.

Pope, Alexander. The happy man, 145.

Popularity. *See* Reputation.

Poverty. *See* Riches.

Practice. *See* Habit.

Praise. *See* Flattery, Censure.

Prayer. *See* Religious injunctions

Prejudice. *See* Sincerity.

Presumption: Beware thy meddling hand . . . beyond thy reach of knowledge (Pythagoras), 88.

Pride. — Haughtiness. — Arrogance. — Scorn: Arrogance because of knowledge. . . . Inspire not men with fear. . . . Be neither haughty nor mean (Ptah-hotep), 33, 34, 38; The Lord scorneth the scorners. . . . The Lord hateth haughty eyes. . . . When pride cometh, then cometh shame. . . . By pride cometh only contention (Proverbs), 50, 51, 52, 53; Treat no one with disdain. . . . The scorned may sleep in peace; . . .

the scorner perisheth (Manu), 65, 67 ; Say not, Who shall control me. . . . Laugh no man to scorn (Ecclesiasticus), 116, 117; God will not love him who loves to look at the pomposity of pride (Welsh Triad), 171, 172 ; Trample pride under foot (Thomas à Kempis), 204 ; Disdain not thy inferiors. . . . Despise no man's folly and ignorance (Rhodes), 207, 208 ; Contemn no poor man, mock no simple man (Ascham), 219 ; Be not haughty towards the old, the infirm, &c. . . . tremble lest you be as unfortunate (Mexican precept), 222, 226 ; If thou seest anything in thyself which may make thee proud, look a little further, &c. (Quarles), 292 ; Shun pride and baseness, tutors to contempt, of yourself and others (Osborne), 294; A truly virtuous man prides himself on nothing (La Rochefoucauld), 311 ; One kind of pride is as much a virtue as the other is a vice (Halifax), 319; Have courage to speak to a friend in a seedy coat. . . . To own that you are poor . . . to laugh at your personal defects . . . to wear your old garments, &c. (Stanislaus), 357, 358; Pride costs more than hunger, thirst, and cold (Jefferson), 411; A great mistake : to hold oneself too high and rate oneself too cheap (Goethe), 414; We have two great vices to beat down, pride and sensuality (Lacordaire), 453. See, also, Humility.

Privacy : He lives happily that lives hiddenly or privately. . . . It doubles man's life (Penn), 334 ; The happy man . . . doomed to an obscure but tranquil state, is pleased with it (Cowper), 394.

Profanity : Thou shalt not take the name of the Lord thy God in vain (Decalogue), 42 ; Ye shall not swear by my name (Leviticus), 44 ; Buddhistic command against, 79; Beware of cursing (Wyclif), 197; Let never oath be heard to come out of your mouth (Sidney), 247.

Profusion. See Expenditure.

Promises : He that sweareth to his own hurt and changeth not (Psalm), 46, 411 ; Pay that which thou vowest (Ecclesiastes), 58; Let not bill, witness, or possession be stronger in your sight than a promise by word of mouth (Maimonides), 167; Rarely promise, constantly perform (Penn), 328 ; Undertake not what you cannot perform, but be careful to keep your promise (Washington), 404.

Prosperity. — Adversity. — Fortune : Behavior in prosperity (Ptah-hotep), 38 ; In the day of prosperity be joyful, and in the day of adversity consider : God hath made the one side by side with the other. . . . The race is not to the swift. . . . Remember the days of darkness (Ecclesiastes), 61, 62; Whether fortune comes or goes take no notice of her (Seneca), 141; If God send adversity, accept it patiently. . . . If prosperity, thank him humbly (St. Louis), 174 ; So use prosperity that adversity may not abuse thee. . . . Seest thou good days ? prepare for evil times (Quarles), 290, 292 ; It requires greater virtues to support good than bad fortune (La Rochefoucauld), 310. See, also, Fortune.

Proverbs, selections from the Book of, 5, 6, 47.

Prudence. — Caution. — Deliberation. — Forethought. — Rashness. — Recklessness : Let wary thought each enterprise forerun. . . . After long consultation, engage in speaking or acting (Pythagoras), 88, 90 ; Whatsoever thou takest in hand, remember the end. . . . Go not in a way wherein thou mayest fall . . . Put all in writing (Ecclesiasticus), 118, 124, 125 ; The prudent man thinks before he acts (Thomas à Kempis), 203 ; Accustom the mind to judge the proportion and value of things. . . . Beware of being carried to things beyond our strength. . . . Do not engage too peremptorily in anything (Bacon), 268, 269 ; Do not despise an evil because it is small. . . . Have no days of carelessness ; destiny loves to play tricks. . . . Look into the inside of things. . . . Keep always something behind in store (Gracian), 287 ; Wise venturing is the most commendable part of prudence (Halifax), 315 ; Have courage to be content with small profits (Stanislaus), 358 ; Use not today what to-morrow may want (Chesterfield), 363 ; What we plan, what we undertake, should be so clearly mapped out, &c. . . . Distinguish between what is attainable and what is not (Goethe), 414, 415 ; Better debate a question without settling it than settle it without debate (Joubert), 419 ; To do what we do carelessly is to lose time inevitably (Swetchine), 438 ; May prudence, fortitude, and truth, erect your brow (Burns), 423 ; Prudence is at the beginning of all the cardinal virtues (Lacordaire), 452.

Psalm, The Fifteenth, 46, 410.

Ptah-hotep, the precepts of, 1, 32.

Public opinion. *See* Opinion, public.

Punctuality : A necessary part of good manners is a punctual observance of time (Swift), 350.

Purity. *See* Chastity.

Purpose : The masterpiece of man is to know how to live to purpose (Montaigne), 250 ; Imitate nature, which does nothing in vain (Bacon), 269 ; Be busy to purpose ; for a busy man and a man of business are two different things (Penn), 340 ; Let every man ask himself with which of his faculties he can somehow influence his age (Goethe), 416 ; The hero is he who is immovably centred (Emerson), 459.

Pythagoras, The Golden Verses of. Pythagoric sentences, 85.

Quarles, Francis, selections from the Enchiridion of, 289.

Quarrelling. *See* Contention.

Questioning : The superior man is anxious to question others (Confucius), 102 ; Be not curious in unnecessary matters (Ecclesiasticus), 114 ; Be not ashamed to inquire (Maimonides), 166 ; Ask questions of good men (Mediæval precept), 178.

Quintus Fixlein's " Rules of Life," 426.

Raleigh, Sir Walter. Instructions to his son and to posterity, 254.

Rashness. *See* Prudence.

Reading. *See* Books.

Reason. — Judgment : Let reason e'en thy meanest actions guide. . . . The reasoning art is oft an erring guide. . . . By using reason as guide you will avoid crimes (Pythagoras), 87, 92 ; Socrates became perfect, improving himself by everything, attending to nothing but reason (Epictetus), 153 ; If thou findest anything better than thy own mind's self-satisfaction in things done according to right reason, turn to it (Marcus Aurelius), 159 ; I will employ my life in cultivating my reason and advancing in the knowledge of truth (Descartes), 298 ; He

that doth not use his reason is a tame beast ; he that abuses it is a wild one (Halifax), 316 ; Let memory fail so long as you can rely on your judgment (Goethe), 415 ; Whose law is reason ; who depends upon that law (Wordsworth), 429.

Rebuke. *See* Reproof.

Recklessness. *See* Prudence.

Recreation. *See* Pleasure.

Refinement : Judge refinement by the test of conscience. . . . What is base no polish can make sterling (Cowper), 396. *See, also*, Taste.

Reformation. *See* Self-improvement, Self-control.

Refusing : A gilded No satisfies more than a dry Yes (Gracian), 285.

Regret : Let the past be past forever (Goethe), 416.

Religious injunctions : (Decalogue), 42 ; (Leviticus), 44 ; (Proverbs), 48 ; (Ecclesiastes), 58, 62, 63 ; (Manu), 66, 67, 70 ; (Hesiod), 73 ; (Buddha), 80 ; (Pythagoras), 86, 91 ; (Ahikar), 105 ; (Ecclesiasticus), 117, 125 ; (Jesus), 133, 134, 135 ; (Welsh Triads), 171 ; (St. Louis), 174 ; (La Tour), 190 ; (Wyclif), 195 ; (Suffolk), 200 ; (Ascham), 219 ; (Mexican), 222 ; (Wyatt), 231, 233, 236 ; (Burleigh), 239 ; (Sidney), 245 ; (Raleigh), 258 ; (Lyly), 263 ; (Essex-Bacon), 275 : (Wotton), 283 ; (Quarles), 291 ; (Browne), 300 ; (Penn), 330, 332, 333, 336 ; (Fénelon), 343 ; (Addison), 353 ; (Stanislaus), 358 ; (Edwards), 366-374 ; (Franklin), 382 ; (Chatham), 389, 390 ; (Jefferson), 410 ; (Burns), 422, 423 ; (Lacordaire), 453-454. *See, also*, Profanity, Commandments.

Renown. *See* Fame.

Repentance. *See* Penitence.

Reproach. *See* Reproof.

Reproof. — Rebuke. — Reproach. — Admonition : Better the rebuke of the wise than the song of fools (Ecclesiastes), 60 ; Take rebuke patiently (Rhodes), 207 ; Take all admonitions thankfully (Washington), 403. *See, also*, Correction.

Reputation. — Popularity : A good name better than precious ointment (Ecclesiastes), 59 ; Get the love of the congregation (Ecclesiasticus), 115 ; I advise thee not to affect or neglect popularity too much (Burleigh), 243 ; Popularity is a crime from the moment it is sought. . . . The invisible thing called a *good name* is made up of the breath of numbers (Halifax), 314, 319; We are only really alive when we enjoy the good will of others (Goethe), 414.

Resentment. *See* Anger.

Resignation *See* Contentment.

Resolution: Make few resolutions, but keep them (Penn), 332. *See, also,* Firmness, Doing, Persuasion, Stubbornness.

Respect. *See* Courtesy, Filial Duty, Elders, Authority, Honor.

Rest. *See* Bodily Care.

Retaliation. — Revenge. — Self-defence: Smite not him who smites thee (Mahabharata), 96; Whosoever smiteth thee on thy right cheek, turn to him the other (Jesus), 132; The best way of avenging thyself is not to become like the wrong-doer (Marcus Aurelius), 160; Glory in forbearance, because that is the true strength and real victory (Maimonides), 168; Hath any wronged thee? be bravely reveng'd: slight it and the work's begun; forgive it and 't is finisht (Quarles), 291; Write thy wrongs in water (Browne), 302; Be not provoked by injuries to commit them (Penn), 329; Never to do anything out of revenge (Edwards), 367.

Reticence. *See* Speech.

Revels: Beware of secret corners and night sitting up (Ascham), 220.

Revenge. *See* Retaliation.

Reverence. *See* Filial Duty, Elders, Authority, Religious Injunctions.

Rhodes, Hugh. Rule of honest living, from the "Boke of Nurture," 206.

Ribaldry. — Obscenity: If anything obscene be said, don't laugh at it (Erasmus), 217, 218; Let never word of ribaldry come out of your mouth (Sidney), 247. *See, also,* Modesty, Chastity.

Riches. — Wealth. — Poverty. — Want: Riches to be used as by a steward of the good things of God (Ptah-hotep), 38; The hand of the diligent maketh rich. . . . Riches profit not in the day of wrath. . . . He that trusteth in his riches shall fall. . . . There is that maketh himself rich, yet hath nothing, &c. . . . Wealth gotten by vanity shall be diminished. . . . Better is little with the fear of the Lord (Proverbs), 51, 52, 53, 54; He that loveth silver shall not be satisfied with silver. . . . When goods increase they are increased that eat them. . . . A grievous evil [is] riches kept by the owner to his hurt (Ecclesiastes), 59; Let us live happily, though we call nothing our own (Dhammapada), 83; Wealth, the perishing, uncertain good. . . . The non-possession of unnecessary goods the greatest wealth. . . . Impossible to be a lover of riches and a lover of Divinity (Pythagoras), 87, 91, 93, 94; Endive and gall not more bitter than poverty (Ahikar), 105; Set not thy heart upon thy goods. . . . When thou art rich, think upon poverty (Ecclesiasticus), 116, 121; Riches not to be reckoned amongst goods (Cicero), 128; Where thy treasure is, there will thy heart be (Jesus), 134; I will despise riches as much when I have them as when I have them not (Seneca), 141; Seek not riches basely (Raleigh), 257; Happy is he who, having nothing, yet hath all (Wotton), 283; He is rich, not that possesses much, but that covets no more. . . . Command thy money, lest she command thee. . . . Be not too greedy, &c. (Quarles), 290; A slave unto Mammon makes no servant unto God. . . . Take no satisfaction in dying but living rich. . . . Unto some it is wealth enough not to be poor (Browne), 300, 301, 304; The things to be bought with money are such as least deserve a price (Halifax), 315; Seek not to be rich, but happy; the one lies in bags, the other in content (Penn), 328; Even riches shall not make thee unhappy, if, &c. . . . The distribution is more equal than the fool can believe (Chesterfield), 363, 364; Gather gear by ev'ry wile that's justified by honor (Burns), 422; It is a mercy to the rich that there are poor. . . . We are rich only through what we give (Swetchine), 438; It is usually only when we have lost our possessions that we begin to find out their value (Schopenhauer), 444.

Richter, Jean Paul Friedrich. Quintus Fixlein's "Rules of Life," 426.

Ridicule. — Sarcasm. — Satire. — Raillery; Mocks follow them that delight therein (Wyatt), 233; Be not scurrilous in conversation nor satirical in jests (Burleigh), 243; Let your mirth be void of scurrility and biting words. . . . A wound by a word often harder of cure than that given with the sword (Sidney), 246; Jest not openly at those that are simple (Raleigh), 255 ; Let wit rather serve for a buckler to defend than a sword to wound (Osborne), 295.

Righteousness. — Rectitude. — Uprightness : He that walketh uprightly (Psalm), 46, 410 ; The Lord blesseth the habitation of the righteous. . . . Righteousness delivereth from death. . . . The tongue of the righteous is as choice silver. . . . The righteous shall flourish as the green leaf (Proverbs), 50, 52, 53 ; Blessed are they that hunger and thirst after righteousness. . . . Do not your righteousness before men (Jesus), 130, 132 ; Live that thy deeds be so rightful that no man shall blame them with reason (Wyclif), 196 ; Join gospel righteousness with legal right (Browne), 301 ; There is no such thing as a venial sin against morality (Halifax), 314 ; Resolutions to strive for a life of strict righteousness (Edwards), 366-374. See, also, Good, Goodness, Honesty, Justice.

Robbery. See Theft.

Rochefoucauld, Duke de la. Selections from Sentences and Moral Maxims, 310.

Rudeness. See Courtesy.

Sabbath. See Religious injunctions.

Saint Louis. Instructions to his son, 174.

Scandal : Publish not scandal (Thomas à Kempis), 203. See, also, Gossip, Speech.

Schopenhauer, Arthur. Selections from " Aphorisms on the Wisdom of Life," 441.

Scorn. See Pride.

Secrets : Disclose not the secrets of another (Proverbs), 56 ; If you know anything you wish to conceal, tell it by no means to your wife (Mediæval precept), 179 ; What I would have kept as secrets I tell to nobody (Erasmus), 212 ; Keep secret what thou hearest (Mexican precept), 224 ; It is wise not to seek a secret ; honest not to reveal one (Penn), 327, 331 ; Trust neither fools, knaves, women, or young men with secrets (Chesterfield), 360-361.

Self-communion, Meditation : Better to converse more with yourself than with others (Pythagoras), 91 ; Have you known how to meditate and manage your life ? you have performed the greatest work (Montaigne), 250 ; Let your meditation always be systematic (Féne-

lon), 343 ; Resolutions for self-communion (Edwards), 368-372 ; The happy man . . . in contemplation is his bliss (Cowper), 394.

Self-conceit. See Vanity.

Self-control. — Equanimity. — Serenity. — Calmness. — Tranquillity : He that ruleth his spirit is better than he that taketh a city (Proverbs), 6 ; The doctrine of self-control in ancient morals, 6-8 ; Keep thyself calm when contradicted. . . . Be not of an irritable temper. . . . He who agitates himself all day long has not a good moment (Ptah-hotep), 33, 36, 38 ; E'en as a driver checks his restive steeds . . . restrain thy passions. . . . The man who keeps his senses in control gains all the fruit of holy study. . . . Self-subjugation included in the tenfold summary of duty (Manu), 66, 69, 70 ; Self-control, . . . self-restraint and purity, the greatest blessing. . . . The mind that shaketh not, without grief or passion, is the greatest blessing (Buddha), 79, 80 ; He who lives without looking for pleasures, his senses well controlled, Mâra will not overthrow. . . . Self is the lord of self (Dhammapada), 82, 83 ; No one is free who has not the empire of himself (Pythagoras), 92 ; Practice sobriety and self-control (Mahabharata), 98 ; Be tranquil in works and words (Ahikar), 104 ; Habits of perfected self-mastery are spoiled by excess and defect (Aristotle), 108, 109 ; Tranquillity renders life happy (Cicero), 127 ; Suppose that only to be your own which is your own [in your own power] (Epictetus), 150 ; Live a rightful life . . . ruling well thy five senses (Wyclif), 196 ; He that resisteth evil inclinations in their birth shall more easily destroy them when their roots are deep (Thomas à Kempis), 203 ; Never to have a violent aversion or fondness for anything (Erasmus), 213 ; Grandeur of soul consists in knowing how to govern and circumscribe itself. . . . Have you known how to take repose ? You have done more than he who has taken cities (Montaigne), 250 ; In discovering your passions, give not way in little (Essex-Bacon), 274 ; Happy is he . . . whose passions not his masters are (Wotton), 282 ; Overcome your antipathies. . . . Be master of yourself if you would be master of others (Gracian), 285 ; Aim at conquering rather desires than fortune (Descartes), 297 ; Give no quarter unto those vices which are of thy inward family (Browne), 303 ; Resolutions for self-control (Edwards), 368-372 ; It beseemeth not man to allow himself to be ruled by mere instinct (Goethe), 414 ; The passions may all become innocent if well directed (Joubert), 418 ; A power which is our human nature's highest dower (Wordsworth), 429 ; A little self-control at the right moment may prevent much subsequent compulsion (Schopenhauer), 444. *See, also,* Self-improvement, Anger, Passions, Fortitude, Self-watchfulness.

Self-defence. *See* Retaliation.

Self-esteem. *See* Self-respect, Self-knowledge, Self-reliance, Vanity.

Self-examination : Plan for systematic self-examination (Franklin), 379-384 ; Inspect the neighborhood of thy life (Richter), 427 ; Ask thyself first : Wherein am I most faulty ? . . . Then inquire : whence comes this defect ? (Zschokke), 433. *See, also,* Self-knowledge.

Self-improvement : Blow off the impurities of self one by one, little by little (Dhammapada), 84 ; A man may mend his faults with as little labor as cover them (Essex-Bacon), 271 ; If we would amend the world we should amend ourselves (Penn), 328 ; On the overcoming of faults (Zschokke), 432 ; I know of no more encouraging fact than the unquestionable ability of man to elevate his life by a conscious endeavor (Thoreau), 462.

Self - knowledge. — Self - examination : Know thyself (Chilo), 76 : Examine thyself by thyself (Dhammapada), 84 ; With reverence at thy own tribunal stand. . . . You are furious and insane in proportion as you are ignorant of yourself (Pythagoras), 89-91 ; Next to the knowledge of others comes the knowledge of self. But it is not enough for a man only to *know* himself (Bacon), 266, 267 ; Know your pet faults (Gracian), 286 ; Read not books alone, but men, chiefly thyself (Quarles), 290 ; Study thyself betimes and early find what nature bids thee to be (Browne), 301 ; Resolutions for self-examination (Edwards), 368-372 ; Learn

to know yourself, not by contemplation, but action (Goethe), 413 ; More skillful in self-knowledge (Wordsworth), 429.

Self-praise. *See* Vanity.

Self - reliance. — Self - confidence. — Self-containment. — Independence : Depend not on another. . . . Never despise thyself. . . . Think not on destiny, but act thyself (Manu), 68, 69 ; Rouse thyself by thyself (Dhammapada), 84 ; To depend on oneself and on Divinity is alone stable (Pythagoras), 93 ; Give not thy son . . . brother . . . friend power over thee (Ecclesiasticus), 124 ; Happy is he . . . that serveth not another's will (Wotton), 282 ; Have but little to do and do it thyself . . . Be not tied to things without you. . . . Be free ; live at home, in yourselves (Penn), 328, 332 ; Have the courage to be independent (Stanislaus), 359 ; Never trouble another for what you can do yourself (Jefferson), 411 ; Live with the world whoso hath nerve to make the world his purpose serve (Goethe), 416 ; Gather gear . . . for the glorious privilege of being independent (Burns), 422.

Self-respect. — Self-esteem : The soul is its own witness. . . . Grieve thou not thy soul (Manu), 66 ; Let reverence of thyself thy thoughts control (Pythagoras), 87 ; People take a man at his own estimate ; but he must estimate himself at something (Goethe), 415.

Self-watchfulness : If a man holds himself dear let him watch himself carefully (Dhammapada), 83 ; A watch over the senses is the foundation of purity, the discipline of peace (Thomas à Kempis), 203 ; Never open the door to an evil, however small (Gracian), 285 ; Resolutions for self-watchfulness (Edwards), 368-372. *See, also,* Self-control.

Selfishness : If self the wavering balance shake, it 's rarely right adjusted (Burns), 421.

Seneca : Rules for a happy life, 138.

Sensuality. *See* Chastity.

Serenity. *See* Self-control, Equanimity.

Seriousness. *See* Earnestness.

Sermon on the Mount, The, 17, 130.

Servants, Treatment of : Command only to direct (Ptah-hotep), 38 ; The wages shall not abide with thee (Leviticus), 44 ; Be not as a lion in thy house. . . . Let thy soul love a good servant (Ecclesiasticus), 115, 118; Keep rather two too few than one too many (Burleigh), 241; If thou wouldst have a good servant, let thy servant find a wise master (Quarles), 291; Servants may be looked upon as humble friends (Halifax), 317; Towards servants, never accustom yourself to rough and passionate language (Chatham), 392.

Servility. See Flattery.

Seven wise men of Greece, 76.

Shakespeare. Advice of Polonius to Laertes, 281.

Shame. — Shamelessness : Life is easy for a man without shame (Dhammapada), 84; Commit no sin through shame (Spirit of Wisdom), 164. See, also, Fame.

Sidney, Sir Henry : Letter to his son, Sir Philip, 245.

Silence. See Speech.

Simplicity : How few the things are that give a life which flows in quiet like the existence of the gods ! . . . Do what is necessary, . . . the greatest part of what we say and do being unnecessary (Marcus Aurelius), 158, 159; The simplicity of the life of the happy man described (Cowper), 394; Let your affairs be as two or three, and not a hundred or a thousand. . . . Simplify, simplify (Thoreau), 463.

Sincerity. — Candor. — Duplicity. — Prejudice : The superior man is anxious that his speech be sincere (Confucius), 102; Examine the word in thy heart and then utter it (Ahikar), 104; Let thy word be the same. . . . Let thy life be sincere (Ecclesiasticus), 116; To thine own self be true. . . . Thou canst not then be false to any man (Shakespeare), 281; Happy is he . . . whose armor is his honest thought, and simple truth, &c. (Wotton), 282; Sincerity is an opening of the heart; we find it in few (La Rochefoucauld), 310; Nothing needs a trick but a trick; sincerity loathes one (Penn), 329; Have the courage to admit that you have been wrong (Stanislaus), 357; Think innocently and justly; speak accordingly (Franklin), 378, 379, 384; If obliged to differ, do it with all possible candor. . . . Warning against obstinate adherence to false notions only because one has declared for them (Chatham), 388, 389; To think what we do not feel is to lie to oneself (Joubert), 419; Be without

guile, take men as they are (Zschokke), 435. See, also, Earnestness, Falsehood, Hypocrisy.

Sinfulness. See Wickedness.

Skepticism : Buddhistic command against, 79.

Slander. — Evil-speaking. — Backbiting.— Detraction : He that slandereth not (Psalm), 46, 410; He that uttereth a slander is a fool (Proverbs), 52; Buddhistic command against slander, 79; Keep thy tongue from evil speaking (Ahikar), 104; Every other demon attacks in the front, but Slander (Spirit of Wisdom), 164; Let no one before thee speak evil of others behind their backs (St. Louis), 175; Beware of speaking evil (Wyclif), 197; Forbear to speak evil of men, though it be true (Raleigh), 255; It is a more dextrous error to speak well of an evil man than ill of a good man (Quarles), 291; Abhor detraction, the sin of fallen angels (Penn), 333; Resolved, never to speak evil of any one (Edwards), 367, 369; Let your conversation be without malice. . . . Speak not injurious words (Washington), 403, 404.

Sleep : How long, O sluggard ? . . . Love not sleep, lest thou come to poverty (Proverbs), 51, 55; The sleep of a laboring man is sweet (Ecclesiastes), 59; Practice not slothful sleep (Spirit of Wisdom), 164; Give not thyself to slumber (Mexican precept), 227; Let the end of thy first sleep raise thee from repose (Quarles), 290; If you do not rise early you can never make any progress (Chatham), 387.

Sluggishness. See Sleep, Industry.

Social Relationships. See Neighbors, Companions, Friendship, Privacy, Fame, Reputation, Honors, Courtesy, Manners, Familiarity, Benevolence, Giving.

Socrates, 13.

Solon, Saying of, 76.

Sorrow : Sorrow is better than laughter. . . . Better to go to the house of mourning than to the house of feasting (Ecclesiastes), 59; Blessed are they that mourn (Jesus), 130. See, also, Afflictions.

Soul, The : There resides within thee a Being who inspects thy every act. . . . The soul is its own witness ; . . . grieve thou not thy soul (Manu), 66; Let no example, . . . no soothing tongue, prevail upon thee . . . to do thy soul's immortal essence wrong. . . . In all things guard thy soul from wrong. . . . The Divinity has not a place more allied to his nature than a pure soul (Pythagoras), 88, 89, 94 ; In every good work trust thy own soul. . . . Prove thy soul in thy life (Ecclesiasticus), 124.

Speech. — Language. — Words. — Talkativeness. — Reticence : Do not repeat extravagances of language ; nor scatter thy words ; nor speak with heat. . . . Let thoughts be abundant and mouth under restraint (Ptah-hotep), 37, 38, 40 ; In a multitude of words there wanteth not transgression. . . . He that spareth his words hath knowledge. . . . A fool when he holdeth his peace is counted wise. . . . A word fitly spoken is like apples of gold, &c. (Proverbs), 52, 54, 56 ; Be not rash with thy mouth (Ecclesiastes), 58 ; Pleasant speech the greatest blessing (Buddha), 79 ; Be not hasty in thy tongue, and in thy deeds slack. . . . Honor and shame is in talk. . . . Strive not with a man that is full of tongue. . . . Learn before thou speak. . . . He that can rule his tongue shall live without strife. . . . To slip upon a pavement better than to slip with the tongue. . . . Not so many have fallen by the sword as by the tongue. . . . Weigh thy words in a balance (Ecclesiasticus), 115, 116, 119, 121, 122; Be for the most part silent (Epictetus), 152 ; Be not a man of many words (Marcus Aurelius), 158 ; Measure your words with judgment. . . . Speak as one who seeketh to learn, and not as eager for victory. . . . Keep a bridle upon your tongue (Maimonides), 166; He that keeps strict silence shall not offend. . . . Blessed is the prudent tongue (Thomas à Kempis), 202, 203, 204; Abstain ever from words of ribaldry. . . . Love rather words profitable than eloquent and pleasant ; right words than flattering (Rhodes), 206 ; Great part of quarrels come from intemperance of the tongue (Erasmus), 212 ; Keep silence ; nothing is gained by talking (Mexican precept), 225 ; Be rather a hearer. . . . Think upon every word. . . . Remember how nature hath ramparted up the tongue with teeth, lips, &c. (Sidney), 247 ; He that is lavish in words is a niggard in deeds (Raleigh), 256; Give thy thoughts no tongue. . . .

Give every man thine ear, but few thy voice (Shakespeare), 281 ; What is well said is soon said (Gracian), 286 ; If thou desire to be held wise, be so wise as to hold thy tongue (Quarles), 291 ; A man strictly wise can hardly be called a sociable creature (Halifax), 315 ; If thou thinkest twice before thou speakest once, thou wilt speak twice the better (Penn), 327, 330, 331, 334 ; Have courage to speak when necessary and to hold your tongue when it is better (Stanislaus), 357 ; Of much speaking cometh repentance (Chesterfield), 363 ; Speak not but what may benefit others or yourself (Franklin), 377, 379 ; Be a patient, attentive, and well-bred hearer. . . . Dedicate the first parts of life more to hear and to learn (Chatham), 388 ; Think before you speak (Washington), 404 ; Be a listener. . . . Endeavor to establish the habit of silence (Jefferson), 409 ; Keep something to yoursel, ye scarcely tell to ony (Burns), 421. See, also, Geniality, Conversation, Gossip, Scandal, Doing.

Spendthrift ways. See Expenditure.

Spirit of Wisdom, Opinions of the, 163.

Squandering. See Expenditure.

Stage, The: Abstain from stage plays (Buddhist commandments), 78.

Stanislaus, King of Poland : Traits of moral courage in every-day life, 356.

"Stans puer ad mensam," 180.

Steadfastness. See Firmness.

Stinginess. See Giving.

Stoic morality, 13–15.

Strife. See Contention.

Stubbornness. — Obstinacy : A stubborn heart shall fare evil (Ecclesiasticus), 114. See, also, Firmness.

Study. See Education, Books.

Success. — Failure. — Mistakes : People make no mistakes who never wish to do anything worth doing (Goethe), 415 ; They wha fa' in fortune's strife, their fate we should na censure (Burns), 421.

Suffolk, William de la Pole, Duke of. Letter to his son, 200.

Sullenness. See Good Nature.

Surety, Giving : Warnings against (Proverbs), 50, 51, 52, 55 ; (Thales), 76 ; (Ecclesiasticus), 119, 123 ; (Burleigh), 242 ; (Raleigh), 257 ; (Osborne), 294.

Surrey, Earl of. Translation from Martial, 143.

Suspicion. See Trust.

Swetchine, Madame. Selections from "Airelles" and "Thoughts," 437.

Swift, Jonathan. On good manners, 348.

Sympathy : If thou hast any sorrow, tell it to thy confessor, or to some discreet man (St. Louis), 175 ; He shall be sure of shame that feeleth no grief in other men's shames (Wyatt), 233.

System. See Order.

Table manners, Mediæval, 180.

Talebearing. See Gossip.

Talkativeness. See Speech.

Taste : Be common in nothing, above all not in taste (Gracian), 285 ; A man that has a taste of music, painting, and architecture is like one that has another sense (Addison), 355. See, also, Refinement.

Teachableness : Train thy son to be a teachable man (Ptah-hotep) 39 The foolish despise instruction (Proverbs), 48 ; From the experience of others learn wisdom (Chesterfield), 363. See, also, Education.

Teachers, Conduct towards. See Elders.

Teaching. See Education.

Temper, Ill : See Anger, Good nature).

Temperance (in eating and drinking). — Intemperance. — Drunkenness. — Gluttony : Wine is a mocker. . . . Be not among winebibbers. . . . Look not upon the wine (Proverbs), 55, 56 ; Drink thy wine with a merry heart (Ecclesiastes), 61 ; Honor thy food ; . . . avoid excess (Manu), 67 ; One should not become a drinker of intoxicating liquors. . . . Abstinence from strong drink, the greatest blessing (Buddha), 78, 80 ; The strength of the soul is temperance (Pythagoras), 93 ; Injunctions for keeping the mean between excess and defect (Aristotle), 108 ; Take not pleasure in much good cheer (Ecclesiasticus), 121 ; Eat and drink to quench the desires of nature (Seneca), 142 ; If thou findest anything better than temperance, &c., turn to it (Marcus Aurelius), 158, 159; Eat that ye may live. . . . Be careful in taking wine (Maimonides), 169 ; The flesh is tempted by delicious meats and drinks (La Tour), 190 ; Take meat and drink in measure (Wyclif), 195 ; Consider to thyself what nature requireth. . . . Eat without surfeit. Drink without drunkenness (Rhodes), 205 ; Banish swinish drunkards out of thine house (Burleigh),

240 ; Use moderate diet. . . . Seldom drink wine (Sidney), 246 ; There never was any man came to honor that loved wine (Raleigh), 257 ; Without knowledge there can be no temperance (Essex-Bacon), 275 ; Drunkenness makes way for all vices (Quarles), 292 ; Be sober and temperate, that you may truly serve God, which you cannot well do wi.hout health (Browne), 299, 300 ; It is a piece of arrogance to dare to be drunk (Halifax), 316 ; Resolved to maintain the strictest temperance (Edwards), 368, 370; Eat not to dullness ; drink not to elevation (Franklin), 377, 379, 380, 381 ; Avoid taverns, drinkers, smokers etc. . . . We never repent of having eaten too little (Jefferson), 409, 411 ; Temperance is the third cardinal virtue (Lacordaire), 452. See, also, Bodily Care.

Temperance (in the larger sense). See Moderation.

Temptation : If sinners entice thee consent not (Proverbs), 48 ; Be well occupied, and no time idle, for the danger of temptation (Wyclif), 195 ; More pure, as tempted more (Wordsworth), 429 ; Never place thyself in the way of temptation in order to test thy strength (Zschokke), 434 ; Tempt no man, lest thou fall for it (Penn), 329.

Ten commandments. See Religious injunctions.

Thales, saying of, 76.

Thankfulness. See Gratitude.

Theatre. See Stage.

Theft : Thou shalt not steal (Decalogue), 42 ; Ye shall not steal (Leviticus), 44 ; If sinners entice thee consent not (Proverbs), 48 ; One should not take that which is not given (Buddha), 78 ; Combine to put an end to thefts (Confucius), 101 ; Whether it be gold or little things that one steals, the punishment is the same (Ahikar), 104. See, also, Honesty.

Thomas à Kempis. Selections from "The Little Garden of Roses," 202.

Thoreau, Henry David : On the making of life deliberate and simple, 30, 462.

Thoughtlessness. See Earnestness, Prudence.

Thoughts : Keep thought away from evil. . . . Let no man think lightly of evil (Dhammapada), 82, 83 ; The soul is dyed by the thoughts (Marcus Aurelius), 160 ; The hours of a wise man are lengthened by his ideas (Addison), 355 ; All that is wise has been thought already ; we must try, however, to think it again (Goethe), 413.

Thrift. — Economy : He that gathereth in summer is a wise son. . . . He that loveth pleasure shall be a poor man (Proverbs), 51, 55 ; If with a little thou a little blend continual, mighty shall the heap ascend (Hesiod), 75 ; Prize economy (Confucius), 101 ; Better garner with poverty than squander with riches (Ahikar), 104 ; He that spendeth much and getteth nought, may be sorry, &c. (Rhodes), 208; Buy when the markets and seasons serve fittest (Burleigh), 241. See, also, Industry, Expenditure.

Time : Undertake nothing which of necessity takes up a great quantity of time (Bacon), 269 ; Misspending time is a kind of self-homicide (Halifax), 316 ; Divide your day. . . . Save a treasure of time to yourself (Penn), 333 ; The cause of all evils amongst men is the improper use of time (Massillon), 345 ; Employ the present without regretting the loss of the past, or too much depending on the time to come (Chesterfield), 362 ; Resolved never to lose one moment (Edwards), 366 ; Lose no time (Franklin), 378; Never put off till to-morrow what you can do to-day (Jefferson), 411 ; It is for the past and the future we must work. . . . Use well the moment, &c. (Goethe), 416, 417 ; Ordinary people think how they shall spend their time ; a man of intellect tries to use it (Schopenhauer), 441 ; Time is but the stream I go a-fishing in (Thoreau), 464. See, also, Life, Pleasure, Punctuality, Industry.

Tobacco : Have the courage to throw your snuff-box into the fire (Stanislaus), 359.

Tolerance : I let every one enjoy his opinion (Erasmus), 212 ; When I hear another express an opinion which is not mine, I say to myself, he has a right, &c. (Jefferson), 408 ; Let us have heart and head hospitality (Joubert), 419.

Tongue, The. See Speech.

Tranquillity. See Equanimity, Self-control.

Travel : I can see more in histories than if I had rambled for twenty years (Erasmus), 215 ; Suffer not thy sons to pass the Alps (Burleigh), 241 ; Let not your minds be carried away with vain delights, as with traveling into strange countries (Lyly), 260 ; Study what use to make of travel (Essex-Bacon), 270, 273.

Treachery. See Fidelity.

Triumph. See Contention.

Triviality : Those who bestow too much on trifling things become incapable of great ones. . . . Little minds are too much hurt by little things (La Rochefoucauld), 310, 311 ; A man shows his character in the way in which he deals with trifles (Schopenhauer), 444 ; Our life is frittered away by detail (Thoreau), 463.

Trust. — Faith. — Distrust. — Credulity.— Suspicion : Not e'en thy brother on his word believe. . . . Mistrust destroys us, and credulity (Hesiod), 75 ; Open not thy heart to every man (Ecclesiasticus), 119 ; Never put your trust in a stranger (Mediæval precept), 178 ; Be not light of credence, nor suspicious (Rhodes), 207 ; Trust not any man with thy life, credit, or estate (Burleigh), 243 ; Mistrust no man without cause, neither be credulous without proof (Lyly), 262 ; Do not believe and do not love lightly (Gracian), 286 ; Make writing the witness of your contracts (Osborne), 294 ; It is more disgraceful to distrust friends than to be deceived (La Rochefoucauld), 311 ; Only trust thyself. . . . Be not too credulous (Penn), 327, 331, 335 ; Trust no man until thou hast tried him ; yet mistrust not without reason (Chesterfield), 363 ; Mankind are unco weak, an' little to be trusted (Burns), 421. See, also, Anxiety.

Truth. — Truthfulness. See Falsehood.

Unbelief. See Skepticism.

Understanding : Praise of (Proverbs), 49.

Uprightness. See Righteousness, Honesty.

Use. See Habit.

Usefulness : No respect is lasting but that produced by being useful (Halifax), 316.

Usury : He that putteth not out his money to usury (Psalm), 46, 411.

Utilitarian morality, 14.

Vanity. — Self-conceit. — Self-praise. — Boasting : Let another man praise thee (Proverbs), 57 ; In conversation, avoid excessive mention of your own actions and dangers (Epictetus), 153 ; Never speak of yourself (Gracian), 286; Beware of thinking yourself wiser or greater than you are (Osborne), 294; Measure not thyself by thy morning shadow, but by the extent of thy grave. . . . Become not thy own parasite. . . . Busy not thy best member in the encomium of thyself (Browne), 303, 304; Vanity is never at its full growth till it spreadeth into affectation (Halifax), 319; A man ought not to value himself of his achievements, &c. (Washington), 403; Let no one think that people have waited for him as for the Saviour (Goethe), 416; Our vanity is the constant enemy of our dignity (Swetchine), 437.

Veneration. *See* Filial Duty, Elders, Authority, Honor, Religious Injunctions.

Venturing. *See* Prudence.

Vice. *See* Virtue, Chastity.

Victory. *See* Contention.

Violence. *See* Murder, Theft, Oppression, Cruelty.

Virtue: When passing to [the future world] . . . virtue will thy only comrade be. . . . Virtue alone stays by [one] at the tomb (Manu), 68; Steep the ascent and rough the road [to where Virtue dwells] (Hesiod), 72; By virtuous use thy life and manners frame. . . . It is impossible to receive any gift greater than virtue (Pythagoras), 89, 91; Virtue is a mean state between two faulty states, of excess and defect (Aristotle), 110; Every virtue has its particular sweetness (Thomas à Kempis), 202; Endeavor to excel in virtue, seeing in qualities of body we are inferior to beasts (Lyly), 262; Pursue virtue virtuously. . . . Endeavor to make virtues heroical. . . . Make not the consequences of virtue the ends thereof (Browne), 299, 300, 301; Plan for acquiring habits of virtue (Franklin), 376; All the virtues originate in actual wants; all the vices in factitious ones (Swetchine), 437; The four cardinal virtues (Lacordaire), 452. *See, also,* Good, Goodness, Righteousness, Chastity.

Vows: Pay that which thou vowest (Ecclesiastes), 58.

Want. *See* Riches.

Washington, George. Letters of advice to his nephews, and Rules of Civility, 398, 402.

Wastefulness. *See* Expenditure.

Wealth. *See* Riches.

Welsh Triads, 171.

Wickedness. — Sinfulness. — Iniquity: A wicked man is loathsome. . . . Wickedness overthroweth the sinner. . . . The lamp of the wicked shall be put out (Proverbs), 53; Bad men are the most rife (Bias), 76; It shall not be well with the wicked (Ecclesiastes), 60; None sees us, say the sinful; . . . the gods see them, and the omniscient spirit within their breasts. . . . The god of justice and the heart itself. . . . Iniquity fails not to yield its fruit (Manu), 66, 67; Smooth is the track [to the mansion of Sin] (Hesiod), 72; To cease from sin, the greatest blessing (Buddha), 80.

Wife. *See* Marriage.

Willingness: Nothing is troublesome that we do willingly (Jefferson), 411.

Wisdom: The attributes of a wise man (Ptah-hotep), 39; Praise of wisdom (Proverbs), 49–53; Wisdom is as good as an inheritance. . . . Wisdom is a defence (Ecclesiastes), 60; Worthless he that Wisdom's voice defies (Hesiod), 72; The wise man is alone a priest (Pythagoras), 90; Search for wisdom as for silver (Maimonides), 166; Three things produce wisdom: truth, consideration, and suffering (Welsh Triad), 172; Be desirous of wisdom and apt to learn it (Rhodes), 208; Rather go a hundred miles to speak with a wise man than five to see a fair town (Essex-Bacon), 278; Follow not the tedious practice of such as seek wisdom only in learning (Osborne), 294; God send you speed, still daily to grow wiser (Burns), 423. *See also,* Knowledge, Teachableness, Education.

Words. *See* Speech.

Wordsworth, William. Character of the Happy Warrior, 429.

Work. *See* Industry.

Worry. *See* Anxiety.

Wotton, Sir Henry. The Happy Life, 282.

Wrath. *See* Anger.

Wright, Thomas. On mediæval precepts, 178.

Wyatt, Sir Thomas. Letters to his son, 230.

Wyclif. Short rule of life, 194.

Youth. — Old Age. — Growing old: Rejoice, O young man, in thy youth. . . . Remember thy Creator (Ecclesiastes), 62 ; One must do more when old than when young. . . . Errors are not of much consequence in youth. . . . One need only grow old to become gentler in judgment (Goethe), 414, 415 ; Youth should be a savings-bank (Swetchine), 438.

Zschokke, Johann Heinrich Daniel. On the overcoming of faults, 432.

The Riverside Press

Electrotyped and printed by H. O. Houghton & Co.
Cambridge, Mass., U. S. A.